GLENCOE LANGUAGE ARTS

Grammar

AND

Composition

Handbook

GRADE 10

 **Glencoe
McGraw-Hill**

New York, New York
Columbus, Ohio
Woodland Hills, California
Peoria, Illinois

Printed in the United States of America.

Send all inquiries to:
Glencoe/McGraw-Hill
8787 Orion Place
Columbus, Ohio 43240

ISBN 0-07-825117-6

2 3 4 5 6 7 8 9 10   003   06 05 04 03 02 01

Table of Contents at a Glance

Table of Contents

Chapter 16   Research Paper Writing

468

Chapter 17   Business Writing

501

Table of Contents

Part One

● ● ● ● ● ● ● ● ● ● ● ● ● ●

Ready Reference

The **Ready Reference** consists of three parts. The **Glossary of Terms** is a quick reference to language arts terms, defined and cross-referenced to relevant lessons. The **Usage Glossary** lists pairs of words that are easily confused and provides explanation for the correct usage of each word. The third part is **Abbreviations,** which consists of lists of many commonly used abbreviations.

GLOSSARY OF TERMS

abbreviation An abbreviation is a shortened form of a word. Most abbreviations have periods. If you are unsure of how to write an abbreviation, consult a dictionary (pages 82, 353).

EXAMPLE Gerry left at 8:00 **A.M.**

EXAMPLE Did she really leave at 8:00 **A.M.?**

abstract noun An abstract noun names an idea, a quality, or a characteristic (page 95). *See concrete noun.*

EXAMPLES attitude   dignity   loyalty   sadness   temperature

action verb An action verb tells what someone or something does. Some action verbs express physical action. Others express mental action (page 106).

EXAMPLE Ted **waved** the signal flag. **[physical action]**

EXAMPLE He **hoped** for success. **[mental action]**

active voice An action verb is in the active voice when the subject of the sentence performs the action (page 208). *See passive voice.*

EXAMPLE The brown bear **caught** a salmon.

adjective An adjective is a word that modifies a noun or a pronoun by limiting its meaning. An adjective tells *what kind, which one, how many,* or *how much* (page 110).

EXAMPLES

interesting poem   **romantic** story   **many** novels

these ideas   **Irish** ballad   **cracked** pitcher

enough plates   **second** time   **no** excuse

afternoon class   **cheese** sandwich   **football** game

adjective clause An adjective clause is a subordinate clause that modifies a noun or a pronoun. An adjective clause may begin with a relative pronoun *(who, whom, whose, that,* or *which)* or the word *where* or *when.* An adjective clause normally follows the word it modifies (page 167).

EXAMPLE   Magazines **that inform and entertain** are my
            favorites. **[The adjective clause tells *what kind* and
            modifies *Magazines*.]**

adjective phrase An adjective phrase is a prepositional phrase that modifies a noun or a pronoun (page 147).

EXAMPLE   Tim chose the sandwich **with cheese.** **[adjective phrase
            modifying a noun]**

adverb An adverb is a word that modifies a verb, an adjective, or another adverb (page 114).

EXAMPLES

modifying verbs   **Never** swim alone.
                        verb

                        He has **seldom** complained.
                        verb   verb

modifying adjectives   The movie was **very** scary and **too** long.
                                       adjective   adjective

modifying adverbs   She **almost** always waited **quite** patiently.
                            adverb   adverb

EXAMPLES   **When?**   It should arrive **Saturday.**
            Where?   Leave your coat **there.**
            How?   He stacked the books **neatly.**
            To what degree? We were **very** sorry.

adverb clause An adverb clause is a subordinate clause that modifies a verb, an adjective, or another adverb in the main clause. It tells *when, where, how, why, to what extent,* or *under what conditions* (page 168).

EXAMPLE **Before I took the test,** I studied for hours. **[The adverb clause tells *when* and modifies the verb *studied*.]**

adverb phrase An adverb phrase is a prepositional phrase that modifies a verb, an adjective, or another adverb (page 148).

EXAMPLE Andy works well **under pressure. [adverb phrase modifying the adverb *well*.]**

agreement Agreement is the match between grammatical forms. A verb must agree with its subject (page 215). A pronoun must agree with its antecedent (page 242).

EXAMPLE The **freshmen** and **sophomores are debating** today. **[subject-verb agreement]**

EXAMPLE **Lissa** thanked **her** brother for driving **her** to the dance. **[pronoun-antecedent agreement]**

antecedent An antecedent is the word or group of words to which a pronoun refers or that a pronoun replaces. All pronouns must agree with their antecedents in number, gender, and person (page 242).

EXAMPLE ***Octavio Paz*** is one of the greatest poets of **his** era. **[singular masculine pronoun]**

EXAMPLE ***Emily Dickinson*** wrote **her** poems on scrap paper. **[singular feminine pronoun]**

EXAMPLE ***Walt Whitman*** and ***Emily Dickinson*** are famous for **their** poetry. **[plural pronoun]**

apostrophe An apostrophe (') is a punctuation mark used in possessive nouns, possessive indefinite pronouns, and contractions. In contractions it shows that one or more letters have been left out (page 346).

EXAMPLE   Leon didn't bring Celia's book, so she needs to borrow someone's.

appositive An appositive is a noun or a pronoun that is placed next to another noun or pronoun to identify it or give additional information about it (page 149).

EXAMPLE   My friend **Ethan** works at a bookstore after school. **[The appositive *Ethan* identifies the noun *friend*.]**

appositive phrase An appositive phrase is an appositive plus any words that modify the appositive (page 149).

EXAMPLE   He is saving money to travel to Bogotá, **the capital of Colombia. [The appositive phrase, in blue type, identifies *Bogotá*.]**

article Articles are the adjectives *a, an,* and *the. A* and *an* are called **indefinite articles.** They can refer to any one of a kind of person, place, or thing. *A* is used before consonant sounds, and *an* is used before vowel sounds. *The* is the **definite article.** It refers to a specific person, place, or thing (page 113).

EXAMPLES

indefinite   **a** ring, **a** used computer, **an** egg, **an** hour

definite   **the** ring, **the** used computer, **the** egg, **the** hour

auxiliary verb The most common auxiliary verbs are forms of *be* and *have.* They help the main verb express time by forming the various tenses (page 108).

EXAMPLE   We **will** weed the vegetable garden this morning.

READY REFERENCE

EXAMPLE   Sandra **has** already weeded the peppers and the tomatoes.

EXAMPLE   We **were** weeding the flower beds when the rain started.

The other auxiliary verbs are not used primarily to express time. They are often used to emphasize meaning.

EXAMPLE   I **should be** leaving.

EXAMPLE   **Could** he **have** forgotten?

EXAMPLE   Marisa **may** already **be** finished.

case Personal pronouns have three cases, or forms. The three cases are called **nominative, objective,** and **possessive**. The case of a personal pronoun depends on the pronoun's function in a sentence—that is, whether it's a subject, a complement, an object of a preposition, or a replacement for a possessive noun (page 233).

CASE	PERSONAL PRONOUNS		
	SINGULAR PRONOUNS	PLURAL PRONOUNS	FUNCTION IN SENTENCE
nominative	I, you, she, he, it	we, you, they	subject or predicate nominative
objective	me, you, her, him, it	us, you, them	direct object, indirect object, or object of preposition
possessive	my, mine, your, yours, her, hers, his, its	our, ours, your, yours, their, theirs	replacement for possessive noun(s)

clause A clause is a group of words that has a subject and a predicate (verb). A clause can function as a sentence by itself or as part of a sentence (page 164).

EXAMPLE   The curtain rose.

closing A closing is a way to end a letter. It begins with a capital letter and is followed by a comma (pages 295, 331).

EXAMPLES   Yours truly,   Sincerely,
                    Affectionately,   Your friend,

collective noun A collective noun is singular in form but names a group (pages 97, 220).

EXAMPLES   family   herd   company   band   team
                    audience   troop   committee   jury   flock

colon A colon (:) is a punctuation mark. It's used to introduce a list and to separate the hour and the minutes when you write the time of day. It's also used after the salutation of a business letter (page 316).

EXAMPLE   We need these ingredients: milk, eggs, and raisins.

EXAMPLE   The race will start at exactly 2:15 P.M.

EXAMPLE   Dear Senator Mathers:

comma A comma (,) is a punctuation mark that's used to separate items or to set them off from the rest of a sentence (page 320).

EXAMPLE   You'll find spoons, forks, and knives in that drawer.

EXAMPLE   The clowns, who had crammed themselves into the tiny car, all jumped out at once.

comma splice One type of run-on sentence, a comma splice, occurs when two main clauses are joined by a comma only (page 178).

EXAMPLES

comma splice	It rained the entire time the boys were on vacation**,** they still enjoyed the trip.
correct	It rained the entire time the boys were on vacation**.** They still enjoyed the trip.
correct	It rained the entire time the boys were on vacation**, but** they still enjoyed the trip.
correct	It rained the entire time the boys were on vacation**;** they still enjoyed the trip.

common noun A common noun is the general—not the particular—name of a person, place, thing, or idea (page 96). *See proper noun.*

EXAMPLES

person	artist, uncle, poet
place	country, lake, park
thing	shuttle, vehicle, play
idea	era, religion, movement

comparative degree The comparative degree of an adjective or adverb is the form that shows two things being compared (page 256).

EXAMPLE Kim's dog is **smaller** than my dog. **[adjective]**

EXAMPLE My dog ran **more swiftly** than the cat. **[adverb]**

complement A complement is a word or a group of words that completes the meaning of a verb (page 137). *See also direct objects, indirect objects,* and *subject complements (predicate nominatives* and *predicate adjectives).*

EXAMPLE Carlos served **dinner.**

EXAMPLE Maria admires **him** deeply.

complete predicate The complete predicate consists of the simple predicate, or verb, and all the words that modify it or complete its meaning (page 132).

EXAMPLE The team **will be going from Illinois to Rhode Island by way of Cedar Point in Sandusky, Ohio.**

complete subject The complete subject consists of the simple subject and all the words that modify it (page 132).

EXAMPLE **The small black kitten in the top cage** is the one for me.

complex sentence A complex sentence has one main clause and one or more subordinate clauses (page 174).

Main Clause

EXAMPLE I like Toni Cade Bambara's stories
S V

Subordinate Clause

Subordinate
Clause

because they have characters I can believe in.
S   V   S   V   V

Subordinate Clause   Main Clause

EXAMPLE When I read her stories, I enjoy them
S   V   S   V

Subordinate Clause

because they are realistic.
S   V

compound-complex sentence A compound-complex sentence has two or more main clauses and at least one subordinate clause (page 175).

Main Clause   Subordinate Clause

EXAMPLE I read *Frankenstein,* which Mary Shelley wrote,
S V   S   S   V

Main Clause

and I reported on it.
S   V

compound predicate A compound predicate (or compound verb) is made up of two or more verbs or verb phrases that are joined by a conjunction and have the same subject (page 134).

EXAMPLE Maria **opened** her book, **grabbed** a pencil, and **started** her homework.

EXAMPLE Seagulls **will glide** or **swoop** down to the ocean.

compound preposition A compound preposition is a preposition that is made up of more than one word (page 119).

EXAMPLES

according to	because of	next to
ahead of	by means of	instead of
along with	except for	on account of

compound sentence A compound sentence contains two or more main clauses (page 173).

EXAMPLE

Main Clause

Stories about the Old West are entertaining, **and**
S   V   V

Main Clause

stories set in foreign countries are interesting.
S   V   V

EXAMPLE

Main Clause   Main Clause

Stories entertain me, **and** riddles amuse me, **but**
S   V   S   V

Main Clause

poems are my favorite.
S   V

EXAMPLE

Main Clause   Main Clause

Comedies delight us; tragedies often teach us something.
S   V   S   V

compound subject A compound subject is made up of two or more simple subjects that are joined by a conjunction and have the same verb (page 133).

EXAMPLE   **Tomatoes** and **carrots** are colorful vegetables.

EXAMPLE   **Tomatoes** or **carrots** would add color to the salad.

EXAMPLE   **Tomatoes, carrots,** and **peppers** are healthful.

compound verb *See compound predicate.*

concrete noun A concrete noun names an object that occupies space or can be recognized by any of the senses (sight, smell, hearing, taste, and touch) (page 95). *See abstract noun.*

EXAMPLES   air   melody   stone   aroma   heat

conjunction A conjunction is a word that joins single words or groups of words (page 120). *See coordinating conjunction, correlative conjunction, and subordinating conjunction.*

conjunctive adverb A conjunctive adverb is used to clarify the relationship between clauses of equal weight in a sentence. Conjunctive adverbs are preceded by semicolons and followed by commas (page 123).

EXAMPLES

to replace *and*	also, besides, furthermore, moreover
to replace *but*	however, nevertheless, nonetheless, still, though
to state a result	accordingly, consequently, then, therefore, thus
to state equality	equally, indeed, likewise, similarly

EXAMPLE   Janine is not very organized; **accordingly,** she carries a day planner and consults it often.

contraction A contraction is a single word made up of two words that have been combined by omitting letters. Common contractions combine a subject and a verb or a verb and the word *not* (page 348).

EXAMPLES	**you'd**	*is formed from*	you had, you would
	you're		you are
	who's		who is, who has

coordinating conjunction A coordinating conjunction joins words or groups of words that have equal grammatical weight in a sentence (page 120).

and   but   or   so   nor   yet   for

EXAMPLE   One **and** six are seven. **[two nouns]**

EXAMPLE   Merlin was smart **but** irresponsible. **[two adjectives]**

EXAMPLE   Let's put the note on the TV **or** on the refrigerator.
[two prepositional phrases]

EXAMPLE   I wanted a new sun hat, **so** I bought one.
[two complete thoughts]

EXAMPLE   He did not complain, **nor** did he object to our plan.
[two complete thoughts]

EXAMPLE   Lightning struck the barn, **yet** no fire started.
[two complete thoughts]

EXAMPLE   We didn't explore the summit that night, **for** the climb
had exhausted us. **[two complete thoughts]**

correlative conjunction Correlative conjunctions work in pairs to join words and groups of words of equal grammatical weight in a sentence (page 121).

both . . . and   just as . . . so   not only . . . but (also)
either . . . or   neither . . . nor   whether . . . or

EXAMPLE   **Both** he **and** I were there.

EXAMPLE   **Either** she will sew new curtains, **or** I will put up
the old blinds.

EXAMPLE   I **not only** scrubbed **but also** waxed the floor.

dangling modifier Dangling modifiers seem logically to modify no word at all. To correct a sentence that has a dangling modifier, you must supply a word that the dangling modifier can sensibly modify (page 269).

EXAMPLES

dangling   **Working all night long,** the fire was extinguished. **[participial phrase logically modifying no word in the sentence]**

clear   **Working all night long,** the firefighters extinguished the fire. **[participial phrase modifying *firefighters*]**

dangling   **Sleeping soundly,** my dream was interrupted by the alarm. **[participial phrase logically modifying no word in the sentence]**

clear   **Sleeping soundly,** I had my dream interrupted by the alarm. **[participial phrase modifying *I*]**

dash A dash (—) is a punctuation mark. It's usually used in pairs to set off a sudden break or change in thought or speech (page 334).

EXAMPLE   Lionel Washington—he was my Boy Scout troop leader—is running for city council.

declarative sentence A declarative sentence makes a statement. A declarative sentence usually ends with a period but can end with an exclamation mark. This type of sentence is the most frequently used in speaking and writing (page 171).

EXAMPLE   I have four pets.

EXAMPLE   Two of my pets are dogs.

EXAMPLE   That's the cutest puppy I've ever seen!

demonstrative adjective A demonstrative adjective modifies a noun and points out something by answering the question *which one?* or *which ones? This, that, these,* and *those* are demonstrative adjectives when they modify nouns (page 110).

EXAMPLE   Bring **this** ticket with you; give **that** ticket to a friend.

EXAMPLE   We need **these** props; **those** props can be stored.

demonstrative pronoun A demonstrative pronoun points out specific persons, places, things, or ideas (page 102).

DEMONSTRATIVE PRONOUNS

singular	this	that
plural	these	those

EXAMPLE   Bring **this** with you.

EXAMPLE   Give **that** to a friend.

EXAMPLE   We'll need **these** for the show.

EXAMPLE   The director wrote **those.**

dependent clause *See subordinate clause.*

direct address Direct address is a name, a word, or a phrase used in speaking directly to a person. Words used in direct address are set off by commas (page 330).

EXAMPLE   **Christie,** do you like my haircut?

EXAMPLE   You can't park here**, buddy.**

EXAMPLE   I am very proud of you, **Daughter,** and I want you to know it.

direct object A direct object answers the question *what?* or *whom?* after an action verb (page 138).

EXAMPLE   Carlos served **dinner.**

EXAMPLE   Carlos served a Japanese **dinner** and a fabulous **dessert.**

EXAMPLE   Paula called **Carlos** on the telephone.

direct quotation A direct quotation gives the speaker's exact words. It is preceded and followed by quotation marks (page 294).

EXAMPLE   My little brother asked, **"Why can't I go too?"**

double comparison Don't use both *-er* and *more*. Don't use both *-est* and *most*. To do so would be an error called a double comparison (page 260).

EXAMPLES

incorrect   A redwood grows more taller than an oak.

correct   A redwood grows **taller** than an oak.

incorrect   Aunt Ellie is my most kindest aunt.

correct   Aunt Ellie is my **kindest** aunt.

double negative A double negative is the use of two or more negative words to express the same idea. Use only one negative word to express a negative idea (page 266).

EXAMPLES

incorrect   I don't have no stereo equipment.

correct   I do**n't** have **any** stereo equipment.

correct   I have **no** stereo equipment.

incorrect   We haven't seen no concerts this year.

correct   We have**n't** seen **any** concerts this year.

correct   We have seen **no** concerts this year.

emphatic forms of a verb The present tense and the past tense have additional forms, called emphatic forms, that add special force, or emphasis, to the verb. You make the emphatic forms by using *do, does,* or *did* with the base form of the verb (page 205).

EXAMPLES

present emphatic	I **do hope** the train is on time.
	Tom **does have** a plane to catch.
past emphatic	He **did miss** his plane the last time because of a late train.

end mark An end mark is a punctuation mark used at the end of a sentence. Periods, question marks, and exclamation points are end marks (pages 314–315).

EXAMPLE Here is your clean laundry.

EXAMPLE Did you forget your jacket?

EXAMPLE What a gorgeous salad that is!

essential clause Some adjective clauses are necessary to make the meaning of a sentence clear. Such an adjective clause is called an *essential clause,* or a *restrictive clause.* Do not set off an essential clause with commas (page 167).

EXAMPLE Magazines **that have no substance** bore me.

EXAMPLE Many writers **whose works have become famous** began their writing careers at the *New Yorker* magazine.

exclamation point An exclamation point (!) is a punctuation mark used to end a sentence that shows strong feeling (exclamatory). It's also used after strong interjections (page 314).

EXAMPLE Yikes! We'll be late!

exclamatory sentence An exclamatory sentence expresses strong emotion and ends with an exclamation point. Note that exclamatory sentences can be declarative (first example), imperative (second example), or interrogative (third example) while expressing strong emotion. In writing, exclamatory sentences should be used sparingly so as not to detract from their effectiveness (page 171).

EXAMPLE   She is such a beautiful dog!

EXAMPLE   Don't chew on that!

EXAMPLE   What do you think you are doing!

future perfect tense   Use the future perfect tense to express one future action or condition that will begin *and* end before another future event starts.

You form the future perfect tense by using *will have* or *shall have* with the past participle of a verb: *will have practiced, shall have flown* (page 202).

EXAMPLE   By September I **will have saved** fifty dollars.
   [The money will be saved by the time another future event, the arrival of September, occurs.]

future tense   Use the future tense to express an action or a condition that will occur in the future (pages 198–199).

EXAMPLE   Robby **will order** the supplies.

EXAMPLE   I **will pack** the car in the morning.

gender   The gender of a noun may be masculine (male), feminine (female), or neuter (referring to things) (page 242).

EXAMPLES   **man** (masculine)   **aunt** (feminine)   **notebook** (neuter)

gender-neutral language   Language that does not assume the gender of a noun is called gender-neutral language. Use gender-neutral language when the gender is unknown or could be either masculine or feminine (pages 243, 444).

EXAMPLE   An *author* must capture **his or her** readers' interest.

EXAMPLE *Authors* must capture **their** readers' interest.

EXAMPLE *Authors* must capture readers' interest.

gerund A gerund is a verb form that ends in -*ing* and is used in the same ways a noun is used (page 153).

EXAMPLE **Cooking** is an enjoyable activity. **[gerund as subject]**

EXAMPLE My younger sister likes **swimming. [gerund as direct object]**

gerund phrase A gerund phrase contains a gerund plus any complements and modifiers (page 153).

EXAMPLE **Cross-country skiing** is good exercise.

EXAMPLE **Billie Holiday's soulful singing** delighted many audiences.

helping verb *See auxiliary verb.*

hyphen A hyphen (-) is a punctuation mark that's used in compound words (page 349).

EXAMPLE Luis's great-grandfather hung twenty-one bird feeders.

"IT MAY NOT BE A PERFECT WHEEL, BUT IT'S A STATE-OF-THE-ART WHEEL."

Reprinted by permission of Sidney Harris.

imperative sentence An imperative sentence gives a command or makes a request. An imperative sentence usually ends with a period but can end with an exclamation mark. In imperative sentences, the subject *you* is understood (page 171).

EXAMPLE   Get off the table.

EXAMPLE   Duck!

indefinite pronoun An indefinite pronoun refers to persons, places, things, or ideas in a more general way than a noun does (page 104).

INDEFINITE PRONOUNS

always singular	another	either	neither	other
	anybody	everybody	no one	somebody
	anyone	everyone	nobody	someone
	anything	everything	nothing	something
	each	much	one	
always plural	both	few	many	
	others	several		
singular or plural	all	any	enough	most
	none	some		

EXAMPLE   **Everybody** needs food. [The indefinite pronoun *Everybody* refers to people in general.]

EXAMPLE   Did you get **enough** to eat? [The indefinite pronoun *enough* refers to a general, not a specific, amount.]

EXAMPLE   After two bowls of chili, I did not want **another**. [The indefinite pronoun *another* has the antecedent *bowls (of chili)*.]

independent clause An independent clause has a subject and a predicate and expresses a complete thought. It is the only type of clause that can stand alone as a sentence. An independent clause is also called a main clause (page 164).

EXAMPLE   **The curtain rose.**

EXAMPLE   **The cast bowed,** and **the audience applauded.**

indirect object   An indirect object answers the question *to whom? for whom? to what?* or *for what?* after an action verb (page 138).

EXAMPLE   Tyrone served his **sisters** dinner.

indirect quotation   An indirect quotation paraphrases a speaker's words and should not be capitalized or enclosed in quotation marks (page 294). *See direct quotation.*

EXAMPLE   My brother asked **why** he couldn't go.

infinitive   An infinitive is a verb form that is usually preceded by the word *to* and is used as a noun, an adjective, or an adverb (page 154).

EXAMPLE   His goal is **to graduate. [infinitive as predicate nominative]**

EXAMPLE   They have the desire **to win. [infinitive as adjective]**

infinitive phrase   An infinitive phrase contains an infinitive plus any complements and modifiers (page 155).

EXAMPLE   We stopped **to look at the beautiful scenery.**

EXAMPLE   **To be a good friend** is my goal.

intensive pronoun   An intensive pronoun ends with *-self* or *-selves* and is used to draw special attention to a noun or a pronoun already named (pages 102, 239).

EXAMPLE   He **himself** delivered the flowers.

EXAMPLE   You must sign the application **yourself.**

interjection   An interjection is a word or phrase that expresses emotion or exclamation. An interjection has no grammatical connection to other words (page 125).

EXAMPLE **Oh, my!** What is that?

EXAMPLE **Ouch,** it's hot!

interrogative pronoun An interrogative pronoun is used to form questions (page 103).

who	whom	what	which	whose
whoever	whomever	whatever	whichever	

EXAMPLE **Who** is at the door?

EXAMPLE **Whom** would you prefer?

EXAMPLE **Whose** is this plaid coat?

EXAMPLE **Whatever** is that odd noise?

interrogative sentence An interrogative sentence asks a question. It usually ends with a question mark but can end with an exclamation point if it expresses strong emotion (page 171).

EXAMPLE How many pets do you have**?**

EXAMPLE What in the world were you thinking**!**

intransitive verb An intransitive verb is *not* followed by a word that answers the question *what?* or *whom?* (page 106). *See transitive verb.*

EXAMPLE The batter **swung** wildly. **[The verb is followed by a word that tells *how*.]**

inverted order A sentence written in inverted order, in which the predicate comes before the subject, serves to add emphasis to the subject (pages 136, 225).

EXAMPLES

PREDICATE	SUBJECT
Across the field **galloped**	the three **horses.**
In the distance **flowed**	a **river.**

irregular verb An irregular verb forms its past and past participle in some way other than by adding *-ed* or *-d* to the base form (page 189).

EXAMPLES

BASE FORM	PAST FORM	PAST PARTICIPLE
be, am, are, is	was, were	been
swim	swam	swum
put	put	put
write	wrote	written
lie	lay	lain

italics Italics are printed letters that slant to the right. *This sentence is printed in italic type.* Italics are used for the titles of certain kinds of published works, works of art, foreign terms, and other situations. In handwriting, underlining is a substitute for italics (page 343).

EXAMPLE This ***Newsweek*** magazine has an article about Picasso's painting ***Guernica.***

EXAMPLE Cicero's saying ***Omnia praeclara rara*** can be translated as "All excellent things are scarce."

linking verb A linking verb links, or joins, the subject of a sentence (often a noun or a pronoun) with a noun, a pronoun, or an adjective that identifies or describes the subject. A linking verb does not show action. *Be* in all its forms—*am, is, are, was, were*—is the most commonly used linking verb (page 108).

EXAMPLE The person behind the mask **was** you.

EXAMPLE The players **are** ready.

EXAMPLE Archery **is** an outdoor sport.

EXAMPLE They **were** sports fans.

Several other verbs besides *be* can act as linking verbs.

OTHER VERBS THAT CAN BE LINKING VERBS

appear	grow	seem	stay
become	look	sound	taste
feel	remain	smell	turn

EXAMPLE   This salad **tastes** good.

EXAMPLE   The sun **feels** warm on my shoulders.

EXAMPLE   You **look** comfortable.

EXAMPLE   The leaves **turned** brown.

main clause A main clause has a subject and a predicate and expresses a complete thought. It is the only type of clause that can stand alone as a sentence. A main clause is also called an **independent clause** (page 164).

EXAMPLE   **The curtain rose.**

EXAMPLE   **The cast bowed,** and **the audience applauded.**

EXAMPLE   **The curtains closed for several minutes,** but **the applause continued.**

main verb A main verb is the last word in a verb phrase. If a verb stands alone, it's a main verb (page 108).

EXAMPLE   The band members have been **selling** light bulbs for a month.

EXAMPLE   One band member **sold** two cases of light bulbs.

misplaced modifier Misplaced modifiers modify the wrong word, or they seem to modify more than one word in a sentence. To correct a sentence that has a misplaced modifier, move the modifier as close as possible to the word it modifies (page 267).

EXAMPLE

misplaced **Soaring over the edge of the cliff,** the photographer captured an image of the eagle. **[participial phrase incorrectly modifying *photographer*]**

clear The photographer captured an image of the eagle **soaring over the edge of the cliff.** **[participial phrase correctly modifying *eagle*]**

nominative case Use the nominative case for a pronoun that is a subject or a predicate nominative (page 233).

EXAMPLE **We** have raised enough money.

EXAMPLE The lead soprano will be **she.**

nonessential clause An adjective clause that adds information to a sentence but is not necessary to make the meaning of the sentence clear is called a *nonessential clause* or a *nonrestrictive clause.* Always use commas to set off a nonessential clause (pages 168, 324).

EXAMPLE James Thurber, **who was a famous humorist,** wrote for the *New Yorker.*

EXAMPLE His stories, **which include humorous incidents from his childhood in Ohio,** make funny and interesting reading.

nonrestrictive clause *See nonessential clause.*

noun A noun is a word that names a person, a place, a thing, or an idea (page 93).

EXAMPLES

person uncle, doctor, baby, Luisa, son-in-law

place kitchen, mountain, website, West Virginia

thing   apple, tulip, continent, seagull, amplifier

idea   respect, pride, love, appreciation, century

noun clause A noun clause is a subordinate clause that is used as a noun within the main clause of a sentence. You can use a noun clause as a subject, a direct object, an indirect object, an object of a preposition, or a predicate nominative (page 169).

EXAMPLE   **Whoever wins the election** will speak. **[noun clause as subject]**

number Number refers to the form of a word that indicates whether it is singular or plural. A verb must agree with its subject in number (page 215).

	SINGULAR	PLURAL
EXAMPLE	The **athlete exercises.**	The **athletes exercise.**
EXAMPLE	The **cat scratches.**	The **cats scratch.**

O

object complement An object complement answers the question *what?* after a direct object. That is, it *completes* the meaning of the direct object by identifying or describing it (page 139).

EXAMPLE   Residents find the park **peaceful. [adjective]**

EXAMPLE   Maya appointed me **spokesperson** and **treasurer. [nouns]**

EXAMPLE   My grandmother considers the property **hers. [pronoun]**

object of a preposition An object of a preposition is the noun or pronoun that ends a prepositional phrase (page 118).

EXAMPLE   The diamonds in the **vault** are priceless. **[*In* shows the relationship between the diamonds and the object of the preposition, *vault*.]**

objective case Use the objective case for a pronoun that is a direct object, an indirect object, or an object of a preposition (pages 233–234).

EXAMPLE The coach trained **her.** [direct object]

EXAMPLE The prompter gave **me** my cues. [indirect object]

EXAMPLE Third prize was split between **me** and **him.** [object of preposition]

parentheses Parentheses ( ) are punctuation marks used to set off words that define or explain another word (page 335).

EXAMPLE Myanmar **(**formerly Burma**)** is on the Bay of Bengal.

parenthetical expression Parenthetical expressions are side thoughts that add information. Parenthetical expressions should be set off by commas, dashes, or parentheses (pages 326, 335–337).

EXAMPLES in fact   on the other hand   on the contrary
          by the way   to be exact   after all

EXAMPLE **By the way,** did Mom call today?

EXAMPLE I'm responsible for about a hundred tickets—**to be exact,** 106.

participial phrase A participial phrase contains a participle plus any complements and modifiers (page 151).

EXAMPLE The dog saw many ducks **swimming in the lake.**

EXAMPLE **Barking loudly,** the dog approached the water.

participle A participle is a verb form that can function as an adjective (pages 111, 151).

EXAMPLE A **moving** van is parked on our street. [present participle]

EXAMPLE The dogs watched the **striped** cat. [past participle]

passive voice An action verb is in the passive voice when its action is performed on the subject (page 208). *See active voice.*

EXAMPLE   A salmon **was caught** by the brown bear.

past perfect tense Use the past perfect tense to indicate that one past action or condition began *and* ended before another past action or condition started. You form the past perfect tense by using the auxiliary verb *had* with the past participle of a verb: *had praised, had written* (page 201).

EXAMPLE

PAST   PAST PERFECT

Pat **dedicated** her play to the drama teacher who **had encouraged** her long ago. [First the drama teacher encouraged Pat; then years later Patricia acknowledged her teacher's support.]

past tense Use the past tense to express an action or a condition that was started and completed in the past (page 198).

EXAMPLE   The track meet **went** well.

EXAMPLE   Nan **set** a new school record for the shot put.

period A period (.) is a punctuation mark used to end a sentence that makes a statement (declarative) or gives a command (imperative). It's also used at the end of many abbreviations (pages 314, 353).

EXAMPLE   I can't tell whether this recipe specifies "1 tsp." or "1 tbsp." of cinnamon. **[declarative]**

EXAMPLE   Please mail a check to Dr. Benson. **[imperative]**

personal pronoun A personal pronoun refers to a specific person, place, thing, or idea by indicating the person speaking (the first person), the person being spoken to (the second person), or any other person, place, thing, or idea being discussed (the third person). Like a noun, a personal pronoun expresses number; that is, it can be singular or plural (pages 99, 233).

PERSONAL PRONOUNS

	SINGULAR	PLURAL
first person	I, me	we, us
second person	you	you
third person	he, him, she, her, it	they, them

EXAMPLES

first person	The song was dedicated to **me**. [*Me* refers to the person speaking.]
second person	Sam will copy the document for **you**. [*You* refers to the person being spoken to.]
third person	**She** gave **him** the good news. [*She* and *him* refer to the people being talked about.]

phrase A phrase is a group of words that acts in a sentence as a single part of speech (page 147).

positive degree The positive degree of an adjective or adverb is the form that cannot be used to make a comparison. This form appears as the entry word in a dictionary (page 256).

EXAMPLE My dog is **small.**

EXAMPLE The cat ran **swiftly.**

possessive pronoun A possessive pronoun takes the place of the possessive form of a noun (page 100).

POSSESSIVE PRONOUNS

	SINGULAR	PLURAL
first person	my, mine	our, ours
second person	your, yours	your, yours
third person	his, her, hers, its	their, theirs

predicate The predicate is the part of the sentence that says something about the subject (page 131).

EXAMPLE Garth Brooks **will perform.**

predicate adjective A predicate adjective follows a linking verb and points back to the subject and further describes it (page 140).

EXAMPLE   Firefighters are **brave.**

EXAMPLE   Firefighters must be extremely **careful.**

predicate nominative A predicate nominative is a noun or a pronoun that follows a linking verb and points back to the subject to rename it or to identify it further (page 140).

EXAMPLE   Sopranos are **singers.**

EXAMPLE   Many current opera stars are **Italians** or **Spaniards.**

EXAMPLE   Fiona became both a **musician** and an **architect.**

preposition A preposition is a word that shows the relationship of a noun or a pronoun to another word in a sentence (page 118).

| aboard | beneath | in | regarding |
| about | beside | inside | respecting |

EXAMPLE   I read **to** Carlito **from** the new book.

prepositional phrase A prepositional phrase is a group of words that begins with a preposition and ends with a noun or a pronoun that is called the object of the preposition (page 147).

EXAMPLE   The diamonds **in the vault** are priceless. [*In* **shows the relationship between** *The diamonds* **and the object of the preposition,** *vault.*]

EXAMPLE   The telephone rang four times **during dinner.** [*During* **shows the relationship between** *rang* **and the object of the preposition,** *dinner.*]

EXAMPLE   Here is a gift **for you.** [*For* **relates** *gift* **to the object of the preposition,** *you.*]

present perfect tense Use the present perfect tense to express an action or a condition that occurred at some *indefinite*

time in the past. You form the present perfect tense by using *has* or *have* with the past participle of a verb: *has permitted, have cut* (page 200).

EXAMPLE   The living-room clock **has stopped.**

EXAMPLE   They **have brought** the new couch a day early.

present tense   The present tense expresses a constant, repeated, or habitual action or condition. It can also express a general truth or an action or a condition that exists only now. It is sometimes used in historical writing to express past events and, more often, in poetry, fiction, and journalism (especially in sports writing) to convey to the reader a sense of being there. This usage is sometimes called the *historical present tense* (page 195).

EXAMPLE   Isaac **likes** the taste of tea with honey in it. **[not just this cup of tea but every cup of tea; a repeated action]**

EXAMPLE   Emily **bakes** wonderful spice cookies. **[always; a habitual action]**

EXAMPLE   Gold **is** valuable. **[a general truth]**

EXAMPLE   I **see** a hummingbird at the feeder. **[at this very moment]**

EXAMPLE   The goalie **throws** her body across the opening and **blocks** the shot in the final seconds of the game. **[historical present]**

principal parts of verbs   All verbs have four principal parts: a *base form*, a *present participle*, a *simple past form*, and a *past participle*. All the verb tenses are formed from these principal parts (page 187).

EXAMPLES

PRINCIPAL PARTS OF VERBS

BASE FORM	PRESENT PARTICIPLE	PAST FORM	PAST PARTICIPLE
play	playing	played	played
carry	carrying	carried	carried
sing	singing	sang	sung

progressive forms of a verb Each of the six tenses has a progressive form that expresses a continuing action. You make the progressive forms by using the appropriate tense of the verb *be* with the present participle of the main verb (page 204).

EXAMPLE

present progressive	They *are* **traveling.**
past progressive	They *were* **traveling.**
future progressive	They *will be* **traveling.**
present perfect progressive	They *have been* **traveling.**
past perfect progressive	They *had been* **traveling.**
future perfect progressive	They *will have been* **traveling.**

pronoun A pronoun is a word that takes the place of a noun, a group of words acting as a noun, or another pronoun. The word or group of words to which a pronoun refers is called its antecedent (page 98).

EXAMPLE Though Georgia O'Keeffe was born in Wisconsin, **she** grew to love the landscape of the American Southwest. **[The pronoun *she* takes the place of its proper noun antecedent, *Georgia O'Keeffe*.]**

EXAMPLE When Georgia O'Keeffe and Alfred Stieglitz were married in 1924, **both** were famous artists. **[The pronoun *both* takes the place of the nouns *Georgia O'Keeffe* and *Alfred Stieglitz*.]**

EXAMPLE Though O'Keeffe **herself** was a painter, **her** husband was a photographer. **[The pronouns *herself* and *her* take the place of the nouns *O'Keeffe* and *O'Keeffe's*.]**

proper adjective A proper adjective is formed from a proper noun. It begins with a capital letter (page 113).

EXAMPLE Vancouver is a **Canadian** city.

EXAMPLE We visited the **London** Zoo.

proper noun A proper noun is the name of a particular person, place, thing, or idea (page 96). *See common noun.*

EXAMPLES

PROPER NOUNS

person	Michelangelo, Uncle Louis, Maya Angelou
place	Mexico, Lake Superior, Yellowstone National Park
thing	*Challenger*, Jeep, *Romeo and Juliet*
idea	Industrial Age, Judaism, Romanticism

question mark A question mark (?) is a punctuation mark used to end a sentence that asks a question (interrogative) (page 315).

EXAMPLE   Can you imagine what life would be like without television**?**

quotation marks Quotation marks (" ") are punctuation marks used to enclose the exact words of a speaker. They're also used for titles of certain published works (pages 341–342).

EXAMPLE   "Let's record ourselves reading aloud," said Lou, "and give the tape to the children's hospital."

EXAMPLE   They decided on something a bit more cheerful than "The Pit and the Pendulum."

reflexive pronoun A reflexive pronoun always ends with *-self* or *-selves* and refers, or reflects back, to the subject of a clause, indicating that the same person or thing is involved. A reflexive pronoun always adds information to a sentence (pages 101–102, 239).

EXAMPLE Jim uses a stopwatch to time **himself** on the track.

EXAMPLE She taught **herself** to play the piano.

EXAMPLE We imagined **ourselves** dancing in a forest glade.

regular verb A regular verb forms its past and past participle by adding *-ed* or *-d* to the base form (page 189).

EXAMPLES

REGULAR VERBS

BASE FORM	PAST FORM	PAST PARTICIPLE
climb	climbed	climbed
skate	skated	skated
trot	trotted	trotted

relative pronoun A relative pronoun is used to begin a subordinate clause (pages 103–104).

RELATIVE PRONOUNS

who	whoever	which	that
whom	whomever	whichever	what
	whose	whatever	

EXAMPLE The driver **who** arrived last parked over there. **[The relative pronoun *who* begins the subordinate clause *who arrived last*.]**

EXAMPLE The meal **that** you prepared was delicious. **[The relative pronoun *that* begins the subordinate clause *that you prepared*.]**

restrictive clause *See essential clause.*

run-on sentence A run-on sentence is two or more complete sentences written as though they were one sentence (page 178). *See comma splice.*

Glossary of Terms **35**

EXAMPLE	**run-on**	It rained the entire time the boys were on vacation they still enjoyed the trip.
	run-on	It rained the entire time the boys were on vacation but they still enjoyed the trip.
	run-on	It rained the entire time the boys were on vacation, they still enjoyed the trip.
	correct	It rained the entire time the boys were on vacation. **T**hey still enjoyed the trip.
	correct	It rained the entire time the boys were on vacation, **b**ut they still enjoyed the trip.
	correct	It rained the entire time the boys were on vacation; they still enjoyed the trip.

salutation A salutation is the greeting in a letter. The first word and any proper nouns in a salutation should be capitalized. In a friendly letter, the salutation ends with a comma; in a business letter, the salutation ends with a colon (pages 295, 317, 331).

EXAMPLE **M**y dear cousin **N**ancy,

Dear **C**ouncilwoman **R**amos:

semicolon A semicolon (;) is a punctuation mark used to join the main clauses of a compound sentence (page 318).

EXAMPLE Juliana will sing the melody; Maurice and Lee will harmonize.

sentence A sentence is a group of words that expresses a complete thought (page 130).

EXAMPLE Hector Hugh Munro wrote stories using the pseudonym Saki.

sentence fragment A sentence fragment is an error that occurs when an incomplete sentence is punctuated as though it were complete (page 177).

EXAMPLE

fragment	**The two weary hikers walking for hours.** **[lacks complete predicate]**
complete sentence	The two weary hikers had been walking for hours.

simple predicate The simple predicate is the verb or verb phrase that expresses an action or a state of being about the subject of the sentence (page 131).

EXAMPLE The team **will be going** from Illinois to Rhode Island by way of Cedar Point in Sandusky, Ohio.

simple sentence A simple sentence contains only one main clause and no subordinate clauses (page 172).

EXAMPLE Stories entertain.

EXAMPLE Long, complicated, fantastic stories with aliens, space travelers, and happy endings entertain and educate men, women, and children all over the world.

simple subject The simple subject is the key noun or pronoun (or word or word group acting as a noun) that tells what the sentence is about (page 131).

EXAMPLE The black **kitten** in the top cage is the one for me.

subject The subject is the part of the sentence that names whom or what the sentence is about (page 131).

EXAMPLE **Dogs** were barking.

subject complement A subject complement follows a subject and a linking verb and identifies or describes the subject (page 139). *See predicate nominative and predicate adjective.*

EXAMPLE   Sopranos are **singers.**

EXAMPLE   The star of the opera was **she.**

EXAMPLE   The singer grew **hoarse.**

subordinate clause A subordinate clause, also called a dependent clause, has a subject and a predicate but does not express a complete thought. It cannot stand alone as a sentence (page 164).

EXAMPLE   **When the dog barked,** the baby cried.

EXAMPLE   Dogs **that obey** are a joy.

EXAMPLE   **Whoever joins the circus** will travel across the country.

subordinating conjunction A subordinating conjunction joins two clauses, or ideas, in such a way as to make one grammatically dependent on the other. The idea, or clause, that a subordinating conjunction introduces is said to be "subordinate," or dependent, because it cannot stand by itself as a complete sentence (page 122).

after	as though	since	until
although	because	so long as	when
as	before	so (that)	whenever

EXAMPLE   We can skate on the pond **when** the ice is thicker.

EXAMPLE   We can't skate **until** the ice is thicker.

superlative degree The superlative degree of an adjective or adverb is the form that shows three or more things being compared (page 256).

EXAMPLE   Of the three dogs, Ray's dog is the **smallest** one.

EXAMPLE   The squirrel ran **most swiftly** of all.

syllable When a word must be divided at the end of a line, it is generally divided between syllables or pronounceable parts. Because it is often difficult to decide where a word should be divided, consult a dictionary. In general, if a word contains two consonants occurring between two vowels or if it contains double consonants, divide the word between the two consonants (page 352).

EXAMPLES profes-sor   foun-tain   struc-ture
              tomor-row   lin-ger   sup-per

tense Tenses are the forms of a verb that help to show time. There are six tenses in English: *present, past, future, present perfect, past perfect,* and *future perfect* (page 195).

EXAMPLE

present tense	I **sing.**
past tense	I **sang.**
future tense	I **shall** (*or* **will**) **sing.**
present perfect tense	I **have sung.**
past perfect tense	I **had sung.**
future perfect tense	I **shall** (*or* **will**) **have sung.**

PEANUTS reprinted by permission of United
Feature Syndicate, Inc.

transitive verb A transitive verb is an action verb followed by a word or words that answer the question *what?* or *whom?* (page 106). *See intransitive verb.*

EXAMPLE The batter **swung** the bat confidently. **[The action verb *swung* is followed by the noun *bat*, which answers the question *swung what?*]**

verb A verb is a word that expresses action or a state of being and is necessary to make a statement (page 105).

EXAMPLE   The bicyclist **grinned.**

EXAMPLE   The riders **seem** enthusiastic.

verbal A verbal is a verb form that functions in a sentence as a noun, an adjective, or an adverb. Verbals are *participles, gerunds,* and *infinitives.* Each of these can be expanded into phrases (page 151).

EXAMPLE   **Exhausted,** the team headed for the locker room. **[past participle]**

EXAMPLE   **Swimming** is my sport. **[gerund]**

EXAMPLE   I want **to win. [infinitive]**

verb phrase A verb phrase consists of a main verb and all its auxiliary, or helping, verbs (page 108). The most common auxiliary verbs are forms of *be* and *have.* They help the main verb express time by forming the various tenses.

EXAMPLE   We **will weed** the vegetable garden this morning.

EXAMPLE   We **were weeding** the flower beds when the rain started.

The other auxiliary verbs are not used primarily to express time. They are often used to emphasize meaning.

EXAMPLE   I **should be leaving.**

EXAMPLE   **Could** he **have forgotten?**

verbal phrase A verbal phrase is a verbal plus any complements and modifiers (page 151).

EXAMPLE **Frightened by the barking dogs,** the kittens ran to their mother. **[participial phrase]**

EXAMPLE **Swimming twenty laps a day** is my goal. **[gerund phrase]**

EXAMPLE I like **to sing the fight song. [infinitive phrase]**

voice Voice is the form a verb takes to explain whether the subject performs the action or the action is performed upon the subject. An action verb is in the active voice when the subject of the sentence performs the action. An action verb is in the passive voice when its action is performed on the subject (page 208).

EXAMPLE The brown bear **caught** a salmon. **[active voice]**

EXAMPLE A salmon **was caught** by the brown bear. **[passive voice]**

USAGE GLOSSARY

This glossary presents some particularly troublesome matters of usage. The glossary will guide you in choosing between words that are often confused. It will also alert you to certain words and expressions you should avoid when you speak or write for school or business.

a, an Use *a* before words that begin with a consonant sound. Use *an* before words that begin with a vowel sound.

EXAMPLES **a** poem, **a** house, **a** yacht, **a** union, **a** one-track mind

EXAMPLES **an** apple, **an** icicle, **an** honor, **an** umbrella, **an** only child

accede, exceed *Accede* means "to agree." *Exceed* means "to go beyond."

EXAMPLE I **acceded** to Mom's wishes.

EXAMPLE Don't **exceed** the speed limit.

accept, except *Accept* is a verb that means "to receive" or "to agree to." *Except* is usually a preposition meaning "but." *Except* may also be a verb that means "to leave out or exclude."

EXAMPLE Will you **accept** our thanks?

EXAMPLE The president **accepted** the terms of the treaty.

EXAMPLE Everyone will be there **except** you. **[preposition]**

EXAMPLE The government **excepts** people with very low incomes from paying taxes. **[verb]**

access, excess *Access* means "admittance." An *excess* is a surplus.

EXAMPLE The thief gained **access** to the building with a stolen key.

EXAMPLE We have an **excess** of musical talent in our class.

adapt, adopt *Adapt* means "to change to meet new requirements" or "to adjust." *Adopt* means "to accept and take as one's own."

EXAMPLE   I can **adapt** to new surroundings easily.

EXAMPLE   We can **adapt** this old bathrobe for a Roman senator's costume.

EXAMPLE   I think that dog has **adopted** you.

advice, advise *Advice*, a noun, means "an opinion offered as guidance." *Advise*, a verb, means "to give advice" or "to counsel."

EXAMPLE   Why should I **advise** you when you never accept my **advice**?

affect, effect *Affect* is a verb that means "to cause a change in" or "to influence the emotions of." *Effect* may be a noun or a verb. As a noun, it means "result." As a verb, it means "to bring about or accomplish."

EXAMPLE   The mayor's policies have **affected** every city agency.

EXAMPLE   The mayor's policies have had a positive **effect** on every city agency. **[noun]**

EXAMPLE   The mayor has **effected** positive changes in every city agency. **[verb]**

ain't *Ain't* is unacceptable in speaking and writing unless you're quoting someone's exact words or writing dialogue. Use *I'm not; you, we,* or *they aren't; he, she,* or *it isn't.*

all ready, already *All ready* means "completely ready." *Already* is an adverb that means "before" or "by this time."

EXAMPLE   The band was **all ready** to play its last number, but the fans were **already** leaving the stadium.

all right, alright The spelling *alright* is not acceptable in formal writing. Use *all right*.

EXAMPLE Don't worry; everything will be **all right**.

all the farther, all the faster These expressions are not acceptable in formal speech and writing. Use *as far as* and *as fast as*.

EXAMPLE Five hundred miles was **as far as** [*not* **all the farther**] we could drive in a single day.

EXAMPLE This is **as fast as** [*not* **all the faster**] I can pedal.

all together, altogether Use *all together* to mean "in a group." Use *altogether* to mean "completely" or "in all."

EXAMPLE Let's cheer **all together**.

EXAMPLE You are being **altogether** silly.

EXAMPLE I have three dollars in quarters and two dollars in dimes; that's five dollars **altogether**.

allusion, illusion An *allusion* is an indirect reference. An *illusion* is a false idea or appearance.

EXAMPLE Her speech included an **allusion** to one of Robert Frost's poems.

EXAMPLE The shimmering heat produced an **illusion** of water on the road.

almost, most Don't use *most* in place of *almost*.

EXAMPLE Marty **almost** [*not* **most**] always makes the honor roll.

a lot, alot, allot *A lot* should always be written as two words. It means "a large number or amount." Avoid using *a lot* in formal writing; be specific. The verb *allot* means "to assign or set aside" or "to distribute."

EXAMPLE   **A lot** [*not* **Alot**] of snow fell last night.
        ***Better:* A great deal** of snow fell last night.

EXAMPLE   The legislature will **allot** funds for a new capitol.

altar, alter   An *altar* is a raised structure at which religious
ceremonies are performed. *Alter* means "to change."

EXAMPLE   The bride and groom approached the **altar**.

EXAMPLE   The wardrobe manager **altered** some of the costumes
        to fit the new cast members.

among, between   In general use *among* to show a relationship
in which more than two persons or things are considered as
a group.

EXAMPLE   The committee will distribute the used clothing **among**
        the poor families in the community.

EXAMPLE   There was confusion **among** the players on the field.

   In general, use *between* to show a relationship involving
two persons or things, to compare one person or thing with
an entire group, or to compare more than two items within
a group.

EXAMPLE   Mr. and Mrs. Ito live halfway **between** Seattle and
        Portland. **[relationship involving two places]**

EXAMPLE   What was the difference **between** Frank Sinatra and
        other vocalists of the twentieth century?
        [one person compared with a group]

EXAMPLE   Emilio could not decide **between** the collie, the cocker
        spaniel, and the beagle. **[items within a group]**

amount, number   *Amount* and *number* both refer to quantity.
Use *amount* for things that can't be counted. Use *number*
for things that can be counted.

EXAMPLE   Fort Knox contains a vast **amount** of gold.

EXAMPLE   Fort Knox contains a large **number** of gold bars.

and/or This expression, once common in legal language, should be avoided in general writing. Change *and/or* to "this *or* that *or both*."

EXAMPLE We'll go hiking **or** skiing **or both**. [*not* We'll go hiking and/or skiing.]

anxious, eager *Anxious* comes from *anxiety;* therefore, it implies uneasiness or apprehension. It is not a synonym for *eager,* which means "filled with enthusiasm."

EXAMPLE Jean was **anxious** about her test results.

EXAMPLE She was **eager** [*not* anxious] to begin college.

anyways, anywheres, everywheres, nowheres, somewheres Write and speak these words without the final *s: anyway, anywhere, everywhere, nowhere, somewhere.*

ascent, assent An *ascent* is a rise or an act of climbing. *Assent* as a verb means "to agree or consent"; as a noun, it means "agreement" or "consent."

EXAMPLE We watched the **ascent** of the balloon.

EXAMPLE Will your parents **assent** to our plans? [verb]

EXAMPLE They were happy to give their **assent** to the plans. [noun]

a while, awhile Use *a while* after a preposition. Use *awhile* as an adverb.

EXAMPLE She read for **a while**.

EXAMPLE She read **awhile**.

bad, badly *Bad* is an adjective; use it before nouns and after linking verbs to modify the subject. *Badly* is an adverb; use it to modify action verbs.

EXAMPLE   Clara felt **bad** about the broken vase.

EXAMPLE   The team performed **badly** in the first half.

bare, bear *Bare* means "naked." A *bear* is an animal.

EXAMPLE   Don't expose your **bare** skin to the sun.

EXAMPLE   There are many **bears** in Yellowstone National Park.

base, bass One meaning of *base* is "a part on which something rests or stands." *Bass* pronounced to rhyme with *face* is a type of voice. When *bass* is pronounced to rhyme with *glass*, it's a kind of fish.

EXAMPLE   Who is playing first **base**?

EXAMPLE   We need a **bass** singer for the part.

EXAMPLE   We caught several **bass** on our fishing trip.

because of, due to Use *because of* with action verbs. Use *due to* with linking verbs.

EXAMPLE   The game was canceled **because of** rain.

EXAMPLE   The cancellation was **due to** rain.

being as, being that Some people use these expressions instead of *because* in informal conversation. In formal speaking and writing, use *because.*

EXAMPLE   **Because [*not* Being as]** their car broke down, they were late.

EXAMPLE   They were late **because [*not* being that]** their car broke down.

beside, besides *Beside* means "at the side of" or "next to." *Besides* means "in addition to."

EXAMPLE   Katrina sat **beside** her brother at the table.

EXAMPLE   **Besides** yogurt and fruit, the lunchroom serves muffins and bagels.

blew, blue *Blue* is the color of a clear sky. *Blew* is the past tense of *blow*.

EXAMPLE She wore a **blue** shirt.

EXAMPLE The dead leaves **blew** along the driveway.

boar, bore A *boar* is a male pig. *Bore* means "to tire out with dullness"; it can also mean "a dull person."

EXAMPLE Wild **boars** are common in parts of Africa.

EXAMPLE Please don't **bore** me with your silly jokes.

born, borne *Born* means "given life." *Borne* means "carried" or "endured."

EXAMPLE The baby was **born** at three o'clock in the morning.

EXAMPLE Migrant workers have **borne** many hardships over the years.

borrow, lend, loan *Borrow* means "to take something with the understanding that it will be returned." *Lend* means "to give something with the understanding it will be returned." *Borrow* and *lend* are verbs. *Loan* is a noun. Some people use *loan* as a verb, but most authorities prefer *lend*.

EXAMPLE May I **borrow** your bicycle for an hour?

EXAMPLE Will you **lend** me five dollars? **[verb]**

EXAMPLE I'll repay the **loan** on Friday. **[noun]**

bow When *bow* is pronounced to rhyme with *low,* it means "a knot with two loops." When *bow* rhymes with *how,* it means "to bend at the waist."

EXAMPLE Can you tie a good **bow**?

EXAMPLE Actors **bow** at the end of a play.

brake, break As a noun, a *brake* is a device for stopping something or slowing it down. As a verb, *brake* means "to stop or slow down"; its principal parts are *brake, braking, braked,* and *braked.* The noun *break* has several meanings: "the result of breaking," "a fortunate chance," or "a short rest." The verb *break* also has many meanings. A few are "to smash or shatter," "to destroy or disrupt," "to force a way through or into," or "to surpass or excel." Its principal parts are *break, breaking, broke,* and *broken.*

EXAMPLE   Rachel, please put a **brake** on your enthusiasm. **[noun]**

EXAMPLE   He couldn't **brake** the car in time to avoid the accident. **[verb]**

EXAMPLE   To fix the **break** in the drainpipe will cost a great deal of money. **[noun]**

EXAMPLE   Don't **break** my concentration while I'm studying. **[verb]**

bring, take   *Bring* means "to carry from a distant place to a closer one." *Take* means "to carry from a nearby place to a more distant one."

EXAMPLE   Will you **bring** me some perfume when you return from Paris?

EXAMPLE   Remember to **take** your passport when you go to Europe.

bust, busted   Don't use these words in place of *break, broke, broken,* or *burst.*

EXAMPLE   Don't **break** [*not* bust] that vase!

EXAMPLE   Who **broke** [*not* busted] this vase?

EXAMPLE   Someone has **broken** [*not* busted] this vase.

EXAMPLE   The balloon **burst** [*not* busted] with a loud pop.

EXAMPLE   The child **burst** [*not* busted] into tears.

buy, by *Buy* is a verb. *By* is a preposition.

EXAMPLE   I'll **buy** the gift tomorrow.

EXAMPLE   Stand **by** me.

can, may *Can* indicates ability. *May* expresses permission or possibility.

EXAMPLE   I **can** tie six kinds of knots.

EXAMPLE   "You **may** be excused," said Dad. **[permission]**

EXAMPLE   Luanna **may** take some college classes during her senior year. **[possibility]**

can't hardly, can't scarcely These phrases are considered double negatives. Don't use *hardly* or *scarcely* with *not* or the contraction *n't.*

EXAMPLE   I **can [*not* can't] hardly** lift this box.

EXAMPLE   The driver **can [*not* can't] scarcely** see through the thick fog.

capital, capitol A *capital* is a city that is the seat of a government. *Capital* can also mean "money or property." As an adjective, capital can mean "involving execution" or "referring to an uppercase letter." *Capitol,* on the other hand, refers only to a building in which a legislature meets.

EXAMPLE   What is the **capital** of Vermont?

EXAMPLE   Anyone starting a business needs **capital**.

EXAMPLE   **Capital** punishment is not used in this state.

EXAMPLE   Hester Prynne embroidered a **capital** *A* on her dress.

EXAMPLE   The **capitol** has a gold dome.

carat, caret, carrot, karat A *carat* is a unit of weight for measuring gems. (A similar word, *karat,* is a measure for expressing the fineness of gold.) A *caret* is a proofreader's mark indicating an insertion. A *carrot* is a vegetable.

EXAMPLE   She was wearing a one-**carat** diamond set in a ring of eighteen-**karat** gold.

EXAMPLE   Draw a **caret** at the point where you want to insert a word.

EXAMPLE   Lottie fed her horse a **carrot**.

cent, scent, sent A *cent* is a penny. A *scent* is an odor. *Sent* is the past tense and past participle of *send.*

EXAMPLE   I haven't got one **cent** in my pocket.

EXAMPLE   The **scent** of a skunk is unpleasant.

EXAMPLE   I **sent** my grandma a birthday card.

choose, chose *Choose* is the base form; *chose* is the past tense. The principal parts are *choose, choosing, chose,* and *chosen.*

EXAMPLE   Please **choose** a poem to recite in class.

EXAMPLE   Brian **chose** to recite "The Charge of the Light Brigade."

cite, sight, site To *cite* is to quote or refer to. *Cite* can also mean "to summon to appear in a court of law." As a noun, *sight* means "vision." As a verb, *sight* means "to see." As a noun, a *site* is a place or a location; as a verb, *site* means "to place or locate."

EXAMPLE   Consuela **cited** three sources of information in her report.

EXAMPLE   The officer **cited** the driver for speeding.

EXAMPLE   My **sight** is perfect. **[noun]**

EXAMPLE We **sighted** a scarlet tanager on our hike. [verb]

EXAMPLE The board of education has chosen a **site** for the new high school. [noun]

EXAMPLE The school will be **sited** on Meadow Boulevard. [verb]

clothes, cloths *Clothes* are what you wear. *Cloths* are pieces of fabric.

EXAMPLE Please hang all your **clothes** in your closet.

EXAMPLE Use these **cloths** to wash the car.

coarse, course *Coarse* means "rough," "crude," "not fine," "of poor quality." *Course* can mean "a school subject," "a path or way," "order or development," or "part of a meal." *Course* is also used in the phrase *of course.*

EXAMPLE To begin, I will need some **coarse** sandpaper.

EXAMPLE Mrs. Baldwin won't tolerate **coarse** language.

EXAMPLE Are you taking any math **courses** this year?

EXAMPLE The hikers chose a difficult **course** through the mountains.

complement, complementary; compliment, complimentary
As a noun, *complement* means "something that completes"; as a verb, it means "to complete." As a noun, *compliment* means "a flattering remark"; as a verb, it means "to praise." *Complementary* and *complimentary* are the adjective forms of the words.

EXAMPLE This flowered scarf will be the perfect **complement** for your outfit. [noun]

EXAMPLE This flowered scarf **complements** your outfit perfectly. [verb]

EXAMPLE Phyllis received many **compliments** on her speech. [noun]

EXAMPLE Many people **complimented** Phyllis on her speech. [verb]

EXAMPLE Either hat would be **complementary** to that outfit. [adjective]

EXAMPLE The hostess was especially **complimentary** to Phyllis. [adjective]

compose, comprise *Compose* means "to make up." *Comprise* means "to include."

EXAMPLE The mayor, the superintendent of schools, and the police chief **compose** the committee.

EXAMPLE The committee **comprises** the mayor, the superintendent of schools, and the police chief.

consul; council, councilor; counsel, counselor A *consul* is a government official living in a foreign city to protect his or her country's interests and citizens. A *council* is a group of people gathered for the purpose of giving advice. A *councilor* is one who serves on a council. As a noun, *counsel* means "advice" or "an attorney." As a verb, *counsel* means "to give advice." A *counselor* is one who gives counsel.

EXAMPLE The **consul** protested to the foreign government about the treatment of her fellow citizens.

EXAMPLE The city **council** met to discuss the lack of parking facilities at the sports field.

EXAMPLE The defendant received **counsel** from his **counsel**. [nouns]

EXAMPLE The attorney **counseled** his client to plead innocent. [verb]

continual, continually; continuous, continuously *Continual* describes action that occurs over and over but with pauses between occurrences. *Continuous* describes an action that

continues with no interruption. *Continually* and *continuously* are the adverb forms of the adjectives.

EXAMPLE I could not concentrate because of the **continual** banging of the screen door and the **continuous** blare of the radio.

EXAMPLE This television ad is aired **continually**; I've seen it six times tonight.

EXAMPLE The rain fell **continuously**.

could of, might of, must of, should of, would of After the words *could, might, must, should,* and *would,* use the helping verb *have* or its contraction, *'ve,* not the word *of.*

EXAMPLE **Could** you **have** prevented the accident?

EXAMPLE You **might have** swerved to avoid the other car.

EXAMPLE You **must have** seen it coming.

EXAMPLE I **should've** warned you.

dear, deer *Dear* is a word of affection and is used to begin a letter. It can also mean "expensive." A *deer* is an animal.

EXAMPLE Talia is my **dear** friend.

EXAMPLE We saw a **deer** at the edge of the woods.

desert, dessert *Desert* has two meanings. As a noun, it means "dry, arid land" and is accented on the first syllable. As a verb, it means "to leave" or "to abandon" and is accented on the second syllable. A *dessert* is something sweet eaten after a meal.

EXAMPLE This photograph shows a sandstorm in the **desert**. **[noun]**

EXAMPLE I won't **desert** you in your time of need. **[verb]**

EXAMPLE Strawberry shortcake was served for **dessert**.

different from, different than In most cases, *different from* is the correct choice. Use *different than* only if *than* introduces a subordinate clause.

EXAMPLE Square dancing is **different from** ballroom dancing.

EXAMPLE I felt **different than** I had felt before.

diner, dinner A *diner* is someone who dines or a place to eat. A *dinner* is a meal.

EXAMPLE The **diners** at the corner **diner** enjoy the corned beef hash.

EXAMPLE **Dinner** will be served at eight.

discover, invent *Discover* means "to come upon something for the first time." *Invent* means "to produce something original."

EXAMPLE Marie Curie **discovered** radium.

EXAMPLE Eli Whitney **invented** the cotton gin.

doe, dough A *doe* is a female deer. *Dough* is a mixture of flour and a liquid.

EXAMPLE A **doe** and a stag were visible among the trees.

EXAMPLE Knead the **dough** for three minutes.

doesn't, don't *Doesn't* is a contraction of *does not.* It is used with *he, she, it,* and all singular nouns. *Don't* is a contraction of *do not.* It is used with *I, you, we, they,* and all plural nouns.

EXAMPLE She **doesn't** know the answer to your question.

EXAMPLE The twins **don't** like broccoli.

emigrate, immigrate Use *emigrate* to mean "to leave one country and go to another to live." Use *immigrate* to mean

"to come to a country to settle there." Use the preposition *from* with *emigrate*. Use *to* or *into* with *immigrate*.

EXAMPLE Karl **emigrated** from Germany.

EXAMPLE He **immigrated** to the United States.

eye, I An *eye* is what you see with; it's also a small opening in a needle. *I* is a personal pronoun.

EXAMPLE **I** have something in my **eye**.

farther, further Use *farther* in referring to physical distance. Use *further* in all other situations.

EXAMPLE San Antonio is **farther** south than Dallas.

EXAMPLE We have nothing **further** to discuss.

fewer, less Use *fewer* with nouns that can be counted. Use *less* with nouns that can't be counted. *Less* may also be used with numbers that are considered as single amounts or single quantities.

EXAMPLE There are **fewer** students in my math class than in my physics class.

EXAMPLE I used **less** sugar than the recipe recommended.

EXAMPLE David had **less** than two dollars in his pocket. [*Two dollars* **is treated as a single sum, not as individual dollars.**]

EXAMPLE I can be there in **less** than thirty minutes. [*Thirty minutes* **is treated as a single period of time, not as individual minutes.**]

figuratively, literally *Figuratively* means "not truly or actually but in a symbolic way." *Literally* means "truly" or "actually."

EXAMPLE   Dad hit the ceiling, **figuratively** speaking.

EXAMPLE   You can't take him **literally** when he talks about the fish he's caught.

flaunt, flout   *Flaunt* means "to make a showy display." *Flout* means "to defy."

EXAMPLE   Enrique **flaunted** his knowledge of computer science at every opportunity.

EXAMPLE   Darla **flouted** the law by jaywalking.

flour, flower   *Flour* is used to bake bread. A *flower* grows in a garden.

EXAMPLE   Sift two cups of **flour** into a bowl.

EXAMPLE   A daisy is a **flower**.

for, four   *For* is a preposition. *Four* is a number.

EXAMPLE   Wait **for** me.

EXAMPLE   I have **four** grandparents.

formally, formerly   *Formally* is the adverb form of *formal,* which has several meanings: "according to custom, rule, or etiquette"; "requiring special ceremony or fancy clothing"; or "official." *Formerly* means "previously."

EXAMPLE   The class officers will be **formally** installed on Thursday.

EXAMPLE   Ed was **formerly** employed by Kwik Kar Kleen.

go, say   Don't use forms of *go* in place of forms of *say.*

EXAMPLE   I tell her the answer, and she **says** [*not* goes], "I don't believe you."

EXAMPLE   I told her the news, and she **said** [*not* went], "Are you serious?"

good, well *Good* is an adjective; use it before nouns and after linking verbs to modify the subject. *Well* is an adverb; use it to modify action verbs. *Well* may also be an adjective meaning "in good health."

EXAMPLE You look **good** in that costume.

EXAMPLE Joby plays the piano **well**.

EXAMPLE You're looking **well** in spite of your cold.

grate, great A *grate* is a framework of bars set over an opening. *Grate* also means "to shred by rubbing against a rough surface." *Great* means "wonderful" or "large."

EXAMPLE The little girl dropped her lollipop through the **grate**.

EXAMPLE Will you **grate** this cheese for me?

EXAMPLE You did a **great** job!

had of Don't use *of* between *had* and a past participle.

EXAMPLE I wish I **had known** [*not* had of known] about this sooner.

had ought, hadn't ought, shouldn't ought *Ought* never needs an auxiliary verb. Use *ought* by itself.

EXAMPLE You **ought** to win the match easily.

EXAMPLE You **ought** not to blame yourself. *or* You **shouldn't** blame yourself.

hanged, hung Use *hanged* when you mean "put to death by hanging." Use *hung* in all other instances.

EXAMPLE This state **hanged** three convicts between 1900 and 1950.

EXAMPLE We **hung** Yoko's painting over the fireplace.

healthful, healthy *Healthful* means "favorable to one's health," or "wholesome." *Healthy* means "in good health."

EXAMPLE   We chose **healthful** picnic foods: whole-grain breads, juices, cheese, and fresh fruits.

EXAMPLE   A **healthy** person is likely to live longer than an unhealthy one.

hear, here   *Hear* is a verb meaning "to be aware of sound by means of the ear." *Here* is an adverb meaning "in or at this place."

EXAMPLE   I can **hear** you perfectly well.

EXAMPLE   Please put your books **here**.

he, she, it, they   Don't use a pronoun subject immediately after a noun subject, as in *The **girls they** baked the cookies*. Omit the unnecessary pronoun. *The **girls** baked the cookies.*

EXAMPLE   The girls baked the cookies. [*not* **The girls they baked the cookies.**]

holey, holy, wholly   *Holey* means "having holes." *Holy* means "sacred." *Wholly* means "completely."

EXAMPLE   I hate wearing **holey** socks.

EXAMPLE   Religious travelers make pilgrimages to **holy** places.

EXAMPLE   That dog is **wholly** devoted to you.

how come   In formal speech and writing, use *why* instead of *how come.*

EXAMPLE   **Why** weren't you at the meeting? [*not* **How come you weren't at the meeting?**]

imply, infer   *Imply* means "to suggest." *Infer* means "to draw a conclusion from something."

EXAMPLE   The baby's crying **implied** that he was hungry.

EXAMPLE   I **inferred** from the baby's crying that he was hungry.

in, into, in to Use *in* to mean "inside" or "within." Use *into* to show movement from the outside to a point within. Don't write *into* when you mean *in to.*

EXAMPLE Jeanine was sitting outdoors **in** a lawn chair.

EXAMPLE When it got too hot, she went **into** the house.

EXAMPLE She went **in to** get out of the heat.

ingenious, ingenuous *Ingenious* means "clever," "inventive," "imaginative." *Ingenuous* means "innocent," "childlike," "sincere."

EXAMPLE What an **ingenious** plan you have dreamed up!

EXAMPLE Her **ingenuous** enthusiasm for the cafeteria food made us smile.

inside of Don't use *of* after the preposition *inside.*

EXAMPLE **Inside [*not* Inside of]** the cupboard were several old photograph albums.

irregardless, regardless Use *regardless.* Both the prefix *ir-* and the suffix *–less* have negative meanings; therefore, *irregardless* is a double negative, which is incorrect.

EXAMPLE **Regardless [*not* Irregardless]** of what the critics said, I liked that movie.

its, it's *Its* is the possessive form of *it. It's* is a contraction of *it is* or *it has.*

EXAMPLE The dishwasher has finished **its** cycle.

EXAMPLE **It's [It is]** raining again.

EXAMPLE **It's [It has]** been a pleasure to meet you, Ms. Donatello.

kind of, sort of Don't use these expressions as adverbs. Use *somewhat* or *rather* instead.

EXAMPLE   We were **rather** sorry to see him go. [*not* **We were kind of sorry to see him go.**]

kind of a, sort of a, type of a Omit the word *a*.

EXAMPLE   What **kind of** dog is that? [*not* **What kind of a dog is that?**]

knead, need *Knead* means "to mix or work into a uniform mass." As a noun, a *need* is a requirement. As a verb, *need* means "to require."

EXAMPLE   **Knead** the clay to make it soft.

EXAMPLE   I **need** a new jacket.

knight, night A *knight* was a warrior of the Middle Ages. *Night* is the time of day during which it is dark.

EXAMPLE   A handsome **knight** rescued the fair maiden.

EXAMPLE   **Night** fell, and the moon rose.

later, latter *Later* is the comparative form of *late*. *Latter* means "the second of two."

EXAMPLE   They will arrive on a **later** flight.

EXAMPLE   He arrived **later** than usual.

EXAMPLE   Both Scott and Sabrina are running for class president; I'm voting for the **latter**.

lay, lie *Lay* means "to put" or "to place." Its principal parts are *lay, laying, laid,* and *laid.* Forms of *lay* are usually followed by a direct object. *Lie* means "to rest or recline" or "to be positioned." Its principal parts are *lie, lying, lay,* and *lain.* Forms of *lie* are never followed by a direct object.

EXAMPLE   **Lay** your coat on the bed.

EXAMPLE   The children are **laying** their beach towels in the sun to dry.

EXAMPLE   Dad **laid** the baby in her crib.

EXAMPLE   Myrna had **laid** the book beside her purse.

EXAMPLE   **Lie** down for a few minutes.

EXAMPLE   The lake **lies** to the north.

EXAMPLE   The dog is **lying** on the back porch.

EXAMPLE   This morning I **lay** in bed listening to the birds.

EXAMPLE   You have **lain** on the couch for an hour.

lead, led   As a noun, *lead* has two pronunciations and several meanings. When it's pronounced to rhyme with *head*, it means "a metallic element." When it's pronounced to rhyme with *bead*, it can mean "position of being in first place in a race or contest," "example," "clue," "leash," or "the main role in a play."

EXAMPLE   **Lead** is no longer allowed as an ingredient in paint.

EXAMPLE   Jason took the **lead** as the runners entered the stadium.

EXAMPLE   Follow my **lead**.

EXAMPLE   The detective had no **leads** in the case.

EXAMPLE   Only dogs on **leads** are permitted in the park.

EXAMPLE   Who will win the **lead** in this year's musical production?

As a verb, *lead* means "to show the way," "to guide or conduct," "to be first." Its principal parts are *lead, leading, led,* and *led.*

EXAMPLE   Ms. Bachman **leads** the orchestra.

EXAMPLE   The trainer was **leading** the horse around the track.

EXAMPLE   An usher **led** us to our seats.

EXAMPLE   Gray has **led** the league in hitting for two years.

learn, teach   *Learn* means "to receive knowledge." *Teach* means "to give knowledge."

EXAMPLE   Manny began to **learn** to play the piano at the age of six.

EXAMPLE   Ms. Guerrero **teaches** American history.

leave, let   *Leave* means "to go away." *Let* means "to allow to."

EXAMPLE   I'll miss you when you **leave**.

EXAMPLE   **Let** me help you with those heavy bags.

like, as, as if, as though   *Like* can be a verb or a preposition. It should not be used as a subordinating conjunction. Use *as, as if,* or *as though* to introduce a subordinate clause.

EXAMPLE   I **like** piano music. [verb]

EXAMPLE   Teresa plays the piano **like** a professional. [preposition]

EXAMPLE   Moira plays **as** [*not* like] her teacher taught her to play.

EXAMPLE   He looked at me **as if** [*not* like] he'd never seen me before.

EXAMPLE   You sound **as though** [*not* like] you disagree.

like, say   Don't use the word *like* in place of forms of *say*.

EXAMPLE   I tell him to scroll down, and **he says** [*not* he's like], "What's scrolling down?"

EXAMPLE   I told her to turn left, and **she said** [*not* she was like], "Left!"

loath, loathe   *Loath* means "reluctant or unwilling." *Loathe* means "to hate."

EXAMPLE   Jeanine was **loath** to accept the responsibility.

EXAMPLE   Leonardo **loathes** sports.

loose, lose   The adjective *loose* means "free," "not firmly attached," or "not fitting tightly." The verb *lose* means "to misplace" or "to fail to win."

EXAMPLE   Don't **lose** that **loose** button on your shirt.

EXAMPLE   If we **lose** this game, we'll be out of the tournament.

mail, male   *Mail* is what turns up in your mailbox. A *male* is a man.

EXAMPLE   We received four pieces of **mail** today.

EXAMPLE   The **males** in the chorus wore red ties.

main, mane   *Main* means "most important." A *mane* is the long hair on a horse's neck.

EXAMPLE   What is your **main** job around the house?

EXAMPLE   The horse's **mane** was braided with colorful ribbons.

mean, medium, average   The *mean* of a set of numbers is a middle point. To get the arithmetic mean, you add up all the items in the set and divide by the number of items. The *medium* is the middle number when the items are arranged in order of size. The *average*, a noun, is the same as the arithmetic mean; as an adjective, *average* is "usual" or "typical."

EXAMPLE   The **mean** value of houses in a neighborhood is found by adding together all their selling prices and dividing the sum by the number of houses.

EXAMPLE   We lined up all the ponies from smallest to biggest, and Taminka chose the **medium** one, the one in the center of the row.

EXAMPLE   Let's figure out the **average** of all our test scores; then we can tell whether as a class we've improved.

EXAMPLE   This crop of tomatoes is nothing unusual; it's pretty **average**.

meat, meet *Meat* is food from an animal. Some meanings of *meet* are "to come face to face with," "to make the acquaintance of," and "to keep an appointment."

EXAMPLE Some people don't eat **meat**.

EXAMPLE **Meet** me at the library at three o'clock.

miner, minor *Miner* is a noun that means "one who works in a mine." *Minor* can be a noun or an adjective. As a noun, it means "a person under legal age." As an adjective, it means "small in importance."

EXAMPLE Coal **miners** often suffer from a disease known as black lung.

EXAMPLE **Minors** are restricted by law from certain activities.

EXAMPLE Several well-known actors had **minor** roles in the film.

minute When *minute* is pronounced min'it, it means "sixty seconds" or "a short period of time." When *minute* is pronounced mī noot', it means "very small."

EXAMPLE I'll be with you in a **minute**.

EXAMPLE Don't bother me with **minute** details.

moral, morale As a noun, a *moral* is a lesson taught by a fable or a story. As an adjective, *moral* means "decent," "right," "proper." *Morale* means "mental attitude."

EXAMPLE Did you understand the **moral** of that story?

EXAMPLE Jackson has strong **moral** principles.

EXAMPLE The team's **morale** would be improved by a win.

nauseated, nauseous *Nauseated* means "feeling nausea," or "experiencing nausea, as in sea-sickness." *Nauseous*, on the other hand, means "causing nausea," or "sickening."

EXAMPLE   My **nauseated** family could not stand to look any longer at the **nauseous** dish of scrambled eggs and leftovers I had placed in front of them.

object   *Object* is stressed on the first syllable when it means "a thing." *Object* is stressed on the second syllable when it means "oppose."

EXAMPLE   Have you ever seen an unidentified flying **object**?

EXAMPLE   Mom **objected** to the proposal.

off   Don't use *off* in place of *from*.

EXAMPLE   I'll borrow some money **from** [*not* off] my brother.

off of   Don't use *of* after the preposition *off*.

EXAMPLE   He fell **off** [*not* off of] the ladder, but he didn't hurt himself.

ordinance, ordnance   An *ordinance* is a law. *Ordnance* is a word for military weapons and equipment.

EXAMPLE   Our town has an **ordinance** against lying on the sidewalk.

EXAMPLE   Private Malloy was assigned to guard the **ordnance**.

ought to of   Don't use *of* in place of *have* after *ought to*.

EXAMPLE   You **ought to have** [*not* ought to of] known better.

outside of   Don't use *of* after the preposition *outside*.

EXAMPLE   I'll meet you **outside** [*not* outside of] the library.

overlook, oversee   Overlook can mean "to look past or miss," and "to look down at from above." *Oversee* means "to supervise workers or work."

EXAMPLE Lynn calculated the net profit we made from the car wash, but she had **overlooked** the cost of the lemonade and snacks provided for the workers.

EXAMPLE The ridgetop cabin **overlooks** the whole valley.

EXAMPLE Part of the caretaker's job is to **oversee** the garden staff, the groundskeeping staff, and the security staff.

pair, pare, pear A *pair* is two. *Pare* means "to peel." A *pear* is a fruit.

EXAMPLE I bought a new **pair** of socks.

EXAMPLE **Pare** the potatoes and cut them in quarters.

EXAMPLE Would you like a **pear** or a banana?

passed, past *Passed* is the past form and the past participle of the verb *pass*. *Past* can be an adjective, a preposition, an adverb, or a noun.

EXAMPLE We **passed** your house on the way to school. **[verb]**

EXAMPLE The **past** week has been a busy one for me. **[adjective]**

EXAMPLE We drove **past** your house. **[preposition]**

EXAMPLE At what time did you drive **past**? **[adverb]**

EXAMPLE I love Great-grandma's stories about the **past**. **[noun]**

pause, paws A *pause* is a short space of time. *Pause* also means "to wait for a short time." *Paws* are animal feet.

EXAMPLE We **pause** now for station identification.

EXAMPLE I wiped the dog's muddy **paws**.

peace, piece *Peace* means "calmness" or "the absence of conflict." A *piece* is a part of something.

EXAMPLE We enjoy the **peace** of the countryside.

EXAMPLE   The two nations have finally made **peace**.

EXAMPLE   May I have another **piece** of pie?

persecute, prosecute   *Persecute* means "to torment." *Prosecute* means "to bring legal action against."

EXAMPLE   Bullies sometimes **persecute** younger, weaker children.

EXAMPLE   The government **prosecuted** Al Capone for tax evasion.

personal, personnel   *Personal* means "private" or "individual." *Personnel* are employees.

EXAMPLE   Employees should not make **personal** telephone calls during working hours.

EXAMPLE   All **personnel** will receive a bonus in July.

plain, plane   *Plain* means "not fancy," "clear," or "a large area of flat land." A *plane* is an airplane or a device for smoothing wood; it can also mean "a flat surface."

EXAMPLE   He wore a **plain** blue tie.

EXAMPLE   The solution is perfectly **plain** to me.

EXAMPLE   Buffalo once roamed the **plains**.

EXAMPLE   We took a **plane** to Chicago.

EXAMPLE   Jeff used a **plane** to smooth the rough wood.

EXAMPLE   The two metal surfaces of this machine must be perfect **planes**.

precede, proceed   *Precede* means "to go before" or "to come before." *Proceed* means "to continue" or "to move along."

EXAMPLE   Our band **preceded** the homecoming floats as the parade **proceeded** through town.

precedence, precedents *Precedence* means "superiority of rank or position." *Precedents* are previous events that serve as examples for future actions or decisions.

EXAMPLE Doing your schoolwork has **precedence** over playing computer games.

EXAMPLE The legal **precedents** for the decision were clear and numerous.

principal, principle As a noun, *principal* means "head of a school"; it can also mean "a sum of money borrowed or invested." As an adjective, *principal* means "main" or "chief." *Principle* is a noun meaning "basic truth or belief" or "rule of conduct."

EXAMPLE Mr. Washington, our **principal**, will speak at the morning assembly. **[noun]**

EXAMPLE What was your **principal** reason for joining the club? **[adjective]**

EXAMPLE The **principle** of fair play is important in sports.

quiet, quit, quite The adjective *quiet* means "silent" or "motionless." The verb *quit* means "to stop" or "to give up or resign." The adverb *quite* means "very" or "completely."

EXAMPLE Please be **quiet** so I can think.

EXAMPLE Shirelle has **quit** the swim team.

EXAMPLE We were **quite** sorry to lose her.

raise, rise *Raise* means "to cause to move upward." It can also mean "to breed or grow" and "to bring up or rear." Its principal parts are *raise, raising, raised,* and *raised.*

Forms of *raise* are usually followed by a direct object. *Rise* means "to move upward." Its principal parts are *rise, rising, rose,* and *risen.* Forms of *rise* are never followed by a direct object.

EXAMPLE **Raise** your hand if you know the answer.

EXAMPLE My uncle is **raising** chickens.

EXAMPLE Grandma and Grandpa Schwartz **raised** nine children.

EXAMPLE Steam **rises** from boiling water.

EXAMPLE The sun is **rising**.

EXAMPLE The children **rose** from their seats when the principal entered the room.

EXAMPLE In a short time, Loretta **had risen** to the rank of captain.

rap, wrap *Rap* means "to knock." *Wrap* means "to cover."

EXAMPLE **Rap** on the door.

EXAMPLE **Wrap** the presents.

rational, rationale *Rational,* an adjective, means "sensible," "sane." A *rationale* is a reason for doing something. *Rationale* is a noun.

EXAMPLE Melody always behaves in a **rational** manner.

EXAMPLE I didn't understand Clive's **rationale** for quitting his job.

read, reed *Read* means "to understand the meaning of something written." A *reed* is a stalk of tall grass.

EXAMPLE Will you **read** Jimmy a story?

EXAMPLE We found a frog in the **reeds** beside the lake.

real, really *Real* is an adjective; use it before nouns and after linking verbs to modify the subject. *Really* is an adverb; use it to modify action verbs, adjectives, and other adverbs.

EXAMPLE   Winona has **real** musical talent.

EXAMPLE   She is **really** talented.

real, reel *Real* means "actual." A *reel* is a spool to wind something on, such as a fishing line.

EXAMPLE   I have a **real** four-leaf clover.

EXAMPLE   My dad bought me a new fishing **reel**.

reason is because Don't use *because* after *reason is.* Use *that* after *reason is,* or use *because* alone.

EXAMPLE   The **reason** I'm tired **is that** I didn't sleep well last night.

EXAMPLE   I'm tired **because** I didn't sleep well last night.

respectfully, respectively *Respectfully* means "with respect." *Respectively* means "in the order named."

EXAMPLE   The audience listened **respectfully** as the poet read his latest work.

EXAMPLE   Sue, Jerry, and Chad will be president, secretary, and treasurer, **respectively**.

root, rout, route, en route A *root* is a part of a plant. As a verb, *rout* means "to defeat"; as a noun, it means "a defeat." A *route* is a road or way for travel. *En route* means "on the way."

EXAMPLE   A carrot is a **root**.

EXAMPLE   The Tigers **routed** the Bears in last week's game. **[verb]**

EXAMPLE   The game ended in a **rout** for the Bears. **[noun]**

EXAMPLE   Let's take the **route** that runs along the river.

EXAMPLE   We stopped for lunch **en route**.

row When *row* is pronounced to rhyme with *low,* it means "a series of things arranged in a line" or "to move a boat by using oars." When *row* is pronounced to rhyme with *how,* it means "a noisy quarrel."

EXAMPLE   We sat in the last **row** of the theater.

EXAMPLE   Let's **row** across the lake.

EXAMPLE   My sister and I had a serious **row** yesterday, but today we've forgotten about it.

S

said, says *Said* is the past form and the past participle of *say. Says* is used in the present tense with *he, she, it,* and all singular nouns. Don't use *says* when you should use *said.*

EXAMPLE   At dinner last night, Neil **said** he wasn't hungry.

EXAMPLE   He always **says** that, but he eats everything anyway.

sail, sale A *sail* is part of a boat. It also means "to travel in a boat." A *sale* is a transfer of ownership in exchange for money.

EXAMPLE   As the boat **sails** away, the crew raise the **sail.**

EXAMPLE   The **sale** of the house was completed on Friday.

sea, see A *sea* is a body of water. *See* means "to be aware of with the eyes."

EXAMPLE   The **sea** is rough today.

EXAMPLE   I can **see** you.

set, sit *Set* means "to place" or "to put." Its principal parts are *set, setting, set,* and *set.* Forms of *set* are usually followed by a direct object. *Sit* means "to place oneself in a seated position" or "to be in a seated position." Its principal parts are *sit, sitting, sat,* and *sat.* Forms of *sit* are not followed by a direct object.

Set is an intransitive verb when it's used with *sun* to mean "the sun is going down" or "the sun is sinking below the horizon." When *set* is used in this way, it is not followed by a direct object.

EXAMPLE   Lani **set** the pots on the stove after the sun **set**.

EXAMPLE   The children **sit** quietly at the table.

sew, sow   *Sew* means "to work with needle and thread." When *sow* is pronounced to rhyme with *how*, it means "a female pig." When *sow* is pronounced to rhyme with *low*, it means "to plant."

EXAMPLE   Can you **sew** a button on a shirt?

EXAMPLE   The **sow** has five piglets.

EXAMPLE   Some farmers **sow** corn in their fields.

shear, sheer   *Shear* has to do with cutting or breaking off. *Sheer* can mean "thin and fine," "utter or complete," or "steep."

EXAMPLE   It's time to **shear** the sheep.

EXAMPLE   He decided to **shear** off his beard.

EXAMPLE   The bride's veil was made of a **sheer** fabric.

EXAMPLE   You are talking **sheer** nonsense.

EXAMPLE   It was a **sheer** drop from the top of the cliff.

shined, shone, shown   Both *shined* and *shone* are past tense forms and past participles of *shine*. Use *shined* when you mean "polished"; use *shone* in all other instances.

EXAMPLE   Clete **shined** his shoes.

EXAMPLE   The sun **shone** brightly.

EXAMPLE   Her face **shone** with happiness.

Shown is the past participle of *show*; its principal parts are *show, showing, showed,* and *shown*.

EXAMPLE   You **showed** me these photographs yesterday.

EXAMPLE   You have **shown** me these photographs before.

slow, slowly *Slow* may be used as an adverb only in such expressions as *Go slow* or *Drive slow*. In other instances where an adverb is needed, *slowly* should be used. You can't go wrong if you always use *slow* as an adjective and *slowly* as an adverb.

EXAMPLE We took a **slow** ferry to the island.

EXAMPLE The ferry moved **slowly** through the water.

some, somewhat Don't use *some* as an adverb in place of *somewhat*.

EXAMPLE The team has improved **somewhat** [*not* some] since last season.

son, sun A *son* is a male child. A *sun* is a star.

EXAMPLE Kino is Mr. and Mrs. Akawa's **son**.

EXAMPLE We watched as the **sun** rose [over the horizon].

stationary, stationery *Stationary* means "fixed" or "unmoving." *Stationery* is writing paper.

EXAMPLE This classroom has **stationary** desks.

EXAMPLE Rhonda likes to write letters on pretty **stationery**.

straight, strait *Straight* means "not crooked or curved"; it can also mean "direct" or "directly." A *strait* is a narrow waterway connecting two larger bodies of water. In the plural, it can also mean "difficulties" or "distress."

EXAMPLE Can you draw a **straight** line without a ruler?

EXAMPLE We drove **straight** to the airport.

EXAMPLE The **Strait** of Gibraltar connects the Mediterranean Sea and the Atlantic Ocean.

EXAMPLE People who don't control their spending often find themselves in financial **straits**.

sure, surely *Sure* is an adjective; use it before nouns and after linking verbs to modify the subject. *Surely* is an adverb; use it to modify action verbs, adjectives, and other adverbs.

EXAMPLE　Are you **sure** about that answer?

EXAMPLE　You are **surely** smart.

tail, tale A *tail* is what a dog wags. A *tale* is a story.

EXAMPLE　The dog's **tail** curled over its back.

EXAMPLE　Everyone knows the **tale** of Goldilocks and the three bears.

tear When *tear* is pronounced to rhyme with *ear*, it's a drop of fluid from the eye. When *tear* is pronounced to rhyme with *bear*, it means "a rip" or "to rip."

EXAMPLE　A **tear** fell from the child's eye.

EXAMPLE　**Tear** this rag in half.

than, then *Than* is a conjunction used to introduce the second part of a comparison.

EXAMPLE　LaTrisha is taller **than** LaToya.

EXAMPLE　Ted ordered more food **than** he could eat.

Then has several related meanings that have to do with time: "at that time," "soon afterward," "the time mentioned," "at another time." *Then* can also mean "for that reason" or "in that case."

EXAMPLE　My grandmother was a young girl **then**.

EXAMPLE　We ate lunch and **then** washed the dishes.

EXAMPLE　I look forward to seeing you **then**.

EXAMPLE　Sometimes I feel completely confident; **then** I feel totally incompetent.

EXAMPLE   "It's raining," said Joy.

"**Then** we can't go," wailed her brother.

that there, this here   Don't use *there* or *here* after *that, this, those,* or *these.*

EXAMPLE   I can't decide whether to read **this** [*not* this here] magazine or **that** [*not* that there] book.

EXAMPLE   Fold **these** [*not* these here] towels and hang **those** [*not* those there] shirts in the closet.

that, which, who   *That* may refer to people or things. *Which* refers only to things. *Who* refers only to people.

EXAMPLE   The poet **that** wrote *Leaves of Grass* is Walt Whitman.

EXAMPLE   I have already seen the movie **that** is playing at the Bijou.

EXAMPLE   The new play, **which** closed after a week, received poor reviews.

EXAMPLE   Students **who** do well on the test will receive scholarships.

their, there, they're   *Their* is a possessive form of *they;* it's used to modify nouns. *There* means "in or at that place." *They're* is a contraction of *they are.*

EXAMPLE   A hurricane damaged **their** house.

EXAMPLE   Put your books **there**.

EXAMPLE   **They're** our next-door neighbors.

theirs, there's   *Theirs* is a possessive form of *they* used as a pronoun. *There's* is a contraction of *there is.*

EXAMPLE   **Theirs** is the white house with the green shutters.

EXAMPLE   **There's** your friend Chad.

them   Don't use *them* as an adjective in place of *those.*

EXAMPLE   I'll take one of **those** [*not* them] hamburgers.

this kind, these kinds Use the singular forms *this* and *that* with the singular nouns *kind, sort,* and *type.* Use the plural forms *these* and *those* with the plural nouns *kinds, sorts,* and *types.*

EXAMPLE Use **this kind** of lightbulb in your lamp.

EXAMPLE Do you like **these kinds** of lamps?

EXAMPLE Many Pakistani restaurants serve **that sort** of food.

EXAMPLE **Those sorts** of foods are nutritious.

EXAMPLE **This type** of dog makes a good pet.

EXAMPLE **These types** of dogs are good with children.

thorough, through, threw *Thorough* means "complete." *Through* is a preposition meaning "into at one side and out at another." *Through* can also mean "finished." *Threw* is the past tense of *throw.*

EXAMPLE We gave the bedrooms a **thorough** cleaning.

EXAMPLE A breeze blew **through** the house.

EXAMPLE At last I'm **through** with my homework.

EXAMPLE Lacey **threw** the ball.

to, too, two *To* means "in the direction of"; it is also part of the infinitive form of a verb. *Too* means "very" or "also." *Two* is the number after *one.*

EXAMPLE Jaleela walks **to** school.

EXAMPLE She likes **to** study.

EXAMPLE The soup is **too** salty.

EXAMPLE May I go, **too**?

EXAMPLE We have **two** kittens.

toward, towards People in Great Britain use *towards,* but the preferred form in the United States is *toward.*

EXAMPLE Smiling, she walked **toward** me.

try and Use *try to.*

EXAMPLE   Please **try to** [*not* **try and**] be on time.

type, type of Don't use *type* as an adjective.

EXAMPLE   What **type of** music [*not* **what type music**] do you like?

uninterested, disinterested *Uninterested* means "not interested," "unenthusiastic," and "indifferent." *Disinterested* means "impartial," "unbiased, not favoring either side in a dispute."

EXAMPLE   I threw the collie a biscuit, but, supremely **uninterested**, he let it lie where it fell.

EXAMPLE   The judge listened carefully to all the witnesses in that tangled case before handing down her **disinterested** and even-handed decision.

unless, without Don't use *without* in place of *unless.*

EXAMPLE   **Unless** [*not* **Without**] I earn some money, I can't go to camp.

used to, use to The correct form is *used to.*

EXAMPLE   We **used to** [*not* **use to**] live in Cleveland, Ohio.

waist, waste Your *waist* is where you wear your belt. As a noun, *waste* means "careless or unnecessary spending" or "trash." As a verb, it means "to spend or use carelessly or unnecessarily."

EXAMPLE   She tied a colorful scarf around her **waist**.

EXAMPLE   Buying those skis was a **waste** of money.

EXAMPLE   Put your **waste** in the dumpster.

EXAMPLE   Don't **waste** time worrying.

wait, weight *Wait* means "to stay or remain." *Weight* is a measurement.

EXAMPLE   **Wait** right here.

EXAMPLE   Her **weight** is 110 pounds.

wait for, wait on *Wait for* means "to remain in a place in anticipation of something expected." *Wait on* means "to act as a server."

EXAMPLE   **Wait for** me at the bus stop.

EXAMPLE   Nat and Tammy **wait on** diners at The Golden Griddle.

way, ways Use *way*, not *ways*, in referring to distance.

EXAMPLE   It's a long **way** [*not* ways] to Tipperary.

weak, week *Weak* means "feeble" or "not strong." A *week* is seven days.

EXAMPLE   She felt **weak** for a **week** after the operation.

weather, whether *Weather* is the condition of the atmosphere. *Whether* means "if"; it is also used to introduce the first of two choices.

EXAMPLE   The **weather** in Portland is mild and rainy.

EXAMPLE   Tell me **whether** you can go.

EXAMPLE   I can't decide **whether** to fly or drive.

when, where Don't use *when* or *where* incorrectly in writing a definition.

EXAMPLE   A simile is a comparison using *like* or *as*. [*not* A simile is **when you compare two things using** *like* or *as*.]

EXAMPLE A watercolor wash is a thin coat of paint applied to paper that has been dampened with water. [*not A watercolor wash is where you dampen the paper before applying paint.*]

where Don't use *where* in place of *that*.

EXAMPLE I see **that** [*not* where] the Cubs are in the basement again.

where . . . at Don't use *at* after *where*.

EXAMPLE **Where** is your mother? [*not* Where is your mother at?]

who, whom *Who* is the nominative case. Use it for subjects and predicate nominatives. *Whom* is the objective case. Use it for direct objects, indirect objects, and objects of prepositions.

EXAMPLE **Who** is that woman with the red umbrella?

EXAMPLE **Whom** did you see at the mall?

who's, whose *Who's* is a contraction of *who is* or *who has*. *Whose* is the possessive form of *who*.

EXAMPLE **Who's** [Who is] conducting the orchestra?

EXAMPLE **Who's** [Who has] read this book?

EXAMPLE **Whose** umbrella is this?

wind When *wind* rhymes with *finned*, it means "moving air." When *wind* rhymes with *find*, it means "to wrap around."

EXAMPLE The **wind** is strong today.

EXAMPLE **Wind** the bandage around your ankle.

wood, would *Wood* comes from trees. *Would* is an auxiliary verb.

EXAMPLE **Would** you prefer a **wood** bookcase or a metal one?

wound When *wound* is pronounced to rhyme with *sound*, it is the past tense of *wind*. When *wound* is pronounced wo͞ond, it means "an injury in which the skin is broken."

EXAMPLE I **wound** the bandage around my ankle to cover the **wound**.

your, you're *Your* is the possessive form of *you*. *You're* is a contraction of *you are*.

EXAMPLE **Your** arguments are convincing.

EXAMPLE **You're** doing a fine job.

ABBREVIATIONS

An abbreviation is a short way to write a word or a group of words. Abbreviations should be used sparingly in formal writing except for a few that are actually more appropriate than their longer forms. These are *Mr., Mrs.,* and *Dr.* (*doctor*) before names, *A.M.* and *P.M.,* and *B.C.* and *A.D.*

Some abbreviations are written with capital letters and periods, and some with capital letters and no periods; some are written with lowercase letters and periods, and some with lowercase letters and no periods. A few may be written in any one of these four ways and still be acceptable. For example, to abbreviate *miles per hour,* you may write *MPH, M.P.H., mph,* or *m.p.h.*

Some abbreviations may be spelled in more than one way. For example, *Tuesday* may be abbreviated *Tues.* or *Tue.* *Thursday* may be written *Thurs.* or *Thu.* In the following lists, only the most common way of writing each abbreviation is given.

When you need information about an abbreviation, consult a dictionary. Some dictionaries list abbreviations in a special section in the back. Others list them in the main part of the book.

MONTHS

Jan.	January	none	July
Feb.	February	Aug.	August
Mar.	March	Sept.	September
Apr.	April	Oct.	October
none	May	Nov.	November
none	June	Dec.	December

DAYS

Sun.	Sunday	Thurs.	Thursday
Mon.	Monday	Fri.	Friday
Tues.	Tuesday	Sat.	Saturday
Wed.	Wednesday		

TIME AND DIRECTION

CDT	central daylight time	MST	mountain standard time
CST	central standard time	PDT	Pacific daylight time
DST	daylight saving time	PST	Pacific standard time
EDT	eastern daylight time	ST	standard time
EST	eastern standard time	NE	northeast
		NW	northwest
		SE	southeast
MDT	mountain daylight time	SW	southwest

A.D.	in the year of the Lord (Latin *anno Domini*)
B.C.	before Christ
B.C.E.	before the common era
C.E.	common era
A.M.	before noon (Latin *ante meridiem*)
P.M.	after noon (Latin *post meridiem*)

MEASUREMENT

The same abbreviation is used for both the singular and the plural meaning of measurements. Therefore, *ft.* stands for both *foot* and *feet,* and *in.* stands for both *inch* and *inches.* Note that abbreviations of metric measurements are commonly written without periods. U.S. measurements, on the other hand, are usually written with periods.

Metric System

Mass and Weight

t	metric ton
kg	kilogram
g	gram
cg	centigram
mg	milligram

Capacity

kl	kiloliter
l	liter
cl	centiliter
ml	milliliter

Length

km	kilometer
m	meter
cm	centimeter
mm	millimeter

U.S. Weights and Measures

Weight

wt.	weight
lb.	pound
oz.	ounce

Capacity

gal.	gallon
qt.	quart
pt.	pint
c.	cup
tbsp.	tablespoon
tsp.	teaspoon
fl. oz.	fluid ounce

Length

mi.	mile
rd.	rod
yd.	yard
ft.	foot
in.	inch

MISCELLANEOUS MEASUREMENTS

p.s.i.	pounds per square inch
MPH	miles per hour
MPG	miles per gallon
d.p.i.	dots per inch
rpm	revolutions per minute
C	Celsius, centigrade
F	Fahrenheit
K	kelvin
kn	knot
kW	kilowatt

COMPUTER AND INTERNET

CPU	central processing unit
CRT	cathode ray tube
DOS	disk operating system
e-mail	electronic mail
K	kilobyte
URL	uniform resource locator
DVD	digital video disc
d.p.i	dots per inch
WWW	World Wide Web
ISP	internet service provider
DNS	domain name system

UNITED STATES (U.S.)

In most cases, state names and street addresses should be spelled out. The postal abbreviations in the following lists should be used with ZIP codes in addressing envelopes. They may also be used with ZIP codes for return addresses and inside addresses in business letters. The traditional state abbreviations are seldom used nowadays, but occasionally it's helpful to know them.

State	Traditional	Postal
Alabama	Ala.	AL
Alaska	none	AK
Arizona	Ariz.	AZ
Arkansas	Ark.	AR
California	Calif.	CA
Colorado	Colo.	CO
Connecticut	Conn.	CT
Delaware	Del.	DE
District of Columbia	D.C.	DC
Florida	Fla.	FL
Georgia	Ga.	GA
Hawaii	none	HI
Idaho	none	ID
Illinois	Ill.	IL
Indiana	Ind.	IN
Iowa	none	IA
Kansas	Kans.	KS
Kentucky	Ky.	KY
Louisiana	La.	LA
Maine	none	ME
Maryland	Md.	MD
Massachusetts	Mass.	MA
Michigan	Mich.	MI
Minnesota	Minn.	MN
Mississippi	Miss.	MS

Missouri	Mo.	MO
Montana	Mont.	MT
Nebraska	Nebr.	NE
Nevada	Nev.	NV
New Hampshire	N.H.	NH
New Jersey	N.J.	NJ
New Mexico	N. Mex.	NM
New York	N.Y.	NY
North Carolina	N.C.	NC
North Dakota	N. Dak.	ND
Ohio	none	OH
Oklahoma	Okla.	OK
Oregon	Oreg.	OR
Pennsylvania	Pa.	PA
Rhode Island	R.I.	RI
South Carolina	S.C.	SC
South Dakota	S. Dak.	SD
Tennessee	Tenn.	TN
Texas	Tex.	TX
Utah	none	UT
Vermont	Vt.	VT
Virginia	Va.	VA
Washington	Wash.	WA
West Virginia	W. Va.	WV
Wisconsin	Wis.	WI
Wyoming	Wyo.	WY

POSTAL ADDRESS ABBREVIATIONS

The following address abbreviations are recommended by the U.S. Postal Service to speed mailing. In most writing, these words should be spelled out.

Alley	ALY	North	N
Annex	ANX	Parkway	PKY
Avenue	AVE	Place	PL
Boulevard	BLVD	Plaza	PLZ
Center	CTR	River	RIV
Circle	CIR	Road	RD
Court	CT	South	S
Drive	DR	Square	SQ
East	E	Station	STA
Estates	EST	Street	ST
Expressway	EXPY	Terrace	TER
Heights	HTS	Trace	TRCE
Highway	HWY	Trail	TRL
Island	IS	Turnpike	TPKE
Lake	LK	Viaduct	VIA
Lane	LN	Village	VLG
Lodge	LDG	West	W
Mount	MT		

ADDITIONAL ABBREVIATIONS

ac	alternating current
dc	direct current
AM	amplitude modulation
FM	frequency modulation
RF	radio frequency
ASAP	as soon as possible

e.g.	for example (Latin *exempli gratia*)
etc.	and others, and so forth (Latin *et cetera*)
i.e.	that is (Latin *id est*)
Inc.	incorporated
ISBN	International Standard Book Number
lc	lowercase
misc.	miscellaneous
p.	page
pp.	pages
re	with regard to
R.S.V.P.	please reply (French *répondez s'il vous plaît*)
SOS	international distress signal
TM	trademark
uc	uppercase
vs.	versus
w/o	without

CLOSE TO HOME JOHN McPHERSON

WELCOME TO
SLIM POINT BEACH

AIR TEMP.: 87° F
WATER TEMP.: 71° F
SAND TEMP.: 749° F

AAAH!

© 1995 John McPherson/Dist. by Universal Press Syndicate

5-29

Part Two

● ● ● ● ● ● ● ● ● ● ●

Grammar, Usage, and Mechanics

Chapter 1

Parts of
Speech

● ● ● ● ● ● ● ● ● ● ● ● ●

PRETEST **Identifying Parts of Speech**

For each numbered word in the paragraph below, write one of these words to identify its part of speech: noun, pronoun, verb, adjective, adverb, preposition, conjunction, interjection.

If only the schools[1] we all spend so much of our lives in came[2] equipped with[3] gardens! I[4] don't mean little[5] plots of[6] petunias that some[7] adult hired by the school takes[8] care of. No, schools should really[9] have gardens, big stretches[10] of rich[11] soil[12] that students[13] could painstakingly[14] cultivate.[15] They[16] could easily[17] provide fresh tomatoes[18] and[19] lettuce for[20] the lunchroom for at least part of the year. Every[21] classroom in[22] the school could have a view of perfectly[23] beautiful[24] hollyhocks or[25] roses in the spring and chrysanthemums in the fall. It[26] would be quite lovely, yet [27] it would cost hardly anything. Ah, well.[28] At least we[29] have[30] the petunias.

1.1 NOUNS

A **noun** is a word that names a person, a place, a thing, or an idea.

EXAMPLES	PERSON	uncle, doctor, baby, Luisa, son-in-law
	PLACE	kitchen, mountain, website, West Virginia
	THING	apple, tulip, continent, seagull, amplifier
	IDEA	respect, pride, love, appreciation, century

SINGULAR AND PLURAL NOUNS

Nouns can be singular or plural, depending on whether they name *one* person, place, thing, or idea or *more than one.*

To form the plural of most nouns, simply add *–s.* Other plural nouns are formed in different ways. For nouns ending in *s, ch, sh, x,* or *z,* add *–es* to form the plural. For nouns ending in *y* preceded by a consonant, change the *y* to *i* and add *–es.* For most nouns ending in *f* or *fe,* change the *f* to *v* and add *–s* or *–es.* Other nouns have irregular plurals (for example, *man/men, child/children, woman/women*). Some nouns do not change form from singular to plural (for example, *sheep/sheep*).

| EXAMPLES | SINGULAR | girl, switch, hobby, life, goose, fish |
| | PLURAL | girls, switches, hobbies, lives, geese, fish |

GRAMMAR/USAGE/MECHANICS

Write the plural form of each noun. Consult a dictionary if you need help.

1. table   **5.** mouse   **9.** fly

2. building   **6.** fan   **10.** wolf

3. history   **7.** dish

4. leaf   **8.** watch

POSSESSIVE NOUNS

The possessive form of a noun can show possession, ownership, or the general relationship between two nouns. Add an apostrophe and *–s* to form the possessive of any singular noun, even one that already ends in *s*. Use an apostrophe alone to form the possessive of a plural noun that ends in *s*.

EXAMPLES	SINGULAR POSSESSIVE	PLURAL POSSESSIVE
	the **kitten's** tail	the **kittens'** tails
	her **dress's** collar	her **dresses'** collars
	the **wife's** speech	the **wives'** speeches
	the **cookie's** decoration	the **cookies'** decorations
	the **story's** villain	the **stories'** villains
	the **watch's** battery	the **watches'** batteries

Add an apostrophe and *–s* to form the possessive of a plural noun that does not end in *s*.

EXAMPLES   the **oxen's** stalls

the **children's** books

the **women's** trophies

Rewrite each phrase below using the possessive form of the noun in parentheses.

1. Mr. (Spears) car
2. the (dog) bone
3. the (oxen) yoke
4. the (geese) formation
5. (Jess) hat

6. the (containers) lids
7. the (octopus) arms
8. the (Wilsons) house
9. (cheese) odor
10. the (match) flame

COMPOUND NOUNS

A **compound noun** is a noun made of two or more words. Compound nouns may be open, hyphenated, or closed.

EXAMPLES		
OPEN	gray fox, press secretary, line of sight
HYPHENATED	mother-in-law, tenth-grader, good-bye
CLOSED	folksinger, headlight, postmaster

CONCRETE AND ABSTRACT NOUNS

A **concrete noun** names an object that occupies space or can be recognized by any of the senses (sight, smell, hearing, taste, touch).

EXAMPLES	air	melody	stone	aroma	heat

An **abstract noun** names an idea, a quality, or a characteristic.

EXAMPLES	attitude	dignity	loyalty	sadness	temperature

COMMON AND PROPER NOUNS

A **common noun** is the general—not the particular—name of a person, place, thing, or idea.

EXAMPLES		COMMON NOUNS
	PERSON	artist, uncle, poet
	PLACE	country, lake, park
	THING	shuttle, vehicle, play
	IDEA	era, religion, movement

A **proper noun** is the name of a particular person, place, thing, or idea.

EXAMPLES		PROPER NOUNS
	PERSON	Michelangelo, Uncle Louis, Maya Angelou
	PLACE	Mexico, Yellowstone National Park, Lake Superior
	THING	*Challenger*, Jeep, *Romeo and Juliet*
	IDEA	Industrial Age, Judaism, Romanticism

A **proper noun** is capitalized. A common noun is usually not capitalized unless it is the first word of a sentence.

PRACTICE Common, Proper, Concrete, and Abstract Nouns

Identify each noun by writing common *or* proper. *If a noun is common, also write* concrete *or* abstract *to further identify it.*

1. The Grand Coulee Dam is the largest concrete dam anywhere in the world.

2. One of the world's most famous races occurs in Monte Carlo.

3. The hottest area in the United States is Death Valley, California.

4. Melissa already has far too many books to fit on her shelves.

5. India is the largest existing democracy.

6. Many people admired Princess Diana and felt a great loss when she died.

7. That chihuahua is not my idea of a dog.

8. To pursue happiness is often to lose it.

9. I don't know why Petra is angry.

10. A purple turtle sits on the top of my computer.

Collective Nouns

A **collective noun** is singular in form but names a group.

EXAMPLES
family	herd	company	band	team
audience	troop	committee	jury	flock

A collective noun is sometimes considered singular and sometimes considered plural. If you are talking about a group as a whole acting together, consider the collective noun singular. (Sometimes the word *its* will refer to the collective noun used as a singular noun.) If you are talking about the individual members of a group, consider the collective noun plural. (Sometimes the word *their* will refer to the collective noun used as a plural noun.)

EXAMPLES **SINGULAR** The **jury** *is* ready with *its* verdict.

PLURAL The **jury** *are* comparing *their* interpretations of the evidence.

Write each collective noun. Label it S *if it's singular and* P *if it's plural.*

1. The decorating committee disagree about everything.

2. The couple in the film were Meg Ryan and Tom Hanks.

3. The mob is howling outside the gates of the embassy.

4. Ideally, a union represents all the workers.

5. Every night, the audience gives the play a standing ovation.

6. We like to harmonize at our house, and the family sing all the different parts.

7. In this story, an entire class decides to volunteer at a homeless shelter.

8. The Chamber of Commerce is a powerful force for development in this city.

9. While they're warming up, the orchestra play different exercises at different tempos.

10. Congress passes many more bills than most of us ever hear about.

1.2 PRONOUNS

A **pronoun** is a word that takes the place of a noun, a group of words acting as a noun, or another pronoun. The word or group of words to which a pronoun refers is called its **antecedent**.

EXAMPLE Though Georgia O'Keeffe was born in Wisconsin, **she** grew to love the landscape of the American Southwest. [The pronoun *she* takes the place of its proper noun antecedent, *Georgia O'Keeffe*.]

EXAMPLE When Georgia O'Keeffe and Alfred Stieglitz were married in 1924, **both** were famous artists. [The pronoun *both* takes the place of the nouns *Georgia O'Keeffe* and *Alfred Stieglitz*.]

| EXAMPLE | Though O'Keeffe **herself** was a painter, **her** husband was a photographer. [**The pronouns** *herself* **and** *her* **take the place of** *O'Keeffe* **and** *O'Keeffe's*.] |

All pronouns in English can be put into these categories: personal and possessive pronouns, reflexive and intensive pronouns, demonstrative pronouns, interrogative pronouns, relative pronouns, and indefinite pronouns.

PERSONAL AND POSSESSIVE PRONOUNS

A **personal pronoun** refers to a specific person, place, thing, or idea by indicating the person speaking (the first person), the person or people being spoken to (the second person), or any other person, place, thing, or idea being discussed (the third person).

Like a noun, a personal pronoun expresses number; that is, it can be singular or plural.

PERSONAL PRONOUNS		
	SINGULAR	**PLURAL**
FIRST PERSON	I, me	we, us
SECOND PERSON	you	you
THIRD PERSON	he, him, she, her, it	they, them

EXAMPLE	FIRST PERSON	The song was dedicated to **me**. [*Me* refers to the person speaking.]
	SECOND PERSON	Sam will copy the document for **you**. [*You* refers to the person being spoken to.]
	THIRD PERSON	**She** gave **him** the news. [*She* and *him* refer to the people being talked about.]

Chapter 1 Parts of Speech   **99**

Third-person singular pronouns also express **gender**. *He* and *him* are masculine; *she* and *her* are feminine; *it* is neither masculine nor feminine but neuter.

A **possessive pronoun** takes the place of the possessive form of a noun.

POSSESSIVE PRONOUNS		
	SINGULAR	**PLURAL**
FIRST PERSON	my, mine	our, ours
SECOND PERSON	your, yours	your, yours
THIRD PERSON	his, her, hers, its	their, theirs

Notice that no possessive personal pronoun contains an apostrophe. Take particular note that the possessive pronoun *its* in the preceding chart has no apostrophe. It is a serious but common error to mistake *its* and *it's*.

EXAMPLE   The pup is chasing **its** tail. [possessive pronoun]

EXAMPLE   **It's** a pity we have no camera. [contraction for *It is*]

Some possessive pronouns must be used before nouns. Others can stand alone.

EXAMPLE   USED BEFORE A NOUN   This is **your** keyboard.

EXAMPLE   USED ALONE   This keyboard is **yours**.

PRACTICE   Personal Pronouns

Write each pronoun. Identify it by writing first person, second person, *or* third person. *Then write* singular *or* plural. *If the pronoun is possessive, write* possessive.

1. After getting a *D* on his paper, Yuri began to study harder than he had before.

2. My tooth hurt, so I went to the dentist.

3. I saw you at the mall last night, but I am pretty sure you didn't see me.

4. The falling branch just missed hitting her on the head, and it did knock off her glasses.

5. Have you ever been to the Grand Canyon?

6. This is your sweater. Have you seen mine?

7. A camel has a hump on its back, but the animal does not store water in it.

8. May and Emily put their bikes by the side of our house.

9. Marcello turned on the lawn sprinkler when my back was turned.

10. Mr. Earl can sit and watch his garden for hours at a time, with his dog beside him.

REFLEXIVE AND INTENSIVE PRONOUNS

Reflexive and intensive pronouns are formed by adding –*self* or –*selves* to certain personal and possessive pronouns.

REFLEXIVE AND INTENSIVE PRONOUNS		
	SINGULAR	**PLURAL**
FIRST PERSON	myself	ourselves
SECOND PERSON	yourself	yourselves
THIRD PERSON	himself, herself, itself	themselves

Notice that there is no such word as *hisself*, *theirself*, or *theirselves*.

A **reflexive pronoun** refers, or reflects back, to the subject of the sentence, indicating that the same person or thing is involved. A reflexive pronoun always adds information to a sentence.

EXAMPLE Jim uses a stopwatch to time **himself** on the track.

EXAMPLE She taught **herself** to play the piano.

EXAMPLE We imagined **ourselves** dancing in a forest glade.

An **intensive pronoun** adds emphasis to another noun or pronoun in the same sentence.

EXAMPLE He **himself** delivered the flowers.

EXAMPLE You must sign the application **yourself**.

EXAMPLE Mariko **herself** made the bridesmaids' dresses.

EXAMPLE Pepe, Jaime, and César designed the float **themselves**.

An intensive pronoun does not add information to a sentence. If the intensive pronoun is left out, the sentence still has the same meaning. Often, but not always, an intensive pronoun comes immediately after its antecedent.

DEMONSTRATIVE PRONOUNS

A **demonstrative pronoun** points out specific persons, places, things, or ideas.

DEMONSTRATIVE PRONOUNS

SINGULAR	this	that
PLURAL	these	those

EXAMPLE   **This** is your locker.

EXAMPLE   **That** is your assignment.

EXAMPLE   **These** are the shrubs to be trimmed.

EXAMPLE   My uniform is cleaner than **those**.

INTERROGATIVE AND RELATIVE PRONOUNS

An **interrogative pronoun** is used to form questions.

INTERROGATIVE PRONOUNS

who	whom	whose
what	which	whoever
whomever	whatever	whichever

EXAMPLE   **Who** is at the door?

EXAMPLE   **Whom** would you prefer?

EXAMPLE   **Whose** is this plaid coat?

EXAMPLE   **What** is for lunch?

EXAMPLE   **Which** of these books is your favorite?

EXAMPLE   **Whatever** were you thinking of?

A **relative pronoun** is used to begin a special subject-verb word group called a subordinate clause. (See Chapter 4.)

RELATIVE PRONOUNS			
who	whoever	which	that
whom	whomever	whichever	what
	whose	whatever	

EXAMPLE   The driver **who** arrived last parked over there. [**The relative pronoun *who* begins the subordinate clause *who arrived last*.**]

EXAMPLE   The meal **that** you prepared was delicious. [**The relative pronoun *that* begins the subordinate clause *that you prepared*.**]

INDEFINITE PRONOUNS

An **indefinite pronoun** refers to persons, places, things, or ideas in a more general way than a noun does.

EXAMPLE   **Everybody** needs food. [**The indefinite pronoun *Everybody* refers to people in general.**]

EXAMPLE   Did you get **enough** to eat? [**The indefinite pronoun *enough* refers to a general, not a specific, amount.**]

EXAMPLE   After two bowls of chili, I did not want **another**. [**The indefinite pronoun *another* has the antecedent *bowls (of chili)*.**]

SOME INDEFINITE PRONOUNS				
all	both	everything	nobody	others
another	each	few	none	several
any	either	many	no one	some
anybody	enough	most	nothing	somebody
anyone	everybody	much	one	someone
anything	everyone	neither	other	something

Write each pronoun. Identify it by writing reflexive, intensive, demonstrative, interrogative, relative, *or* indefinite.

1. That was the hottest day of the year, and the family had to help Richard move themselves.
2. Someone in the back of the room asked, "What is the largest tree in the world?"
3. Leaving the meeting late, Elizabeth found herself all alone on the dark street and headed quickly for home.
4. Those are the only shoes Joan has to wear with the blue dress. Anybody can see that!
5. Whatever is Will doing up in the tree, and who told the boy that it was all right to be there?
6. Which of the white houses on this block is Preston's? Is that the one?
7. Somebody with no sense walked right across the garden, stepped on Benjamin's newly planted petunias, and crushed some.
8. Sylvia has enough presents; the birthday girl should be generous and not keep all those herself.
9. No, Marsha can't have the bananas or the apples; those are Ted's.
10. No one has ever hit more than seventy home runs in a single major league season, but several have been in the ballpark.

1.3 VERBS

A **verb** is a word that expresses action or a state of being and is necessary to make a statement.

EXAMPLES The bicyclist **grinned**. The right gear **is** important.

EXAMPLES A spectator **cheered** loudly. The riders **seem** enthusiastic.

The primary characteristic of a verb is its ability to express time—present, past, and future. Verbs express time by means of *tense* forms.

EXAMPLE **PRESENT TENSE** They **watch** the race together.

EXAMPLE **PAST TENSE** They **watched** the race together.

EXAMPLE **FUTURE TENSE** They **will watch** the race together.

ACTION VERBS

An **action verb** tells what someone or something does.

Some action verbs express physical action. Others express mental action.

EXAMPLE **PHYSICAL ACTION** Ted **waved** the signal flag.

EXAMPLE **MENTAL ACTION** He **hoped** for success.

A **transitive verb** is followed by a direct object—that is, a word or words that answer the question *what?* or *whom?*

EXAMPLE The batter **swung** the bat confidently. [The action verb *swung* is followed by the noun *bat*, which answers the question *swung what?*]

An **intransitive verb** is *not* followed by a direct object.

EXAMPLE The batter **swung** wildly. [The verb is followed by a word that tells *how*.]

To decide whether a verb in a sentence is transitive or intransitive, ask *what?* or *whom?* after the verb. If the answer is given in the sentence, the verb is transitive. If the answer is not given in the sentence, the verb is intransitive.

PRACTICE **Transitive and Intransitive Verbs**

Write each verb. Identify it by writing transitive *or* intransitive. *If it is transitive, write the word or words that answer the questions* what? *or* whom?

1. Thomas Morris, an Australian athlete, once skipped rope from Melbourne to Adelaide, Australia.
2. Manuel, the head chef of the finest restaurant in the hotel, baked fourteen different kinds of cakes for the wedding reception.
3. He also expertly sculpted a swan out of ice that stood five feet tall, with fresh flowers at its base and piles of fruit between its wings.
4. During the Great Depression of the 1930s, poverty-stricken contestants competed in dance marathons for days at a time.
5. Sometimes they fell asleep on their feet, leaning against each other.
6. My sister Elena and I stayed at the school until four o'clock for play rehearsal.
7. Then we ran most of the way home.
8. Monique chewed a carrot thoughtfully and waited for a telephone call.
9. The big yellow cat watched her, a gleam of mischief in his dark gold eyes.
10. My father mowed the entire lawn yesterday with the push mower, and my brother, Allen, and I weeded most of the flower beds.

LINKING VERBS

A **linking verb** links, or joins, the subject of a sentence (often a noun or a pronoun) with a noun, a pronoun, or an adjective that identifies or describes the subject. A linking verb does not show action.

Be in all its forms—*am, is, are, was, were*—is the most commonly used linking verb.

EXAMPLES The person behind the mask **was** you.

The players **are** ready.

EXAMPLES Archery **is** an outdoor sport.

They **were** sports fans.

Several other verbs besides *be* can act as linking verbs.

OTHER VERBS THAT CAN BE LINKING VERBS			
look	remain	seem	become
stay	grow	appear	sound
taste	smell	feel	turn

EXAMPLES This salad **tastes** good.

The sun **feels** warm on my shoulders.

EXAMPLES You **look** comfortable.

The leaves **turned** brown.

VERB PHRASES

The verb in a sentence may consist of more than one word. The words that accompany the main verb are called **auxiliary**, or helping, **verbs**.

A **verb phrase** consists of a main verb and all its auxiliary, or helping, verbs.

AUXILIARY VERBS	
FORMS OF *BE*	am, is, are, was, were, being, been
FORMS OF *HAVE*	has, have, had, having
OTHER AUXILIARIES	can, could may, might must do, does, did shall, should will, would

The most common auxiliary verbs are forms of *be* and *have*. They help the main verb express time by forming the various tenses.

EXAMPLE We **will weed** the vegetable garden this morning.

EXAMPLE Sandra **has** already **weeded** the peppers and the tomatoes.

EXAMPLE We **were weeding** the flower beds when the rain started.

The other auxiliary verbs are not used primarily to express time. They are often used to emphasize meaning.

EXAMPLE I **should be leaving**.

EXAMPLE **Could** he **have forgotten**?

EXAMPLE Marisa **may** already **be finished**.

PRACTICE Verbs and Verb Phrases: Transitive, Intransitive, and Linking

Write each verb and verb phrase. Identify it by writing transitive, intransitive, *or* linking.

1. During the hurricane, the large oak tree blew over.
2. Maple trees look beautiful in the autumn.
3. It was raining on the day of Queen Elizabeth's coronation.
4. We put the new piano in the corner.
5. Samantha's birthday cake tasted awful.
6. That particular type of exercise has always been difficult for me.

7. My brother Gary hates arguments.

8. Adam is staying at the cabin in the woods until next week at least.

9. The Gateway Arch towers over St. Louis.

10. I didn't feel very well yesterday.

1.4 ADJECTIVES

An **adjective** is a word that modifies a noun or a pronoun by limiting its meaning. An adjective tells *what kind, which one, how many,* or *how much.*

EXAMPLES

red barn	**that** notebook	**seven** apples
interesting poem	**romantic** story	**many** novels
these ideas	**Irish** ballad	**cracked** pitcher
enough plates	**second** time	**no** excuse
afternoon class	**cheese** sandwich	**football** game

Pronouns can also serve as adjectives. For example, possessive pronouns (*my, our, your, his, her, its,* and *their*) act as adjectives when they modify nouns. Demonstrative pronouns (*this, that, these,* and *those*) can also be considered demonstrative adjectives when they modify nouns. Similarly, nouns can serve as adjectives. Possessive nouns, like possessive pronouns, can be used as adjectives. In fact, any noun that modifies another noun can be considered an adjective.

EXAMPLES **my** kitten [possessive adjective]

those bicycles [demonstrative adjective]

Lucy's report [possessive noun acting as adjective]

leather shoes [noun acting as adjective]

Two verb forms can also act as adjectives: the present participle, which ends in *–ing*, and the past participle, which either ends in *–ed* or is irregularly formed.

EXAMPLES   a **spinning** top   some **burned** toast   a **fallen** tree

Adjectives may appear in various positions in relation to the words they modify.

EXAMPLE   How **suspenseful** this *movie* is!

EXAMPLE   That **suspenseful** *movie* was very popular.

EXAMPLE   The *movie* is **suspenseful**.

EXAMPLE   The critics considered the *movie* **suspenseful**.

EXAMPLE   The *movie*, relentlessly **suspenseful**, ended suddenly.

PRACTICE   Adjectives and the Words They Modify

Write each adjective and the word it modifies. Don't write articles.

1. The shrew is a small, ferocious mammal.
2. Delicate white curtains hung at the tall windows of our old house.
3. Marcus was not paying close attention, and he fell through the cracked ice on the lake.
4. In the empty house, dried flowers hung on the faded yellow wall.
5. The flowers were amazingly beautiful in the bright sunlight.
6. My younger sister hates to have her beautiful curly hair brushed.
7. Shooting stars are really meteorites.
8. Please submit a glossy photograph with your application.
9. The book looks interesting, but it is too long for me to read in a week.
10. The leaves on the tree were turning orange, and those on the ground were brown.

FORMS OF ADJECTIVES

Many adjectives have different forms to indicate their degree of comparison. The **positive form** indicates no comparison. The **comparative form** compares two nouns or pronouns. The **superlative form** compares more than two nouns or pronouns.

EXAMPLES	POSITIVE	COMPARATIVE	SUPERLATIVE
	smooth	smoother	smoothest
	happy	happier	happiest
	thin	thinner	thinnest
	beautiful	more beautiful	most beautiful
	good, well	better	best
	bad	worse	worst
	many, much	more	most
	little	less	least

PRACTICE Comparative and Superlative Adjectives

Write the correct comparative or superlative form of the adjective in parentheses. Consult a dictionary if necessary.

1. Dictionaries are usually (thick) than novels.
2. *War and Peace,* by Tolstoy, is one of the (long) books ever written.
3. When she won the gold medal, Nikki was the (happy) person in the stadium.
4. From all reports, it is much (hot) in the Sahara than in the country of Norway.
5. Of the two boys, Glen is a (good) skier.
6. David is the (cute) of the McDonald twins, at least according to Jenny.

7. I think your dog Rutherford is the (peculiar) dog I have ever seen.

8. The Olympic team of China is known to be one of the (strong) in the world.

9. Lake Erie is not the (large) of the Great Lakes, but it is certainly very large.

10. There are faster birds and fish, but the cheetah is the (fast) land animal.

ARTICLES

Articles are the adjectives *a, an,* and *the*. *A* and *an* are called **indefinite articles**. They can refer to any one of a kind of person, place, thing, or idea. *A* is used before consonant sounds, and *an* is used before vowel sounds. *The* is the **definite article**. It refers to a specific person, place, thing, or idea.

EXAMPLES

INDEFINITE	He found **a** ring.	I ate **an** egg.
	I have **a** used computer.	It's almost **an** hour since he left.
DEFINITE	He found **the** ring.	I ate **the** egg.
	I have **the** used computer.	It's almost **the** hour for lunch.

PROPER ADJECTIVES

A **proper adjective** is formed from a proper noun. It begins with a capital letter.

EXAMPLE Vancouver is a **Canadian** city.

EXAMPLE We visited the **London** Zoo.

The following suffixes, along with others, are often used to form proper adjectives: *-n, -ian, -an, -ese, -ic,* and *-ish*. Sometimes there are other changes as well. Check the spelling in a dictionary if necessary.

EXAMPLES	PROPER NOUNS	PROPER ADJECTIVES
	Queen Victoria	Victorian
	Egypt	Egyptian
	Mexico	Mexican
	Lebanon	Lebanese
	Celt	Celtic
	Ireland	Irish

PRACTICE Proper Adjectives

Rewrite each phrase, changing the noun in boldfaced type into a proper adjective. Consult a dictionary if necessary.

1. waterfalls of **Venezuela**
2. history of **South Africa**
3. farmlands of **Canada**
4. hills of **Ireland**
5. island of **Tanzania**
6. pasta of **Italy**
7. automobiles of **Japan**
8. festivals of **Uruguay**
9. rivers of **Norway**
10. kangaroos of **Australia**

1.5 ADVERBS

An **adverb** is a word that modifies a verb, an adjective, or another adverb by making its meaning more specific.

The following sentences illustrate the use of adverbs to modify verbs, adjectives, and adverbs.

EXAMPLES

MODIFYING VERBS

Never swim alone.
verb

He has **seldom** complained.
verb   verb

MODIFYING ADJECTIVES

The movie was **very** scary and **too** long.
adjective   adjective

MODIFYING ADVERBS

She **almost** always waited **quite** patiently.
adverb   adverb

Adverbs modify by answering these questions: *When? Where? How? To what degree?*

EXAMPLES

WHEN?	It should arrive **Saturday**.
	I changed the schedule **again**.
WHERE?	Leave your coat **there**.
	He drove **south**.
HOW?	He stacked the books **quickly** and **neatly**.
	Carefully I counted them.
TO WHAT DEGREE?	We were **very** sorry.
	We had arrived **quite** late.

When an adverb modifies a verb or a verb phrase, it may sometimes be placed in various positions relative to the verb or verb phrase. When an adverb modifies an adjective or another adverb, it usually comes directly before the modified word.

EXAMPLES   **MODIFYING A VERB**

Now the room *is* ready.
The room **now** *is* ready.
The room *is* **now** ready.
The room *is* ready **now**.

MODIFYING AN ADJECTIVE	The ice is **dangerously** *soft*.
	You look **terribly** *tired*.
MODIFYING AN ADVERB	I answered **too** *slowly*.
	It **almost** *never* rains this hard.

NEGATIVE WORDS AS ADVERBS

The word *not* and the contraction *n't* (as in *don't* and *won't*) are adverbs. Other negative words can function as adverbs of time and place.

EXAMPLES The bell has **not** rung. The toy is **nowhere** to be seen.

She is **scarcely** awake. I have **never** danced with her.

PRACTICE Adverbs

Write each adverb and the word it modifies. Then tell whether the modified word is a verb, *an* adjective, *or another* adverb.

1. The sound he made as he slept was barely noticeable.
2. The dog bit the man unintentionally.
3. Rachel ran out of the burning building quickly.
4. Simone hardly knew her own sister, who had been at boarding school for four years.
5. Everyone I know thought the movie was terribly boring and almost too long to bear.
6. The people of Sweden are frequently blonde.
7. The lion tamers approached the escaped lioness very carefully.
8. I will gladly help you with your history homework if you will help me practice my lines for the play.
9. Fearfully, she turned to see if anyone was behind her.
10. He stumbled sleepily across the floor and reached for the coffee thirstily.

ADVERBS THAT COMPARE

Like adjectives, some adverbs have different forms to indicate their degree of comparison. The comparative form of an adverb compares two actions. The superlative form of an adverb compares more than two actions.

For most adverbs of only one syllable, add *–er* to make the comparative form and *–est* to make the superlative form.

EXAMPLES

POSITIVE	COMPARATIVE	SUPERLATIVE
runs **fast**	runs **faster**	runs **fastest**
pays **soon**	pays **sooner**	pays **soonest**
works **hard**	works **harder**	works **hardest**

Most adverbs that end in *–ly* or have more than one syllable use the word *more* to form the comparative and *most* to form the superlative.

EXAMPLES

POSITIVE	COMPARATIVE	SUPERLATIVE
eats **healthfully**	eats **more healthfully**	eats **most healthfully**
checks **often**	checks **more often**	checks **most often**
snores **loudly**	snores **more loudly**	snores **most loudly**

Some adverbs form the comparative and superlative irregularly.

EXAMPLES

POSITIVE	COMPARATIVE	SUPERLATIVE
swims **well**	swims **better**	swims **best**
dives **badly**	dives **worse**	dives **worst**
cares **little**	cares **less**	cares **least**
sees **far**	sees **farther**	sees **farthest**
researches **far**	researches **further**	researches **furthest**

Chapter 1 Parts of Speech   **117**

Write the comparative and superlative forms of each
adverb. Consult a dictionary if necessary.

1. seriously	**5.** late	**9.** badly
2. quietly	**6.** well	**10.** clumsily
3. near	**7.** quick	
4. sincerely	**8.** tenderly	

1.6 PREPOSITIONS

A **preposition** is a word that shows the relationship of
a noun or a pronoun to another word in a sentence.

A **prepositional phrase** is a group of words that begins
with a preposition and ends with a noun or a pronoun
that is called the **object of the preposition**.

EXAMPLE   The diamonds **in** the vault are priceless. [*In* shows the
relationship between *diamonds* and the object of the preposition, *vault*.]

EXAMPLE   The telephone rang four times **during** dinner. [*During*
shows the relationship between *rang* and the object of the
preposition, *dinner*.]

EXAMPLE   Here is a gift **for** you. [*For* relates *gift* to the object of the
preposition, *you*.]

COMMONLY USED PREPOSITIONS

aboard	beneath	in	regarding
about	beside	inside	respecting
above	besides	into	since
across	between	like	through
after	beyond	near	throughout
against	but (except)	of	to

along	by	off	toward
amid	concerning	on	under
among	despite	onto	underneath
around	down	opposite	until
as	during	out	up
at	except	outside	upon
before	excepting	over	with
behind	for	past	within
below	from	pending	without

A **compound preposition** is a preposition that is made up of more than one word.

COMPOUND PREPOSITIONS		
according to	because of	instead of
ahead of	by means of	next to
along with	except for	on account of
apart from	in addition to	on top of
aside from	in front of	out of
as to	in spite of	owing to

Some words may be used as either prepositions or adverbs. A word is used as a preposition if it has a noun or a pronoun as its object. A word is used as an adverb if it does not have an object.

EXAMPLES

WORD USED AS PREPOSITION
I left my boots **outside** the back door.
The speech was **over** my head.
Everyone came **aboard** the boat.

WORD USED AS ADVERB
I left my boots **outside**.
The speech was **over**.
Everyone came **aboard**.

Chapter 1 Parts of Speech **119**

Write each prepositional phrase. Underline the preposition and draw a circle around the object of the preposition.

1. There is a large group of people playing a baseball game over that hill.
2. Grizzly bears are commonly found in North America.
3. It started to rain during the third inning.
4. They decided to have their picnic beside the creek.
5. Over the river and through the woods was the way to Grandma's condominium.
6. After the movie, Megan walked Jeremy home.
7. Chicago is the largest city in the Midwest, but it is not the capital of Illinois.
8. Thomas Edison was a collector of birds, owning 5,000 at one time.
9. During the American Revolution, many brides wore red, a sign of rebellion.
10. The first Cadillac was sold for $750.

1.7 CONJUNCTIONS

A **conjunction** is a word that joins single words or groups of words.

COORDINATING CONJUNCTIONS

A **coordinating conjunction** joins words or groups of words that have equal grammatical weight in a sentence.

COORDINATING CONJUNCTIONS						
and	but	or	so	nor	yet	for

EXAMPLE One **and** six are seven. [two nouns]

EXAMPLE Merlin was smart **but** irresponsible. [two adjectives]

EXAMPLE   Let's put the note on the TV **or** on the refrigerator. [**two prepositional phrases**]

EXAMPLE   I wanted a new sun hat, **so** I bought one. [**two complete thoughts**]

EXAMPLE   He did not complain, **nor** did he object to our plan. [**two complete thoughts**]

EXAMPLE   Lightning struck the barn, **yet** no fire started. [**two complete thoughts**]

When used as a coordinating conjunction, *for* means "for the reason that" or "because."

EXAMPLE   We didn't explore the summit that night, **for** the climb had exhausted us.

CORRELATIVE CONJUNCTIONS

Correlative conjunctions work in pairs to join words and groups of words of equal grammatical weight in a sentence.

CORRELATIVE CONJUNCTIONS		
both . . . and	just as . . . so	not only . . . but (also)
either . . . or	neither . . . nor	whether . . . or

Correlative conjunctions make the relationship between words or groups of words a little clearer than do coordinating conjunctions.

EXAMPLES

COORDINATING CONJUNCTIONS
He **and** I were there.

She will sew new curtains, **or** I will put up the old blinds.

I scrubbed **and** waxed the floor.

CORRELATIVE CONJUNCTIONS
Both he **and** I were there.

Either she will sew new curtains, **or** I will put up the old blinds.

I **not only** scrubbed **but also** waxed the floor.

Write all conjunctions. Then identify them as either coordinating *or* correlative.

1. Diana got poor grades in school, so she didn't go to college.
2. Both Marilyn and Susan wanted to go to the library.
3. I was hoping for a good grade on my paper, but I really knew better.
4. The car was in great shape, yet it wasn't what Jo wanted.
5. Not only did Wilt Chamberlain score 100 points in an NBA game, but he also played for the Harlem Globetrotters.
6. Ancient Egyptians buried people in underground tombs and pyramids.
7. Joseph couldn't decide whether to read *Catcher in the Rye* or *The Martian Chronicles.*
8. A car has either manual transmission or automatic.
9. People did not expect slave Elizabeth Freeman to sue for her freedom in 1781 nor to win; she did both.
10. The day turned out to be neither bright nor breezy.

SUBORDINATING CONJUNCTIONS

A **subordinating conjunction** joins two clauses, or thoughts, in such a way as to make one grammatically dependent on the other.

The thought, or clause, that a subordinating conjunction introduces is said to be "subordinate," or dependent, because it cannot stand by itself as a complete sentence.

EXAMPLE We can skate on the pond **when** the ice is thicker.

EXAMPLE We can't skate **until** the ice is thicker.

EXAMPLE **Because** the ice is still too thin, we must wait for a hard freeze.

COMMON SUBORDINATING CONJUNCTIONS

after	as though	since	until
although	because	so long as	when
as	before	so (that)	whenever
as far as	considering (that)	than	where
as if	if	though	whereas
as long as	inasmuch as	till	wherever
as soon as	in order that	unless	while

PRACTICE **Subordinating Conjunctions**

Write each subordinating conjunction.

1. Considering that he is only five feet, three inches tall, it amazed me to see Mugsy Bogues play in the NBA.
2. Everything was great until Jose looked down.
3. Inasmuch as Congress was in session, I hoped to see senators and representatives.
4. While the family was in Florida, Kathy walked the dog.
5. I did my homework right away because I wanted to have friends over.
6. Although the White Sox had clinched the division, the Indians continued to play their hardest.
7. Write me a letter if you get a chance.
8. "Where there's smoke, there's fire."
9. Don't behave as if you didn't know better.
10. Since you're here, you might as well stay.

CONJUNCTIVE ADVERBS

A **conjunctive adverb** is used to clarify the relationship between clauses of equal weight in a sentence.

Conjunctive adverbs are usually stronger, more precise, and more formal than coordinating conjunctions. Notice that only a comma is used with a coordinating conjunction to separate the clauses. When a conjunctive adverb is used between clauses, a semicolon precedes the conjunctive adverb and a comma follows it.

EXAMPLES

COORDINATING CONJUNCTION	The civilization of the Incas was advanced, **but** they never invented the wheel.
CONJUNCTIVE ADVERB	The civilization of the Incas was advanced; **however,** they never invented the wheel.

There are many conjunctive adverbs, and they have many uses, as the following examples show.

EXAMPLES

TO REPLACE *AND*	also, besides, furthermore, moreover
TO REPLACE *BUT*	however, nevertheless, nonetheless, still
TO STATE A RESULT	accordingly, consequently, then, therefore, thus
TO STATE EQUALITY	equally, indeed, likewise, similarly

PRACTICE **Conjunctive Adverbs**

Write each underlined word. If it's a coordinating conjunction, label it CC. *If it's a conjunctive adverb, label it* CA.

1. George Washington Carver did not work just with peanuts; <u>indeed</u>, he developed 536 dyes from other plants.

2. Billie Holiday had a very hard childhood, <u>yet</u> she became one of the greatest jazz singers of all time.

3. Stephen Hawking is physically disabled; <u>however</u>, he has one of the finest minds since Einstein.

4. Baseball is played with a round ball, <u>and</u> the game of lacrosse is, too.

5. A tree, which had fallen in the previous night's storm, was blocking the road, <u>so</u> we had to turn around and go back the way we came.

6. Molly was a top-notch student; <u>likewise</u>, she was an all-conference softball pitcher.

7. After the long hike, David was exhausted; <u>furthermore</u>, he was hungry and cold.

8. Some people can detect sweetness in a solution of 1 part sugar to 200 parts water, <u>but</u> butterflies can detect 1 in 300,000.

9. Maureen fell down the first few times she tried to ride a bike; <u>nevertheless</u>, she kept trying and finally learned.

10. Carl could not turn in his homework, <u>for</u> he came to school without his book bag.

1.8 INTERJECTIONS

An **interjection** is a word or a phrase that expresses emotion or exclamation. An interjection has no grammatical connection to other words.

EXAMPLES **Oh, my!** What is that?   **Yikes**, I'll be late!

Ouch! It's hot!   **Ah**, that's better.

PRACTICE Interjections

Identify each interjection.

1. Mrs. Howell stopped and cried out, "Oh, my! Those flowers in the back garden are breathtakingly beautiful."

2. "Yikes!" said Dena with a shudder as she hopped backwards. "That anaconda is the biggest snake I've ever seen outside a book."

3. "Great Googaly Moogaly! It's the Indies!" said Christopher Columbus as he sailed towards America.

4. "Shucks!" said Harve in disgust. "Where did I put that ear of corn?"

5. "Rats!" said Bill, as he dialed the exterminator. "We have rodents in the basement again."

6. Vera looked at the space between Pat's upheld hands. "Wow! That was a big fish that got away."

7. "I dropped my wallet in the park," said Frida. "But someone returned it, thank goodness!"

8. "Well, would you look who's here!" said Jarvis sarcastically when Clyde arrived. "It's my old friend from summer camp."

9. "Eee!" Mel screamed. "Was that a sea monster or just a long strand of kelp?"

10. Bella looked at the goulash on the stove. "Aaagh! Is that alive?"

PRACTICE Parts of Speech

Use each word below in two sentences as two different parts of speech. You will write a total of twenty sentences. In each sentence, circle the word. After each sentence, give the word's part of speech.

EXAMPLE block

ANSWER Walk the dog around the (block.) noun

(Block) that play! verb

1. bowl
2. dance
3. past
4. record
5. another
6. fly
7. frame
8. light
9. so
10. that

Rewrite the following passage, correcting errors in spelling, capitalization, grammar, and usage. Add any missing punctuation. Write legibly to be sure one letter is not mistaken for another. There are ten mistakes.

Mary Antin

[1]During the 1890s, thousands of people came to the United States from Europe. [2]Most of them was Jewish people who were fleeing from discrimination. [3]The writer Mary Antin was one of those people, having come from Russia in 1894 at the age of thirteen. [4]Her family settled in Massachusetts, and Mary loved the freedom she finds in her new country. [5]She later said that she felt she had experienced "a second birth." [6]Not long after Mary came to America, she wrote to her uncle in Russia, describing the familys' journey. [7]That letter would later play an important role in her life.

[8]Because she spoke no english, the teenager was placed in a kindergarten class when she started school in the United States. [9]However, she completed grammar school in only for years and, in the meantime, had her poems published in Boston newspapers. [10]Then, a friend who knew how poor the family was showed a copy of Mary's letter to her Uncle to a publisher. [11]In 1899, it was published as a small book, and the money that came in from it's sale enabled Mary to attend a private high school and, later, college.

[12]In 1912, Mary Antin published an autobiography called *The Promised Land*. [13]It became the most famous immigrant autobiography in the country selling 85,000 copies during her lifetime. [14]For most of the twentieth century, it spoke vividly to others who had been threw the immigrant experience.

GRAMMAR/USAGE/MECHANICS

For each numbered word in the paragraph below, write one of these words to identify its part of speech: noun, pronoun, verb, adjective, adverb, preposition, conjunction, interjection.

I'm sitting quietly[1] at[2] the window,[3] thinking about[4] my day. My mother fixed[5] my favorite[6] breakfast, for[7] no reason at all. It wasn't my birthday or[8] anything. On the school bus,[9] my best[10] friend said,[11] "Hey[12], great shirt!" My English teacher[13] handed back[14] my paper and[15] said it was the best I had ever[16] written. During[17] softball practice,[18] I[19] hit a home run. When[20] I got home, my father[21] was waiting for[22] me at the bus stop. He had come home from work early[23] and just thought[24] it would be nice to meet me[25] there. He had[26] my dog with him.

Now I'm just[27] thinking about my whole[28] experience. In one way, it wasn't special,[29] but in another way it was. I guess[30] you could say it was just a good day.

Chapter 2

Parts of the Sentence

● ● ● ● ● ● ● ● ● ● ● ● ● ● ● ●

PRETEST **Simple and Complete Subjects
and Predicates**

*Identify each underlined word or group of words in the
paragraph by writing one of these labels:* simple subject,
complete subject, simple predicate, *or* complete predicate.

<u>My downstairs neighbor</u>[1] is moving tomorrow. That <u>makes me sad</u>.[2] The
family <u>has three small children</u>.[3] Maybe I <u>am</u>[4] just used to having them
around. I <u>don't know</u>.[5] <u>Marcello, the oldest</u>[6], is quiet and kind of tough for a
six-year-old. Matthias <u>talks</u>[7] all the time. The <u>baby</u>,[8] Nicholas, <u>just looks
around with his big blue eyes and smiles</u>.[9] In the morning, down the back
stairs <u>they</u>[10] all <u>troop</u>.[11] Suddenly, <u>the whole backyard</u>[12] is filled with running, laughing kids. How can <u>three kids</u>[13] make so much noise? <u>Don't ask
me!</u>[14] I <u>am really going to miss them</u>.[15]

Identify each underlined word or group of words by writing one of these labels: direct object, indirect object, object complement, predicate nominative, predicate adjective.

16. Juanita uses a potter's <u>wheel</u> very well.

17. Kristen taught <u>Eliza</u> mathematics.

18. Harvey helped <u>Esther</u> with painting her house.

19. Before school, Sue ate a quick <u>breakfast</u>.

20. The decision made her <u>speechless</u>.

21. Reginald got his <u>sister</u> a dog at the pound.

22. The committee elected Georgina its <u>president</u>.

23. Watch out! That dog is <u>mean</u>.

24. The atmosphere of the restaurant in the woods near town seemed <u>peaceful</u>.

25. Bob named his cat <u>Grunge</u>.

26. Does your father water the <u>plants</u> on your back porch every morning?

27. Albert Einstein was <u>one</u> of the most intelligent men of the twentieth century.

28. Charles Lindbergh made a solo <u>flight</u> across the Atlantic Ocean.

29. The strawberry is a very healthful <u>fruit</u>.

30. Baxter rang the <u>doorbell</u> twice.

2.1 SIMPLE SUBJECTS AND SIMPLE PREDICATES

A **sentence** is a group of words that expresses a complete thought.

Every sentence has two basic parts, a *subject* and a *predicate*.

The **subject** is the part of the sentence that names whom or what the sentence is about.

The **predicate** is the part of the sentence that says something about the subject.

Both the subject and the predicate can consist of more than one word.

The **simple subject** is the key noun or pronoun that tells what the sentence is about.

The **simple predicate** is the verb or verb phrase that expresses an action or a state of being about the subject of the sentence.

Remember, a simple predicate that is a verb phrase consists of a verb and any auxiliary, or helping, verbs.

EXAMPLES	SIMPLE SUBJECT	SIMPLE PREDICATE
	Garth Brooks	will perform.
	Dogs	were barking.
	Michael Jordan	jumped.
	Things	change.

You find the simple subject by asking *who?* or *what?* about the verb. For example, in the first sentence above, the proper noun *Garth Brooks* answers the question *Who will perform?*

PRACTICE **Simple Subjects and Simple Predicates**

Write each simple subject and simple predicate. Underline the simple predicate.

1. Bright clouds drifted across the sky.
2. Quietly, the smooth green lizard slipped down the rock.
3. Stella just broke her paperweight.
4. Amazingly, one little mosquito has forty-seven teeth!

5. Suddenly and without warning, the heavy plate fell off the table.

6. Thomas Jefferson wrote the Declaration of Independence secretly.

7. Babe Didrikson excelled in golf and baseball as well as track.

8. A python can be twenty-five feet long and over 220 pounds in weight.

9. After the game, the softball players hungrily wolfed down sandwiches and watermelon.

10. Japanese artists prefer thick ink for their finest work.

2.2 COMPLETE SUBJECTS AND COMPLETE PREDICATES

In most sentences, the addition of other words and phrases to the simple subject and the simple predicate expands or modifies the meaning of the sentence.

The **complete subject** consists of the simple subject and all the words that modify it.

The **complete predicate** consists of the simple predicate, or verb, and all the words that modify it or complete its meaning.

EXAMPLES	COMPLETE SUBJECT	COMPLETE PREDICATE
	Talented Garth Brooks	will perform his biggest hits.
	Large dogs	were barking at strangers on the sidewalk.
	The athletic Michael Jordan	jumped above the rim.
	Many things	change daily.

Complete Subjects and Complete Predicates

Identify each underlined complete subject or complete predicate by writing CS *or* CP.

1. Lions <u>spend a great deal of their time simply lying in the sun</u>.
2. <u>The museum of natural history</u> had an exhibition about dinosaurs.
3. Damascus, Syria, <u>is the oldest capital city in the world</u>.
4. <u>Almost all Americans</u> eat entirely too much sugar and have done so for decades.
5. Rap music <u>was created by African Americans in the inner cities of America</u>.
6. <u>Madame C. J. Walker's determination</u> made her the first self-made woman millionaire in the United States.
7. <u>French artists Auguste Renoir and Claude Monet</u> were two of the great Impressionist painters.
8. The old train <u>chugged slowly out of the station on its last journey</u>.
9. <u>Ripe peaches with beautiful red and orange skins</u> taste wonderful in the summer.
10. <u>Never do that again</u>.

2.3 COMPOUND SUBJECTS AND COMPOUND PREDICATES

A **compound subject** is made up of two or more simple subjects that are joined by a conjunction and have the same verb.

The conjunctions most commonly used to join the subjects in a compound subject are *and* and *or.*

EXAMPLE   **Tomatoes** and **carrots** are colorful vegetables.

EXAMPLE   **Tomatoes** or **carrots** would add color to the salad.

Correlative conjunctions may also be used to join compound subjects.

EXAMPLE   Neither the **tomato** nor the **pepper** grows underground.

EXAMPLE   Both the **tomato** and the **pepper** are rich in vitamin C.

When there are more than two subjects, the conjunction is usually used only between the last two subjects, and the subjects are separated by commas.

EXAMPLE   **Tomatoes, carrots,** and **peppers** are healthful.

Some sentences have more than one simple predicate.

A **compound predicate** (or **compound verb**) is made up of two or more verbs or verb phrases that are joined by a conjunction and have the same subject.

EXAMPLE   Horses **gallop** and **charge**.

EXAMPLE   Maria **opened** her book, **grabbed** a pencil, and **started** her homework.

In compound verbs that contain verb phrases, the auxiliary verb may or may not be repeated before the second verb.

EXAMPLE   Seagulls **will glide** or **swoop** down to the ocean.

EXAMPLE   We **have tested** these procedures and **have found** them good.

A sentence may have both a compound subject and a compound predicate.

EXAMPLE   **Butterflies** and **hummingbirds dart** and **dip** in the air.

Write CS if a sentence has a compound subject. Write CP if there is a compound predicate. Then write the simple subjects and the simple predicates.

1. Harold and Claudia took turns driving to school.
2. Lemons and limes are both citrus fruits.
3. My mother always drinks her coffee with cream and never adds sugar.
4. Chicago's Navy Pier, a major tourist attraction in that city, has a giant Ferris wheel and attracts millions of people every year.
5. My friend Jenny walked her two border collies and fed her goldfish.
6. Neither Alissa nor Ernesto particularly liked pepperoni on a pizza.
7. Yolanda's new hiking boots rubbed against her heels and gave her blisters.
8. I have never walked longer nor seen a more beautiful sunset.
9. *Star Wars* had a great many special effects and was a very expensive movie to make.
10. Long, warm days and short, cool nights make summer in Wisconsin delightful.

2.4 ORDER OF SUBJECT AND PREDICATE

In English the subject comes before the verb in most sentences. Some exceptions to this normal word order are discussed on the next page.

In **commands** and **requests,** the subject is usually not stated. The predicate is the entire sentence. The pronoun *you* is understood to be the subject.

EXAMPLES [You] **Run!** [You] **Give** it to me. [You] Please **be** careful.

Questions frequently begin with a verb or a helping verb or the words *who, whom, what, when, where, why,* or *how.*

EXAMPLE **Was** she correct?

EXAMPLE **Have** you **read** Gary Soto's stories?

EXAMPLE **Whom** did he invite?

In these cases, the subject generally follows the verb or helping verb. To find the subject of a question, rearrange the words to form a statement.

EXAMPLES	SUBJECT	PREDICATE
	She	was correct.
	You	have read Gary Soto's stories.
	He	did invite whom.

A sentence written in **inverted order,** in which the predicate comes before the subject, serves to add emphasis to the subject.

EXAMPLES	PREDICATE	SUBJECT
	Across the field **galloped**	the three **horses.**
	In the distance **flowed**	a **river.**

Remember, a word in a prepositional phrase is never the subject.

When the word *there* or *here* begins a sentence and is followed by a form of the verb *to be,* the subject follows the verb. The word *there* or *here* is never the subject.

There **is**   a **chill** in the air.

Here **are**   my **thoughts** on the matter.

You can find the subject in an inverted sentence by asking *who?* or *what?* about the predicate.

EXAMPLES What galloped across the field? The three horses did.

What is in the air? A chill is.

PRACTICE **Identifying Simple Subjects and Predicates in Sentences With Unusual Order**

Write each simple subject and simple predicate. If a subject is understood, write [You].

1. Why are you angry with me?

2. Meet me for lunch next Tuesday.

3. Into the garden crawled a ladybug on a mission.

4. Put down that cookie!

5. What are you doing with that bucket?

6. Completely disgusting is the smell of wet dog.

7. Across the field galloped the black horse.

8. Return your library books immediately!

9. Down the hill and over the rocks rolled the ball.

10. Has one single flower in your entire garden bloomed yet this year?

2.5 COMPLEMENTS

A **complement** is a word or a group of words that completes the meaning of a verb.

There are four kinds of complements: *direct objects, indirect objects, object complements,* and *subject complements.*

DIRECT OBJECTS

A **direct object** answers the question *what?* or *whom?* after an action verb.

The subject of a sentence usually performs the action indicated by the verb. That action may be directed toward or received by someone or something—the direct object. Direct objects are nouns, pronouns, or words acting as nouns, and they may be compound. Only transitive verbs have direct objects.

EXAMPLE Carlos served **dinner.** [Carlos served *what?*]

EXAMPLE Maria admires **him** deeply. [Maria admires *whom?*]

EXAMPLE Carlos served a Mexican **dinner** and a fabulous **dessert.** [Carlos served *what?*]

INDIRECT OBJECTS

An **indirect object** answers the question *to whom? for whom? to what?* or *for what?* after an action verb.

A sentence can have an indirect object only if it has a direct object. Two clues can help you identify indirect objects. First, an indirect object always comes between the verb and the direct object.

EXAMPLE Tyrone sent **me** a letter. [Tyrone sent a letter *to whom?*]

EXAMPLE Kim saved **Rosa** and **Manuel** seats. [Kim saved seats *for whom?*]

Second, if you add the word *to* or *for* in front of an indirect object, you haven't changed the meaning of the sentence.

EXAMPLE   Debra sent Todd a postcard.

Debra sent a postcard to Todd.

Notice that in the second sentence, the proper noun *Todd* is no longer an indirect object. It has become the object of a preposition (see p. 118).

OBJECT COMPLEMENTS

An **object complement** answers the question *what?* after a direct object. That is, it *completes* the meaning of the direct object by identifying or describing it.

Object complements occur only in sentences with direct objects and only in those sentences with the following action verbs or with similar verbs that have the general meaning of "make" or "consider":

appoint	consider	make	render
call	elect	name	think
choose	find	prove	vote

An object complement usually follows a direct object. It may be an adjective, a noun, or a pronoun.

EXAMPLE   Residents find the park **peaceful.** [adjective]

EXAMPLE   Maya appointed me **spokesperson** and **treasurer.** [nouns]

EXAMPLE   My grandmother considers the property **hers.** [pronoun]

SUBJECT COMPLEMENTS (PREDICATE NOMINATIVES, PREDICATE ADJECTIVES)

A **subject complement** follows a subject and a linking verb and identifies or describes the subject.

There are two kinds of subject complements: *predicate nominatives* and *predicate adjectives*.

A **predicate nominative** is a noun or a pronoun that follows a linking verb and points back to the subject to rename it or to identify it further.

EXAMPLE   Sopranos are **singers.**

EXAMPLE   The star of the opera was **she.**

EXAMPLE   Many current opera stars are **Italians** or **Spaniards.**

Predicate nominatives are usually found in sentences that contain forms of the linking verb *be*. A few other linking verbs (for example, *become* and *remain*) can also be followed by predicate nominatives.

EXAMPLE   Fiona became both a **musician** and an **actress.**

EXAMPLE   That experience remains a cherished **memory** for me.

A **predicate adjective** follows a linking verb and points back to the subject and further describes it.

EXAMPLE   Firefighters are **brave.**

EXAMPLE   Firefighters must be extremely **careful.**

EXAMPLE   Most firefighters are **dedicated** and **hardworking.**

Predicate adjectives may follow any linking verb.

EXAMPLE   I feel very **confident.**

EXAMPLE   My sister appeared **angry.**

EXAMPLE   The spoiled milk smelled **bad.**

EXAMPLE	Heidi seemed **intelligent** and **efficient**.
EXAMPLE	The trumpet sounded **sour.**
EXAMPLE	The soup tasted **salty**.
EXAMPLE	Overnight the maple leaves all turned **red.**

PRACTICE Complements

Write each complement and identify it by writing DO *for a direct object,* IO *for an indirect object,* OC *for an object complement,* PN *for a predicate nominative, and* PA *for a predicate adjective.*

1. Jeffrey drank his soda very quickly.
2. Hamish sent his mother a package of brightly colored ribbons for her birthday.
3. The jury found the defendant guilty in one day.
4. Through hard work and dedication, Mohammed became a scientist.
5. Jamie walked five miles yesterday.
6. Bill asked Fred a very difficult question.
7. Elaine's field hockey skills remain unpolished.
8. Estella watched the play at the little theater in town with great interest.
9. Peter is a good writer.
10. When not enough people showed up to vote, we had to appoint Joe club chairman.
11. A band of more than 20,000 members played music in Oslo, Norway, in 1964.
12. Aristotle taught Alexander the Great many things.
13. Jerald donated two trees to the park.
14. Lucy cut her own hair yesterday.
15. Most critics consider horror movies inferior.

16. Rain battered the roof all afternoon.

17. Pearl has remained my best friend for years.

18. That television show is really stupid.

19. Josh ate Sammy's french fries at the restaurant.

20. Today after school, Maria told Nikki a secret.

PRACTICE Proofreading

Rewrite the following passage, correcting errors in spelling, capitalization, grammar, and usage. Add any missing punctuation. Write legibly to be sure one letter is not mistaken for another. There are ten mistakes.

Nellie Bly

[1]The famous Nellie Bly came from a poor and abusive household to become the most famous Journalist of her time. [2]Born on May 5, 1864, Elizabeth Jane Cochran was eighteen years old when she writes an anonymous letter to the *Pittsburgh Dispatch* objecting to an editorial about women. [3]The papers' editor asked the letter writer to step forward. [4]She did, and he gave her a job and the name Nellie Bly.

[5]In the next few years, Nellie Bly invented the field of investigative reporting. [6]She posed as a garment worker to expose horribly working conditions. [7]When the paper's advertisers complained, she was assigned to cover fashions. [8]Instead, she went to mexico, where she exposed political corruption. [9]Thrown out of the country by an outraged government she went straight to New York.

[10]working for the *New York World*, Bly committed herself to a mental institution for women to expose conditions there. [11]Her report begun a movement to reform the care of the mentally ill. [12]She continued her investigative work [13]Then, the newspaper decided to send a man around the world in eighty days. [14]Nellie Bly was furious. [15]She, if anyone, had earned the right to undertake the mission she threatened to beat the other reporter's time if the paper didn't send her. [16]The editor gave in, and Nellie Bly completed the trip in seventy-two days.

Identify each underlined word or group of words in the paragraph by writing one of these labels: simple subject, complete subject, simple predicate, complete predicate.

People[1] around the world have made masks for thousands of years.[2] The face[3] seems to be endlessly fascinating, as well as symbolic. Some masks have been used for religious rituals.[4] Others[5] are part of the dance or drama of a culture. Wood, paper, metal, and various decorative objects[6] have all been widely used in mask-making. Some of the most beautiful masks[7] are used in Japanese Kabuki theater. African masks,[8] of course, are[9] also very beautiful and powerful. They have strongly influenced modern art in all parts of the world.[10]

POSTTEST **Complements**

Identify each underlined word or group of words by writing one of these labels: direct object, indirect object, object complement, predicate nominative, predicate adjective.

11. What did you buy Michael for his birthday?
12. Please don't chew your gum so loudly.
13. You should do your homework before you go out.
14. The first animal successfully cloned was a sheep.
15. Sing the national anthem before you play.
16. When we got into a fight, my friend called me a jerk.
17. Tony's mother is a volunteer firefighter.
18. Is your friend Howard an only child?
19. Brianne is rather petite.
20. Early risers saw a rainbow in the park.
21. Can you make that sentence clearer?
22. Spiders seem awfully scary to me.

GRAMMAR/USAGE/MECHANICS

23. The owner removed <u>them</u> from the store.
24. Marco threw <u>Janet</u> the <u>volleyball</u>.
25. Max chose <u>Vernon</u> first for the baseball game.
26. Some talk show hosts give their <u>audiences</u> <u>gifts</u>.
27. Did Habib take <u>Monica</u> her new <u>dress</u>?
28. Louis Armstrong remains a <u>legend</u> long after his death.
29. The photographer secretly took a <u>picture</u>.
30. Thunder and lightning accompanied the <u>storm</u>.

Chapter 3

Phrases

● ● ● ● ● ● ● ● ● ● ● ● ● ● ●

PRETEST   **Prepositional Phrases**

Write the prepositional phrases. For each, write the word or words modified by the phrase. Then write ADJ *for adjective or* ADV *for adverb to identify the type of phrase.*

1. At one time, there was a television show that lasted for only one episode.
2. One Sunday morning news show, however, has been on the air for half a century.
3. How can some shows continue for long periods of time while others are gone in an instant?
4. Well, the style of a show is very important.
5. During most seasons, one kind of program will be most fashionable.
6. One season, game shows might come into prime time.
7. At another time, reality programming might be popular.
8. With the high costs of production, every show must be "best."
9. Writers and producers with high values may sometimes forget them.
10. As a result, programming of a lower moral and artistic quality can become common.

Identify each italicized word or words by writing one of these labels: appositive, participle, gerund, infinitive.

11. Dickinson, the great American *poet,* lived very quietly.
12. *Keeping* calm was the only way *to win* the argument.
13. *Dreaming* of the future, I neglected *to pay* attention.
14. The plant *sitting* on the windowsill is an aloe vera.
15. By *telling* stories, Georgia entertained the children.
16. Fabrics *used* for drapes are supposed *to be* somewhat stiff, with some resistance to sunlight.
17. I just want *to sit* down with a good book.
18. By *standing* on the trunk, I was able *to get* the lid down.
19. *Written* in the first half of the twentieth century, the work of John Steinbeck will be long remembered.
20. Kathy, a hard *worker,* finds time *to relax* with her friends.

PRETEST Phrases

Identify each italicized group of words by writing one of these labels: prepositional phrase, appositive phrase, participial phrase, gerund phrase, infinitive phrase.

21. The little brown house *in the forest* smelled pleasantly of gingerbread.
22. The three bowls of porridge in the cottage had different *cooling off* rates.
23. *For construction work,* brick does better than straw.
24. *Talking to strange animals in the forest* is unwise.
25. *Seeing her in a bedjacket and sleeping cap,* a wise child recognizes her own grandmother.
26. He granted the usual reward for service to a magical being, *three wishes.*
27. *Letting down her hair,* the maiden braced herself against the wall *by the window.*

28. Fictional characters never seem *to learn about the punishments for lying.*

29. *Having defeated the dragon,* the knight decided to break for lunch.

30. *By the way,* I can't help but wonder if there is anything a magic fish cannot swallow.

3.1 PREPOSITIONAL PHRASES

A **phrase** is a group of words that acts in a sentence as a single part of speech.

A **prepositional phrase** is a group of words that begins with a preposition and ends with a noun or a pronoun, which is called the **object of the preposition.**

EXAMPLE The staircase leads **to the attic.**
[*Attic* **is the object of the preposition** *to.*]

EXAMPLE The staircase is too steep **for her.**
[*Her* **is the object of the preposition** *for.*]

For a list of common prepositions, see page 118.

Be careful to distinguish between the preposition *to* (*to the store,* **to** *Detroit*) and the *to* that marks an infinitive (*to see,* **to** *revise*). See page 154 for more about infinitives.

Adjectives and other modifiers may be placed between a preposition and its object. Also, a preposition may have more than one object.

EXAMPLE The staircase leads **to the crowded, dusty attic and the roof.** [adjectives added, two objects]

A prepositional phrase usually functions as an adjective or an adverb. When it is used as an adjective, it modifies a noun or a pronoun and is called an *adjective phrase.* An adjective phrase usually follows the word it modifies.

EXAMPLE They used the staircase **on the left.**
[adjective phrase modifying the noun *staircase*]

EXAMPLE Which **of the staircases** leads downstairs?
[adjective phrase modifying the pronoun *which*]

When a prepositional phrase is used as an adverb, it modifies a verb, an adjective, or an adverb and is called an *adverb phrase.*

EXAMPLE **At midnight** I went downstairs **to the kitchen.**
[adverb phrases modifying the verb *went*]

EXAMPLE My grandfather explained that a daily walk

is healthful **for him.** [adverb phrase modifying the adjective *healthful*]

EXAMPLE She skis very well **for a beginner.**
[adverb phrase modifying the adverb *well*]

An adverb phrase that modifies a verb may appear in different positions in a sentence.

EXAMPLE She wore a beautiful diamond ring **on her finger.**
[adverb phrase modifying *wore*]

EXAMPLE **On her finger,** she wore a beautiful diamond ring.
[adverb phrase modifying *wore*]

EXAMPLE She wore **on her finger** a beautiful diamond ring.
[adverb phrase modifying *wore*]

Writing Tip

Place adjective and adverb phrases exactly where they belong. A misplaced phrase can be confusing. See pages 267–268 for more about misplaced modifiers.

Write the prepositional phrases. For each, write the word or words modified by the phrase. Then write ADJ *for adjective or* ADV *for adverb to identify the type of phrase.*

1. The white horse with the long black tail was the tallest we could see.
2. Above the doorway hung a set of deer antlers.
3. Jack crawled under the fallen tree.
4. Howie and Michelle finished the soccer game with very dirty uniforms.
5. The price of gasoline varies with supply and demand.
6. Bob nearly hit the lady in the crosswalk.
7. When I was in a building with large glass windows during the storm, I became frightened.
8. The bird with bright green wings flew off suddenly.
9. If you are looking for the fish market, it is around the corner.
10. I think your earring fell under the table.

3.2 APPOSITIVES AND APPOSITIVE PHRASES

An **appositive** is a noun or a pronoun that is placed next to another noun or pronoun to identify it or give additional information about it.

EXAMPLE My friend **Ethan** works at a bookstore after school. [The appositive *Ethan* identifies the noun *friend*.]

An **appositive phrase** is an appositive plus any words that modify the appositive.

EXAMPLE He is saving money to travel to Bogotá, **the capital of Colombia.** [The appositive phrase, in blue type, identifies Bogotá.]

Use commas to set off any appositive or appositive phrase that is not essential to the meaning of the sentence.

EXAMPLE Ethan's friend **Julie** works at the store. **[The appositive *Julie* is essential because Ethan has more than one friend.]**

EXAMPLE Eric, **Ethan's twin brother,** does not work. **[The appositive phrase is not essential because Ethan has only one twin brother.]**

Usually an appositive or an appositive phrase follows the noun or pronoun it identifies or explains. Occasionally an appositive phrase precedes the noun or pronoun.

EXAMPLE **A hard worker,** Ethan will save money quickly.

PRACTICE Appositives and Appositive Phrases

Write each appositive or appositive phrase and the noun or pronoun that is identified or explained by the appositive.

1. Reggie, my pet Rottweiler, weighs eighty-five pounds.
2. The coldest of all the planets in our solar system is Pluto, the ninth planet from the Sun.
3. I just read *To Kill a Mockingbird,* my new favorite book.
4. The largest mammal in the world, the blue whale, can reach 100 feet in length.
5. The White Sox are playing the best team in baseball, the Yankees, on Saturday.
6. The building at 1600 Pennsylvania Avenue, the White House, is where the president lives.
7. Erwin's sister Julia has the best grades in the class.
8. I finished the project on Thursday, the last possible day.
9. The third president of the United States, Thomas Jefferson, was the main author of the Declaration of Independence.
10. Frederick Douglass, a former enslaved person, was a great orator.

3.3 VERBALS AND VERBAL PHRASES

A **verbal** is a verb form that functions in a sentence as a noun, an adjective, or an adverb.

A **verbal phrase** is a verbal plus any complements and modifiers.

Verbals are *participles, gerunds,* and *infinitives.* Each of these can be expanded into phrases.

PARTICIPLES AND PARTICIPIAL PHRASES

A **participle** is a verb form that can function as an adjective.

Present participles always end in *–ing* (*moving*). *Past participles* often end in *–ed* (*striped*), but some are irregularly formed (*broken*). Many commonly used adjectives are actually participles.

EXAMPLE   A **moving** van is parked on our street.

EXAMPLE   The dogs barked at the **striped** cat.

EXAMPLE   The **broken** window suggested **frightening** possibilities.

When a participle is part of a verb phrase, the participle is not functioning as an adjective.

EXAMPLES

PARTICIPLE AS AN ADJECTIVE   The **confused** child was afraid.

PARTICIPLE IN A VERB PHRASE   The teacher **has confused** our names.

A **participial phrase** contains a participle plus any complements and modifiers.

Participial phrases can be placed in various positions in a sentence. They always act as adjectives.

EXAMPLE   The dog saw many ducks **swimming in the lake.**

EXAMPLE   **Barking loudly,** the dog approached the water.

EXAMPLE   The ducks, **startled by the noise,** rose and flew away quickly.

EXAMPLE   The **sorely disappointed** dog returned to the campsite.

A participial phrase at the beginning of a sentence is usually followed by a comma.

PRACTICE   Participles and Participial Phrases

Write the participles and participial phrases. Then write the word or words each participle or participial phrase modifies.

1. One of the joys of the garden is a freshly picked tomato.
2. Known all over the world, Charlie Chaplin once received 73,000 letters in two days.
3. After the game, tape helped protect Jim's sprained ankle from further damage.
4. Remembering their giver, Jan refused to throw away the wilted, brown flowers.
5. Kindly helping an older woman across the street, Margaretta felt useful.
6. Broken beyond repair, my mother's favorite vase lay in a pool of water.
7. Saturn, orbiting slowly around the Sun, has many rings that look like solid disks.
8. Trying to swing on a broken vine, mighty Tarzan fell into the lake.
9. The bird could only walk around the backyard because it had an injured wing.
10. Patrick, feeling that he was not accepted by his teammates, quit the team.

GERUNDS AND GERUND PHRASES

A **gerund** is a verb form that ends in *–ing* and is used in the same ways a noun is used.

EXAMPLE **Cooking** is an enjoyable activity. [gerund as subject]

EXAMPLE My younger sister likes **swimming**.
[gerund as direct object]

EXAMPLE Tony gives **baking** his best effort.
[gerund as indirect object]

EXAMPLE How much money have you saved for **shopping?**
[gerund as object of preposition]

EXAMPLE Dustin's favorite sport is **skiing**.
[gerund as predicate nominative]

EXAMPLE My hobbies, **drawing** and **painting,** require patience.
[gerunds as appositives]

A **gerund phrase** contains a gerund plus any complements and modifiers.

EXAMPLE **Cross-country skiing** is good exercise.

EXAMPLE **Billie Holiday's soulful singing** delighted many audiences.

Although both a gerund and a present participle end in *-ing,* they function as different parts of speech. A gerund is used as a noun, whereas a present participle is used as part of a verb phrase or as an adjective.

EXAMPLES

PARTICIPLE AS AN ADJECTIVE **Reading her new book,** Isabella became sleepy.

PARTICIPLE IN A VERB PHRASE Isabella **was reading** in the window seat.

GERUND **Reading** is Isabella's favorite pastime.

PRACTICE

PRACTICE **Gerunds and Gerund Phrases**

Write the gerunds and gerund phrases. Identify the way each is used by writing one of these labels: subject, direct object, indirect object, object of a preposition, predicate nominative, appositive.

1. One really negative habit is taking advantage of people.
2. Oscar was arrested for going too fast.
3. The hyena was frightened away by the monkeys' howling.
4. Talking is the only hobby I really enjoy.
5. Isabel likes arguing too much to be a good coach.
6. One of my favorite pastimes is fishing.
7. Eli's job, gardening, is difficult but rewarding.
8. Fighting constantly is a sign of emotional problems.
9. Celia's jealousy lent her joking a bitter edge.
10. I'm not particularly good at shopping.
11. Watching sports movies really doesn't count as exercise.
12. My hobby, collecting baseball cards, can be expensive.
13. Jane gives bird-watching her full attention.
14. The whole team loves playing basketball on the out-door court at the park.
15. This time, apologizing is not enough.

INFINITIVES AND INFINITIVE PHRASES

An **infinitive** is a verb form that is usually preceded by the word *to* and is used as a noun, an adjective, or an adverb.

When you use the word *to* before the base form of a verb, *to* is not a preposition but part of the infinitive form of the verb.

EXAMPLE   **To stand** can be uncomfortable. **[infinitive as subject]**

EXAMPLE   Infants first learn **to creep**. **[infinitive as direct object]**

EXAMPLE   His goal is **to graduate**. **[infinitive as predicate nominative]**

EXAMPLE   They have the desire **to win.** [infinitive as adjective]

EXAMPLE   I was ready **to leave.** [infinitive as adverb]

An **infinitive phrase** contains an infinitive plus any complements and modifiers.

EXAMPLE   We stopped **to look at the beautiful scenery.**

EXAMPLE   **To be a good friend** is my goal.

EXAMPLE   Obedience school teaches dogs **to behave well.**

PRACTICE Infinitives and Infinitive Phrases

Write the infinitives and infinitive phrases. For each, write noun, adjective, *or* adverb *to tell how the infinitive or infinitive phrase is being used.*

1. Jeff needed campaign funds to run for office.
2. James didn't want to miss yearbook pictures again.
3. To win the contest, Lauren needed a really big fish.
4. I don't know why Sarah feels the need to bite her nails.
5. Who wants to watch baseball on television?
6. Are you prepared to give your all for the team?
7. The first woman to present a case before the Supreme Court was Belva Lockwood, in 1879.
8. Gerry played to win.
9. Just to know I did my best is enough for me.
10. I walked awhile to clear my mind.

PRACTICE Appositives and Verbals

Identify each italicized term by writing one of these labels: appositive, participle, gerund, infinitive.

1. *To work* hard is the lot of most parents.
2. Dora and Emily were caught *passing* notes in class.
3. *Bicycling* through mountains is a strenuous activity.

4. The horse galloped through the mountain meadow, *moving* with great grace.

5. Diane gives *writing* her full attention.

6. I have no desire *to wash* the dishes.

7. Jimmy Carter, *the thirty-ninth president of the United States,* has a submarine named after him.

8. My neighbor's *barking* German shepherd gives me a headache.

9. *Seeing* a baby bird on the ground under the tree, I replaced it in its nest.

10. Geri hated *to pick* berries.

PRACTICE Phrases

Identify each italicized group of words by writing one of these labels: prepositional phrase, appositive phrase, participial phrase, gerund phrase, infinitive phrase.

1. *Working on the mayor's campaign,* I felt very useful and happy.

2. I'm going to my room *to call my friend*.

3. Sylvia, *my good friend,* paints many pictures *of the flowers in the garden*.

4. *Living in a eucalyptus tree* suits the koala so well it needs nothing else.

5. *To be a good nurse* requires dedication.

6. The plant life *in the ocean* accounts for 85 percent *of all the world's plants*.

7. Thomas Edison was a collector of birds, *owning five thousand of them at one time*.

8. *Baking cupcakes* is not as easy as it might seem, but it's worth the effort.

9. Gerry has been known *to call Heather ten times in one day*.

10. *Talking to friends* is my favorite pastime.

Rewrite the following passage, correcting errors in spelling, capitalization, grammar, and usage. Add any missing punctuation. Write legibly to be sure one letter is not mistaken for another. There are ten mistakes.

Willa Cather

¹Although she was born in Virginia, writer Willa Cather grew up in Red Cloud Nebraska. ²It was not a big town. ³The class of 1890 at Red Cloud High School her graduating class contained exactly three students. ⁴Cather moved on after graduation to the larger city of Lincoln, where she attends the University of Nebraska. ⁵While at the university, she began publishing short storys and articles in the school newspaper. ⁶After college, she got a job as the editor of a women's magazine, called the "Home Monthly."

⁷By 1906, Cather was living in New York, still writing, and sometimes getting her poems and short stories published. ⁸In 1912, her first novel, *Alexander's Bridge,* came out. ⁹It was followed 2 years later by her popular and respected *O Pioneers!* ¹⁰Before much time passed she was able to support herself as a writer. ¹¹she sold the rights to one of her novels, *A Lost Lady,* to a film producer. ¹²However, she hated the film, and refused to allow any of her other books to be adapted. ¹³Today she is considered one of America's most important novelists.

Write the prepositional phrases. For each, write the word or words modified by the phrase. Then write ADJ for adjective or ADV for adverb to identify the phrase.

1. The picture in that beautiful frame is of my grandfather.
2. Lady Astor discovered she had mice in the walls.
3. I'll buy a paper at the drugstore around the corner.
4. The area around the sun is unimaginably hot.
5. Kim and Taylor danced under the stars.

6. My family spends time in rural Missouri.
7. In the early twentieth century, Aida Overton Walker was one of the first African American Broadway stars.
8. Gretchen hid a flashlight under her pillow to read at night.
9. Shakespeare had a vocabulary of roughly 24,000 words.
10. The "countdown" so beloved by the space program was first used by director Fritz Lang in a science fiction film.

POSTTEST Appositives and Verbals

Identify each italicized word or words by writing one of these labels: appositive, participle, gerund, infinitive.

11. Nigeria is the most densely *populated* country in Africa.
12. By *developing* commercially practical electricity, Thomas Edison ended the age of steam power in this country.
13. A sturgeon, *a giant fish,* lives for more than 150 years.
14. *Feeling* a little ill, Maria went home at lunchtime.
15. Maggie Lena Walker, *the first woman bank president in the United States,* was from Richmond, Virginia.
16. *Coming* out of the clouds, the sun shone on the garden.
17. Mignon likes *to attend* the free concerts in the park.
18. The Charleston, *a lively dance,* was popular in the 1920s.
19. Solar energy could be very useful for *heating.*
20. The cadets spent the day *marching.*

POSTTEST Phrases

Identify each italicized group of words by writing one of these labels: prepositional phrase, appositive phrase, participial phrase, gerund phrase, infinitive phrase.

21. *Knowing this new information,* I would never choose that product.

22. In spite of his love for movies, Eric prefers to go *to the museum*.

23. *Looking for a book on beads,* I found instead a book on precious gems.

24. *Learning history* makes the world seem richer.

25. *After lunch,* I plan *to take a nap*.

26. All Larry wants *to do* is watch videos.

27. Elvis Presley is one of the few performers ever to make twenty albums *selling more than a million copies each.*

28. Earl, *my teddy bear,* sits in the window of my bedroom and watches for me *to come home*.

29. *Gus's constant whining* is getting on my nerves.

30. Are you going out *without a hat?*

Chapter 4

Clauses and Sentence Structure

• • • • • • • • • • • • • • •

PRETEST   **Main and Subordinate Clauses**

Write each boldfaced clause and label it M *for main or* S *for subordinate. Then identify each subordinate clause as adjective* (ADJ), *adverb* (ADV), *or noun* (N).

1. *To Kill a Mockingbird* is a powerful book **that was made into a wonderful movie.**

2. When I go away next year, **I will travel to Spain.**

3. **What I dislike about winter** is snow.

4. **Only Sheila knows** what Dan said to her.

5. Vanessa studied the Revolutionary War in her history class; **however, she liked learning about the Civil War even more.**

6. **When Paul doesn't know how to spell a word,** he looks it up in the dictionary and tries to remember it for the future.

7. **Al had refereed the game** that had attracted the biggest crowd of the season.

8. The movie **that we rented** reminded me of *Star Wars.*

9. **Because Anthea has band practice after school,** she is hungry when she gets home.

10. When I first saw you, **you were wearing jeans.**

11. Kasi will fix the salad **because her salad dressing is excellent.**

12. When you are in Boston, **you should try the clam chowder.**

13. Did you know **that the best recipe for chicken salad includes grapes?**

14. **After it stayed above freezing for a few days,** my snowman melted into a puddle.

15. Fred's hat, **which I picked out,** looks good with that jacket.

16. **Gary likes neither coffee nor tea,** but his uncle likes them both.

17. Bubbles, **because they entertain everyone,** are a great party favor.

18. **If I have to write any more,** I may not be able to use my hand tomorrow.

19. Yes, that woman is **who you think she is.**

20. Those TV game shows **that everyone watches** can be exciting.

Identify each sentence by writing S *for simple,* C *for compound,* CX *for complex, or* CC *for compound-complex.*

21. I had to sleep on the floor because my grandparents didn't have an extra bed.

22. The moon was startlingly bright, and the stars were beautiful.

23. The summer afternoon was too hot for hot food or a heavy meal.

24. Please, don't leave the door open after you let out that pesky cat.

25. I can't stand the smell of vinegar; no one else in my family thinks that it has an offensive odor.

26. Pati picked up the brown teddy bear and gave it to her little brother.

27. Vera will be sure to call you when she gets home.

28. If it's hot outside, my parents give me extra water bottles for camp, and my counselors give us extra water breaks.

29. Because he was looking for street signs, Ivan almost missed the light.

30. I always get the grilled chicken sandwich at this restaurant; however, I think I'll try the turkey club this time.

PRETEST Kinds of Sentences

Identify each sentence by writing D *for declarative,* IT *for interrogative,* IM *for imperative, or* E *for exclamatory.*

31. Scott, go to the office.

32. I hope that I do well on the geography test; I studied for three hours.

33. Has Victoria told you about her trip to San Diego?

34. Wow, look at that sunset!

35. Stop writing, put down your pencils, and pass your tests forward.

36. What will Sylvia do if her ride does not show up on time?

37. The picture from the homecoming dance made Melissa look attractive.

38. Let's go, Bulls!

39. Rewind the video before you return it and try to return it on time.

40. May I borrow a quarter?

PRETEST **Fragments and Run-ons**

Identify each numbered item by writing F *for fragment,* R *for run-on sentence, or* S *for sentence.*

41. I think the story makes it clear that the figure in the bed wasn't really Little Red Riding Hood's grandmother.

42. Before you start to explain yourself.

43. Did you know that people used to think the Sun revolved around Earth?

44. Completely fed up with your bickering!

45. He who thinks like others is not thinking, he needs to think for himself.

46. When you go to the museum, make sure you see the exhibit about the human heart it is more interesting than you might expect.

47. I just start laughing sometimes.

48. The ornate candlesticks holding pale, tapered candles that decorated the dinner table.

49. You look around the store, I'll stay here in case they return.

50. Blue and gray are Mina's favorite colors; they go with almost everything.

4.1 MAIN CLAUSES

A **clause** is a group of words that has a subject and a predicate (verb). A clause can function as a sentence by itself or as part of a sentence.

A **main clause** has a subject and a predicate and expresses a complete thought. It is the only type of clause that can stand alone as a sentence. A main clause is also called an **independent clause.**

Every sentence must have at least one main clause. In the following examples, the clauses express complete thoughts, so they are main clauses. Note that a coordinating conjunction is not part of a main clause.

EXAMPLE

Main Clause

The curtain rose.
Subject   Verb

EXAMPLE

Main Clause   Main Clause

The cast bowed, and the audience applauded.
Subject   Verb   Subject   Verb

Both the subject and the predicate of a main clause may be compound.

EXAMPLE

Main Clause

The actors and crew smiled and bowed, and
Subject   Subject   Verb   Verb

Main Clause

the audience cheered and clapped.
Subject   Verb   Verb

4.2 SUBORDINATE CLAUSES

A **subordinate clause,** also called a **dependent clause,** has a subject and a predicate but does not express a complete thought, so it cannot stand alone as a sentence.

There are three types of subordinate clauses: *adjective clauses,* which modify nouns or pronouns; *adverb clauses,* which modify verbs, adjectives, or adverbs; and *noun clauses,* which function as nouns.

A subordinate clause is dependent on the rest of the sentence because a subordinate clause does not make sense by itself. A subordinating conjunction or a relative pronoun usually introduces a subordinate clause. (See Lesson 1.2 on page 104 for a list of relative pronouns. See Lesson 1.7 on page 123 for a list of subordinating conjunctions.)

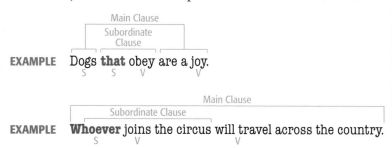

EXAMPLE **When** the dog barked, the baby cried.

In some cases, a relative pronoun can also function as the subject or some other part of a subordinate clause.

EXAMPLE Dogs **that** obey are a joy.

EXAMPLE **Whoever** joins the circus will travel across the country.

In the first example, the subordinating conjunction *when* placed before *the dog barked* creates a word group—*when the dog barked*—that cannot stand alone as a main clause. Although the clause has a subject and a predicate, it does not express a complete thought.

In the second example, the relative pronoun *that* begins a subordinate clause that comes between the subject and the verb of the main clause. *That* also serves as the subject of the subordinate clause, and *obey* is its verb. *That obey* cannot, however, stand alone.

In the third example, the subordinate clause functions as the subject of the sentence. *Whoever* functions as the subject of the subordinate clause, *whoever joins the circus. Joins* is the verb, and *the circus* is the direct object. *Whoever joins the circus* cannot, however, stand alone.

PRACTICE Subordinate Clauses

Write the subordinate clause from each sentence.

1. After Laura gets home from school, she eats a piece of fruit.
2. Our tour guide was a woman who had lived in Spain.
3. The movie that Sue rented was creepy.
4. Jim and Clare went to a Chicago Cubs' game that was played in Wrigley Field.
5. The car, which they bought last year, is in the shop.
6. That we weren't going to Nebraska was a disappointment to all of us.
7. Mom waited at the corner that was always crowded.
8. Chili is Lila's favorite food when it's cold outside.
9. Becka's orange shirt, which Tom had given her for her birthday, made her stand out in the crowd.
10. Unless someone volunteers, Jane will walk the puppy.

PRACTICE Main and Subordinate Clauses

Copy the sentences. Underline the main clauses once and the subordinate clauses twice.

1. While I wash the dishes, you set the table.
2. What Kasim enjoys is reading a book on a beautiful day under his favorite tree.
3. Martha truly believes that she will be president of the United States.

4. Cara uses a computer to perform calculations that she cannot do on her own.
5. He may not be home when you call.
6. Li can't go to the park this afternoon because she is going to the art fair.
7. Whoever swims in the deep end is required to pass the swim test.
8. If it rains, Sam has an extra umbrella.
9. The sand, which felt soft under his bare feet, was almost white.
10. A bald eagle's feathers weigh more than double its bones, which are hollow.

4.3 ADJECTIVE CLAUSES

An **adjective clause** is a subordinate clause that modifies a noun or a pronoun.

An adjective clause may begin with a relative pronoun (*who, whom, whose, that,* or *which*) or the word *where* or *when.* An adjective clause normally follows the word it modifies.

EXAMPLE   Magazines **that inform and entertain** are my favorites.

EXAMPLE   Several writers **whom I admire** contribute to magazines.

EXAMPLE   The store **where I buy magazines** sponsors readings by contributors.

Sometimes the relative pronoun is dropped from the beginning of an adjective clause.

EXAMPLE   *National Geographic* is the magazine **I like best.**
[**The relative pronoun *that* has been omitted.**]

Some adjective clauses are necessary to make the meaning of a sentence clear. Such an adjective clause is called an *essential clause,* or a *restrictive clause.* It must not be set off with commas.

EXAMPLE Magazines **that have no substance** bore me.

EXAMPLE Many writers **whose works have become famous** began their writing careers at the *New Yorker* magazine.

An adjective clause that is not necessary to make the meaning of the sentence clear, even though it may add information to a sentence, is called a *nonessential clause* or a *nonrestrictive clause.* Always use commas to set off a nonessential clause.

EXAMPLE James Thurber**, who was a famous humorist,** wrote for the *New Yorker.*

EXAMPLE His stories**, which include humorous incidents from his childhood in Ohio,** make funny and interesting reading.

When choosing between *that* and *which* to introduce an adjective clause, use *that* to begin an essential clause and *which* to begin a nonessential clause.

EXAMPLE Magazines **that include art and literature** are interesting and educational.

EXAMPLE The *New Yorker***, which includes fiction and poetry,** competes with *Vanity Fair.*

4.4 ADVERB CLAUSES

An **adverb clause** is a subordinate clause that modifies a verb, an adjective, or an adverb. It tells *when, where, how, why, to what extent,* or *under what conditions.*

Adverb clauses begin with subordinating conjunctions (page 122). An adverb clause can come either before or after the main clause. When an adverb clause comes first, separate it from the main clause with a comma. (See Lesson 11.6.)

EXAMPLE **Before I took the test,** I studied for hours. [The adverb clause tells *when* and modifies the verb *studied*.]

EXAMPLE I studied longer **than I had ever studied before.** [The adverb clause tells *to what extent* and modifies the adverb *longer*.]

EXAMPLE I was happy **because I passed the test.** [The adverb clause tells *why* and modifies the adjective *happy*.]

Elliptical adverb clauses have words left out of them. You can easily supply the omitted words because they are understood or implied.

EXAMPLE She can swim faster **than I.** [*Can swim* has been omitted.]

EXAMPLE **While walking,** she listens to the radio. [*She is* has been omitted.]

4.5 NOUN CLAUSES

A **noun clause** is a subordinate clause that is used as a noun within the main clause of a sentence.

You can use a noun clause as a subject, a direct object, an indirect object, an object of a preposition, or a predicate nominative.

EXAMPLE **Whoever wins the election** will speak. [noun clause as subject]

EXAMPLE The reporter will do **whatever is required** to get an interview. [noun clause as direct object]

EXAMPLE The senator will give **whoever asks** an interview. [noun clause as indirect object]

EXAMPLE A news story should begin with **whatever gets the reader's attention.** [noun clause as object of a preposition]

EXAMPLE That is **why she included specific data in the article.** [noun clause as predicate nominative]

The following are some words that can be used to introduce noun clauses.

how	whatever	which	whose
however	when	whichever	why
if	where	who, whom	
that	wherever	whoever	
what	whether	whomever	

Sometimes the introductory word is dropped from a noun clause.

EXAMPLE I believe **most readers will be entertained by this article.** [*That* has been omitted from the beginning of the clause.]

PRACTICE **Kinds of Subordinate Clauses**

Write the subordinate clause from each sentence. Then write ADJ if it's an adjective clause, ADV if it's an adverb clause, or N if it's a noun clause.

1. Whoever wins the game will be the champion.
2. Before he stepped up to the plate, Sammy Sosa checked with his third base coach.
3. Sue reluctantly ate what was on her plate.
4. My mom, who has two published novels, hasn't written a book in a couple of years.
5. Next week we play the team that is in first place.
6. Fletcher eats a banana whenever he wants a snack.
7. Because Si likes to swim, he joined the YMCA.
8. The winner was the dog that had the red collar.
9. The key to the puzzle is what the eye does not see.
10. Rick needed a glue stick and a pair of scissors before he could start his project.

4.6 FOUR KINDS OF SENTENCES

Sentences are often classified according to their purpose. There are four purposes that sentences may have: to make a statement, to give an order or make a request, to ask a question, and to express strong emotion.

A **declarative sentence** makes a statement.

EXAMPLE   I have four pets.

EXAMPLE   Two of my pets are dogs.

A declarative sentence usually ends with a period but can end with an exclamation mark. This type of sentence is the most frequently used in speaking and writing.

An **imperative sentence** gives a command or makes a request.

EXAMPLE   Get off the table.

EXAMPLE   Zelda, please leave the cats alone.

An imperative sentence usually ends with a period but can end with an exclamation mark. In imperative sentences, the subject *you* is understood.

An **interrogative sentence** asks a question.

EXAMPLE   How many pets do you have?

EXAMPLE   Do you like rottweilers?

An interrogative sentence usually ends with a question mark but can end with an exclamation mark if it expresses strong emotion.

An **exclamatory sentence** expresses strong emotion.

EXAMPLE   She is such a beautiful dog!

EXAMPLE   Don't chew on that!

EXAMPLE   What do you think you're doing!

An exclamatory sentence ends with an exclamation point. Note that sentences are not only exclamatory but can be declarative (first example on the previous page), imperative (second example), or interrogative (third example) while expressing strong emotion. In writing, exclamatory sentences should be used sparingly so as not to detract from their effectiveness.

PRACTICE **Kinds of Sentences**

Identify each sentence by writing D *for declarative,* IT *for interrogative,* IM *for imperative, or* E *for exclamatory.*

1. Janice held up a gift certificate from her grandparents.
2. How many hats do you have, anyway?
3. What an amazing play that was!
4. Please, give me some help with this.
5. The energetic music made Josephine tap her feet and snap her fingers.
6. Why do I always have to feed the cat?
7. Hara writes stories that have surprise endings.
8. Get out of there, dog!
9. What kind of answer was that?
10. Make sure you vote in the upcoming election.

4.7 SIMPLE AND COMPOUND SENTENCES

Sentences are sometimes classified by their structure. The four sentence structures are *simple, compound, complex,* and *compound-complex.*

A **simple sentence** contains only one main clause and no subordinate clauses.

A simple sentence may contain a compound subject, a compound predicate, or both. The subject and the predicate can be expanded with adjectives, adverbs, prepositional phrases, appositives, and verbal phrases.

EXAMPLE Stories entertain. **[simple sentence]**

EXAMPLE Stories and riddles entertain and amuse. **[simple sentence with compound subject and compound predicate]**

EXAMPLE Stories about the Old West entertain adults and children alike. **[simple sentence including a prepositional phrase, a direct object, and an adverb]**

A **compound sentence** contains two or more main clauses.

The main clauses in a compound sentence may be joined in any of four ways.

1. Usually they are joined by a comma and a coordinating conjunction (*and, but, or, so, nor, yet, for*).

EXAMPLE Stories about the Old West are entertaining**, and** stories set in foreign countries are interesting.

EXAMPLE Stories entertain me**, and** riddles amuse me**, but** poems are my favorite.

2. Main clauses in a compound sentence may be joined by a semicolon used alone.

EXAMPLE Talented oral storytellers are rare; Spalding Gray is exceptional.

3. Main clauses in a compound sentence may be joined by a semicolon and a conjunctive adverb (such as *however, therefore, nevertheless*).

EXAMPLE Stories entertain and amuse**; however,** poems are delightful.

4. Main clauses in a compound sentence may be joined by a semicolon and an expression such as *for example.*

EXAMPLE Many authors write stories and poems**; for example,** Sherman Alexie is known for both his stories and his poems.

Identify each sentence by writing S for a simple sentence or C for a compound sentence.

1. Megan, my second cousin, and Peter, her brother, walked six miles the other day.

2. Vern made hot cocoa, and his uncle supplied the marshmallows.

3. My dad fixes breakfast and cleans the kitchen on Sundays.

4. Anya checks her e-mail often, but she doesn't always respond right away.

5. Don't let his calm face fool you; that lion could hurt you.

6. George and Alicia hiked through the forest and camped next to a creek.

7. You should try to get a good night's sleep.

8. Pam loves jewelry; however, she has sensitive skin and can't wear it.

9. The airplane circled overhead and then flew toward the airport.

10. The rainbow in the sky was incredible; the sun was warm.

4.8 COMPLEX AND COMPOUND-COMPLEX SENTENCES

A **complex sentence** has one main clause and one or more subordinate clauses.

Main Clause

EXAMPLE I like Toni Cade Bambara's stories
S V

Subordinate Clause

because they have good characters.
S   V

EXAMPLE

| Subordinate Clause | Main Clause |

When I read her stories, I enjoy them
S   V   S   V

| Subordinate Clause |

because they are believable.
        S   V

A **compound-complex sentence** has two or more main clauses and at least one subordinate clause.

EXAMPLE

| Main Clause | Subordinate Clause |

I read *Frankenstein*, which Mary Shelley wrote,
S   V   S   V

| Main Clause |

and I reported on it.
    S   V

GRAMMAR/USAGE/MECHANICS

PRACTICE   Complex and Compound-Complex Sentences

Identify each sentence by writing CX *for complex sentence or* CC *for compound-complex sentence. Then write the subordinate clause from each sentence.*

1. If you want to go, you have to find a ride for us.

2. I should lift weights more often, but it's difficult when I work five days a week.

3. *My Fair Lady*, which is Ryan's favorite musical, is known for the song "Wouldn't It Be Loverly?" but my favorite song in it is "On the Street Where You Live."

4. I hope that my brothers will come home soon.

5. With three teenagers, the Langs want a house that has at least two bathrooms.

6. I'm going to the beach on Friday, which is supposed to be a warm day, and I want you to go with me.

7. Bobby's knees hurt after he fell, but he hobbled home without too much trouble.

8. When Amin opened the refrigerator, there was not a bit of cheese left.
9. Because her day had been exhausting, Camille relaxed in the evening.
10. Quinn didn't like the music that was favored by his sister, but he tried to understand her point of view.

Frank and Ernest

DO YOU WANT THIS TYPED UP JUST THE WAY YOU SAID IT, OR SHALL I CHOP IT UP INTO SENTENCES?

THAVES

PRACTICE Simple, Compound, Complex, and Compound-Complex Sentences

Copy the following sentences. Identify each sentence by writing S for simple, C for compound, CX for complex, and CC for compound-complex. Underline each main clause once and each subordinate clause twice.

1. Bill and Al went to the north end of the park, turned left, and drove for two blocks.
2. When Yuri fed the horses, he also fed the chickens.
3. Julia fished in the lake, but Johanna sat under the tree and read a book.

4. Carl listened to the drums and decided that he wanted to play.
5. Before I told my side of the story, Steve had confessed, and Peter cried.
6. If you choose one of the books from the stack, I will help you read it.
7. Rafe watched the clock; time moved more slowly.
8. The prince rode his horse across the meadow and jumped over the fence.
9. The girl who has been a good friend of mine distributed the gifts.
10. The child hid behind the mailbox, so her babysitter could not see her.

4.9 SENTENCE FRAGMENTS

A **sentence fragment** is an error that occurs when an incomplete sentence is punctuated as though it were complete.

There are three things you should look for when you review your work for sentence fragments. First look for a group of words without a subject. Then look for a group of words without a complete predicate, especially a group that contains a verbal or a verbal phrase. Finally, be sure you haven't punctuated a subordinate clause as if it were a complete sentence.

Many times you can correct a sentence fragment by attaching it to a main clause. Other times you may need to add words to make the sentence complete.

FRAGMENT	COMPLETE SENTENCE
Beck and Ally started the hike on the main trail. **Wanted to explore a remote area of the park.** [lacks subject]	Beck and Ally started the hike on the main trail, but they wanted to explore a remote area of the park.
The two weary hikers walking for hours. [lacks complete predicate]	The two weary hikers had been walking for hours.
The concerned and tired hikers. [lacks complete predicate and contains verbal]	The concerned and tired hikers found a faint trail.
When they stopped to rest. They checked their compass and trail guide. [subordinate clause]	When they stopped to rest, they checked their compass and trail guide.

Sentence fragments can be used to produce special effects, such as adding emphasis or showing realistic dialogue. Remember that professional writers use sentence fragments carefully and intentionally. In most of the writing you do, including your writing for school, you should avoid sentence fragments.

4.10 RUN-ON SENTENCES

A **run-on sentence** is two or more complete sentences written as though they were one sentence.

There are two types of run-on sentences. The first occurs when two main clauses are joined by a comma only. This is an error called a *comma splice.*

EXAMPLE

RUN-ON   It rained the entire time Gabriel and Jeffrey were on vacation, they still enjoyed the trip.

GRAMMAR/USAGE/MECHANICS

The second type of run-on sentence occurs when two main clauses have no punctuation separating them. This can occur with or without a conjunction.

EXAMPLES

RUN-ON   It rained the entire time Gabriel and Jeffrey were on vacation they still enjoyed the trip.

RUN-ON   It rained the entire time Gabriel and Jeffrey were on vacation but they still enjoyed the trip.

You can correct a run-on sentence in several ways. The method you choose in correcting your writing will depend on the relationship you want to show between the two clauses.

EXAMPLES

METHOD OF CORRECTING RUN-ON	COMPLETE SENTENCE
Add end punctuation between the clauses and make two sentences.	It rained the entire time Gabriel and Jeffrey were on vacation. **T**hey still enjoyed the trip.
Separate the clauses with a comma and a coordinating conjunction.	It rained the entire time Gabriel and Jeffrey were on vacation, **but** they still enjoyed the trip.
Separate the clauses with a semicolon.	It rained the entire time Gabriel and Jeffrey were on vacation; they still enjoyed the trip.
Add a semicolon and a conjunctive adverb between the clauses.	It rained the entire time Gabriel and Jeffrey were on vacation; **however,** they still enjoyed the trip.
Change one of the main clauses to a subordinate clause. Add a comma if the subordinate clause comes first.	**Although** it rained the entire time Gabriel and Jeffrey were on vacation, they still enjoyed the trip.

Identify each numbered item by writing F for fragment or R for run-on sentence. Then rewrite each item, correcting the error.

1. Given the number of people that we expected to come.
2. Hardly a cloud in the sky as Veronica drove through the country.
3. This is the way to the store that is the way to the movie theater.
4. Don't act as if you're perfect you make mistakes!
5. The poor little kitten has a hurt paw must have stepped on something sharp.
6. Because you are my favorite teacher.
7. Some people are nicer than others I guess that is why I like some people more than others.
8. Running down the driveway and waving at the car!
9. Gathered all of his strength for his last attempt.
10. The shirts are red, the pants are black.

PRACTICE Proofreading

Rewrite the following passage, correcting errors in spelling, capitalization, grammar, and usage. Add any missing punctuation. Write legibly to be sure one letter is not mistaken for another. There are ten mistakes.

Ida B. Wells-Barnett

[1]Ida B. Wells was born in Holly Springs Mississippi, on July 16, 1862, to parents who were slaves. [2]She would have been a slave to if the civil war had not brought emancipation. [3]She become the wage earner for her family at an early age when her parents both died in a yellow fever epidemic. [4]She taught school and atended Rust College in the summers.

[5]Riding on a train one day she was told to move to a "colored car." [6]She refused and was taken by force off the train. [7]She sued the railroad

but had lost her suit. [8]An event that only intensified her determination to fight for racial justice.

[9]Wells wrote for several newspapers. [10]She is most famous for her crusade against lynching, she brought this problem wide attention.

[11]In 1895, she married Ferdinand Barnett a newspaper owner. [12]They worked together, using his newspaper to fight for justice.

POSTTEST **Main and Subordinate Clauses**

Identify each boldfaced, numbered clause as M for main or S for subordinate. Then identify each subordinate clause as adjective (ADJ), adverb (ADV), or noun (N).

Although he was born in Missouri,[1] Thomas Lanier Williams changed his name to "Tennessee."

I never knew[2] **that United States Presidents don't have to be men.**[3]

If you have any questions,[4] **call me.**[5]

Gunsmoke, **which starred James Arness,**[6] was the top-rated national television show of the 1960s.

William Howard Taft is the only president[7] **who also served on the Supreme Court.**[8]

Because the dog is frightened,[9] treat it gently.

Louis Braille invented the system **that allows blind people to read**[10] **when he was just fifteen years old.**[11]

When I'm finished here,[12] we'll go.

Sam Houston, **who was the first governor of Texas,**[13] had previously been governor of Tennessee.

On Venus, a day is almost as long as a year on Earth.[14]

Did you know[15] **that Mount Everest is named after Sir George Everest?**[16]

John fell[17] **when he tripped over the cat.**[18]

The holiday **that is celebrated by the most countries in the world**[19] is New Year's Day.

Whatever you decide[20] is fine.

Identify each sentence by writing S *for simple,* C *for compound,* CX *for complex, or* CC *for compound-complex.*

21. Felix watched the bird circle its prey, took out his camera, and snapped a picture.

22. The picnic was more fun than we had expected because our neighbors brought their new puppy.

23. The first main step of cell division is mitosis; the phases of mitosis are prophase, metaphase, anaphase, and telophase.

24. The dictionary helped me confirm the definition of *instrumental,* and I don't think Cy was correct when he said that he was instrumental to our team's success.

25. Before I went running, I watched the sun rise over the mountains; it was worth getting up early.

26. Where Ari hid the old and smelly potato was a mystery.

27. After the lettuce was added, the olives were hidden.

28. Did you know that Duke Ellington's real name was Edward Kennedy Ellington, but he was known as "Duke" from childhood?

29. Death Valley is the hottest place in North America and the lowest place in the Western Hemisphere.

30. The average summer temperature in Death Valley is 125 degrees, but many kinds of animals live there.

POSTTEST Kinds of Sentences

Identify each sentence by writing D *for declarative,* IT *for interrogative,* IM *for imperative, or* E *for exclamatory.*

31. Can you tell me what the difference is between a tsunami and a tidal wave?

32. There's no way you are going to believe this, but we struck oil!

33. Half of any bone's weight comes from minerals, primarily calcium.

34. Get lost!

35. Did Christopher say that his family is moving to Australia next month?

36. Jennifer, take out the garbage right now and clean up that hideous mess.

37. Please write a two-page report on Samuel Clemens and turn it in by Monday.

38. Are you serious?

39. Help me hide Peter's gift so he doesn't find it before his birthday.

40. Henry Wadsworth Longfellow was a published poet by the age of thirteen.

POSTTEST Fragments and Run-ons

Identify each numbered item by writing F *for fragment,* R *for run-on sentence, or* S *for sentence.*

41. Hardly a mistake, if I do say so myself.

42. The leaves from the tree have fallen the grass is turning brown.

43. Don't underestimate the persuasive power of a good argument.

44. The book looked boring, but Harry needed something on the subject and bought it anyway.

45. The gorgeous flowers in Aunt June's garden.

46. People in glass houses shouldn't throw stones, they wouldn't want anyone to throw stones at them.

47. A penny saved is a penny earned.

48. Earning five dollars for walking dogs.

49. The things children say.

50. Monet is famous he was an Impressionist painter.

Chapter 4 Clauses and Sentence Structure **183**

Verb Tenses and Voice

● ● ● ● ● ● ● ● ● ● ● ● ● ● ●

PRETEST **Verb Forms**

Write the correct form of the verb in parentheses.

1. It was a sizzling line drive, but Juan (catch) it.
2. Yesterday we (go) to the air show.
3. Right now, I (think) I know the answer to that question.
4. An hour ago, my boss (pay) me for three weeks of work.
5. When their team pulled ahead by three runs, my team (give) up.
6. My brother has (hold) the remote just out of my reach for an hour.
7. We (believe) that when the ice had frozen over we could walk on it safely.
8. By next Sunday, Jo will have (bring) four new members to the club.
9. I just (buy) a new watch.
10. What did the king's men do when Humpty Dumpty (fall) off the wall?

11. As the plane flew in, the pilot (speak) over the intercom.
12. Carrie could have (blow) bubbles all day.
13. The telephone (ring) four times before the answering machine picked up.
14. Now, I always (begin) my homework before breakfast.
15. While hibernating, a woodchuck (breathe) only ten times an hour.
16. Tammy snagged the ball and (throw) it to first base.
17. I have (play) the game quite a few times.
18. After his first defeat, Mr. Lee (fight) the case all the way to the Supreme Court.
19. Earlier, I (bite) into a pit in my piece of cherry pie.
20. For a week, Helga has (drink) nothing but water.

GRAMMAR/USAGE/MECHANICS

PRETEST Verb Tenses

Identify the italicized verb tense by writing one of these labels: present, past, future, present perfect, past perfect, future perfect.

21. Megan *has read* this book already.
22. Each morning, I *swim* all the way across the lake.
23. Ned *will graduate* at the top of his class.
24. As the game got tougher, Jamal *rose* to the occasion.
25. By the time the parade went by, Robbie *had run* to the window.
26. I *will sell* my old bicycle for twenty-five dollars.
27. Helen *has driven* from here to the bank four times today.
28. By this evening, Paolo *will have flown* the kite he made himself, and we will know if it works.
29. Sean *changed* channels with the remote *he had found* in the couch.
30. *Will* the Vasquezes *have lived* in our neighborhood for fifteen years next week?

PRETEST Progressive and Emphatic Forms

Identify the italicized verb form by writing one of these labels: present progressive, past progressive, future progressive, present perfect progressive, past perfect progressive, future perfect progressive, present emphatic, past emphatic.

31. Why *was* it *raining* on a sunny day?

32. I *am getting* upset with the current situation.

33. Greg *has* long *been debating* whether to go to the camp for the summer or get a job.

34. I really *do want* you to come to my party on Wednesday.

35. Jeff *will be skipping* practice tomorrow afternoon.

36. Alf *had been* soundly *sleeping* in the chair in the living room for an hour.

37. Moira *was playing* the oboe in the school band for a year.

38. We *will have been driving* for more than two days before we get to El Paso.

39. Dora *is* not *stopping* by my house for a visit.

40. Yes, I *did drop* the pie while I was taking it out of the oven.

PRETEST Consistency of Verb Tense and Voice

Rewrite each sentence, correcting verbs in the wrong tense or change verbs in passive voice to active voice.

41. After the first charge was made by the cavalry, the cannons were brought in by the infantry.

42. The curtains that were washed by Terry earlier will now be hung out by her to dry.

43. "Hound Dog" was sung by "Big Mama" Thornton before it was sung by Elvis Presley.

44. Because of her excitement about her favorite band's new release, Erika drove to the store and buys a CD.

45. Richard voted for Colleen in the school election, and she votes for Sean.

46. We were strolling across the meadow when the cows we watched suddenly began to moo loudly.

47. As the gardening club watched, Vince shows how to prune a bonsai tree.

48. The high jumpers will have finished before the sprinters began.

49. After we had all been given the correct costumes by the costume designer, we were told how to take care of them by her.

50. If a Spartan man had not been married by the age of thirty, he loses his right to vote.

5.1 PRINCIPAL PARTS OF VERBS

All verbs have four **principal parts:** a *base form,* a *present participle,* a *simple past form,* and a *past participle.* All the verb tenses are formed from these principal parts.

EXAMPLES

PRINCIPAL PARTS OF VERBS

BASE FORM	PRESENT PARTICIPLE	PAST FORM	PAST PARTICIPLE
play	playing	played	played
watch	watching	watched	watched
break	breaking	broke	broken
hire	hiring	hired	hired
be	being	was, were	been

You can use the base form (except the base form of *be*) and the past form by themselves as main verbs. To function as the simple predicate in a sentence, the present participle and the past participle must always be used with one or more auxiliary verbs.

EXAMPLE   Monkeys **climb.** [base or present form]

EXAMPLE   Monkeys **climbed.** [past form]

EXAMPLE   Monkeys **are climbing.** [present participle with the auxiliary verb *are*]

EXAMPLE   Monkeys **have climbed.** [past participle with the auxiliary verb *have*]

PRACTICE   Principal Parts of Verbs

Write the correct form of the principal part of the verb in parentheses.

1. John Adams (past form of *serve*) as the second president of the United States.
2. Allison is (present participle of *announce*) the winner at the awards dinner.
3. Wayne seems to (base form of *try*) harder than anyone else I know.
4. Sherry had been (present participle of *work*) hard on the set for hours.
5. Critics have long (past participle of *consider*) Walt Whitman an important American poet.
6. Who (past form of *move*) the chair?
7. Before long, Alisha will be (present participle of *dance*) with the city ballet.
8. My friend Josh has (past participle of *receive*) good grades for years.
9. Nicholas (past form of *advise*) me to get some sleep.
10. Frank will probably be (present participle of *move*) to Portland at the end of the school year.

5.2 REGULAR AND IRREGULAR VERBS

A **regular verb** forms its past and past participle by adding *-ed* or *-d* to the base form.

REGULAR VERBS		
BASE FORM	**PAST FORM**	**PAST PARTICIPLE**
climb	climbed	climbed
skate	skated	skated
learn	learned	learned

Some regular verbs undergo spelling changes when *-ed* is added.

EXAMPLES spy + **-ed** = spie**d**

trot + **-ed** = trot**ted**

refer + **-ed** = refer**red**

An **irregular verb** forms its past and past participle in some way other than by adding *-ed* or *-d* to the base form.

EXAMPLES

COMMON IRREGULAR VERBS		
BASE FORM	**PAST FORM**	**PAST PARTICIPLE**
be, am, are, is	was, were	been
bear	bore	borne
beat	beat	beaten *or* beat
become	became	become

Common Irregular Verbs, continued

BASE FORM	PAST FORM	PAST PARTICIPLE
begin	began	begun
bite	bit	bitten *or* bit
blow	blew	blown
break	broke	broken
bring	brought	brought
burst	burst	burst
buy	bought	bought
cast	cast	cast
catch	caught	caught
choose	chose	chosen
come	came	come
creep	crept	crept
cut	cut	cut
dive	dived *or* dove	dived
do	did	done
draw	drew	drawn
drink	drank	drunk
drive	drove	driven
eat	ate	eaten
fall	fell	fallen
feel	felt	felt
find	found	found
fling	flung	flung
fly	flew	flown

Common Irregular Verbs, continued

BASE FORM	PAST FORM	PAST PARTICIPLE
freeze	froze	frozen
get	got	got *or* gotten
give	gave	given
go	went	gone
grow	grew	grown
hang*	hung *or* hanged	hung *or* hanged
have	had	had
hit	hit	hit
hold	held	held
keep	kept	kept
know	knew	known
lay**	laid	laid
lead	led	led
leave	left	left
lend	lent	lent
let	let	let
lie**	lay	lain
lose	lost	lost
make	made	made
pay	paid	paid
put	put	put
read	read	read
ride	rode	ridden
ring	rang	rung

Common Irregular Verbs, continued

BASE FORM	PAST FORM	PAST PARTICIPLE
rise**	rose	risen
run	ran	run
say	said	said
see	saw	seen
seek	sought	sought
sell	sold	sold
set***	set	set
shake	shook	shaken
shine****	shone *or* shined	shone *or* shined
shrink	shrank *or* shrunk	shrunk *or* shrunken
sing	sang	sung
sink	sank	sunk
sit***	sat	sat
sleep	slept	slept
speak	spoke	spoken
spend	spent	spent
spring	sprang *or* sprung	sprung
steal	stole	stolen
sting	stung	stung
swear	swore	sworn
swim	swam	swum
swing	swung	swung
take	took	taken
teach	taught	taught

BASE FORM	PAST FORM	PAST PARTICIPLE
tear	tore	torn
tell	told	told
think	thought	thought
throw	threw	thrown
wear	wore	worn
weave	wove	woven
win	won	won
write	wrote	written

*Use *hanged* to refer to death by hanging. For all other uses, *hung* is correct.

**For more detailed instruction on *lay* versus *lie* and *rise* versus *raise,* see the Usage Glossary pages 61 and 69.

***For more detailed instruction on *sit* versus *set,* see the Usage Glossary page 72.

****Shone* is intransitive. (The sun *shone.*) *Shined* is transitive. (I *shined* my shoes.)

PRACTICE **Past Forms and Past Participles**

Copy and complete the chart. Make sure that you have spelled each form correctly.

BASE FORM	PAST FORM	PAST PARTICIPLE
1. ring		
2. find		
3. pay		

Practice, Past Forms and Past Participles, continued

BASE FORM	PAST FORM	PAST PARTICIPLE
4. wait		
5. draw		
6. lend		
7. creep		
8. lose		
9. write		
10. bury		
11. begin		
12. freeze		
13. shake		
14. grow		
15. swing		
16. catch		
17. worry		
18. make		
19. spring		
20. bother		
21. lead		
22. break		
23. weave		
24. seek		
25. climb		

Write the correct form of the verb in parentheses.

1. Rea has (be) my best friend for years.
2. My first attempt at a toy boat (sink) like a stone when I tried it out.
3. Mr. Willis, the assistant principal, has (speak) at every graduation for years.
4. Last August, we (go) kayaking on the river.
5. Dennis (fall) off his platform shoes.
6. He must have (break) his ankle!
7. Well, he will be (lie) in bed for at least a week.
8. Lewis (win) the last two contests, but I don't think he'll pull it off this time.
9. You probably will have (catch) a bad cold before opening night.
10. The other day, Jim (make) a really nice fishing pole for his sister.

5.3 TENSE OF VERBS

The **tenses** of a verb are the forms that help to show time.

There are six tenses in English: *present, past, future, present perfect, past perfect,* and *future perfect.*

PRESENT TENSE

The present-tense form of a verb is the same as the verb's base form, except for the third-person singular, which adds *-s* or *-es.* The exceptions are the verb *have* (which has the third-person singular form *has*) and the verb *be.*

PRESENT TENSE OF THE VERB *STAY*

	SINGULAR	PLURAL
FIRST PERSON	I **stay.**	We **stay.**
SECOND PERSON	You **stay.**	You **stay.**
THIRD PERSON	She, he, or it **stays.**	They **stay.**
	Joanie **stays.**	The dogs **stay.**

PRESENT TENSE OF THE VERB *BE*

	SINGULAR	PLURAL
FIRST PERSON	I **am** sure.	We **are** sure.
SECOND PERSON	You **are** sure.	You **are** sure.
THIRD PERSON	She, he, or it **is** sure.	They **are** sure.
	Henry **is** sure.	The children **are** sure.

The **present tense** expresses a constant, repeated, or habitual action or condition. It can also express a general truth.

EXAMPLE   Isaac **likes** the taste of tea with honey in it. [not just this cup of tea but every cup of tea; a repeated action]

EXAMPLE   Emily **bakes** wonderful spice cookies. [always; a habitual action]

EXAMPLE   Gold **is** valuable. [a general truth]

The **present tense** can also express an action or a condition that exists only now.

EXAMPLE   Krista **feels** good about her score on the science test. **[not always but just now]**

EXAMPLE   I **see** a hummingbird at the feeder. **[at this very moment]**

The **present tense** is sometimes used in historical writing to express past events and, more often, in poetry, fiction, and journalism (especially in sports writing) to convey to the reader a sense of being there. This usage is sometimes called the *historical present tense.*

EXAMPLE   Washington **continues** to beg the Continental Congress for supplies.

EXAMPLE   The goalie **throws** her body across the opening and **blocks** the shot in the final seconds of the game.

PRACTICE   Present Tense

Write a sentence using each of the following verb forms. The content of your sentence should express the kind of present tense indicated in parentheses.

1. runs (a repeated or habitual action)
2. flows (a constant action)
3. is (a general truth)
4. sits (a repeated action)
5. have (at this very moment)
6. wears (a repeated or habitual action)
7. stands (a constant action)
8. makes (a repeated or habitual action)
9. like (at this very moment)
10. grows (a general truth)

PAST TENSE

Use the **past tense** to express an action or a condition that was started and completed in the past.

EXAMPLE   The track meet **went** well.

EXAMPLE   Nan **set** a new school record for the shot put.

EXAMPLE   The sprinters **ran** like antelopes.

EXAMPLE   The coach **praised** the hurdlers.

Nearly all regular and irregular verbs (except *be*) have just one past-tense form, such as *climbed* or *ran*. The verb *be* has two past-tense forms, *was* and *were*.

EXAMPLES

PAST TENSE OF THE VERB *BE*

	SINGULAR	PLURAL
FIRST PERSON	I **was** sure.	We **were** sure.
SECOND PERSON	You **were** sure.	You **were** sure.
THIRD PERSON	She, he, or it **was** sure. Maude **was** sure.	They **were** sure. The dancers **were** sure.

FUTURE TENSE

Use the **future tense** to express an action or a condition that will occur in the future.

You form the future tense of any verb by using the auxiliary verb *shall* or *will* with the base form: *I shall study; you will go.* Note: In modern American English, *shall* is very seldom used except for questions in which *I* or *we* is the subject: *Shall I call you? Shall we go now?*

EXAMPLE   Robby **will order** the supplies.

EXAMPLE   I **will pack** the car in the morning.

There are three other ways to express future time besides using the future tense. They are as follows:

1. Use *going to* with the present tense of *be* and the base form of a verb.

EXAMPLE   Robby **is *going to* order** the supplies.

2. Use *about to* with the present tense of *be* and the base form of a verb.

EXAMPLE   Robby **is *about to* order** the supplies.

3. Use the present tense with an adverb or an adverb phrase that shows future time.

EXAMPLE   Robby **leaves *tomorrow*.**

EXAMPLE   Robby **arrives *on tomorrow's train*.**

PRACTICE   Future Tense

Rewrite each sentence so that the verb expresses the future tense in the four ways taught in this lesson. For each sentence given here, be sure you have four different responses.

1. Audrey ran the high hurdles.
2. The new student council president was sworn in.
3. The Cuban dance company performed.
4. The basketball team played in the finals.
5. Crispus put the finishing touches on the parade float.

PRACTICE   Present, Past, and Future Tenses

Identify the italicized verb tense by writing one of these labels: present, past, future.

1. I *think* a lot about the farm we used to visit.
2. Every day, we *played* in the farmyard.
3. I *liked* to kick up the red dust in the road.

4. I still *look* at old aluminum windmills with great fondness.

5. *Will* any other farm ever *seem* as interesting to me as that farm?

6. I *know* my mother didn't like it very much.

7. She *grew* up there and was used to it.

8. She probably just *saw* a dirty old house, a bunch of skinny chickens, and some broken-down fences.

9. I *understand* that, of course.

10. In my mind's eye, though, I *will* always *picture* that farm as a refuge from ordinary, everyday, city things.

5.4 PERFECT TENSES

PRESENT PERFECT TENSE

Use the **present perfect tense** to express an action or a condition that occurred at some *indefinite time* in the past.

You form the present perfect tense by using *has* or *have* with the past participle of a verb: *has permitted, have cut.*

Do not be confused by the word *present* in the name of the present perfect tense. This tense expresses past time. The word *present* refers to the tense of the auxiliary verb *has* or *have.*

EXAMPLE   The living-room clock **has stopped.**

EXAMPLE   They **have brought** the new couch a day early.

The present perfect tense can refer to completed action in past time only in an indefinite way. Adverbs such as *yesterday* cannot be added to make the time more specific.

EXAMPLE   Chandra **has completed** her project.

EXAMPLE   Jack **has** always **wanted** to visit Mexico.

To be specific about completed past time, you would normally use the simple past tense.

EXAMPLE Chandra **completed** her project yesterday.

EXAMPLE Jack **wanted** to visit Mexico last summer.

The present perfect tense can also be used to express the idea that an action or a condition *began in the past and is still happening.* To communicate this idea, you would normally add adverbs (or adverb phrases or clauses) of time.

EXAMPLE The mall **has displayed** our artwork for two weeks.

EXAMPLE We **have kept** a spare house key under this rock ever since I left my key at school.

PAST PERFECT TENSE

Use the **past perfect tense** to indicate that one past action or condition began *and* ended before another past action or condition started.

You form the past perfect tense by using the auxiliary verb *had* with the past participle of a verb: *had praised, had written.*

Past

EXAMPLE Patricia **dedicated** her play to the drama teacher who

Past Perfect

had encouraged her long ago. [First the drama teacher encouraged Patricia; then years later Patricia acknowledged her teacher's support.]

Past Perfect

EXAMPLE The meat loaf **had dried** to shoe leather by the time I

Past

remembered to check it. [First the meat loaf dried up; then I remembered to check it.]

FUTURE PERFECT TENSE

Use the **future perfect tense** to express one future action or condition that will begin *and* end before another future event starts.

You form the future perfect tense by using *will have* or *shall have* with the past participle of a verb: *will have practiced, shall have flown.*

EXAMPLE By September I **will have saved** fifty dollars. [The money will be saved by the time another future event, the arrival of September, occurs.]

EXAMPLE Before Maggie's baby is born, I **will have made** a quilt for the child's crib. [The quilt will be made before another future event, the baby's birth, occurs.]

PRACTICE Perfect Tenses

Read the verb in parentheses. Then write it in the tense indicated in brackets.

1. She (read) all the Harry Potter books. [present perfect]
2. Before we leave today, we (finish) the prom decorations. [future perfect]
3. Jo (keep) a secret for more than three years. [past perfect]
4. If our luck holds, we (reach) the cabins and settled in before the rains begin. [future perfect]
5. Galen (train) for the meet all summer. [past perfect]
6. I (scorch) three pans in cooking class. [present perfect]
7. Either your mother shrank your clothes, or you (grow) out of that coat. [present perfect]
8. By dinner, Cornel (meet) Jaron's bus. [future perfect]
9. Megan (see) Sean three or four times before she decided he was cute. [past perfect]
10. Jason (fall), but he can get up. [present perfect]

VERB-TENSE TIME LINE

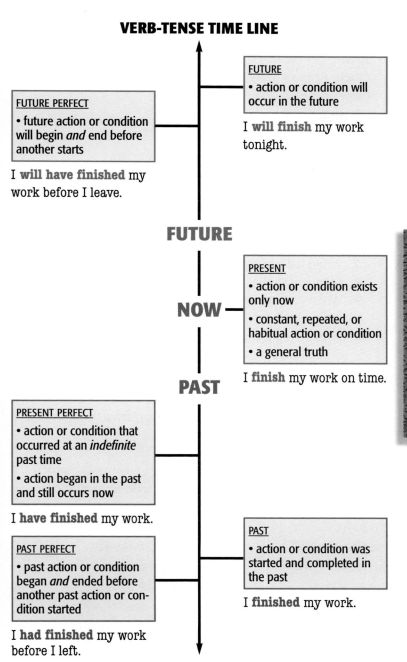

FUTURE PERFECT
• future action or condition will begin *and* end before another starts

I **will have finished** my work before I leave.

FUTURE
• action or condition will occur in the future

I **will finish** my work tonight.

FUTURE

PRESENT
• action or condition exists only now
• constant, repeated, or habitual action or condition
• a general truth

I **finish** my work on time.

NOW

PAST

PRESENT PERFECT
• action or condition that occurred at an *indefinite* past time
• action began in the past and still occurs now

I **have finished** my work.

PAST PERFECT
• past action or condition began *and* ended before another past action or condition started

I **had finished** my work before I left.

PAST
• action or condition was started and completed in the past

I **finished** my work.

GRAMMAR/USAGE/MECHANICS

Identify the italicized verb tense by writing one of these labels: present, past, future, present perfect, past perfect, future perfect.

1. Last week, I *went* with my family on vacation to the Ozarks.
2. I *had been* sick all week before we left.
3. Fortunately, I now *feel* much better.
4. We *have enjoyed* ourselves a lot so far.
5. We *will leave* next Friday, I think.
6. I'm hoping that by then I *will have learned* to ride a horse pretty well.
7. When *will* you *come* to visit?
8. I *think* of that as a kind of vacation, too.
9. When you *came* to visit last summer with your family, it was great.
10. I *have thought* often about all the hiking, swimming, and bike riding we did.

5.5 PROGRESSIVE AND EMPHATIC FORMS

Each of the six tenses has a **progressive** form that expresses a continuing action.

You make the progressive forms by using the appropriate tense of the verb *be* with the present participle of the main verb.

EXAMPLES

PRESENT PROGRESSIVE	They *are* **traveling.**
PAST PROGRESSIVE	They *were* **traveling.**
FUTURE PROGRESSIVE	They *will be* **traveling.**
PRESENT PERFECT PROGRESSIVE	They *have been* **traveling.**
PAST PERFECT PROGRESSIVE	They *had been* **traveling.**
FUTURE PERFECT PROGRESSIVE	They *will have been* **traveling.**

The present tense and the past tense have additional forms, called **emphatic forms,** that add special force, or emphasis, to the verb.

You make the emphatic forms by using *do, does,* or *did* with the base form of the verb.

EXAMPLES

PRESENT EMPHATIC   I **do hope** the train is on time.

Tom **does have** a plane to catch.

PAST EMPHATIC   He **did miss** his plane the last time because of a late train.

PRACTICE Progressive and Emphatic Forms

Identify the italicized verb form by writing one of these labels: present progressive, past progressive, future progressive, present perfect progressive, past perfect progressive, future perfect progressive, present emphatic, past emphatic.

1. Carpenters *are working* in the apartment downstairs.
2. They *have been making* noise since early this morning.
3. They *were using* a power saw all day yesterday.
4. I *am getting* really tired of it.
5. My neighbor *has been saying* for a week that they are almost finished.
6. Of course, they *had been working* for more than two weeks before that.
7. In fact, by Friday, they *will have been bothering* me for almost a month.
8. I *do know* that the work needs to get done.
9. I *will be trying* as hard as I can to be patient.
10. However, I *did tell* my landlord from the beginning that I really hate noise.

5.6 CONSISTENCY OF TENSES

Don't shift, or change, tenses when two or more events occur at the same time.

GRAMMAR/USAGE/MECHANICS

EXAMPLES	**INCORRECT**	The soloist **stopped** suddenly and **coughs** loudly. **[The tense needlessly shifts from the past to the present.]**
	CORRECT	The soloist **stopped** suddenly and **coughed** loudly. **[Now it is clear that both events happened at nearly the same time.]**
	INCORRECT	The radio operator **removes** his headphones. He **rushed** to the captain with the message. **[The tense needlessly shifts from the present to the past.]**
	CORRECT	The radio operator **removes** his headphones. He **rushes** to the captain with the message. **[It is clear that both events happened at nearly the same time.]**

Do shift tenses to show that one event precedes or follows another.

EXAMPLES	**INCORRECT**	By the time we **found** the campsite, the others **ate** all the hot dogs. **[The two past-tense verbs give the mistaken impression that both events–the finding of the campsite and the eating of the hot dogs–happened at the same time.]**
	CORRECT	By the time we **found** the campsite, the others **had eaten** all the hot dogs. **[The shift from the past tense *(found)* to the past perfect tense *(had eaten)* clearly shows that the others ate the hot dogs before the campsite was found.]**

Keep a statement about a general truth in the present tense even if other verbs are in the past tense.

EXAMPLE We **remembered** that the freezing point of water **is** thirty-two degrees Fahrenheit.

PRACTICE Consistency of Tenses

Find the first verb that appears in each sentence. Then write the consistent tense of the verb in parentheses.

1. Having run out of gas, we arrived for the awards banquet quite late, and found that everyone else (ate, had eaten).
2. Wes tripped over a skate and (fell, falls) with a resounding crash.
3. By the time the school play opens tomorrow night, I (will have gone, went) over Gisa's lines with her an enormous number of times.
4. Rico's parents raised him to believe that honesty (is, was) the best policy.
5. Mr. Lavelli, a neighbor of ours, dislikes it when the apples from our tree (fell, fall) over the fence onto his property.
6. When Cheryl received her driver's license, she (gasps, gasped) with horror at her picture.
7. Our guide explained that old forests (had, have) less undergrowth than younger ones.
8. As Stan worked with the younger players, he (encourages, encouraged) them.
9. The chorus teacher chose Millie for the solo in next month's concert because she (showed, will show) such talent.
10. Upon reaching the edge of town, we realized that we (turned, had turned) at the wrong corner.

5.7 VOICE OF VERBS

An action verb is in the **active voice** when the subject of the sentence performs the action.

EXAMPLE   The brown bear **caught** a salmon.

An action verb is in the **passive voice** when its action is performed on the subject.

EXAMPLE   A salmon **was caught** by the brown bear.

Generally the active voice is stronger, but at times the passive voice is preferable or even necessary. If you don't want to call attention to the performer of the action or don't know who the performer is, use the passive voice.

EXAMPLE   All the costumes **were ruined.** [You may not want to identify the culprit.]

EXAMPLE   The bank **was robbed.** [You may not know who the culprit is.]

You form the passive voice by using a form of the auxiliary verb *be* with the past participle of the verb. The tense of a passive verb is determined by the tense of the auxiliary verb.

EXAMPLE   The song **is sung** by the choir. [present tense, passive voice]

EXAMPLE   The song **was sung** by the choir. [past tense, passive voice]

EXAMPLE   The song **will be sung** by the choir. [future tense, passive voice]

PRACTICE   Active and Passive Voice

Rewrite each sentence, changing active verbs to passive and passive verbs to active.

1. George W. Gale Ferris built a huge "pleasure wheel" for the World's Columbian Exposition in 1893.
2. Bulls cannot see color.

3. Enough debris was sent into the air by the eruption of the volcano to block the sun.
4. The human eye can see stars that are trillions of miles away.
5. Unidentified flying objects were first called "flying saucers" by an airplane pilot in 1947.
6. Sierra Leone's farmers grow a wide variety of crops.
7. To my surprise, I was bitten by the cute little dog.
8. The same place can be struck by lightning many times.
9. The explosion shattered windows all over town.
10. The first widely used synthetic plastic was invented by a man looking for a cheap way to make billiard balls.

PRACTICE Proofreading

Rewrite the following passage, correcting errors in spelling, capitalization, grammar, and usage. Add any missing punctuation. Write legibly to be sure one letter is not mistaken for another. There are ten mistakes.

Hank Williams

¹Hiram Williams, who become known as Hank Williams, was born in Alabama in 1923. ²His parents were poor, and the family live in a log house that was also a small general store. ³Hank's mother, who was a church organist, learned him music. ⁴At the age of seven, Hank started working, selling peanuts on the street. ⁵He also shone shoes. ⁶At the same time, he was learning to play a guitar that his mother had buyed him for $3.50.

⁷At the age of twelve, he won a songwriting contest. ⁸By the age of fourteen, he had formed a band that played at hoedowns, square dances, pie suppers, and other local events. ⁹It's name was "Hank Williams and the Drifting Cowboys."

¹⁰In his late teens, Hank does whatever he could to make a living. ¹¹He road in rodeos, joined a traveling medicine show, and worked in shipyards. ¹²In about 1946, he got a contract with a Nashville publishing

company as a songwriter, and that was the begining of a great career. [13]He wrote and recorded such great songs as "Cold, Cold Heart," "Jambalaya," and "Long Gone Lonesome Blues." [14]As "the father of country music," he proved that country music could sell outside the South. [15]Who knows what he could accomplish if he had not died at twenty-nine?

POSTTEST Verb Forms

Write the correct form of the verb in parentheses.

1. You have probably (hear, heard) of the Portuguese explorer Ferdinand Magellan.
2. Many people think he sailed around the world and was the first to have (did, done) so.
3. Magellan's voyage (shrank, shrinked) the world, but he himself did not finish that voyage.
4. Magellan (leaved, left) from Spain in 1519 with the financial backing of the teenaged king.
5. Under his command he (has, had) five ships and more than two hundred men.
6. He and his crew (seeked, sought) a route around the world with a stop at the Spice Islands.
7. By the time he (reaches, reached) South America, Magellan had (gone, went) all the way across the Atlantic.
8. The ships did not (find, found) a passage to the Pacific before summer (ends, ended) in the Southern Hemisphere and had to winter over in what is now southern Argentina.
9. In October, Magellan's ships (swinged, swung) around the tip of the South American continent.
10. Then, the mutinous crew of one of the ships (chose, chosen) to sail back to Spain without warning.
11. Magellan had (put, putted) down other mutinies, but this one (was, been) successful.
12. The voyage across the Pacific (took, taken) the remaining ships far longer than Magellan had expected.

13. As weeks passed, it was clear that the journey had (become, became) a complete disaster.
14. Crossing the Pacific (took, taken) months.
15. After nearing starvation many times, the voyagers (finded, found) the Philippines and docked there.
16. Magellan quickly (maked, made) friends with one of the island kings.
17. Suddenly, he (finded, found) himself involved in island warfare.
18. On April 27, 1521, Magellan (losed, lost) his life in a battle.
19. Juan Sebastian del Cano, one of the ships' captains, had one of the ships (broke, broken) up and burned.
20. The remaining men (leave, left) the Philippines, and one ship actually (make, made) it around the world and home.

POSTTEST Verb Tenses

Identify the italicized verb tense by writing one of these labels: present, past, future, present perfect, past perfect, future perfect.

21. On Saturday, there *was* an important game at the park between the Tigers and the first place Dodgers.
22. The Tigers coach *noticed* something odd.
23. "That kid Tony *runs* like a duck," the coach said to his friend.
24. "Really? I *have* not *noticed* that before."
25. "*Will* you *watch* when he comes up again?"
26. "Sure. He *has hit* well all week and probably will again."
27. At his next at bat, Tony hit a line drive with the new stance he *had taught* himself.
28. "I *call* that a double," said the coach's friend.
29. "He *will* only *make* it to first," said the coach.
30. "Well, he's a good learner. By next week, maybe he *will have learned* to run."

Identify the italicized verb form by writing one of these labels: present progressive, past progressive, future progressive, present perfect progressive, past perfect progressive, future perfect progressive, present emphatic, past emphatic.

31. People *have been writing* about wild youth for thousands of years.

32. "What *is happening* to our young people?" asked Plato more than two millennia ago.

33. He charged that young people *were disrespecting* their elders and ignoring the laws.

34. Of course, Plato *did stand* in a long tradition of criticism of the young.

35. Adults *had been making* charges like these long before Plato.

36. By the time today's youth have grandchildren, they *will have been dealing* with these issues for years.

37. People *will be worrying* about the problem of youth as long as there are people.

38. Personally, I *do think* the problems are overstated.

39. For example, violent crime rates among young people *have been going* down for almost four decades.

40. At the same time, adults *are passing* more and more laws aimed at young people every day.

Rewrite each sentence. Correct verbs in the wrong tense or change verbs in passive voice to active voice.

41. Artists' work may not be appreciated by people during the artists' lifetimes.

42. Their work may go up in value dramatically after they died.

43. Vincent van Gogh will be a good example of this.

44. He has painted more than fifteen hundred paintings before he died.

45. Only one painting was sold by him, *The Red Vineyard.*

46. Historians think he gets only thirty dollars for this painting.

47. Respect was needed by him as much as money was, but neither was received.

48. Now, of course, van Gogh's paintings sold for millions of dollars.

49. Van Gogh would have been supported in luxury all his life for the current sale price of only one of his paintings.

50. Instead, only auction houses have been made rich by his talent, while he has died in disappointment and poverty.

Chapter 6

Subject-Verb Agreement

• • • • • • • • • • • • • • •

PRETEST **Subject-Verb Agreement**

*Write the main word or words from the subject of each
sentence. Then write the correct verb from the choices in
parentheses.*

  1. Raisins (is, are) just dried grapes.
  2. The hands on my watch (glows, glow) in the dark.
  3. The flock (follows, follow) its shepherd.
  4. (Do, Does) anyone know the answer to my question?
  5. Most of us (is, are) still in high school.
  6. Neither the airplanes nor the helicopter (has, have)
     enough gas.
  7. The horse and the rhinoceros (belongs, belong) to the
     same order of mammals.

8. Vegetables (is, are) good for you.
9. The colors of the sunset (glow, glows) brilliantly.
10. My teammate and friend (is, are) Willa.
11. Both a parrot and a parakeet (makes, make) noise.
12. The band (tunes, tune) their instruments.
13. All of the campers (get, gets) tired of listening to the camp counselor talk.
14. The admiration of the majority of people (is, are) not necessarily the most important thing.
15. There (goes, go) my two favorite people.
16. My hobby (is, are) homemade movies.
17. Across the meadow (comes, come) a doe.
18. Maria and I (enjoys, enjoy) walking in the park.
19. Twenty-five dollars (is, are) not a lot to pay for a shrub of that size.
20. Either Roy or his children (has, have) a cold.
21. Molasses (is, are) as sweet and sticky as honey.
22. Several of them (is coming, are coming) to dinner.
23. Many a leaf and twig (is, are) falling.
24. Why (was, were) the dog so aggressive?
25. Misery and pain (was, were) the result of my carelessness.

6.1 AGREEMENT OF SUBJECTS AND VERBS

A verb must agree with its subject in number.

Number refers to the form of a word that indicates whether it is singular or plural. A singular subject indicates *one* and requires a singular verb. Plural subjects indicate *more than one* and require plural verbs. With most regular verbs, add *-s* or *-es* to form the singular.

EXAMPLES

SINGULAR

The **athlete exercises.**

PLURAL

The **athletes exercise.**

An exception to the rule occurs with the pronouns *I* and *you*. Both require the form of a verb without *-s* or *-es,* even when *you* refers to one person. The only exception is *be*—when *I* is the subject, the verb form is *am.*

EXAMPLE   **I love** animals.

EXAMPLE   **You are** my best friend.

Whether functioning as main verbs or auxiliary verbs, *be, have,* and *do* change in form to show agreement.

EXAMPLES

SINGULAR	PLURAL
I **am** happy.	We **are** happy.
The dog **has** food.	The dogs **have** food.
I **do** trust you.	He **does** trust you.

When *be, have,* and *do* are used as auxiliary verbs, they indicate the number of a verb phrase. Notice that the following main verbs do not change form.

EXAMPLES

SINGULAR	PLURAL
He **has seen** the movie.	They **have seen** the movie.
She **is going** to work.	They **are going** to work.
Does she **stay** here?	**Do** they **stay** here?

Note that *were* is plural except in two cases: first, when its subject is the second-person singular personal pronoun, *you;* and second, when it is the verb in a statement that is contrary to fact.

EXAMPLES   **You were** the skateboard king. [singular subject]
If I were a lottery winner, I would buy you that car.
[The subordinate clause containing *were* is contrary to fact.]

Write the correct verb from the choices in parentheses.

1. Matilda (walks, walk) through the park.
2. Drew (goes, go) to the store for his father.
3. The garbage truck (picks, pick) up our trash.
4. (Does, Do) you have any chewing gum?
5. Dorothy (is, are) going to follow the yellow brick road.
6. He (enjoys, enjoy) reading in bed at night.
7. They (talks, talk) on the phone every day.
8. Monkeys (hangs, hang) by their tails.
9. The pickers (has, have) dropped a few apples.
10. Tell me if you (is, are) nervous.

6.2 INTERVENING PHRASES

Don't mistake a word in an intervening phrase for the subject of a sentence.

The simple subject is never in a prepositional phrase.

EXAMPLE   The **foliage** on the trees **provides** shade. [The singular verb *provides* agrees with the singular subject, *foliage*, not with the plural object of the preposition, *trees*.]

EXAMPLE   The **spices** in the food **are** tasty. [The plural verb *are* agrees with the plural subject, *spices*, not with the object of the preposition, *food*.]

If a singular subject is linked to another noun by a phrase, the subject is still considered singular. Expressions such as *accompanied by, as well as, in addition to, plus*, and *together with* introduce phrases that modify the subject without changing its number.

EXAMPLE   **Sleet,** in addition to snow, **is** a driver's nightmare.

EXAMPLE   **Paula,** along with her friends, **goes** to the mall.

Most of the following sentences contain an error in Subject-Verb Agreement. For each sentence, write the subject and the corrected verb. If a sentence is already correct, write C.

1. The colors of last night's sunset was the most brilliant in many weeks.
2. The bright red apples in the wooden bowl look almost too good to eat.
3. The bottom rungs on the old ladder breaks from the large man's weight.
4. Henry, along with a couple of his friends, is coming for supper.
5. The lights in the living room is bright.
6. The heat, together with the humidity, are making it difficult for both teams.
7. The hedgehog, as well as the shrew and the mole, are fond of eating insects.
8. The flavors of the restaurant's famous taco was distinctive and wonderful.
9. The passengers in the plane stay calm during the unexpected turbulence.
10. The recipe for our grandmother's famous rolls need to be doubled at Thanksgiving.

6.3 AGREEMENT WITH COMPOUND SUBJECTS

A compound subject that is joined by *and* or *both … and* is plural unless its parts belong to one unit or they both refer to the same person or thing.

EXAMPLES

PLURAL The **lion** and the **tiger are roaring.**
    Both **skiing** and **skating are** fun.

SINGULAR **Peanut butter** and **jelly is** my favorite type of
    sandwich. **[one unit]**
    His best **friend** and **companion is** George. **[one person]**

With compound subjects joined by *or* or *nor* (or by
either…or or *neither…nor*), the verb agrees with the
subject closer to it.

EXAMPLES

SINGULAR My **dog** or my **cat is** responsible for this mess.
    Neither the **cows** nor the **goat eats** bananas.

PLURAL Either the **dog** or the **cats are** responsible for this mess.
    Neither the **cows** nor the **goats eat** bananas.

PRACTICE **Agreement with Compound Subjects**

*Write the complete subject of each sentence. Then write
the correct verb from the choices in parentheses.*

1. Fran and her friends, Edna and Emma, (orders, order)
   Chinese food for their party.
2. Both the salamander and the frog (is, are) amphibious
   animals.
3. Spaghetti and meatballs (is, are) what I always order at
   that restaurant.
4. Neither elephants nor zebras (lives, live) in the
   American wilderness.
5. Who or what (digs, dig) those big holes in our
   neighbor's yard?
6. Either my mom or my grandparents (drives, drive) me
   to my doctor's appointments.
7. Gary and she (is going, are going) to play in the snow
   with their new sleds.

GRAMMAR/USAGE/MECHANICS

8. Floyd, the boy who lives next door to me, and Elton (plans, plan) to go to the concert.

9. Willie and Inez (wants, want) to buy more land for their farm.

10. My mathematics teacher and basketball coach (is, are) Mr. Serra.

6.4 AGREEMENT WITH SPECIAL SUBJECTS

COLLECTIVE NOUNS

A **collective noun** names a group of persons, things, or animals.

When a collective noun subject refers to a group as a whole, it requires a singular verb. When a collective noun subject refers to each member of a group individually, it requires a plural verb.

EXAMPLES

SINGULAR   His **family is** from Italy.

PLURAL   His **family are getting** haircuts today.

When deciding the number of the verb needed for a collective noun subject, look for the pronouns *its* and *their*. When a collective noun is referred to by *its*, the collective noun requires a singular verb. When a collective noun is referred to by *their*, the collective noun needs a plural verb.

EXAMPLES

SINGULAR   The **committee submits** *its* report.

PLURAL   The **committee sign** *their* names.

SPECIAL NOUNS

Certain nouns that end in *s*, such as *mathematics*, *molasses*, and *news*, require singular verbs.

EXAMPLES **Mathematics is** my favorite subject.

The news was good.

Certain other nouns that end in *s*, such as *scissors, pants, binoculars,* and *eyeglasses,* require plural verbs.

EXAMPLES **The scissors were** sharp.

Your **eyeglasses need** cleaning.

Many other nouns that end in *s*, such as *mumps, measles, ethics, statistics,* and *politics,* depending on the meaning, may require either a singular or a plural verb. In general, if the noun refers to a whole, such as a disease or a science, it requires a singular verb. If it refers to qualities, activities, or individual items, it requires a plural verb.

EXAMPLES

SINGULAR **Measles is** a childhood disease.

PLURAL **Measles cover** the sick child's body.

SINGULAR **Statistics is** an interesting subject.

PLURAL **Statistics show** that women live longer than men.

MANY A, EVERY, AND *EACH*

When *many a, every,* or *each* precedes a subject, whether simple or compound, the subject is considered singular.

EXAMPLE *Many a* **student lives** in this dorm.

EXAMPLE *Many a* **giraffe** and **elephant inhabits** this nature preserve.

EXAMPLE *Every* **player has won** at least one game.

EXAMPLE *Every* **chair, bench,** and **table was taken.**

EXAMPLE *Each* **poem was studied.**

EXAMPLE *Each* **story** and **novel was read.**

NOUNS OF AMOUNT

When a plural noun of amount refers to one unit, it acts as a singular subject. When it refers to individual units, it acts as a plural subject.

EXAMPLES   SINGULAR **Three dollars is** not too much.

PLURAL **Three dollars are** on the table.

When a fraction or a percentage refers to a singular word, it requires a singular verb. When it refers to a plural word, it requires a plural verb.

EXAMPLES

SINGULAR **One-fourth** of the cookie dough **is** in the bowl.

PLURAL **One-fourth** of the cookies **are** in this box.

Units of measurement usually require singular verbs.

EXAMPLE **Ten kilometers works** out to one myriameter.

TITLES

A title of a creative work always acts as a singular subject, even if a noun within the title is plural.

EXAMPLE **"Glory Days" describes** high school experiences.

COUNTRIES AND CITIES

The names of countries and cities require singular verbs.

EXAMPLE **New Orleans hosts** Mardi Gras every spring.

| PRACTICE | Agreement with Special Subjects |

Write the correct verb form from the choices in parentheses.

1. Statistics (is, are) the class I have right before lunch.

2. Did you know that the Philippines (gets, get) thousands of tourists?

3. The team (has, have) great hopes for Saturday.
4. Each dog and cat (needs, need) a loving home.
5. Ten years (is, are) a decade.
6. The city council (votes, vote) according to their own political beliefs.
7. "Snowflakes" (is, are) a poem about a father passing away during winter.
8. Marion's plaid Bermuda shorts (has, have) a rip on the right leg.
9. Ethics (is, are) important for the development of healthy values and a solid belief system.
10. Many a college baseball star never (plays, play) professional ball.

6.5 INDEFINITE PRONOUNS AS SUBJECTS

Some indefinite pronouns are always singular, some are always plural, and others may be singular or plural.

INDEFINITE PRONOUNS	
SINGULAR	another, anybody, anyone, anything, each, either, everybody, everyone, everything, neither, nobody, no one, nothing, one, somebody, someone, something
PLURAL	both, few, many, others, several
SINGULAR OR PLURAL	all, any, enough, most, much, none, some

Singular indefinite pronouns require singular verbs. Plural indefinite pronouns require plural verbs.

EXAMPLES   SINGULAR   **Everybody is** going to the concert.
            PLURAL   **Few have** the patience she has.

The number of the pronouns in the last group in the chart depends on the words to which they refer. If the pronoun refers to a singular word, then it requires a singular verb. If the pronoun refers to a plural word, it requires a plural verb.

SINGULAR Most of the pie **was eaten.** [*Most* refers to *pie*, a singular noun]

PLURAL Most of the cookies **were** still there. [*Most* refers to *cookies*, a plural noun]

The indefinite pronouns *any* and *none* can be singular subjects even when they refer to a plural word. It depends on whether you are thinking of each thing separately or of several things acting as one group.

EXAMPLES

Any of these bikes **is** ready. [Any one bike is ready.]
Any of these bikes **are** ready. [All these bikes are ready.]
None of these pens **has** a cap. [Not one pen has a cap.]
None of these pens **have** caps. [No pens have caps.]

Bizarro © by Dan Piraro. Reprinted with permission of Universal Press Syndicate. All rights reserved.

GRAMMAR/USAGE/MECHANICS

Write the correct verb from the choices in parentheses for each sentence.

1. She ate some porridge, but enough (remains, remain) for the bears.
2. Each of the poems we read (has, have) rhyme and rhythm.
3. Both (is, are) plausible explanations for the extinction of dinosaurs.
4. (Does, Do) anyone know who this person is?
5. Everything (is going, are going) wrong in this plan.
6. There are many spoons, but all (is, are) being used.
7. Every time the cabinet door is opened all of the dog food (spills, spill) on the floor.
8. Not one of the team members (plays, play) any other sport.
9. Many (argues, argue) that aliens do exist.
10. Nobody (believes, believe) that my dog ate my science homework.

From the chart in this lesson, choose five indefinite pronouns that are always singular, and write sentences using each as a subject. Then do the same for five that are always plural and five that can be either singular or plural. Underline the verb in each sentence.

6.6 AGREEMENT IN INVERTED SENTENCES

In an **inverted sentence,** the subject follows the verb.

Inverted sentences often begin with prepositional phrases. Don't mistake the object of the preposition for the subject.

GRAMMAR/USAGE/MECHANICS

EXAMPLES

SINGULAR   Across the seas **sails** the young **immigrant.**

PLURAL   In the jungle **roar** the **lions.**

In sentences beginning with *there* or *here,* the subject follows the verb. The words *there* and *here* never function as the subject of a sentence.

EXAMPLES

SINGULAR   Here **comes** the **bus.**
           There **goes** your **friend.**

PLURAL   Here **come** the **buses.**
           There **go** your **friends.**

In questions an auxiliary verb usually comes before the subject. Look for the subject between the auxiliary verb and the main verb.

EXAMPLES

SINGULAR   **Does** that **woman teach** English?

PLURAL   **Do** those **women teach** English?

PRACTICE   Agreement in Inverted Sentences

Most of the following sentences contain an error in Subject-Verb Agreement. For each sentence, write the incorrect verb and the correct verb. If a sentence is already correct, write C.

1. Past the other animals runs the leader of the pack.
2. Under the giant oak tree sit the lazy farmhand.
3. Here lies the remains of the ancient civilization.
4. Up the stairs crawl the tired child.
5. What kind of music does Anna and Nora listen to?
6. There is no cows in the park.
7. Over the river and through the woods, to Grandmother's house go we.
8. Which of the doors are Maria going to choose?

9. Here are three good reasons why I'm right.
10. Down the rabbit hole tumbles Alice and her friend.

PRACTICE **Subject-Verb Agreement with Special Subjects, in Inverted Sentences, and with Indefinite Pronouns**

Write the subject of each sentence. Then write the correct verb from the choices in parentheses.

1. In front of all the others (runs, run) Tracy.
2. Everything (needs, need) updating.
3. Rarer than most other mammals (is, are) the marsupial.
4. Something (is, are) wrong with those dogs.
5. The choir (dresses, dress) in their own rooms.
6. German measles (is, are) a dangerous disease for teenagers.
7. Few actually (sees, see) what happens after the crash.
8. Through the darkness of the night sky (falls, fall) a shooting star.
9. Fifty dollars (is, are) too much to pay for a ticket.
10. Sports (follows, follow) the weather in this newscast.

6.7 AGREEMENT WITH SUBJECT, NOT PREDICATE NOMINATIVE

Don't be confused by a predicate nominative that is different in number from the subject. Only the subject affects the number of the linking verb.

EXAMPLE The first **act was** jugglers. [The singular verb *was* agrees with the singular subject, *act,* not with the plural predicate nominative, *jugglers.*]

EXAMPLE Airline **tickets were** the first prize. [The plural verb *were* agrees with the plural subject, *tickets,* not with the singular predicate nominative, *prize.*]

Write the subject of each sentence. Then write the correct verb from the choices in parentheses.

1. Air (is, are) combined molecules.
2. Alexander's great-uncle's main interest (was, were) antique cars.
3. Cecilia's lovely eyes (was, were) her most distinctive feature.
4. At the youth center, the workers (is, are) a good example for many kids.
5. Potholes (has been, have been) a problem for automobile tires in this town.
6. According to many people, a nation's greatest resource (is, are) its children.
7. Melinda's favorite exhibit at the zoo (is, are) the polar bears.
8. Those files over there (is, are) the research of my assistant.
9. Long walks (is, are) a favorite activity of mine.
10. The loud, bleating cries of the sheep (was, were) the result of a thunderstorm.

PRACTICE Proofreading

Rewrite the following passage, correcting errors in spelling, capitalization, grammar, and usage. Add any missing punctuation. Write legibly to be sure one letter is not mistaken for another. There are ten mistakes.

Agnes De Mille

[1]Agnes De Mille was born in 1905 in New York City. [2]Her father was a successful playwright, and the brother of film director Cecil B. De Mille.

GRAMMAR/USAGE/MECHANICS

³Cecil and he worked in the new film industry. ⁴Many a girl have dreamed of the life young Agnes lived.

⁵After Agnes grew up, she became a famous dancer and choreographer which is someone who composes dances. ⁶She also wrote about her families' life in America, both in New York and in Hollywood. ⁷Her first book, *Dance to the Piper,* describes how difficult it was for her to become a dancer.

⁸Agnes De Mille was not as tall and thin as dancers generally are. ⁹Usually, neither choreographers nor a casting director envision short women as ballerinas. ¹⁰The most successful dancers in a ballet or musical tends to be tall. ¹¹Also, De Mille was interested in unusual kinds of dances and liked to create them. ¹²Some was funny; others had a harsh edge. ¹³Interesting, original ballets involving American themes was her true strength. ¹⁴She finally became widely known and quite successful creating dances for Broadway musicals.

¹⁵De Mille's fame was ensured by her choreography for a brilliant new musical *Oklahoma*. ¹⁶In fact, she changed dancing in American musicals forever. ¹⁷Today, her collection of books about dance and about her life are almost as important as her dances.

POSTTEST Subject-Verb Agreement

Write the main word or words from the subject of each sentence or clause. Then write the correct verb from the choices in parentheses.

1. The boys and their mother (hurries, hurry) to make the flight to Los Angeles.

2. Abigail Adams (is, are) well known as both John Adams's wife and his best friend.

3. (Does, Do) everybody here remember Roy Rogers, King of the Cowboys?

4. Felicia, together with her guinea pig and cat, (arrives, arrive) for a week's stay.

5. Either (seems, seem) good to me.
6. Through the china shop (runs, run) the bulls.
7. The passengers on the bus (moves, move) to the back when I ride.
8. The names for the states Iowa, Oklahoma, Kansas, and Illinois (comes, come) from Native American words.
9. The last act of the show (was, were) singers and dancers in old-fashioned clothes.
10. Seventy-five percent of the voters (favors, favor) the incumbent mayor.
11. Under the cabin there (lives, live) a family of raccoons.
12. The constant noise of the barking dogs (drives, drive) the neighbors crazy.
13. Macaroni and cheese (is, are) Nita's favorite meal.
14. Out of the water (leaps, leap) the dolphins.
15. All of the kids (enjoys, enjoy) eating the homemade bread.
16. (Does, Do) they know where the office is?
17. Mickey Mantle, a switch-hitting center fielder, and Yogi Berra, a strong-armed catcher, (is, are) among the best-loved baseball players of their era.
18. Four quarts (equals, equal) a gallon.
19. A bus, as well as dozens of cabs, (passes, pass) as June and Karin talk.
20. Niagara Falls (is, are) well worth seeing.
21. What time (is, are) my parents coming home?
22. One of the boys (is, are) sure to help me.
23. *Ghostbusters* (stars, star) Dan Aykroyd and Bill Murray.
24. Good manners (is, are) an important tool in the business world as well as in society.
25. In the thirteenth century, Italian merchants, like Marco Polo, (travels, travel) the "Silk Road" to the court of Kublai Khan.

Chapter 7

Using Pronouns Correctly

● ● ● ● ● ● ● ● ● ● ● ● ● ● ●

PRETEST **Using Pronouns Correctly**

For each sentence, write the correct pronoun from the choices in parentheses.

1. We helped Simon and (he, him) with their homework.

2. (We, Us) sophomores are going to tonight's student talent show together.

3. They had to do it (theirselves, themselves), or they wouldn't be able to face Rowena.

4. That is (he, him) over by the lockers, talking to the girl with red hair.

5. The spelling bee came down to just two of us, Hiroshi and (me, myself).

6. My friends and (I, me) went to my house.

7. The selection committee will make (its, their) decision public this afternoon.

8. I'll bet you can't guess which of the girls, Jackie or (she, her), is older.

9. Coming from (he and she, him and her), this kind of thing doesn't really surprise me.

10. As soon as you and (I, me) finish this, let's eat.

11. Mrs. Santos had to decide (who, whom), among the four of them, would make the best Romeo.

12. I was pretty sure that the bee was going to sting either Shaw or (I, me).

13. Cal's mom appreciates the effort his sister and (he, him) make to help around the house.

14. It was clear that Julie was injured more than (I, me), so I went for help.

15. Sylvia seemed to deeply resent (us, our) laughing at her clumsiness.

16. Since Jody is the captain, it should be (she, her) who gets to go first.

17. (Whoever, Whomever) needs medical attention the most is treated first.

18. Everyone is supposed to return (his or her, their) own lunch tray.

19. In Iowa (people, they) often refer to the mid-day meal as "dinner" and to the evening meal as "supper."

20. (You, Your) going to the store will be a big help to me.

21. The subcommittee, John and (I, me), did much of our research on the Internet.

22. I know that I'm not as smart as (he, him).

23. I can't imagine (who, whom) would want to go kayaking in ice-cold water.

24. Pardon me, to (who, whom) were you speaking?

25. My computer is only a year old, and (it's, its) already out-of-date.

7.1 CASE OF PERSONAL PRONOUNS

Pronouns that refer to persons or things are called **personal** pronouns.

Personal pronouns have three **cases,** or forms. The three cases are called **nominative, objective,** and **possessive.** The case of a personal pronoun depends on the pronoun's function in a sentence—that is, whether it is a subject, a complement, an object of a preposition, or a replacement for a possessive noun.

Study the chart to see the different forms of personal pronouns.

PERSONAL PRONOUNS			
CASE	**SINGULAR PRONOUNS**	**PLURAL PRONOUNS**	**FUNCTION IN SENTENCE**
NOMINATIVE	I, you, she, he, it	we, you, they	subject or predicate nominative
OBJECTIVE	me, you, her, him, it	us, you, them	direct object, indirect object, or object of preposition
POSSESSIVE	my, mine, your, yours, her, hers, his, its	our, ours, your, yours, their, theirs	replacement for possessive noun(s)

Use these rules to avoid errors in the case of personal pronouns.

1. Use the nominative case for a personal pronoun in a compound subject.

EXAMPLE   Mindy and **I** play tennis.

EXAMPLE   **She** and **I** are equally matched.

2. Use the objective case for a personal pronoun in a compound object.

EXAMPLE May my mom sit between you and **me?**

EXAMPLE Ahmad spoke to Rick and **me.**

EXAMPLE This is for you and **her.**

Hint: When you are choosing a pronoun for a sentence that has a compound subject or a compound object, try saying the sentence to yourself without the conjunction and the other subject or object.

EXAMPLE The ball bounced toward **[Mindy and] me.**

Note: It is considered courteous to place the pronoun *I* or *me* last in a series.

EXAMPLE **Lou, Sandy,** and **I** will be line judges. **[nominative case]**

EXAMPLE He aimed his camera at **Julie** and **me.** **[objective case]**

3. Use the nominative case for a personal pronoun after a linking verb.

EXAMPLE The best line judge is **he.**

EXAMPLE Is it **I?**

EXAMPLE The oldest guest is **she.**

This rule is changing. In informal speech, people often use the objective case after a linking verb; they say, *It's me, It was him.* Some authorities even recommend using the objective case in informal writing to avoid sounding artificial. To be strictly correct, however, use the nominative case after a linking verb, especially in formal writing.

4. Never spell possessive personal pronouns with apostrophes.

EXAMPLE This wrist brace is **hers.**

EXAMPLE The cooler is **theirs.**

EXAMPLE That one is **yours.**

It's is a contraction for *it is* or *it has*. Don't confuse *it's* with the possessive pronoun *its*.

EXAMPLE   **It's** too late to play tennis. Give me the racket and **its** case.

5. Use possessive pronouns before gerunds (*-ing* forms used as nouns).

EXAMPLE   I don't like **his** calling the shots.

EXAMPLE   **Our** objecting would do no good.

PRACTICE   **Case of Personal Pronouns**

Write the correct personal pronoun from the choices in parentheses.

1. Laura and (he, him) did the best work.
2. The cat rested (its, it's) head on my arm as I read.
3. Are you sure (you, your) driving is a good idea?
4. He drives Elena and (I, me) crazy.
5. I like these beads; are (they, them) yours?
6. Both (he, him) and (I, me) are eager to go to lunch with (she, her).
7. Lou wedged in between Gilly and (I, me).
8. (Their's, Theirs) is the only project still missing.
9. Does Rick plan to join the girls and (we, us) at the game?
10. Please do Lily and (I, me) a huge favor and pick (she, her) up after school.

Frank and Ernest

© 1995 Thaves / Reprinted with permission. Newspaper dist. by NEA, Inc.

7.2 PRONOUNS WITH AND AS APPOSITIVES

Use the nominative case for a pronoun that is an appositive to a subject or a predicate nominative.

EXAMPLE The producers, **Mrs. Singh** and **she,** have raised enough money. [*Producers* is the subject of the sentence.]

EXAMPLE The leads will be two sophomores, **Liam** and **she.** [*Sophomores* is a predicate nominative.]

Use the objective case for a pronoun that is an appositive to a direct object, an indirect object, or an object of a preposition.

EXAMPLE The director rehearsed the leads, **Liam** and **her.** [*Leads* is a direct object.]

EXAMPLE The prompter gave the minor actors, **Barbara** and **me,** our cues. [*Actors* is an indirect object.]

EXAMPLE Fancy costumes went to the dancers, **Keesha** and **him.** [*Dancers* is the object of the preposition *to.*]

It is considered courteous to place the pronoun *I* or *me* last in a pair or series of appositives.

EXAMPLE The lighting crew, **Rob, Luellen,** and **I,** are ready for the technical rehearsal. [nominative case]

EXAMPLE Our soundtrack was recorded by a local pair, **Rob** and **me.** [objective case]

When a pronoun is followed by an appositive, choose the case of the pronoun that would be correct if the appositive were omitted.

EXAMPLE   **We beginners** hope to learn fast. [*We*, which is in the nominative case, is correct because *we* is the subject of the sentence.]

EXAMPLE   The director has helped **us beginners.** [*Us*, which is in the objective case, is correct because *us* is the direct object.]

Hint: When you are choosing the correct pronoun, it is helpful to say the sentence to yourself leaving out the appositive.

EXAMPLE   **We** hope to learn fast.

EXAMPLE   The director has helped **us.**

PRACTICE   **Pronouns with and as Appositives**

Write the correct pronoun from the choices in parentheses.

1. The planning committee, Rob, Laura, and (I, me), got together to assess the situation.
2. I wish the instructions were clearer for the newcomers, the Carlsons and (we, us).
3. The conductor led (we, us) new band members through the piece.
4. If our dreams come true, the coach will pick the tallest girls, Rita and (I, me), to start the big game.
5. The debate team, Edwina and (I, me), lost.
6. They thought that (we, us) older students could help.
7. Two firefighters, Su Lin and (she, her), complained about being called firemen.
8. The head lifeguard showed the new trainees, Debra and (I, me), how to rescue a drowning person.
9. The best double-play combination, Max, Frank, and (I, me), are so good because we practice every day.
10. Please draw the travelers, Kris and (she, her), a map.

7.3 PRONOUNS AFTER *THAN* AND *AS*

When words are left out of an adverb clause that begins with the word *than* or *as*, choose the case of the pronoun that you would use if the missing words were fully expressed.

EXAMPLE You ride a skateboard more skillfully than **I**. [That is, . . . *than I ride a skateboard.* **The nominative pronoun *I* is the subject of the adverb clause *than I ride a skateboard.***]

EXAMPLE The loud thunder bothered Lindsay as much as **me**. [That is, . . . *as much as it bothered me.* **The objective pronoun *me* is the direct object in the adverb clause *as much as it bothered me.***]

In some sentences, the correct pronoun depends on the meaning intended by the speaker or writer.

EXAMPLE Aliko liked Cadeo more than **I** [liked Cadeo].

EXAMPLE Aliko liked Cadeo more than [he liked] **me**.

PRACTICE Pronouns After *Than* and *As*

Rewrite each sentence, choosing the correct pronoun from the choices in parentheses. Justify your choice by adding the necessary words to complete the incomplete comparison.

1. Is Juanita taller than (I, me)?
2. Patrick was nicer to the new neighbors than (we, us).
3. I don't think Francesca is as funny as (they, them).
4. He ran much faster than Gus and (she, her).
5. Mario enjoys jazz more than (we, us); we like rock.

6. Mom always gave the dog more food than (I, me).

7. Artie liked Jackie as much as (she, her).

8. Does he really play any better than (we, us)?

9. Grandpa had as much fun as (they, them).

10. Are you as hungry as (I, me)?

7.4 REFLEXIVE AND INTENSIVE PRONOUNS

Observe the following rules when you use reflexive and intensive pronouns.

1. Don't use *hisself*, *theirself*, or *theirselves*. All three are incorrect forms. Use *himself* and *themselves*.

EXAMPLE   Pablo designed the sailboat **himself.**

EXAMPLE   My brothers **themselves** remodeled the basement.

2. Use a reflexive pronoun when a pronoun refers to the subject of a sentence.

EXAMPLES

INCORRECT	CORRECT
I bought me a book.	I bought **myself** a book.
He found him a chair.	He found **himself** a chair.

3. Don't use a reflexive pronoun unnecessarily. Remember that a reflexive pronoun must refer to the subject, but it must not take the place of the subject.

EXAMPLES

INCORRECT	CORRECT
Mama and myself are here.	Mama and **I** are here.
Ron and yourself are lucky.	Ron and **you** are lucky.

Most of the sentences below contain errors in pronoun use. Rewrite the incorrect sentences, correcting the errors by replacing the incorrect pronouns. If a sentence is already correct, write C.

1. The cat washed itself constantly.
2. Grandma claims that the dishes won't wash theirselves.
3. My youngest nephew, Jay, is very proud that he can dress hisself.
4. Dad wants to go with Amy and myself.
5. I wanted a new bat, so I got me one.
6. Donna and I buried ourself up to our waists in the wet sand at the beach.
7. My friends arranged a surprise party that was a total shock to myself.
8. A pair of lions sunned themselves lazily on the rocks in the desert.
9. Geraldo gave Sara and myself boxes of chocolate.
10. Jeff himself built that beautiful table.

7.5 *WHO* AND *WHOM* IN QUESTIONS AND SUBORDINATE CLAUSES

THE USES OF *WHO*

Use the nominative pronouns *who* and *whoever* for subjects.

EXAMPLE **Whoever** made these cookies? [*Whoever* is the subject of the verb *made.*]

EXAMPLE Ask them **who** will be home for dinner. [*Who* is the subject of the noun clause *who will be home for dinner.*]

In questions that have an interrupting expression (such as *did you say* or *do you think*), it often helps to drop the interrupting phrase to make it easier to decide whether to use *who* or *whom*.

EXAMPLE **Who** do you think will win the contest? [Think, "*Who* will win the contest?" *Who* is the subject of the verb *will win*.]

THE USES OF *WHOM*

Use the objective pronouns *whom* and *whomever* for the direct object or the indirect object of a verb or a verbal and for the object of a preposition.

EXAMPLE **Whomever** are you calling first? [*Whomever* is the direct object of the verb *are calling*. Think, "You are calling whomever first?"]

EXAMPLE They told her **whom** she could invite to the show. [*Whom* is the direct object of the verb *could invite* in the noun clause *whom she could invite to the show*. Think, "She could invite whom to the show?"]

EXAMPLE Picasso is a painter about **whom** I have read quite a bit. [*Whom* is the object of the preposition *about* in the adjective clause *about whom I have read quite a bit*. Think, "I have read quite a bit about whom?"]

EXAMPLE **Whom** did you say the new kitten likes best? [*Whom* is the direct object of the verb *likes*. Drop the interrupting phrase *did you say* and think, "The new kitten likes whom best?"]

In informal speech, many people generally use *who* in place of *whom* in sentences such as *Who did you call?* In writing and in formal speaking situations, however, make the distinctions between *who* and *whom*.

GRAMMAR/USAGE/MECHANICS

For each sentence, write the correct pronoun from the choices in parentheses.

1. (Who, Whom) did your parents want you to invite to the party?
2. (Who, Whom) is Jeremiah calling at this hour?
3. (Whoever, Whomever) ate the last piece of pizza was very inconsiderate.
4. When he saw the broken window, he asked, "(Who, Whom) did it?"
5. The pitcher replied, "(Who, Whom) wants to know?"
6. After Nora said I had a package, I asked her, "From (who, whom)?"
7. After the final test, everyone in the class wondered (who, whom) had passed.
8. (Who, Whom) do you know here?
9. I thought I had met everyone in the room; (who, whom) are you talking about?
10. She hoped (whoever, whomever) was going to come would show up soon.

7.6 PRONOUN-ANTECEDENT AGREEMENT

An **antecedent** is the noun to which a pronoun refers or that a pronoun replaces. All pronouns must agree with their antecedents in number, gender, and person.

AGREEMENT IN NUMBER AND GENDER

A pronoun must agree with its antecedent in number (singular or plural) and gender (masculine, feminine, or neuter).

A pronoun's antecedent may be a noun, another pronoun, or a phrase or a clause acting as a noun. In the following examples, the pronouns appear in blue type and their antecedents appear in italic blue type. Notice that they agree in both number and gender.

EXAMPLE *Octavio Paz* is one of the greatest poets of his era. [singular masculine pronoun]

EXAMPLE *Emily Dickinson* wrote her poems on scrap paper. [singular feminine pronoun]

EXAMPLE *Walt Whitman* and *Emily Dickinson* are famous for their poetry. [plural pronoun]

EXAMPLE This poetry *book,* despite its tattered cover, is valuable. [singular neuter pronoun]

Traditionally, a masculine pronoun was used when the gender of an antecedent was not known or might be either masculine or feminine. When you are reading literature written before the 1970s, remember that *his* may mean *his*, it may mean *her*, or it may mean *his or her*.

EXAMPLE An *author* must capture his readers' interest.

This usage has recently changed, however. Many people now feel that the use of masculine pronouns excludes half of humanity. Use gender-neutral language when the gender is unknown or could be either masculine or feminine. Here are three ways to avoid using a masculine pronoun when the antecedent may be feminine:

1. Use *his or her*, *he or she*, and so on.
2. Make the antecedent plural and use a plural pronoun.
3. Eliminate the pronoun.

EXAMPLE An *author* must capture his or her readers' interest.

EXAMPLE *Authors* must capture their readers' interest.

EXAMPLE *Authors* must capture readers' interest. [no pronoun]

Rewrite each sentence in three different ways, using gender-neutral language.

1. The chef in a top-quality restaurant must take his work very seriously.
2. A good painter understands the value of keeping his brushes clean.
3. A nurse works hard to ensure her patient's recovery.
4. An equestrian must know how to control her horse in the show ring.
5. An accountant needs to keep his desk neat.

AGREEMENT WITH COLLECTIVE NOUNS

When the antecedent of a pronoun is a collective noun, the number of the pronoun depends on whether the collective noun is meant to be singular or plural.

EXAMPLE   The *orchestra* played its last song of the concert. [The collective noun *orchestra* conveys the singular sense of one unit. Therefore, the singular pronoun *its* is used.]

EXAMPLE   The *orchestra* carried their instruments off the stage. [The collective noun *orchestra* conveys the plural sense of several people performing separate acts. Therefore, the plural pronoun *their* is used.]

EXAMPLE   The *team* tried on their new uniforms. [The collective noun *team* conveys the plural sense of several people performing separate actions. Therefore, the plural pronoun *their* is used.]

EXAMPLE   The *team* heard its fans cheering as it ran onto the field. [The collective noun *team* conveys the singular sense of one unit. Therefore, the singular pronouns *its* and *it* are used.]

GRAMMAR/USAGE/MECHANICS

*Write the correct pronoun from the choices in parentheses.
Then write the collective noun that is the subject of each
sentence, and tell whether it is singular or plural in the
sentence.*

1. The cast had learned (its, their) lines individually a
week before the first rehearsal.
2. The city council voted to give (its, their) approval to a
huge development that would bring thousands of new
jobs to the community.
3. The soccer team voted to paint (its, their) locker room
black and white.
4. The pep squad called (its, their) parents when the bus
broke down.
5. The local plumbers' union decided (it, they) would
withdraw from the national organization.

AGREEMENT IN PERSON

A pronoun must agree in person (first, second, or
third person) with its antecedent.

Do not use *you*, a second-person pronoun, to refer to
an antecedent in the third person. Either change *you* to an
appropriate third-person pronoun or replace it with a
suitable noun.

EXAMPLES

POOR   Suki and Jim are going to visit the Everglades, where
you can see alligators.

BETTER   Suki and Jim are going to visit the Everglades, where
they can see alligators.

BETTER   Suki and Jim are going to visit the Everglades, where
tourists can see alligators.

When the antecedent of a pronoun is another pronoun, be sure the two pronouns agree in person. Avoid unnecessary shifts from *they* to *you, I* to *you,* or *one* to *you.*

EXAMPLES

POOR   **They** often visit the Centerville Fruit Farm, where **you** can pick **your** own strawberries.

BETTER   **They** often visit the Centerville Fruit Farm, where **they** can pick **their** own strawberries.

EXAMPLES

POOR   **I** hiked on trails that amazed **you** with their beauty.

BETTER   **I** hiked on trails that amazed **me** with their beauty.

EXAMPLES

POOR   When **one** travels by train, **you** can learn a lot.

BETTER   When **one** travels by train, **one** can learn a lot.

BETTER   When **you** travel by train, **you** can learn a lot.

PRACTICE   **Agreement in Person**

Rewrite each item, correcting the inappropriate use of you *by substituting a third-person pronoun or a suitable noun.*

1. Morgan lives in Centerville, where you can recycle just about everything.
2. I enjoy going to Chicago Cubs games because you get to sit in that nice, old stadium.
3. Jessie's songs are filled with witty lyrics and clever rhymes that make you laugh.
4. I like a travel book that makes you feel as though you're really traveling with the author.
5. When one is really tired, you can fall asleep almost anywhere.

AGREEMENT WITH INDEFINITE PRONOUN ANTECEDENTS

In general, use a singular personal pronoun when the antecedent is a singular indefinite pronoun. Use a plural personal pronoun when the antecedent is a plural indefinite pronoun.

INDEFINITE PRONOUNS					
ALWAYS SINGULAR	another	either	neither	other	
	anybody	everybody	no one	somebody	
	anyone	everyone	nobody	someone	
	anything	everything	nothing	something	
	each	much	one		
ALWAYS PLURAL	both	few	many	others	several
SINGULAR OR PLURAL	all	any	enough	most	none	some

EXAMPLE **Each** of the girls must bring **her** own toolbox.

EXAMPLE **One** of the boys has **his** own safety glasses.

EXAMPLE **Many** of the workers take **their** toolboxes home at night.

Note that the plural nouns in the prepositional phrases—*of the girls, of the boys*—do not affect the number of the personal pronouns. *Her* and *his* are singular because *each* and *one*, their antecedents, are singular.

When no gender is specified, use gender-neutral wording.

EXAMPLE **Everyone** must bring **his or her** own jacket.

GRAMMAR/USAGE/MECHANICS

If you find the previous sentence a bit awkward, the best solution may be to reword the sentence. You might use a plural indefinite pronoun or a suitable noun (such as *people*) to replace the singular indefinite pronoun. You might even eliminate the personal pronoun entirely.

EXAMPLE *All* must bring **their** own jackets.

EXAMPLE *People* must bring **their** own jackets.

EXAMPLE *Everyone* must bring **a** jacket. [no pronoun]

PRACTICE **Gender-Neutral Agreement with Indefinite Pronoun Antecedents**

Rewrite each item in three ways, using gender-neutral language.

1. Each of the employees is required to turn in his time card every day.
2. Anyone who bungee jumps must be out of her mind.
3. Everyone who votes is exercising his rights.
4. Has everyone found her way to the gym?
5. Everyone likes to feel that he is well liked.

7.7 CLEAR PRONOUN REFERENCE

Make sure that the antecedent of a pronoun is clearly stated. Make sure that a pronoun doesn't refer to more than one antecedent.

VAGUE PRONOUN REFERENCE

Don't use the pronoun *this, that, which, it, any,* or *one* without a clearly stated antecedent.

EXAMPLES VAGUE Seung is a wonderful magician, and **this** was evident in last night's show. [What was evident? His magic skill was evident, but the word *skill* is not specifically mentioned.]

GRAMMAR/USAGE/MECHANICS

CLEAR	Seung is a wonderful magician, and **his skill** was evident in last night's show.
VAGUE	The senator loved public speaking, and **that** greatly boosted his popularity. [**What boosted his popularity? His speeches did, but the word** *speeches* **is not specifically mentioned.**]
CLEAR	The senator loved public speaking, and **his speeches** greatly boosted his popularity.
VAGUE	Last week our garage burned, **which** started from a kerosene heater. [**What started from a kerosene heater? A fire started, but the word** *fire* **is not specifically mentioned.**]
CLEAR	Last week a fire, **which** started from a kerosene heater, burned our garage.
VAGUE	The Supreme Court is deliberating on the question of disability, and **it** will affect anti-discrimination lawsuits. [**What will affect lawsuits? The Supreme Court's decision will do so, but the word** *decision* **is not specifically mentioned.**]
CLEAR	The Supreme Court is deliberating on the question of disability, and **its decision** will affect anti-discrimination lawsuits.

GRAMMAR/USAGE/MECHANICS

PRACTICE **Clear Pronoun Reference**

Rewrite each item, replacing vague pronouns with specific words.

1. Marta stopped to buy milk, but it was closed.
2. I like to work in my vegetable garden, which makes me very tired.
3. I wrote to George several times last year, but they were never answered.

4. That huge oak tree blew down in the storm last night, and that made a huge noise.

5. Derek went to see the new science fiction movie, but it was full when he got there.

UNCLEAR AND INDEFINITE PRONOUN REFERENCE

If a pronoun seems to refer to more than one antecedent, either reword the sentence to make the antecedent clear or eliminate the pronoun.

EXAMPLES

UNCLEAR ANTECEDENT	After the tickets slipped between the reports, **they** were lost. [Which word is the antecedent of *they*? Were the tickets or the reports lost?]
CLEAR ANTECEDENT	The tickets were lost when **they** slipped between the reports.
NO PRONOUN	When the tickets slipped between the reports, **the tickets** were lost.

The pronouns *you* and *they* should not be used as if they were indefinite pronouns. Instead, you should name the performer of the action. In some cases, you may be able to reword the sentence in such a way that you do not name the performer of the action and you do not use a pronoun.

EXAMPLES

INDEFINITE	In Japan **you** bow after saying hello.
CLEAR	In Japan **people** bow after saying hello.
INDEFINITE	In some countries, **they** take naps after lunch.
CLEAR	In some countries, **people** take naps after lunch.
CLEAR	In some countries, **it is customary** to take a nap after lunch.

*Rewrite each sentence, correcting any unclear or indefi-
nite pronoun references.*

1. My sister resembles Oprah Winfrey, but she is older.
2. To ski down a mountain, you must first get to the top of
the mountain.
3. In France, they don't think that everything has to be
new and shiny.
4. Randy ran into Alec on the playground, and he got a
bloody nose.
5. They say that Southern California could have another
major earthquake at any time.

PRACTICE Proofreading

*Rewrite the following passage, correcting errors in
spelling, capitalization, grammar, and usage. Add any
missing punctuation. Write legibly to be sure one letter is
not mistaken for another. There are ten mistakes.*

Hans Christian Andersen

¹Hans Christian Andersen was born in 1805 in Odense, Denmark. ²His
parents and him lived in the slums, and he received almost no education.
³At the age of fourteen, he left by hisself for Copenhagen. ⁴He hoped to
succeed as a performer, but he bearly managed to stay alive. ⁵However,
one of the Royal Theatre's directors took an interest in Andersen and
arranged for him attending a grammar school. ⁶Later, this same benefactor
obtained tuition for Andersen's use at a university. ⁷He begun writing plays
and novels but acheived his greatest success with fairy tales.

⁸Andersen's most famousest stories include "The Ugly Duckling" "The
Emperor's New Clothes," and "The Little Mermaid." ⁹They have made many
of his stories into movies and cartoons, and many more have been read by
children and adults throughout the world. ¹⁰His name has become familiar
to whomever appreciates stories that contain humor, wisdom, and insight.

For each sentence, write the correct pronoun from the choices in parentheses.

1. Dan, if you really want to be as good a swimmer as (I, me), you have to practice more.

2. Without a doubt, the best candidate for class president is (she, her).

3. The referee was forced to come to (we, us) players to find out what happened.

4. They finished early because the work was shared by Shawna and (he, him).

5. I wonder (who, whom) left the gym shoes on top of the kitchen table.

6. As Sam walked by the store, he saw (hisself, himself) in the glass window.

7. Are you sure Helen and (they, them) have all the materials they need?

8. With Gloria and (I, me) out of the picture, Jessica had clear sailing.

9. Everyone must do what is right for (him or her, them).

10. It was clear that (whoever, whomever) answered the next question correctly would win.

11. That dog hurt (it's, its) paw on the hot pavement.

12. Although the news was exciting to the students, there was still no excuse for (them, their) running in the hall.

13. Why would you accuse your teammates, Jenny and (I, me), of doing something like that?

14. I wanted to take my dog into the restaurant, but (they, a worker) said that dogs were prohibited by the health code.

15. My friends and (she, her) met for the first time at the party.

16. The rapidly rising flood waters trapped Juan and (me, myself) on top of the roof.

17. Luisa said the volunteer work that Molly and (she, her) do at the children's hospital is fantastically rewarding.

18. Of all the first-graders, the two best-behaved were (he and she, him and her).

19. I have never seen Maggie and Devan's dog, but this must be (their's, theirs).

20. Mom and Dad were really happy about (you, your) deciding to go along.

21. I don't know (who, whom) can help me in this situation.

22. I think that I am faster than (she, her).

23. The letter that arrived today was addressed to both Mom and (I, me).

24. The coach told Cathy that the two best performers in the game were the two newcomers, Wilma and (she, her).

25. All were responsible for (his or her, their) own actions.

Using Modifiers Correctly

● ● ● ● ● ● ● ● ● ● ● ● ● ● ● ●

PRETEST Using Modifiers Correctly

For each sentence, write the correct word or words from the choices in parentheses.

1. Instead of what he actually said before the football game began, the referee should have called out, "May the (good, better, best) team win!"
2. Jared threw the javelin the (farther, farthest) of all the competitors and won the medal.
3. Sylvia rode the horse (more badly, worse, worst) than Kimberly had.
4. Frank has little talent on the piano, but Caroline has (littler, less).
5. People don't enjoy competition if they do not have (a high, a higher, the highest) opinion of their abilities.

6. Kathleen created the (more flamboyant, most flamboyant) outfit of all those in the fashion show.

7. Of all my friends, I'd have to say that Rupa is the (smart, smarter, smartest).

8. Willie has the (darkest, most dark) eyes I've ever seen.

9. I hope I will do (more well, better) on this test than I did on the last one.

10. Which town is (farther, further) away, Smallville or Metropolis?

11. Gina and Frances are both cheerful people who have (many, more, the most) friends.

12. My throat is sore, I ache all over, and I'm just not feeling very (good, well).

13. When my dog ran away, I felt (lonely, lonelier, loneliest) than I ever have in my life.

14. In the tenderest moment of the musical, Greta sang (more softly, softlier) than Zoe had when she played the role.

15. The house was in the (worse, worst) shape of any Marge had yet seen.

PRETEST Double and Incomplete Comparisons, Double Negatives, Misplaced and Dangling Modifiers

Rewrite each sentence, correcting any errors.

16. Peering over the high wall, the ducks on the grass looked like statues.

17. I'm not hardly old enough to drive yet.

18. Abigail's dog behaves better than any dog I've seen.

19. I'm not no good at making snap decisions.

20. All mothers are nicer than his mother.

21. Wrigley Field is different from any ballpark.

22. We saw sun spots visiting the planetarium.

23. Running through the streets, the buildings seemed to tower over me.

24. I only want one of these pomegranates.

25. Brisco watched the news more than anything on television.

26. Squirming miserably while waiting for the light to change, the car felt hotter and hotter to us.

27. I hardly never miss a chance to practice the piano.

28. The Tannenbaums' glimpsed a rainbow out walking.

29. Hilda likes mangoes much more better than oranges.

30. A computer can break down faster than any machine I know about.

8.1 THE THREE DEGREES OF COMPARISON

Most adjectives and adverbs have three degrees: the positive, or base, form; the comparative form; and the superlative form.

The **positive** form of a modifier cannot be used to make a comparison. (This form appears as the entry word in a dictionary.)

The **comparative** form of a modifier shows two things being compared.

The **superlative** form of a modifier shows three or more things being compared.

EXAMPLES

POSITIVE	My dog is **small.**
	The cat ran **swiftly.**
COMPARATIVE	Kim's dog is **smaller** than my dog.
	My dog ran **more swiftly** than the cat.
SUPERLATIVE	Of the three dogs, Ray's dog is the **smallest** one.
	The squirrel ran **most swiftly** of all.

In general, for one-syllable modifiers add *–er* to form the comparative and *–est* to form the superlative.

EXAMPLES green, greener, greenest

The neighbor's grass always looks **greener** than ours.

loud, louder, loudest

That sonic boom was the **loudest** one I've ever heard.

fast, faster, fastest

Her hair grows **faster** than mine.

In some cases, adding *–er* and *–est* requires spelling changes.

EXAMPLES big, bigger, biggest

true, truer, truest

dry, drier, driest

With some one-syllable modifiers, it may sound more natural to use *more* and *most* instead of *–er* and *–est*.

EXAMPLES just, **more** just, **most** just

Of the three, that judge's ruling was the **most just** decision.

For most two-syllable adjectives, add *–er* to form the comparative and *–est* to form the superlative.

EXAMPLES ugly, uglier, ugliest

Your mask is **uglier** than mine.

That is the **ugliest** mask I've ever seen.

If *–er* and *–est* sound awkward with a two-syllable adjective, use *more* and *most* instead.

EXAMPLES afraid, **more** afraid, **most** afraid

No one is **more afraid** of wasps than I am.

Of all of us, I was the **most afraid.**

Chapter 8 Using Modifiers Correctly   **257**

In general, for adverbs ending in *–ly*, use *more* and *most* to form the comparative and superlative degrees. For some *–ly* adverbs, add *–er* and *–est*. Consult a dictionary if necessary.

EXAMPLES   clearly, **more** clearly, **most** clearly

Tom gives directions **more clearly** than most people.

That candidate explains her position **most clearly** of all.

but

early, earli**er,** earli**est**

They arrived **earlier** than we did.

You must have arrived **earliest** of all.

For modifiers of three or more syllables, always use *more* and *most* to form the comparative and superlative degrees.

EXAMPLES   attractive, **more** attractive, **most** attractive

Green looks **more attractive** on you than it does on me.

That oil painting is the **most attractive** one in the exhibit.

Less and *least,* the opposite of *more* and *most,* can also be used with most modifiers to show negative comparison.

EXAMPLES   Are cooked vegetables **less nutritious** than raw vegetables?

Spinach is my **least favorite** green vegetable.

Less and *least* are used before modifiers that have any number of syllables.

Rewrite each sentence to correct the error in comparison. If the sentence is already correct, write C.

1. The bubbles floated more high than the balloon.
2. He writes slowlier than he can think.
3. Above us the full moon shone brightlier than a city streetlight.
4. Your dog, Skipper, is the least vicious dog I have ever met.
5. The horse ran swiftlier than the zebra did.
6. Superman is the invinciblest of the superheroes.
7. Nigel swims more fast than his friend does.
8. Lambs are the most cute animals in the world.
9. Our cat is the biggest of our two pets.
10. As the youngest person in the room, Shawna was able to get up quickliest.

8.2 IRREGULAR COMPARISONS

A few modifiers form their comparative and superlative degrees irregularly. It is helpful to memorize their forms.

MODIFIERS WITH IRREGULAR FORMS OF COMPARISON		
good	better	best
well	better	best
bad	worse	worst
badly	worse	worst
ill	worse	worst
far (distance)	farther	farthest
far (degree, time)	further	furthest
little (amount)	less	least
many	more	most
much	more	most

Write the correct modifier from the choices given in parentheses.

1. My friend Johanna is a (good, better, best) golfer than I will ever be.
2. Joe can throw a ball (far, farthest, furthest) of all the kids on the team.
3. Now I do all my homework so that I can do (well, better, best) in school than before.
4. Please give (much, more, the most) work to Polly than to Melanie.
5. Of the three relay runners, I am the (bad, worse, worst) sprinter.
6. Jeri has (little, less, the least) respect for LuAnn since she was caught cheating.
7. Dalia is (far, farther, further) along in the course than Edwina.
8. I have sighted (many, more, the most) birds today than I did yesterday.
9. I'd never felt (bad, worse, worst) in my life than I did when I caught that flu.
10. Once I recovered, it seemed to me that I felt the (wellest, best) I ever have.

8.3 CORRECTING DOUBLE COMPARISONS

Don't use both *−er* and *more*. Don't use both *−est* and *most*. To do so would be an error called a **double comparison**.

EXAMPLES

INCORRECT A redwood grows more taller than an oak.

CORRECT A redwood grows **taller** than an oak.

INCORRECT Aunt Ellie is my most kindest aunt.

CORRECT Aunt Ellie is my **kindest** aunt.

INCORRECT They will write to us more oftener after school starts.

CORRECT They will write to us **more often** after school starts.

PRACTICE Correcting Double Comparisons

Rewrite each sentence to correct the error in comparison. If the sentence is already correct, write C.

1. I think that Christina is the most happiest person I have met in many years.
2. Small dogs are often more noisier than large dogs, or at least they seem to be.
3. I am more exhausteder than Emily.
4. Austin seemed determined to yell the most loudest of all the cheerleaders.
5. "This is the most extraordinary situation," said the detective to his sidekick.
6. He was the more quieter of the two boys.
7. The Taj Mahal is the most beautifulest building in the world.
8. I swam more slower than the rest of the team, but I finished the race.
9. The Nile is the most longest river on Earth.
10. Climbing trees in autumn is one of the most enjoyable things a kid can do.

8.4 CORRECTING INCOMPLETE COMPARISONS

Don't make an incomplete or unclear comparison by omitting the word *other* or the word *else* when you compare a person or thing with its group.

UNCLEAR Mercury is closer to the sun than any planet.
[*Any planet* **includes Mercury.**]

CLEAR Mercury is closer to the sun than any **other** planet.

UNCLEAR Aunt Elizabeth has more pets than anyone I know.
[*Anyone I know* **includes the aunt.**]

CLEAR Aunt Elizabeth has more pets than anyone **else**
I know.

Be sure your comparisons are between like things—
that is, similar things.

EXAMPLES

UNCLEAR The grace of a basketball player is more obvious than
a baseball player. [**The grace of a basketball player is
being compared illogically with everything about a baseball
player.**]

CLEAR The grace of a basketball player is more obvious than
that of a baseball player.

CLEAR The grace of a basketball player is more obvious than
the grace of a baseball player.

CLEAR The grace of a basketball player is more obvious than **a
baseball player's.**

UNCLEAR The claws of a lion are larger than a house cat. [**The
claws of a lion are being compared illogically with everything about a house cat.**]

CLEAR The claws of a lion are larger than **those of a
house cat.**

CLEAR The claws of a lion are larger than **the claws of a
house cat.**

CLEAR The claws of a lion are larger than **a house cat's.**

Rewrite each sentence, correcting the error in comparison.
If a sentence is already correct, write C.

1. A monkey's strength is greater than a cat.
2. The ears of a lynx are longer than a hyena.
3. The slow loris moves more slowly than any animal.
4. Lincoln was taller than any other president.
5. The fingers of a man are often longer than a woman.
6. This year's results are higher than last year.
7. I tested better than anyone in my state.
8. Rufus swam faster than the rest of the competitors.
9. These hamburgers are better than a restaurant.
10. I'd rather live in the United States than anywhere else.

Rewrite each sentence, correcting the error in comparison.
If a sentence is already correct, write C.

1. Who is the best artist, Rodin or Picasso?
2. Aretha's rendition of the concerto was more better than Baldwin's.
3. Everyone knows that a tree is taller than a bush.
4. The mountains of Nepal are higher than North America.
5. Our debate team is more worse than Groveton's.
6. Nathaniel went further out on a limb than any boy in his class.
7. I feel weller than when I had that terrible cold.
8. Heather dislikes her name more than her sister.
9. I have never known anyone to take a joke farther than Tony does.
10. The baby slept more peacefuler than her mom did.

8.5 *GOOD* OR *WELL; BAD* OR *BADLY*

Always use *good* as an adjective. *Well* may be used as an adverb of manner telling how ably or how adequately something is done. *Well* may also be used as an adjective meaning "in good health."

EXAMPLE Red is a **good** color for you. [adjective]

EXAMPLE You look **good** in red. [adjective after a linking verb]

EXAMPLE I feel **good** when I hear our song. [adjective after a linking verb]

EXAMPLE You dress **well.** [adverb of manner]

EXAMPLE Aren't you feeling **well?** [adjective meaning "in good health"]

Always use *bad* as an adjective. Use *badly* as an adverb.

EXAMPLE That's a **bad** idea. [adjective]

EXAMPLE That milk tastes **bad.** [adjective after a linking verb]

EXAMPLE I feel **bad** about your moving away. [adjective after a linking verb]

EXAMPLE The porch swing is squeaking **badly.** [adverb after an action verb]

Frank and Ernest

© 1998 Thaves / Reprinted with permission. Newspaper dist. by NEA, Inc.

For each sentence, write the correct word or words from the choices in parentheses.

1. Marvin asked his friend, "Is your new job going (good, well)?"
2. The bear was hurt (bad, badly) when it stepped in the hidden trap.
3. I think I have (good, well) taste.
4. You are a horribly (bad, badly) dancer.
5. To his surprise, Alex did really (good, well) on the Spanish test.
6. Sandy wanted (bad, badly) to be chosen to sing a solo with the choir.
7. Matt did a (good, well) job of making a birthday dinner for his sister.
8. As they started to tip over, I realized that the books had been stacked (bad, badly).
9. Pavarotti sings so (good, well) that he puts other tenors to shame.
10. When I lost the bracelet my grandmother had given me, I felt really (bad, badly).

PRACTICE **Regular and Irregular Comparisons**

Give the comparative and superlative forms of each modifier. Consult a dictionary if necessary.

1. friendly
2. rapidly
3. far
4. good
5. beautiful

6. high

7. slowly

8. wonderful

9. little

10. fierce

8.6 CORRECTING DOUBLE NEGATIVES

Don't use two or more negative words to express the same idea. To do so is an error, a **double negative.** Use only one negative word to express a negative idea.

EXAMPLES

INCORRECT	I don't have no stereo equipment.
CORRECT	I do**n't** have **any** stereo equipment.
CORRECT	I have **no** stereo equipment.
INCORRECT	We haven't seen no concerts this year.
CORRECT	We haven't seen **any** concerts this year.
CORRECT	We have seen **no** concerts this year.
INCORRECT	My parrot never says nothing.
CORRECT	My parrot **never** says **anything.**
CORRECT	My parrot says **nothing.**

The words *hardly* and *scarcely* are negative words. Don't use them with other negative words, such as *not.*

EXAMPLES

INCORRECT	I haven't hardly finished.
	He can't scarcely never be on time.
CORRECT	I **have hardly** finished.
	He **can scarcely ever** be on time.

Rewrite each sentence, correcting the double negative. If a sentence is already correct, write C.

1. I don't have no time for this!
2. Millie hadn't hardly studied for the exam, so she failed miserably.
3. Peabody didn't want no dog, but he didn't really like cats neither.
4. Simone didn't tell me nothing about the party, and I wasn't going to ask her no questions.
5. It's annoying that Judy can't go nowhere without her guitar and amplifier.
6. "I don't have no patience with bad grammar," exclaimed my sister, "and neither should you."
7. We didn't think that the train couldn't scarcely stop in time to avoid hitting the car.
8. When Benton was feeling unwell, he hardly ate enough food to keep himself alive, and it seemed he wouldn't ever recover.
9. Reza and I can't hardly wait until it's time to go to the movies tonight.
10. There weren't no indications that the bus was coming anytime soon.

8.7 CORRECTING MISPLACED AND DANGLING MODIFIERS

Misplaced modifiers modify the wrong word, or they seem to modify more than one word in a sentence.

Place modifiers as close as possible to the words they modify in order to make the meaning of the sentence clear.

EXAMPLES

MISPLACED	**Soaring over the edge of the cliff,** the photographer captured an image of the eagle. **[participial phrase incorrectly modifying *photographer*]**
CLEAR	The photographer captured an image of the eagle **soaring over the edge of the cliff.** **[participial phrase correctly modifying *eagle*]**
MISPLACED	He easily spotted the eagle **with his high-powered binoculars. [prepositional phrase incorrectly modifying *eagle*]**
CORRECT	**With his high-powered binoculars,** he easily spotted the eagle. **[prepositional phrase correctly modifying *he*]**

Place the adverb *only* immediately before the word or group of words that it modifies.

If *only* is not positioned correctly in a sentence, the meaning of the sentence may be unclear.

EXAMPLES

UNCLEAR	Dan **only** has art class on Monday. **[Does Dan have only one class on Monday, or does he have art class on no other day than Monday, or is Dan the only person (in a group) who has one class on Monday?]**
CLEAR	Dan has **only** art class on Monday. **[He has no other class that day.]**
CLEAR	Dan has art class **only** on Monday. **[He does not have art class on any other day.]**
CLEAR	**Only** Dan has art class on Monday. **[No one else has art class on Monday.]**

Dangling modifiers seem logically to modify no word at all. To correct a sentence that has a dangling modifier, you must supply a word that the dangling modifier can sensibly modify.

EXAMPLES

DANGLING **Working all night long,** the fire was extinguished. **[participial phrase logically modifying no word in the sentence]**

CLEAR **Working all night long,** the firefighters extinguished the fire. **[participial phrase modifying *firefighters*]**

DANGLING **Sleeping soundly,** my dream was interrupted by the alarm. **[participial phrase logically modifying no word in the sentence]**

CLEAR **Sleeping soundly,** I had my dream interrupted by the alarm. **[participial phrase modifying *I*]**

PRACTICE Correcting Misplaced and Dangling Modifiers

Rewrite each sentence to make the writer's intended meaning clear.

1. Carved in stone, I found the ancient ruins.
2. Walking through the garden, the petunias drooped their scarlet heads.
3. Jordan only told me the story.
4. Jay went to see the new ape in the zoo wearing his jeans.
5. While trying to work on my term paper, my dog kept annoying me.
6. Having gotten rotten, Jim threw out the leftovers.

7. The three children found a lost wallet walking home from school.
8. Using bloodhounds as trackers, the escaped convict was caught.
9. Writing the book, the plot proved hard to come up with.
10. Pram only talked to the monk at the temple once.

PRACTICE   Proofreading

Rewrite the following passage, correcting errors in spelling, capitalization, grammar, and usage. Add any missing punctuation. Write legibly to be sure one letter is not mistaken for another. There are ten mistakes.

Gwendolyn Brooks

[1]Gwendolyn Brooks was born in Topeka, Kansas, but she grows up in Chicago, Illinois. [2]From an early age, she wrote poetry about her life and her feelings. [3]Her early poetry received a boost when she met the poet Langston Hughes who gave her encouragement and made her more determined to get published. [4]The first African American to receive the Pulitzer Prize, Brooks won in 1950 for her book of poetry entitled "Annie Allen," her second collection.

[5]Many people believe that Gwendolyn Brooks was more talented than any contemporary poet. [6]Her poetry is naturaler than more formal poetry, even though it is written with great attention to poetic techniques. [7]Because her work uses the voices of everyday people, the language of home and street, the writing is easier for almost anyone to read and understand.

[8]Brooks, who wasn't never satisfied with language that was less than perfect for her needs, used a keen ear for sound in selecting precisely the right words. [9]Many of her poems are like the gentlest but most power-fulest music. [10]One of her most beautiful books is a long narrative poem. [11]It tells the story of a mother searching for her lost child in a crowded building and of the buildings angry and despairing inhabitents.

For each sentence, write the correct word or words from the choices in parentheses.

1. Babies usually get (sleepy, sleepier, sleepiest) after several hours of activity.

2. The tropical fish swam in the (beautiful, more beautiful, most beautiful) aquarium I have ever seen.

3. My mother says that the music I've been playing lately is (much, more, most) annoying than any other kind of music she's ever heard.

4. Jeremy thought that Maureen looked (good, well) in her new jacket.

5. Madge tried to get away with doing (little, the less, the least) work possible.

6. Her boss did not approve, and she told Madge that she'd never seen an employee do a (bad, badder, worse, worser, worst) job at anything.

7. You shouldn't feel too (bad, badly); Melissa won't hold that mistake against you.

8. When I first met her, I thought she was just (mean, meaner, meanest).

9. She says that my singing is (flat, more flat, flatter, flatly) than that of a lovesick dog!

10. Their music is (more spirited, spiriteder) than some other folk music.

11. The driver sat in his delivery truck for an hour and practiced his (favorite, more favorite, most favorite) trumpet music.

12. The debate went (bad, badly) and I do not feel (good, well) about it.

13. We all thought that the last *Star Wars* movie was the (less, least) exciting movie we had ever seen but that the first one was the (greater, greatest) movie ever made.

GRAMMAR/USAGE/MECHANICS

14. Many people with whom I have talked lately believe that racism is this country's (baddest, worse, worst, worstest) problem.

15. The answer to the problem may be (farther, further) in the future than we would like to think.

POSTTEST Double and Incomplete Comparisons, Double Negatives, Misplaced and Dangling Modifiers

Rewrite each sentence, correcting any errors.

16. Falling from the sky, the barbecue was delayed by rain.

17. I can't scarcely wait for the concert Saturday night, and it won't do no good to tell me to be patient.

18. Julian discovered facts about reptiles reading books.

19. I think that Colorado is more beautiful than any Rocky Mountain state.

20. The frost this spring only killed the daffodils.

21. Don't pay no attention to me this morning; I'm just in a bad mood.

22. Finding the address, the letter was finally mailed.

23. The kids in my new school looked more friendlier than the kids at my last school.

24. Are snow leopards more endangered than any animal?

25. Sitting in a bowl, the painter sketched the fruit.

26. When out in cold weather, your head should be protected by a warm hat.

27. Born on January 1st, my parents welcomed me in with the New Year.

28. Roaring its support, the opposition leader stepped in front of the crowd.

29. The archaeologist found the mummy using very delicate tools.

30. I only have one life to give for my country.

Chapter 9

Diagraming Sentences

• • • • • • • • • • • • • • •

PRETEST **Diagraming Sentences**

Diagram each sentence.

1. Help!
2. Buster both gives and takes.
3. Who is talking so softly?
4. Wolves are predatory.
5. Elephants are large, gray beasts.
6. The marathon winner, my big sister, beat the world record.
7. One of my friends broke her ankle in gym class.
8. Terribly shaken, the refugees entered the camp on the mountain.
9. The vacationers usually spent their time in sunning themselves.
10. Walking the plank was Captain Kidd's idea.
11. The time to eat is decided by the cook.

12. Audrey ate her dinner with enthusiasm, and then she got dessert.
13. Franz, who read the book, wrote a report on it.
14. When Karen won, she was completely surprised.
15. Give your ticket to whoever is standing by the door to the gym.
16. Whatever happens next is unknown.
17. Who knew where he was going after school?
18. The horse and rider jumped over the fence that Sula had put in the field.
19. The lake was in the mountains, and it was fed by the yearly snowmelt.
20. Doug knew that he would be late, but nothing could be done about it.

9.1 DIAGRAMING SIMPLE AND COMPOUND SENTENCES

A **sentence diagram** shows how the various words and parts of a sentence function in the sentence and relate to the sentence as a whole.

It's vital to know the parts of a sentence before you begin diagraming. Diagraming just gives you a visual picture of how these parts relate to one another.

When writing a sentence in a diagram, retain the capitalization but leave out the punctuation.

SUBJECTS AND VERBS

Start your diagram with a horizontal line, called a baseline, intersected by a vertical line. Find the simple subject of the sentence and place it to the left of the vertical line; then place the simple predicate to the right of the vertical line.

EXAMPLE   Senators are meeting.

$$\text{Senators} \mid \text{are meeting}$$

EXAMPLE   Are senators meeting?

$$\text{senators} \mid \text{Are meeting}$$

A sentence with an understood subject is diagramed with the understood subject placed in parentheses.

EXAMPLE   Stop!

$$\text{(you)} \mid \text{Stop}$$

PRACTICE   **Subjects and Verbs**

Diagram each sentence.

1. Sit!
2. Are you going?
3. Ralph has been writing.
4. Trees are blooming.
5. Is it happening?

COMPOUND SUBJECTS AND COMPOUND VERBS

To diagram compound subjects and compound verbs, follow the example diagram. If a pair of correlative conjunctions, such as *both . . . and,* is used, place the conjunctions to the right and left of the dotted line.

EXAMPLE   Both staffers and senators meet and debate.

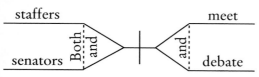

Diagram each sentence.

1. Teddy skipped and jumped.
2. Mary and Alice laughed.
3. Creeks and streams flood.
4. William and Carlos walked and walked.
5. Leaders both inspire and encourage.

ADJECTIVES AND ADVERBS

Both adjectives and adverbs are placed on slanted lines leading from the modified words. An adverb that modifies another modifier is placed on a slanted line parallel to the modifier and is connected to it with a straight line.

EXAMPLE   The older senators speak more frequently.

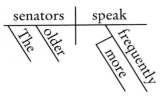

PRACTICE Adjectives and Adverbs

Diagram each sentence.

1. The tall, green giant knelt.
2. Wilbur played gently.
3. Who is pounding so loudly?
4. The old man walks quite slowly.
5. Cold temperatures and dark skies often signal a snowstorm.

DIRECT OBJECTS AND INDIRECT OBJECTS

A direct object appears on the baseline to the right of the verb. The verb and the direct object are separated by a vertical line that does not cross the baseline.

EXAMPLE Experts have given advice.

| Experts | have given | advice |

Indirect objects are placed on a horizontal line below the baseline and are linked to the verb by a slanted line.

EXAMPLE Experts have given senators advice.

| Experts | have given | advice |
senators

PRACTICE **Direct Objects and Indirect Objects**

Diagram each sentence.

1. Did Amos eat that huge sandwich?
2. Melvin handed Alia the book.
3. Dogs give people great joy.
4. Victor gave Edgar a mountain bike.
5. Throw Raul the ball.

SUBJECT COMPLEMENTS AND OBJECT COMPLEMENTS

Subject complements—that is, **predicate nominatives** and **predicate adjectives**—are placed on the baseline to the right of the verb. They are separated from the verb by a slanted line that does not cross the baseline.

EXAMPLE Senators are legislators.

| Senators | are \ legislators |

EXAMPLE That senator is angry.

| senator | is \ angry |
That

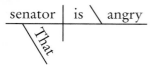

Object complements are diagramed the same way subject complements are, but a direct object comes between the verb and the object complement.

EXAMPLE Everyone considers senators important.

| Everyone | considers | senators \ important |

PRACTICE **Subject Complements and Object Complements**

Diagram each sentence.

1. The backyard is a jungle.
2. Some cats are very lazy.
3. Venecia made her answer much longer.
4. Ned cut his hair short.
5. Neither José nor Jamal considered baseball important.

APPOSITIVES AND APPOSITIVE PHRASES

To diagram an appositive, simply place the word in parentheses beside the noun or pronoun it identifies. To diagram an appositive phrase, place the appositive phrase in parentheses and place any modifying words on slanted lines directly beneath the appositive.

EXAMPLE Washington, the nation's capital, houses Congress.

| Washington (capital) | houses | Congress |

the *nation's*

PRACTICE **Appositives and Appositive Phrases**

Diagram each sentence.

1. My best friend, Marcus, is a great soccer player.
2. I visited my dentist, Dr. Frey.

3. Jake, the school janitor, always keeps the building spotlessly clean.

4. The year's shortest day, December 21, is my cousin's birthday.

5. The caterpillar hungrily chomped my favorite bush, a beautiful lilac.

PREPOSITIONAL PHRASES

To diagram prepositional phrases, follow the example diagram.

EXAMPLE   During campaigns, senators of today address people through television advertisements.

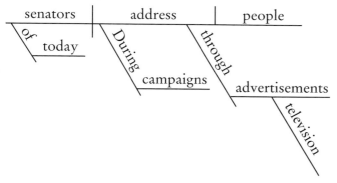

PRACTICE   **Prepositional Phrases**

Diagram each sentence.

1. In 1974, Hank Aaron finally surpassed Babe Ruth's career record for number of home runs.

2. The mayor frequently doodled in the margins of his speeches.

3. In the last minute of the game, our team tied the score.

4. The church is around the corner.

5. Of the three choices, I prefer the last.

PARTICIPLES AND PARTICIPIAL PHRASES

To diagram participles and participial phrases, follow the example diagram.

EXAMPLE Bedraggled, the quarterback rose to his feet.

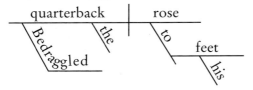

EXAMPLE Hopefully casting his ballot, the senator wanted a victory.

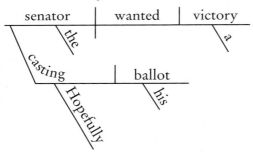

PRACTICE **Participles and Participial Phrases**

Diagram each sentence.

1. Excited, the explorers entered the cave.
2. Looking for Mark, I went to town.
3. My old black dog, lying on the floor, was in everyone's way.
4. Riding beside the train, the cowboy warned the conductor of the washed-out bridge.
5. The old muffler scraping the road caused a shower of bright sparks.

GERUNDS AND GERUND PHRASES

To diagram gerunds and gerund phrases, follow the example diagram.

EXAMPLE   Voting is a way of voicing your opinion.

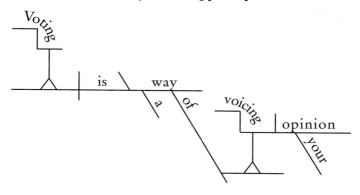

PRACTICE   **Gerunds and Gerund Phrases**

Diagram each sentence.

1. Boxing was originally the sport of gentlemen.
2. Fly-fishing is a highly complex sport.
3. I thoroughly enjoy reading mysteries on stormy evenings.
4. We almost lost hope of finding the lost camper.
5. My favorite exercise is walking slowly to the ice cream store.

INFINITIVES AND INFINITIVE PHRASES

If an infinitive or an infinitive phrase functions as an adverb or an adjective, diagram it as you would diagram a prepositional phrase.

EXAMPLE The place to vote is determined by your residence.

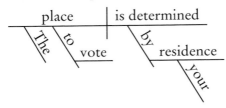

Infinitives and infinitive phrases functioning as nouns are also diagramed like prepositional phrases. However, they are placed on stilts.

EXAMPLE To win an election is to know satisfaction.

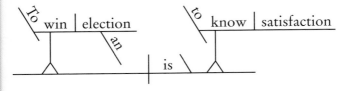

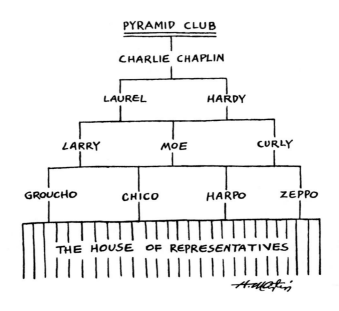

PYRAMID CLUB
CHARLIE CHAPLIN
LAUREL HARDY
LARRY MOE CURLY
GROUCHO CHICO HARPO ZEPPO
THE HOUSE OF REPRESENTATIVES

Diagram each sentence.

1. Oscar stopped at the market to buy some milk.
2. To argue with John is useless.
3. Helena needs to learn some manners.
4. Do not forget to bring your CDs.
5. The car to choose is the one with good mileage.

COMPOUND SENTENCES

A **compound sentence** is two or more simple sentences joined by either a comma and a conjunction or by a semicolon.

Diagram each main clause of a compound sentence separately. If the clauses are connected by a semicolon, use a dotted line to connect the verbs of each main clause. If the main clauses are connected by a conjunction, place the conjunction on a solid horizontal line, and connect it to the verbs of each main clause by dotted lines.

EXAMPLE Voting is a privilege; you must be a citizen.

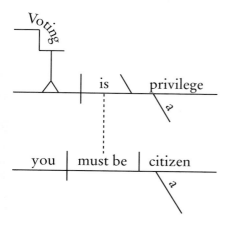

To vote you must register in advance, and you need to bring current identification to the polling place.

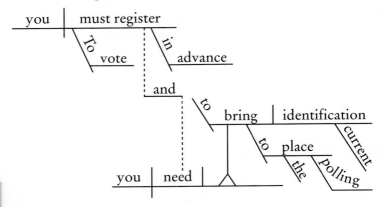

PRACTICE | Compound Sentences

Diagram each sentence.

1. Ice-skating for the first time, Alicia fell often, but Connie glided along gracefully.
2. The foreman stopped the line; the stoppage gave the workers an unexpected break.
3. I kicked the chair, and it broke.
4. In 1956 Mickey Mantle led his league in homers; he also led in RBIs.
5. Do your math homework immediately, or help me in the garage.

9.2 DIAGRAMING COMPLEX AND COMPOUND-COMPLEX SENTENCES

A **complex sentence** has one main clause and one or more subordinate clauses.

ADJECTIVE CLAUSES

To diagram a complex sentence containing an adjective clause, place the main clause in one diagram and the adjective clause in another diagram beneath it. Use a dotted line to connect the introductory word of the clause to the modified noun or pronoun in the main clause.

EXAMPLE The carpenter whom you hired fixed the shelves that were uneven.

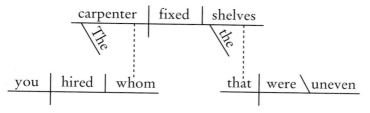

PRACTICE   Adjective Clauses

Diagram each sentence.

1. I know someone who has a pet pig.
2. Maria Sanchez, who is a paramedic, will demonstrate first-aid techniques.
3. The house that was built in the summer was sold to the Wilsons.
4. I like extremely hot chili that has personality.
5. Who wants a room that has no windows?

ADVERB CLAUSES

To diagram a complex sentence containing an adverb clause, place the adverb clause in a separate diagram beneath the main clause. Use a dotted line to connect the verb in the adverb clause to the modified word in the main clause. Write the subordinating conjunction on the dotted line.

EXAMPLE Before carpenters cut the wood, they make a design.

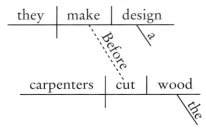

Diagram each sentence.

1. Finish your work when you are riding the bus.
2. Think about this afternoon's activities while you eat.
3. Before the rose bush bloomed, the Marlows' garden had no color.
4. People do not dream unless they are sleeping.
5. After you have decided on a plan, do not bother with other ideas.

NOUN CLAUSES

Diagram the main clause and place the noun clause on a stilt in its appropriate position. The stilt that attaches the noun clause to the sentence may be connected to any point on the noun clause's baseline. You must identify the function of the introductory word of the noun clause. It can be the subject, an object, a predicate nominative, or an adverb in the noun clause; or it might simply connect the noun clause to the main clause. If the latter is the case, place the introductory word on a line of its own above the verb in the noun clause, connecting it to the verb with a dotted vertical line. If it has a function within the clause, diagram it appropriately.

Noun Clause as Subject

EXAMPLE What the carpenter builds is especially sturdy.

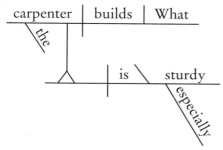

PRACTICE Noun Clause as Subject

Diagram each sentence.

1. Whatever went wrong was not my fault.
2. Which of the answers she gave is correct?
3. Whoever wants my sandwich can have it.
4. What I think about it is not important.
5. Whenever I finish will be a very happy day.

Noun Clause as Direct Object

EXAMPLE We know that the mechanic works long hours.

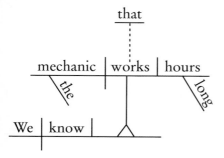

Diagram each sentence.

1. Karen wishes that she could draw well with charcoal pencils.
2. Little Wesley thought that the circus clowns were frightening.
3. I saw that it was no help.
4. Do not ask me what Tom wants.
5. Peter knows where the sports equipment is.

Noun Clause as Object of a Preposition

EXAMPLE The carpenter builds cabinets for whoever requests them.

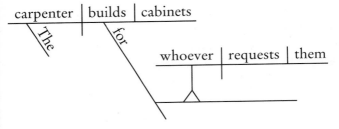

Diagram each sentence.

1. Despite what you said, I am going ahead.
2. Darren walks to school with whoever arrives at the right time.
3. My teacher reminded me about what had been assigned as homework.
4. Julius knew nothing except what Jody told him.
5. Phoebe will give the bicycle to whoever wants it.

GRAMMAR/USAGE/MECHANICS

COMPOUND-COMPLEX SENTENCES

A **compound-complex sentence** has two or more main clauses and at least one subordinate clause.

Diagram a compound-complex sentence as you would diagram a compound sentence.

EXAMPLE   Carpenters who do quality work are usually busy, and they often receive higher pay.

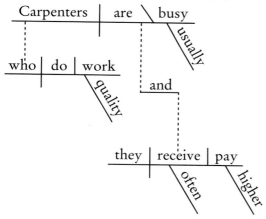

PRACTICE   Compound-Complex Sentences

Diagram each sentence.

1. My parakeet often lays an egg and, while it is in her cage, she will not lay another.
2. Debi laughed when she heard the joke, but I realized that laughter was inappropriate.
3. When she was ten, Susan saved postage stamps, but now she collects coins.
4. The child wandered away, and we did not find her until the sun went down.
5. In Paris, Mata Hari was a dancer whom people admired, but she was also a German spy.

Diagram each sentence.

1. Is he gone?
2. Ross and Emily were married.
3. Come quickly!
4. Do not worry so much.
5. The deer jumped the fences.
6. Jarrett considered Felicia's poem quite beautiful.
7. Estelle loves her shell collection, one of the best in the world.
8. While he goes inside, we will sit in the yard.
9. Running from the dog, the rabbit hid in the garden down the street.
10. Carbon-dating is a good way to learn the age of most fossils.
11. Today, Mom will teach us how she does laundry.
12. To help another person is to help yourself.
13. The local people were fleeing, but the tornado was already there.
14. Pigs can find acorns that are deeply buried.
15. After the concert ended, they went to a restaurant for a late snack.
16. Where the ball lands may decide the game.
17. Who would have believed that Imelda could play the guitar so well!
18. Have you done the trigonometry homework that I assigned yesterday?
19. That grade is for what you did on your essay.
20. Ed and Joe left the house at noon, but Mike waited until evening before he departed.

Chapter 10

Capitalizing

● ● ● ● ● ● ● ● ● ● ● ● ● ● ● ● ● ●

PRETEST Capitalizing

*Rewrite any incorrect sentences, correcting errors in
capitalization. If a sentence is correct, write* C.

1. I like to use webster's *New World dictionary.*
2. My favorite flowers are nasturtiums.
3. Olaf took the Train called *city of New Orleans* from
   Chicago to jackson, Mississippi.
4. The religion known as sikhism combines certain islamic
   and hindu beliefs.
5. Mel goes to a University, but I attend Whitman college.
6. The department of children and family services is
   supposed to protect children.
7. Driving South along the Hudson river, dad pointed to
   the constellation orion.
8. Troy's favorite Song is "crazy," by Patsy Cline.
9. Will asked his Mother, "is this the day of our Field Trip?"

10. Central park is near the Center of New York city.

11. The Teddy Bear was named after president Theodore Roosevelt, who was a fifth cousin of Franklin delano Roosevelt.

12. I'm going to take a World History course next Fall from dr. John "grizzly" Griswald, even though he has an odd nickname.

13. Did you say that the *Washington post* reviewed the book *Lie down with dogs?*

14. Each fourth of July, Emma's Aunt would recite the beginning paragraphs of the declaration of Independence.

15. The bus dropped off the Anderson Brothers at the intersection of Austin and Grand avenues, near the coronet theater.

16. The *Iliad* deals with a war between the greeks and the trojans called the Trojan war.

17. Ben Jonson was a major Elizabethan playwright.

18. There is a large hispanic community in our city, and many signs and instructions are in spanish as well as english.

19. I have to write checks to star electric company, to uncle Jerry, and to North ridge hospital.

20. I wonder why the Dead sea has that name.

21. Secretary of state Ralph Fisher asked the governor, "how do you want me to handle this, governor?"

22. Beth ends letters to her mother with "Much love, Beth."

23. One of Columbus's ships—I think it was the *santa maria*—never made it back to Spain.

24. Harvey took Pictures of the Jefferson memorial.

25. Quentin wrote an outline that began as follows:

I. Modern Literature
   a. European
      1. pre-1900
         A. prose

10.1 CAPITALIZING SENTENCES AND QUOTATIONS

The use of capitalization across the English-speaking world varies. In business writing particularly, people capitalize terms according to company style, which may vary from the rules in this chapter. However, mastering these rules for your own writing will enable you to express yourself clearly in any situation.

Rule 1 Capitalize the pronoun *I* and the first word of a sentence.

EXAMPLE Pets need love and attention.

EXAMPLE Can you watch my dog while I am gone?

Rule 2 Capitalize the first word of a sentence in parentheses that stands by itself. Don't capitalize a sentence within parentheses that is contained within another sentence.

EXAMPLE Games can be tools for learning about computers. (Many games require more computer knowledge than basic use requires.)

EXAMPLE They were looking for software (they hoped to buy no more than two programs) that they could use for writing reports.

Rule 3 Capitalize the first word of a complete sentence that follows a colon. Lowercase the first word of a sentence fragment that follows a colon.

EXAMPLE The poet's love letter was too well written: It intimidated the girl.

EXAMPLE The poet's love letter was passionate, heartwarming, and one thing more: intimidating.

Rule 4 Capitalize the first word of a direct quotation that is a complete sentence.

A **direct quotation** gives the speaker's exact words.

EXAMPLE My little brother asked, "Why can't I go too?"

Unless it begins a sentence, don't capitalize the first word of a direct quotation that cannot stand as a complete sentence.

EXAMPLE Her boss described her as "energetic and intelligent."

Rule 5 Do not capitalize an indirect quotation.

An **indirect quotation** does not repeat a speaker's exact words and should not be enclosed in quotation marks.

EXAMPLE My brother asked why he couldn't go.

An indirect quotation is often introduced with the word *that.*

EXAMPLE She said that she wanted to leave early.

Rule 6 In a traditional poem, the first word of each line is capitalized.

EXAMPLE Let us go then, you and I,
When the evening is spread out against the sky
Like a patient etherized upon a table; . . .
—from "The Love Song of J. Alfred Prufrock" by T. S. Eliot

PRACTICE **Capitalizing Sentences and Quotations**

Copy the sentences, correcting any errors in capitalization. If a sentence is correctly capitalized, write C.

1. Is it true, as i've heard, that Everyone should drink at least eight glasses of water per day?

2. Jerry asked, "who wants to go to the mall?"
3. My kitten, whose name is dandelion, is growing just like a weed.
4. Even though i work out and lift weights, my mother still calls me "A delicate little thing."
5. A writer from the local newspaper asked me, "What do you think about the principal of your new school?"
6. In the years after the Civil War, thousands of African Americans left the south and moved to Kansas. (they were called Exodusters.)
7. The Exodusters founded a great many towns (One of these towns is Nicodemus), and the town of Nicodemus is symbolic of their pioneer spirit.
8. everyone said that Stanley tripped Bob, but Stanley said, "you all are mistaken!"
9. "There isn't much," said Polly, "That I can do about it."
10. Parting really can be, as Shakespeare put it, "Such sweet sorrow."

10.2 CAPITALIZING LETTER PARTS AND OUTLINES

Rule 1 Capitalize the first word in the salutation and the closing of a letter. Capitalize the title and the name of the person addressed.

EXAMPLES

Dear Ms. Romano,   Dear Sir or Madam: Dear General Motors:

With love,   Yours truly,   Sincerely yours,

Rule 2 In a topic outline, capitalize the Roman numerals that label main topics and the letters that label subtopics. Do not capitalize letters that label subdivisions of a subtopic. Capitalize the first word in each heading and subheading.

    I. **M**ain topic
      A. **S**ubtopic
        1. **D**ivision of a subtopic
          a. **S**ubdivision of a subtopic
          b. **S**ubdivision of a subtopic
    II. **M**ain topic

PRACTICE   Capitalizing Letter Parts

Write the letter of the correctly capitalized line in each pair.

1. a. Respectfully Yours,
   b. Respectfully yours,

2. a. Fondly,
   b. fondly,

3. a. Dear Mr. And Mrs. Jackson:
   b. Dear Mr. and Mrs. Jackson:

4. a. Dear Channel 7 News:
   b. dear channel 7 News:

5. a. Best regards,
   b. best regards,

PRACTICE   Capitalizing Outlines

Rewrite the partial outline, correcting any errors in capitalization.

I. Park Activities
  A. Youth Activities
    1. sports
      A. team sports
      B. individual sports
    2. crafts
      A. Lessons and fees
      B. equipment
  B. Adult Activities
    1. Exercise and fitness
      a. Swimming
      b. weight room

10.3 CAPITALIZING PROPER NOUNS AND PROPER ADJECTIVES

A **proper noun** names a particular person, place, thing, or idea.
Proper adjectives are formed from proper nouns.

Rule 1 Capitalize proper nouns and proper adjectives.

EXAMPLES

PROPER NOUNS	PROPER ADJECTIVES
China	Chinese food
Islam	Islamic country

In proper nouns and adjectives made up of more than one word, capitalize all words except articles, coordinating conjunctions, or prepositions of fewer than five letters.

EXAMPLES

PROPER NOUNS	University of Nebraska
	American Society for the Prevention of Cruelty to Animals
PROPER ADJECTIVES	University of Nebraska students
	United States ambassadors

Note: Many proper nouns do not change form when used as adjectives.

Rule 2 Capitalize the names of people and pets and the initials that stand for their names.

EXAMPLES   Connie Chung   Spot and Puff
Eric Cartman   Franklin D. Roosevelt   W. B. Yeats

Foreign names are often compounded with an article, a preposition, or a word meaning "son of" or "father of." These names often follow different rules of capitalization. The capitalization also depends on whether you are using the full name or just the surname, so be sure to look up the names in a reference source for proper capitalization.

EXAMPLES	FULL NAME	SURNAME ALONE
	Alfred de Musset	Musset
	Manuel de Falla	de Falla
	Aziz ibn Saud	Ibn Saud

Capitalize nicknames.

EXAMPLES   Shaq   Babe Ruth   the Sun King

Enclose nicknames in quotation marks when they are used with a person's full name.

EXAMPLE   Louis "Satchmo" Armstrong

Rule 3 Capitalize adjectives formed from people's names.

EXAMPLE   Shakespeare   Shakespearean sonnet
          Napoléon   Napoléonic attire

Rule 4 Capitalize a title or an abbreviation of a title used before a person's name.

EXAMPLES

Mr. Jones	Ms. McGee	Mother Teresa
Dr. Greene	Secretary of State Albright	Chief Sitting Bull

Capitalize a title used in direct address.

EXAMPLE   How is she doing, Doctor?
          The troops are retreating, General.

Don't capitalize a title that follows a person's name.

EXAMPLE   Madeleine Albright, secretary of state, cancelled her visit.

Don't capitalize a title that is simply being used as a common noun.

EXAMPLE   Spiro Agnew was vice president in the 1960s.
          I didn't care whom she nominated for treasurer of the club.

Rule 5 Capitalize the names and abbreviations of academic degrees that follow a person's name. Capitalize *Jr.* and *Sr.*

EXAMPLE   Terrence Odlin, **D**octor of **P**hilosophy

EXAMPLE   Paula Martinéz, **B.A.**

EXAMPLE   Joe Wallace **J**r.

Rule 6 Capitalize a word showing family relationship when it is used either before a proper name or in place of a proper name.

EXAMPLE   Will **A**unt Fern visit this summer?

EXAMPLE   May I go to the movies, **M**om?

Don't capitalize a word showing family relationship if it is preceded by a possessive noun or pronoun.

EXAMPLE   Pilar's **a**unt will visit this summer.

EXAMPLE   Your **m**om said you may go.

Rule 7 Capitalize the names of ethnic groups, nationalities, and languages.

EXAMPLES

ETHNIC GROUPS	**N**ative **A**merican, **C**aucasian, **H**ispanic
NATIONALITIES	**I**talian, **B**razilian, **S**outh **A**frican
LANGUAGES	**R**ussian, **S**wahili, **H**indi, **M**andarin

Rule 8 Capitalize the names of organizations, institutions, political parties and their members, government bodies, business firms, and teams.

EXAMPLES

ORGANIZATIONS	**L**eague of **W**omen **V**oters
	American **M**edical **A**ssociation
	People for the **E**thical **T**reatment of **A**nimals
INSTITUTIONS	**O**hio **S**tate **U**niversity
	Mayo **C**linic
	Metropolitan **M**useum of **A**rt

POLITICAL PARTIES AND MEMBERS	Libertarian Party/Libertarian
	Democratic Party/Democrat
	Socialist Party/Socialist
GOVERNMENT BODIES	House of Commons
	Senate
	Federal Bureau of Investigation
BUSINESS FIRMS	American Electric Power
	Glencoe
	Working Assets Long Distance
TEAMS	Cincinnati Reds
	New York Knicks
	Seattle Seahawks

Note: Don't capitalize words such as *court* and *university* unless they are part of a proper noun.

EXAMPLE   I will attend a university next year.

EXAMPLE   I will attend New York University next year.

Note: When referring to a specific political party or party member, words such as *democrat* and *republican* should be capitalized. However, when used to describe a way of thought or an ideal, such words should be lowercase.

EXAMPLE   They are members of the Democratic Party (*or* party).

EXAMPLE   She supported a democratic government.

EXAMPLE   The Communist Party (*or* party) was powerful in the twentieth century.

EXAMPLE   Marx wrote about communist theories.

Note: Capitalize brand names of products but not the nouns following them.

EXAMPLES   Kornee corn dogs   Land Shark motorcycles

Rule 9 Capitalize the names of roads, parks, towns, cities, counties, townships, provinces, states, regions, countries, continents, other land forms and features, and bodies of water.

EXAMPLES

Fifth Avenue	Hocking Hills	Kansas City
Franklin County	State Park	the Pacific
Guatemala	New York	Northwest
Rocky Mountains	Africa	Mojave Desert
Mediterranean	Long Island	Lake Pontchartrain
Sea	Pacific Ocean	Platte River

Note: Capitalize words such as *city, island,* and *mountains* only when they are part of a proper name.

Capitalize compass points, such as *north, south, east,* and *west,* when they refer to a specific region or when they are part of a proper name. Don't capitalize them when they indicate direction.

EXAMPLES

REGIONS/PROPER NAMES	DIRECTIONS
the South	driving south
East Lansing	eastern Kentucky

Capitalize *northern, southern, eastern,* and *western* when they refer to hemispheres and cultures.

EXAMPLES   Northern Hemisphere   Eastern culture

Capitalize adjectives that are formed from place names.

EXAMPLES   Chinese cuisine   Roman statues   Saharan winds

Rule 10   Capitalize the names of planets and other astronomical bodies.

EXAMPLES

Jupiter	Venus	Uranus
Milky Way	Alpha Centauri	Little Dipper

Rule 11   Capitalize the names of monuments, buildings, bridges, and other structures.

EXAMPLES

Tomb of the Unknowns	Golden Gate Bridge
Empire State Building	Grand Coulee Dam
Taj Mahal	Westminster Abbey

Rule 12 Capitalize the names of ships, planes, trains, and spacecraft. Note that these names are italicized, but the abbreviations before them are not.

EXAMPLES   *Air Force One*   *Columbia*   SS *United States*

Rule 13 Capitalize the names of historical events, special events, and holidays and other calendar items.

EXAMPLES   Texas State Fair   Memorial Day   Olympics

Parent-Teacher Book Fair   Wednesday   December

Historical events require capitalization, as do some historical periods. However, most historical periods are not capitalized. It is best to check a dictionary or other reference source for the proper capitalization of historical periods.

EXAMPLES

HISTORICAL EVENTS   Boston Tea Party, Battle of Gettysburg, French Revolution

HISTORICAL PERIODS   Roaring Twenties, Age of Reason, Dark Ages

eighteenth century, the twenties, baroque period

Note: Historical periods using numerical designations are lowercase unless they are part of a proper name.

Note: Do not capitalize names of the seasons—*spring, summer, fall, winter.*

Rule 14 Capitalize the names of deities and words referring to deities, words referring to a revered being, religions and their followers, religious books, and holy days and events.

EXAMPLES

NAMES OF AND WORDS REFERRING TO DEITIES	Allah	Brahma	God
WORDS REFERRING TO A REVERED BEING	the Prophet	the Baptist	
RELIGIONS	Hinduism	Sikhism	Buddhism
FOLLOWERS	Christian	Muslim	Mormon
RELIGIOUS BOOKS	Koran	I Ching	Talmud
RELIGIOUS HOLY DAYS AND EVENTS	Good Friday	Yom Kippur	Ramadan

Note: When you're referring to ancient Greek or Roman deities, don't capitalize the words *god, gods, goddess,* and *goddesses.*

Rule 15 Capitalize only those school courses that name a language, are followed by a number, or name a specific course. Don't capitalize the name of a general subject.

EXAMPLES	Japanese	foreign language
	Economics 101	economics
	Advanced Calculus	calculus

Rule 16 Capitalize the first word and the last word in the titles of books, chapters, plays, short stories, poems, essays, articles, movies, television series and programs, songs, magazines, newspapers, cartoons, and comic strips. Capitalize all other words except articles, coordinating conjunctions, and prepositions of fewer than five letters.

EXAMPLES

The Mists of Avalon	*Romeo and Juliet*	*Sports Illustrated*
the *New York Times*	"A Room of One's Own"	"Home on the Range"

Note: It is common practice not to capitalize or italicize articles preceding the title of a newspaper or a periodical.

Rule 17 Capitalize the names of documents, awards, and laws.

EXAMPLES

Constitution of the United States

Pulitzer Prize

North American Free Trade Agreement

Treaty of Versailles

New Economic Policy

Nobel Prize

PRACTICE **Capitalizing Proper Nouns and Proper Adjectives**

Copy the sentences, correcting any errors in capitalization. If a sentence is correctly capitalized, write C.

1. Christianity, judaism, and islam are three religions.
2. Columbia university and Cooper union are both schools located in manhattan.
3. Thurgood Marshall was the first African American Supreme Court justice.
4. For several years, the Chicago Bulls dominated Professional Basketball.
5. John f. Kennedy jr. was as famous as his father, j.f.k., and his uncle, Robert "bobby" Kennedy.
6. My Aunt and Kevin's Uncle were both born during the Vietnam war.
7. The Fuller museum of advertising had a display of old magazine ads for Silken Hair Shampoo.

8. The National organization for women tried for many years to get the equal rights amendment passed.

9. While Ronald Reagan was the President of the United States, Margaret Thatcher was the Prime Minister of England.

10. All the planets in our Solar System are named after roman Gods or Goddesses, except the most familiar planet, earth.

11. Last fall, I traveled from East to West across the United States, stopping in towns like Saint Louis in the midwest and Gallup in the southwest.

12. In the 1760s, anti-british colonists formed groups called sons of liberty.

13. For her mathematics requirement, Tisha had to decide between a geometry course and Advanced Algebra.

14. Rosh hashana is the Jewish new year.

15. Chicago holds a food festival in the Summer that is called "taste of Chicago."

16. "One of my favorite books is *Things fall Apart* by the Nigerian writer Chinua Achebe. What's your favorite book, dad?"

17. The south African leader Desmond Tutu won the Nobel peace prize.

18. The agency for International Development is one arm of the U.S. state department.

19. Many Seminole indians have African American ancestors.

20. We toured the fbi, then crossed the Potomac river to see mount Vernon, which was George Washington's home.

Rewrite each item, correcting any errors in capitalization. If an item is already correct, write C.

1. Unlike uncle Calvin, who works for the U.S. navy, Dad is a University professor.
2. The Artist Harriet Powers created a quilt known as "the Creation Of The Animals," which is now owned by the Museum of fine arts in Boston.
3. Dear Sir or madam:

    I am writing to inquire about the photo research position you advertised in last Sunday's edition of The *New York times*. My résumé is enclosed.

    Best Regards,
Su Lin Matsumoto
4. The president often has meetings at Camp David.
5. The Principal of our school has a welcoming party for us after labor day.
6. The indian writer, vikram seth, wrote a collection of modern fables entitled *Beastly Tales from here and there*.
7. Alexander Hamilton, the first secretary of the Treasury, was a leading federalist. (this political party no longer exists.)
8. Federalists favored a strong Federal Government.
9. The caldecott medal is an award given each year to the Illustrator of a picture book for children.
10. I. Early Sculpture
    a. human figures
        1. Greek and roman
        2. african
    B. mythological figures
        1. gods and goddesses
        2. creatures of Nature

SUMMARY OF CAPITALIZATION RULES

NAMES AND TITLES OF PEOPLE

CAPITALIZE	DO NOT CAPITALIZE
M. L. King Jr.	a leader
Miss Jody Pacella	a neighbor
General Schwarzkopf	a general
Uncle Karl	my uncle
Dr. Greene	a doctor

ETHNIC GROUPS, NATIONALITIES, AND LANGUAGES

Maori	an ethnic group
French	a nationality
Yiddish	a language

ORGANIZATIONS, INSTITUTIONS, POLITICAL PARTIES AND THEIR MEMBERS, GOVERNMENT BODIES, BUSINESS FIRMS, AND TEAMS

Girl Scouts of America	an organization
Smithsonian Institution	an institution
Democratic Party / Democrat	democratic theories
Parliament	a governing body
General Motors	an automobile manufacturer
Cleveland Indians	a baseball team

NAMES OF PLACES

Third Street	a street
Portland, Oregon, U.S.A.	a city, state, or country
Galapagos Islands	islands
New England	a region
Pacific Ocean	an ocean

GRAMMAR/USAGE/MECHANICS

Summary of Capitalization rules, continued

PLANETS AND OTHER ASTRONOMICAL BODIES	
CAPITALIZE	DO NOT CAPITALIZE
Jupiter	a planet
Big Dipper	a constellation
MONUMENTS, BUILDINGS, BRIDGES, AND OTHER STRUCTURES	
Washington Monument	a monument
Sears Tower	a skyscraper
JFK Bridge	a bridge
Eiffel Tower	a structure
SHIPS, PLANES, TRAINS, AND SPACECRAFT	
USS Constitution	a ship
Enola Gay	a plane
Apollo 13	a spacecraft
HISTORICAL EVENTS, SPECIAL EVENTS, AND CALENDAR ITEMS	
the Civil War	a war
Kentucky Derby	a race
Inauguration Day	a holiday
July, December	summer, winter
Monday	a day of the week
RELIGIOUS TERMS	
Allah	a deity
Our Lady	a revered being
Catholicism / Catholic	a religion / a religious follower
Koran	a religious book
Passover	a holy day

Summary of Capitalization rules, continued

SCHOOL COURSES	
CAPITALIZE	DO NOT CAPITALIZE
French	a foreign language
Advanced Calculus	calculus
History 152	a history course
TITLES OF WORKS	
Fools of Fortune	a book
"A Rose for Emily"	a short story
National Geographic	a magazine
the *Daily News*	a newspaper
DOCUMENTS, AWARDS, AND LAWS	
the Magna Carta	a document
Distinguished Flying Cross	an award
Atomic Energy Act	a law

GRAMMAR/USAGE/MECHANICS

PRACTICE Proofreading

Rewrite the following passage, correcting errors in spelling, capitalization, grammar, and usage. Add any missing punctuation. Write legibly to be sure one letter is not mistaken for another. There are ten errors.

All Creatures Great and Small

[1]*All Creatures Great and Small* is the first of James Herriot's books (They are largely autobiographical) about being a veterinarian in the English Countryside. [2]We first meet the young Dr. Herriot in 1937. [3]He has just finished veterinary school, and is on his way to his first job interview. [4]The interview is with the far more experienced Dr. Siegfried Farnon in

the town of Darrowby. [5]Darrowby is in an area of England known as yorkshire. [6]On his way to the interview with Dr. Siegfried Herriot thinks of his luck in getting an opportunity for a job during such hard times.

[7]1937 is a time of economic difficulties in England, and Herriot is eager for work, however, he is also nervous and afraid. [8]He has heard many stories about the hard life a Veterinary assistant in the countryside can expect. [9]Of course, he gets the job and began his working life in a building called Skeldale House. [10]The remainder of the book, which is really a series of almost independent stories, tells of his adventures caring for sick animals and by the way, their owners.

POSTTEST Capitalizing

Rewrite any incorrect sentences, correcting errors in capitalization. If a sentence is correct, write C.

1. The Florida department of tourism tries to interest people in visiting the State.
2. My Cousin Bob is a Lieutenant in the United States air force.
3. In Europe, what we call the French and Indian war is known as the Seven years' war.
4. Mike said that He can't make it.
5. Enslaved people used the north star to guide them.
6. The fans were upset by the loss (The team needed to win all its remaining games) that eliminated the Elmwood tigers from competition.
7. My Doctor suggested an addition to my diet: it is broiled chicken.
8. Have scientists found evidence of Life on mars?
9. One of my aunts is Pilar Wallace, m.d., and another is Rachel Kaplan, d.d.s.
10. My Mom wants to know where uncle Willie is planning to go after work.

11. The official Brazilian language is Portuguese, not Spanish.

12. Many Civil War Generals attended the United States military academy, which is also known as west point.

13. The teacher said, "put that magazine away, or i'll have to see you after class."

14. Before beginning his term paper, Nikolai wrote an outline that began as follows:
    I. Early jewish immigration
        a. Portuguese Settlers
            1. Areas of Settlement
            2. Influence in the American revolution
                a. Financial Participation
                b. military participation

15. The structure known as the great wall of China is breathtaking.

16. National Elections can determine whether democrats or republicans control the U.S. senate.

17. The Eighteenth Century was a time of political unheaval.

18. My english class read William Faulkner's story "A rose for Emily."

19. Rachel enjoys her course in Astrophysics, but her Professor demands a great deal of work.

20. When we moved to the midwest, I could no longer find Crumbled Oats Cereal, my favorite breakfast food.

21. My Grandparents are going to visit us for thanksgiving and then go to stay with aunt Sara.

22. The space needle in Seattle is a big tourist attraction.

23. I can't wait for Summer Vacation because my family is going to the Grand canyon.

24. The Christmas letter began: "To Our Friends and Family."

25. Ted is saving for a Car, which he plans to drive to Yellowstone park.

Chapter 11

Punctuation, Abbreviations, and Numbers

• • • • • • • • • • • • • •

PRETEST **Punctuation**

Rewrite each sentence, correcting any errors in punctuation.

1. Great balls of fire: That's delicious
2. Please dont leave your shirt on the bed?
3. James' answer wasnt at all what we expected.

4. Do you want milk, or water, or tea, or juice.

5. I wondered whether she had forgotten all about me since last summer?

6. My sisters impression of the Mayflower, she saw a life-size replica near Plymouth Rock, was that it was a very small ship.

7. I use the following spices in my black-eyed peas, garlic onion red pepper and salt and pepper.

8. The model looked sickly, she was just skin and bones.

9. *Harper's Weekly* one of the oldest American magazines used drawings and engravings to illustrate many of its articles about the Civil War.

10. My group includes Lisa; who is from the Philippines, Faustin, who is from Congo and Michelle who is from Haiti.

11. Common symptoms of a cold are: a stuffy nose, aches, a cough, and a sore throat and the symptoms may last for many days.

12. Then they, listen to this: just got up and left.

13. High in the air above the tiny house: the plane soared.

14. As soon as he was physically able Andrew made his way back home.

15. Beware: this property is guarded by a trained dog.

16. I have to read the contract, (including all the small print), however I forgot my glasses.

17. "Come quickly"! cried the nurse. "A patient has fallen out of bed

18. Mr Parks told me that his daughter is the expresident of that company.

19. I loved being able to see Renoir's painting "Girl with a Watering Can" when we visited the National Gallery didn't you?

20. Sophie Wilson's son in law just got a big promotion and she's extremely proud of him.

Rewrite each item, correcting any errors in the use of abbreviations and numbers.

21. I'm leaving on the 4:30 am flight for Los Angeles, CA.

22. I'm going to need 5 gal. of coffee before I get on that plane!

23. How well do you think N.B.C. did in covering the Olympics?

24. I can never remember if there are 3 or 4 tsp. in a tbsp.

25. Mable's number in the marathon was 431, and mine was twelve.

26. A person's rent should never be more than twenty-five percent of his or her income.

27. My sister borrowed $100 from me last month.

28. Buddhism was founded by Siddhartha around bc 500.

29. One expert on the period from one thousand ad to 1300 AD is Robert Bovenski PhD.

30. Over 6,000,000 people died in the Holocaust.

11.1 THE PERIOD

Use a period at the end of a declarative sentence—a statement—and at the end of an imperative sentence—a polite command or a request.

EXAMPLES **DECLARATIVE SENTENCE** Track practice starts soon.

IMPERATIVE SENTENCE Please sign up for two events.

11.2 THE EXCLAMATION POINT

Use an exclamation point to show strong feeling and to indicate a forceful command.

EXAMPLE What a beautiful day this is!

EXAMPLE Look out!

Use an exclamation point after an interjection that expresses a strong feeling.

EXAMPLES   Yikes!   Hurray!   Ow!   Good heavens!

11.3 THE QUESTION MARK

Use a question mark at the end of a direct question.

EXAMPLE   Who would like a part-time job for the summer?

EXAMPLE   Which call should I answer first?

Don't use a question mark after an indirect question (one that has been reworded so that it is part of a declarative sentence).

EXAMPLE   He asked whether I needed a work permit.

EXAMPLE   I wondered how much the job would pay.

PRACTICE **End Marks**

Rewrite each item, adding the correct end punctuation.

1. Henry, you come here this minute
2. What are you doing on Saturday
3. The plane took off
4. Emily Dickinson composed some of the most beautiful poetry ever written
5. When will the game begin
6. Harrison asked me what the argument could have been about
7. Golly That dinner was expensive
8. Please give me the packing tape
9. Could you please pass the potatoes
10. Thank goodness this day is over

11.4 THE COLON

COLONS TO INTRODUCE

Use a colon to introduce lists, especially after statements that use such words as *these*, *namely*, *the following*, or *as follows*.

EXAMPLE Friday's test will cover **these** areas: the circulatory, the digestive, and the nervous systems.

EXAMPLE He requested **the following:** a screwdriver, a level, and wood screws.

Don't use a colon to introduce a list if the list immediately follows a verb or a preposition. That is, be sure the words preceding the colon form a sentence.

EXAMPLE The best nonanimal sources of protein **are** soybeans, wheat germ, brewer's yeast, nuts, seeds, and whole grains. [The list follows the verb *are* and acts as the sentence's predicate nominative. Don't use a colon.]

EXAMPLE My sister likes to decorate her hamburgers **with** lettuce, tomato, mustard, ketchup, and relish. [The list follows the preposition *with* and acts as the object of the preposition. Don't use a colon.]

Use a colon to introduce material that illustrates, explains, or restates the preceding material.

EXAMPLE I often wish my parents had had more than one child: They worry too much about me.

EXAMPLE The epidemic grew ever more serious: Now children as well as adults were being affected.

A complete sentence following a colon is capitalized.

EXAMPLE Caution: Do not enter until car has come to a complete stop.

Use a colon to introduce a long or a formal quotation. A formal quotation is often preceded by such words as *this, these, the following,* or *as follows.*

EXAMPLE   Mrs. Hoskins asked us to write an essay on **the following** African saying: "It is the rainy season that gives wealth."

Poetry quotations of more than one line and prose quotations of more than four or five lines are generally written below the introductory statement and are indented on the page.

EXAMPLE   In his long poem *The Other Pioneers*, Roberto Félix Salazar describes some of the early settlers of the United States:

> Now I must write
> Of those of mine who rode these plains
> Long years before the Saxon and the Irish came.

OTHER USES OF COLONS

- Use a colon between the hour and the minute of the precise time.
- Use a colon between the chapter and the verse in biblical references.
- Use a colon after the salutation of a business letter.

EXAMPLES   12:30 A.M.   Genesis 7:20–24   Sir:
4:00 P.M.   Ruth 1:16–18   Dear Ms. Davis:

PRACTICE   Colons

Rewrite each item below, correcting any errors in the use of colons and other punctuation.

1. None of these authors won the Nobel Prize for Literature; Leo Tolstoy Mark Twain Virginia Woolf or F Scott Fitzgerald.

2. Dear Sir, or Madam.
3. Some of my favorite animals are these, dogs, cats, horses, pigs, and cows.
4. Genesis 1-1 begins with the following words, "In the beginning . . . "
5. The tools that the nurse laid out for the operation included these. Scalpels, clamps, and sponges.
6. Our dog has the characteristics of a beagle, short hair, floppy ears, a baying voice, a friendly attitude, and a tendency to wander.
7. My ancestors came from: Norway, Ireland, Poland, and Lithuania.
8. Warning: no lifeguard is on duty.
9. My favorite poem begins with the following lines,
   Margaret, are you grieving
   Over Goldengrove unleaving?
10. If you want to start a business you will need: a plan, a budget, and a good product.

11.5 THE SEMICOLON

SEMICOLONS TO SEPARATE MAIN CLAUSES

Use a semicolon to separate main clauses that are not joined by a comma and a coordinating conjunction (*and, but, or, nor, so, yet,* or *for*).

EXAMPLE   Paul Robeson was a talented singer and actor, **and** he was also a famous football player.

EXAMPLE   Paul Robeson was a talented singer and actor; he was also a famous football player.

Use a semicolon to separate main clauses that are joined by a conjunctive adverb (such as *however, therefore, nevertheless, moreover, furthermore,* and *subsequently*) or by an expression such as *for example* or *that is*.

In general, a conjunctive adverb or an expression such as *for example* is followed by a comma.

EXAMPLE Robeson appeared in many plays and musicals**; for example,** he starred in *Othello* and *Porgy and Bess*.

EXAMPLE Robeson appeared in *Show Boat* in 1928**; subsequently,** he acted in the films *Jericho* and *Song of Freedom*.

SEMICOLONS AND COMMAS

Use a semicolon to separate the items in a series when one or more of the items already contain commas.

EXAMPLE Some of the powerful African kingdoms that flourished before the sixteenth century were Kush, which dominated the eastern Sudan; Karanga, which was located around Zimbabwe in southern Africa; Ghana, Mali, and Songhai, which successively controlled the Niger River in West Africa; and Benin, which had its center in what is now Nigeria.

Use a semicolon to separate two main clauses joined by a coordinating conjunction when one or both of the clauses already contain several commas.

EXAMPLE The rule of Mansa Musa, the Moslem emperor of the African kingdom of Mali from 1312 to 1337, is remembered for military success, trade expansion, and Moslem scholarship; but this period is probably most noteworthy as a golden age of peace and prosperity.

Rewrite each item below, correcting any errors in the use of semicolons and other punctuation.

1. The person playing the lead role is Bella, who has a great speaking voice, looks terrific, and does a wonderful job, but the real star of the show is the actor who plays the difficult, moving and hilarious role of Malvolio.

2. None of the many people who were convicted at the notorious Salem witch trials were burned, most were hanged and one was crushed to death.

3. My three nephews are: Malik, who is very dark and rather short, Marion, who is quite tall and has freckles and Tino, who is about average height and has olive skin.

4. Denzel Washington and Julia Roberts starred in *The Pelican Brief,* Washington played an investigative reporter, and Roberts played a woman, who stumbled upon a dangerous secret.

5. I'm getting tired of sitting all the time, moreover I'm really bored by this slide lecture on the development of microbes.

11.6 THE COMMA

As you study the rules for comma usage, keep in mind that to *separate* elements means to place a comma between two equal elements. To *set off* an element means to put a comma before it and a comma after it. Of course, you never place a comma at the beginning or the end of a sentence.

COMMAS IN A SERIES

Use commas to separate three or more words, phrases, or clauses in a series.

EXAMPLE A chair, a table, a lamp, and a sofa were the room's only furnishings.

EXAMPLE The cat ran into the room, across the floor, and up the curtain.

EXAMPLE Skim the section titles, study the picture captions, and make a note of any boldface terms.

Note: The comma before the *and* is called the serial comma. Some authorities do not recommend it. However, many sentences may be confusing without it. We recommend that you always insert the serial comma for clarity.

EXAMPLES **UNCLEAR** Bob, Joe and Tim are ready. [might be telling Bob that two people are ready]

CLEAR Bob, Joe, and Tim are ready. [clearly says that three people are ready]

When all the items in a series are connected by conjunctions, no commas are necessary.

EXAMPLE It was a hot and sunny and humid day in July.

EXAMPLE I want red or black or orange or purple.

Nouns that are used in pairs to express one idea (*thunder and lightning*, *table and chairs*, *bread and butter*) are usually considered single units and should not be separated by commas. If such pairs appear with other nouns or groups of nouns in a series, however, they must be set off from the other items in the series.

EXAMPLE My favorite breakfast is toast, bacon and eggs, and tomato juice.

EXAMPLE Spread out your wet shoes and socks, hat, and jacket on the register.

COMMAS AND COORDINATE ADJECTIVES

Place a comma between coordinate adjectives that precede a noun.

Coordinate adjectives modify a noun equally. To determine whether adjectives are coordinate, try to reverse their order or put the word *and* between them. If the sentence still sounds natural, the adjectives are coordinate.

EXAMPLE   Popeye is a playful, affectionate, intelligent cat.

Don't use a comma between adjectives preceding a noun if the adjectives sound unnatural with their order reversed or with *and* between them. In general, adjectives that describe size, shape, age, and material do not need to be separated by commas.

EXAMPLE   Jelani grew up in a small white frame house.

Commas may be needed between some of the adjectives before a noun and not between others.

EXAMPLE   I like to read in our bright, cozy family room.

In the preceding sentence, *and* would sound natural between *bright* and *cozy*, but it would not sound natural between *cozy* and *family*.

COMMAS AND COMPOUND SENTENCES

Use a comma between the main clauses in a compound sentence.

Place a comma before a coordinating conjunction *(and, but, or, nor, for, so,* or *yet)* that joins two main clauses.

EXAMPLE   I am not going to the concert, **for** I am too busy.

EXAMPLE   Many prospectors searched for years, **but** others found gold at once.

EXAMPLE   Lindy wanted her own guitar, **so** she started saving all of her paper-route income.

Rewrite each item below, correcting any errors in the use of commas and other punctuation.

1. Tom was a triumphant happy jolly man.
2. Joe Kathy and Suzie went to the kitchen to make tuna salad ham and peanut butter and jelly sandwiches.
3. Mrs. Johnson fed her dogs first; then her cats, and then herself.
4. Wyle is a tall, young boy.
5. I went to the bowling alley today; and I'll go shopping tomorrow.

COMMAS AND NONESSENTIAL ELEMENTS

Use commas to set off participles, infinitives, and their phrases if they are not essential to the meaning of the sentence. These nonessential elements are also known as non-restrictive elements.

EXAMPLE She watched, **puzzled,** as the man in the yellow convertible drove away.

EXAMPLE A customer, **complaining loudly,** stepped up to the counter.

EXAMPLE I have no idea, **to be honest,** what you would like for a graduation present.

Frank and Ernest

PERIODICALS

QUESTION MARKICALS AND SEMI-COLONICALS →

THAVES

© 1998 Thaves / Reprinted with permission. Newspaper dist. by NEA, Inc.

Don't set off participles, infinitives, and their phrases if they are essential to the meaning of the sentence. Such essential elements are also known as restrictive elements.

EXAMPLE   The man **standing by the door** is my dad.

EXAMPLE   My mother's car is the one **parked in the driveway.**

EXAMPLE   She went to medical school **to become a doctor.**

EXAMPLE   **To become a doctor** had been her goal for years.

EXAMPLE   I wanted **to go home.**

Use commas to set off a nonessential adjective clause.

A nonessential clause can be considered an extra clause because it gives optional information about a noun. Because it is an extra clause that is not necessary, it is set off by commas.

EXAMPLE   Atlanta**, which is the capital of Georgia,** is the transportation center of the Southeast. [**The adjective clause** *which is the capital of Georgia* **is nonessential.**]

Don't set off an essential adjective clause. Because an essential adjective clause gives necessary information about a noun, it is needed to convey the exact meaning of the sentence.

EXAMPLE   People **who are afraid of heights** don't like to look down from balconies or terraces. [**The adjective clause** *who are afraid of heights* **is essential. It tells which people.**]

EXAMPLE   The paramedics first attended the victims**, who were badly hurt.** [**This clearly states that all the victims were badly hurt.**]

EXAMPLE   The paramedics first attended the victims **who were badly hurt.** [**This clearly states that the paramedics first decided which victims urgently needed help and which victims could wait.**]

Use commas to set off an appositive if it is not
essential to the meaning of a sentence.

A nonessential appositive can be considered interesting
but optional, extra information; it calls for commas.

EXAMPLE   Nelson Mandela, **the president of South Africa,** was
freed from a South African prison in 1990.

EXAMPLE   My mother lives in Escondido, **a town near San Diego.**

A nonessential appositive is sometimes placed before
the noun or pronoun to which it refers.

EXAMPLE   **An insurance executive,** Charles Ives wrote music in
his spare time. **[The appositive,** *an insurance executive,*
precedes the noun it identifies, *Charles Ives.***]**

An essential appositive gives necessary information
about a noun and is not set off with commas.

EXAMPLE   The word *fiesta* came into English from Spanish. **[The
appositive,** *fiesta,* **is needed to identify** *word.***]**

PRACTICE   **Commas and Nonessential Elements**

*Rewrite each item below, correcting any errors in the use
of commas and other punctuation.*

1. The students who understand the lecture, don't often
   have to see the professor during her office hours but
   the other students do.
2. The man, wearing the blue striped shirt, is my Spanish
   teacher; the other is my math teacher.
3. Those pants believe it or not were Jeff's favorite pair.
4. Colette a good friend appeared, to be confused by the
   entire situation.
5. People, who look for the worst in other people, usually
   find it; others try to be more objective.

GRAMMAR/USAGE/MECHANICS

COMMAS WITH INTERJECTIONS, PARENTHETICAL EXPRESSIONS, CONJUNCTIVE ADVERBS, AND ANTITHETICAL PHRASES

Use commas to set off the following:

- interjections (such as *oh, well, alas,* and *good grief*)

- parenthetical expressions (such as *in fact, on the other hand, for example, on the contrary, by the way, to be exact,* and *after all*)

- conjunctive adverbs (such as *however, moreover, therefore,* and *consequently*)

EXAMPLE **Well,** we'd better hit the road.

EXAMPLE **Oh,** I don't know.

EXAMPLE We have to leave, **unfortunately.**

EXAMPLE Last night, **on the other hand,** we could have stayed longer.

EXAMPLE We said we'd be home early; **therefore,** we'd better leave now.

EXAMPLE You might want to come with us, **however.**

Use commas to set off an antithetical phrase.

An **antithetical phrase** uses a word such as *not* or *unlike* to qualify what precedes it.

EXAMPLE You, **not I,** deserve this honor.

EXAMPLE Bicycles, **unlike cars,** produce no pollution.

Rewrite each item below, correcting any errors in the use of commas.

1. Well that's because horses unlike cows have only one stomach.
2. Bessie not Minnie, volunteered to baby-sit for the Jenkins' twins.
3. Cleopatra was a famous queen of Egypt; however most people don't know that she was really Macedonian.
4. Cheese is a favorite of mine, and I really like for example pizza and potatoes *au gratin*.
5. Many sports after all are quite safe; bull riding and hang gliding though can be very dangerous.

COMMAS WITH OTHER ELEMENTS

Set off two or more introductory prepositional phrases or a single long one.

EXAMPLE **On the afternoon of the day of the game,** we made a banner. [three prepositional phrases—*On the afternoon, of the day,* and *of the game*]

EXAMPLE **Because of the rather frightening and extremely unusual circumstances,** the king and his ministers conferred till dawn. [one long prepositional phrase—*Because of the rather frightening and extremely unusual circumstances*]

You need not set off a single short introductory prepositional phrase, but it's not wrong to do so.

GRAMMAR/USAGE/MECHANICS

EXAMPLE In 1789 John Jay became Chief Justice of the Supreme Court of the United States of America. [one short introductory prepositional phrase—*In 1789*]

or

In 1789, John Jay became Chief Justice of the Supreme Court of the United States of America.

Don't use a comma if the introductory prepositional phrase is immediately followed by a verb.

EXAMPLE Over the mantelpiece hung a pair of crossed swords.

EXAMPLE On the stone above the front door of the building was inscribed the date.

Use commas to set off introductory participles and participial phrases.

EXAMPLE **Purring,** the kitten curled up in my lap. [introductory participle]

EXAMPLE **Sitting in a tree,** my little sister called down to us. [introductory participial phrase]

Use commas after all introductory adverbs and adverb clauses.

EXAMPLE **Surprisingly,** no one objected to the new curfew.

EXAMPLE **Hopefully,** Tom and Becky climbed toward the ray of sunlight.

EXAMPLE **Although I like country music,** I did not want to hear his entire collection just then.

EXAMPLE **Until she arrived,** I thought no one else was coming.

Also use commas to set off internal adverb clauses that interrupt the flow of a sentence.

EXAMPLE Evan, **after he had thought about it awhile,** agreed with our conclusion.

In general, don't set off an adverb clause at the end of a sentence unless the clause is parenthetical or the sentence would be misread without the comma.

EXAMPLE Evan agreed with our conclusion after he had thought about it awhile. [no comma needed]

EXAMPLE Those voting against were nine of the twenty councillors, **if you must know.** [parenthetical adverb clause needs comma]

EXAMPLE We were just rehearsing the timing for my scream, **when the bomb exploded.** [comma needed to prevent misreading]

PRACTICE Commas with Other Elements

Rewrite each item below, correcting any errors in the use of commas and other punctuation.

1. You probably won't find the dog's ball, without looking all over the house.
2. Typically Andrew put off doing his work until the last minute.
3. Exhausted James went out with Eddie after they got off work, for a soda.
4. While I enjoy your company I need, a little more time by myself.
5. At the very early age of five Mozart was already composing music.

ADDITIONAL USES OF COMMAS

Use commas to set off a title when it follows a person's name.

EXAMPLE Alicia Wong, **M.D.,** will speak after Jorge Gonzalez, **Ph. D.,** has spoken.

Set off the name of a state or a country when it's used after the name of a city. Set off the name of a city when it's used after a street address. Don't use a comma after the state if it's followed by a ZIP code.

EXAMPLE   Anaheim, California, is the home of Disneyland.

EXAMPLE   Her address is 9 Lee Road, Nome, AK 99762.

In a date, set off the year when it's used with both the month and the day. Don't use a comma if only the month and the year are given.

EXAMPLE   March 17, 2000, was the day I got my driver's license.

EXAMPLE   We moved to Dallas in September 1999.

Use commas to set off the parts of a reference that direct the reader to the exact source.

EXAMPLE   Odysseus becomes reunited with his son, Telemachus, in the *Odyssey*, Book 16, lines 177-219.

Use commas to set off words or names in direct address.

EXAMPLE   **Nathaniel,** do you know where Katie is?

EXAMPLE   I can order the book for you, **sir,** if you like.

Use commas to set off tag questions.

A tag question (such as *shouldn't I?* or *have you?*) suggests an answer to the question that precedes it.

EXAMPLE   You've already seen this movie, **haven't you?**

EXAMPLE   We're not going to be ready on time, **are we?**

Place a comma after the salutation of an informal letter. Place a comma after the closing of all letters. In the inside address, place a comma between the city and state and between the day and year.

EXAMPLE

90 Sherwood Road
New Bedford, MA 02745
July 7, 2000

Dear Dolores,

Very truly yours,

PRACTICE Additional Uses of Commas

Rewrite each item below, correcting any errors in the use of commas and other punctuation.

1. My grandfather was born in Rome Italy in 1943.
2. Sergio Montez Ph.D. is justly proud of himself.
3. Hector what is going on here?
4. Godfrey, is a nice guy don't you think?
5. Dear Grandma
　　　　　　　With hugs and kisses

WRITER'S BLOCK

Chapter 11 Punctuation, Abbreviations, and Numbers **331**

MISUSE OF COMMAS

In general, don't use a comma before a conjunction that connects a compound predicate or compound subject.

EXAMPLES

INCORRECT	She started the car, and drove down the hill. **[compound predicate]**
CORRECT	She started the car and drove down the hill.
INCORRECT	The adults playing softball, and the children playing soccer argued in the field. **[compound subject]**
CORRECT	The adults playing softball and the children playing soccer argued in the field.

Don't use only a comma to join two main clauses unless they are part of a series of clauses. Such a sentence punctuated with a comma alone is called a *run-on sentence* (or a *comma splice* or a *comma fault*). To join two clauses correctly, use a coordinating conjunction with the comma, or use a semicolon.

EXAMPLES

INCORRECT	John Wayne worked in Hollywood for almost fifty years, he made more than 175 films.
CORRECT	John Wayne worked in Hollywood for almost fifty years, **and** he made more than 175 films.
CORRECT	John Wayne worked in Hollywood for almost fifty years; he made more than 175 films.

Don't use a comma between a subject and its verb or between a verb and its complement.

EXAMPLES

INCORRECT	What you do, is your business.
CORRECT	What you do is your business.
INCORRECT	You will need, a sleeping bag, a towel, soap, and a toothbrush.

| CORRECT | You will need a sleeping bag, a towel, soap, and a toothbrush. |

PRACTICE Misuse of Commas

Rewrite each item below, correcting any errors in the use of commas and other punctuation.

1. The dogs in the house, and the cats in the yard, all started yowling at once.
2. Mohandas Gandhi developed a philosophy of passive resistance, and non-cooperation, it has since been adopted by freedom movements all over the world.
3. The track team members all ran sprints, and then did stretches.
4. I went to the store, and bought a six-pack of soda and a half-gallon of milk.
5. Janice, and Juan arrived by supper time, Frances wasn't with them.

PRACTICE Commas

Rewrite each item below, correcting any errors in the use of commas and other punctuation.

1. Say your dad turned twenty-one on August 28 1979 didn't he?
2. Donald told me that he saw these three movies last week: *Dances with Wolves She Wore a Yellow Ribbon* and *The Patriot*.
3. Floundering, in the surf Alfonso yelled "Help I can't swim and I have a cramp in my left foot."
4. Luke can be a smart funny exciting person but his brother is endlessly dull.
5. With a great deal of dread I went to the poetry slam with Max; however it was very entertaining.

6. The almonds salty and crunchy are very good, the walnuts on the other hand, taste terrible
7. Raul has a big, red, bike.
8. Van Gogh was never paid much for his art, in fact he sold only one painting, while he was alive.
9. Grant Hill the basketball star played, for the Detroit Pistons and for Duke University's Blue Devils.
10. I watched the ball game, Pat who is my good friend watched it with me.

11.7 THE DASH

On a typewriter, indicate the dash with two hyphens (--). If you are using a computer, you may make a dash with a certain combination of keystrokes. Refer to the manual of your word-processing program for instructions.

Don't place a comma, a semicolon, a colon, or a period before or after a dash.

DASHES TO SIGNAL CHANGE

Use a dash to indicate an abrupt break or change in thought within a sentence.

EXAMPLE

A small stand sells sugar loaves—the gift to bring when invited to dinner—sugar for the mint tea and for the sweet pastry, so flaky and light, that they bake.

—Anaïs Nin

DASHES TO EMPHASIZE

Use a dash to set off and emphasize extra information or parenthetical comments.

EXAMPLE It was a shiny new car—the first he had ever owned.

EXAMPLE A shiny new car—the first he had ever owned—sat in the driveway.

Don't overuse dashes in your writing. Dashes are most often found in informal or personal letters. In formal writing situations, use subordinating conjunctions (such as *after, until, because,* and *unless*) or conjunctive adverbs (such as *however, nonetheless,* and *furthermore*), along with the correct punctuation, to show the relationships between ideas.

PRACTICE Dashes

Rewrite each item, correcting errors in the use of the dash and other punctuation.

1. Photographers whether amateur—or professional—need to consider the effects of shadows.
2. What we all found so interesting was the Australian wildlife,—kangaroos wallabies, and platypuses.
3. The vines thick and covered—with orange blossoms—, surrounded all the windows of the house.
4. Michael looked up—and saw stars, billions of them in the night sky.
5. Brian—the boy—with the black curly hair is the best player on the team.

11.8 PARENTHESES

PARENTHESES TO SET OFF SUPPLEMENTAL MATERIAL

Use parentheses to set off supplemental, or extra, material.

Commas and dashes as well as parentheses can be used to set off supplemental material; the difference between the three marks of punctuation is one of degree. Use commas to set off supplemental material that is closely related to the rest of the sentence. Use parentheses to set off supplemental material that is not important enough to be considered part of the main statement. Use dashes to set off and emphasize any material that interrupts the main statement.

EXAMPLE Many contemporary women's fashions (business suits and low heels) show the influence of Gabrielle "Coco" Chanel.

A complete sentence within parentheses is not capitalized and needs no period if it is contained within another sentence. If a sentence within parentheses is not contained within another sentence—that is, if it stands by itself—both a capital letter and end punctuation are needed.

EXAMPLE The unisex trend (it still seems to be popular) was started by Chanel, who often wore a man's trench coat.

EXAMPLE Chanel introduced the world's most famous perfume, Chanel No. 5. (This scent is still in great demand.)

PARENTHESES WITH OTHER MARKS OF PUNCTUATION

Place a comma, a semicolon, or a colon *after* the closing parentheses.

EXAMPLE Despite the simple clothes that Chanel designed and wore (the little black dress became her uniform), she became wealthy.

EXAMPLE In the early 1950s, women wore high heels and long skirts with cinched waists (the Dior look); Chanel helped change that.

Place a question mark or an exclamation point *inside* the parentheses if it is part of the parenthetical expression.

EXAMPLE   Chanel believed that simplicity and practicality were more important than obviously expensive, complicated-looking clothes (who would not agree today?).

EXAMPLE   Chanel exerted only a little influence on fashion during World War II (1939–1945), but she reopened her fashion house in 1954 (when she was seventy!).

Place a period, a question mark, or an exclamation point *outside* the parentheses if it is part of the entire sentence.

EXAMPLE   Did you know that Chanel introduced many of today's fashion classics (sweaters, costume jewelry, sling-back shoes)?

EXAMPLE   How astounded I was to find out it was Chanel who made suntans fashionable (in the 1930s)!

PRACTICE   Parentheses

Rewrite each item, correcting errors in the use of parentheses, other punctuation, and capitalization.

1. Abe Lincoln (Not the one you're thinking of) fixed my computer for me.
2. I can see why people might not understand cats, for example, but I'd think that everyone would understand children (for hasn't everyone been one)?
3. Gwendolyn Brooks (who is my favorite poet,) won the Pulitzer Prize for poetry in 1950.

4. The name Gemma (It is a female form of the name James.) has become more popular in the last ten years, but it isn't among the most popular names.

5. Sinead O'Connor, the Irish singer, is still a controversial pop star, (she is the performer who used to shave her head.)

11.9 QUOTATION MARKS

QUOTATION MARKS WITH DIRECT QUOTATIONS

Use quotation marks to enclose a direct quotation.

Place quotation marks around the quotation only, not around purely introductory or explanatory remarks. Generally separate such remarks from the actual quotation with a comma. (For the use of colons to introduce quotations, see page 317.)

EXAMPLE A famous poster asks, "What if they gave a war and nobody came?"

EXAMPLE A Pawnee poem reminds us of "the sacredness of things."

Don't use a comma after a quotation that ends with an exclamation point or a question mark.

EXAMPLE "What is the question?" Gertrude Stein asked.

When a quotation is interrupted by explanatory words such as *he said* or *she wrote*, use two sets of quotation marks.

Separate each part of the quotation from the interrupting phrase with marks of punctuation before and after the phrase. If the second part of the quotation is a complete sentence, begin it with a capital letter and use a period, not a comma, after the interrupting phrase.

EXAMPLE "A thing of beauty," wrote John Keats, "is a joy forever."

EXAMPLE "It wasn't just that he [Babe Ruth] hit more home runs than anybody else," said Red Smith. "He hit them better, higher, farther. . . ."

Do not use quotation marks in an indirect quotation.

EXAMPLE **ORIGINAL QUOTATION** "Dance is life at its most glorious moment," said Pearl Lang.

INDIRECT QUOTATION Pearl Lang has said that dance is life at its most glorious moment.

Use single quotation marks around a quotation within a quotation.

EXAMPLE President John F. Kennedy said, "I am one person who can truthfully say, 'I got my job through the *New York Times*.'"

In writing dialogue, begin a new paragraph and use a new set of quotation marks every time the speaker changes.

EXAMPLE He looked at me proudly. "Was it so hard to do, Daughter?"

"Not so hard as I thought." I pinned the brooch on my dress. "I'll wear it always," I said. "I'll keep it forever."
—Kathryn Forbes

QUOTATION MARKS WITH OTHER MARKS OF PUNCTUATION

Always place a comma or a period *inside* closing quotation marks.

EXAMPLE "The frog does not drink up the pond in which it lives," states a Native American proverb.

EXAMPLE Henry David Thoreau humorously advises, "Beware of all enterprises that require new clothes."

Always place a semicolon or a colon *outside* closing quotation marks.

EXAMPLE Her father said, "We cannot go"; her mother said, "Perhaps we can go next summer"; her elder brother just shrugged.

EXAMPLE This is what I think of Lady Ōtomo's poem "My Heart, Thinking": it is romantic and powerful.

Place the question mark or the exclamation point *inside* the closing quotation marks when it is part of the quotation.

EXAMPLE A famous sonnet by Shakespeare begins with these words: "Shall I compare thee to a summer's day?"

EXAMPLE She cried, "I never want to see you again!"

Place the question mark or the exclamation point *outside* the closing quotation marks when it is part of the entire sentence.

EXAMPLE I've finally memorized all of "Paul Revere's Ride"!

EXAMPLE Why do you keep saying, "I'm sorry"?

If both the sentence and the quotation at the end of the sentence need a question mark (or an exclamation point), use only one punctuation mark, and place it *inside* the closing quotation marks.

EXAMPLE When did he ask, "Why do you want to know?"

EXAMPLE What a surprise it was to hear them shout, "Yahoo!"

Don't use a comma after a quotation that ends with a question mark or an exclamation point.

EXAMPLE "That's incredible!" my father said yet again.

QUOTATION MARKS WITH TITLES, UNUSUAL EXPRESSIONS, AND DEFINITIONS

Use quotation marks to enclose titles of short works, such as short stories, short poems, essays, newspaper articles, magazine articles, book chapters, songs, and single episodes of a television series.

EXAMPLES

"The Legend of Sleepy Hollow" [short story]

"The Raven" [short poem]

"On the Duty of Civil Disobedience" [essay]

"Steven Spielberg's Newest Film" [newspaper article]

"The 1990s in Mexico" [book chapter]

"If I Had a Hammer" [song]

"Division of the Spoils" [episode in a television series]

(For the use of italics with longer titles, see page 343.)

Use quotation marks to enclose unfamiliar slang and other unusual or original expressions.

EXAMPLE My cousin uses the expression "the cat's meow" to describe things she likes.

EXAMPLE The 1920s were known as the "Roaring Twenties."

Be careful not to overuse quotation marks with unusual expressions. Generally, use quotation marks only the first time you use the unusual expression in a piece of writing.

Use quotation marks to enclose a definition that is stated directly.

EXAMPLE   The German noun *Weltanschauung* means "world view" or "philosophy of life."

EXAMPLE   In Japanese the word *ikebana* means "living flowers"; ikebana is the art of arranging cut flowers with other natural objects.

PRACTICE   Quotation Marks

Rewrite each item, correcting errors in the use of quotation marks and other punctuation.

1. "How did your family come to this country"? asked the interviewer.
2. Tecumseh, a Shawnee leader who opposed selling land, is famous for these words: Sell a country! Why not sell the air, the great sea, as well as the earth?
3. In the language of the Sioux, the word *dah-kota* means alliance of friends.
4. The word *revive* comes from the Latin *viv,* meaning live, and the prefix *re-,* meaning again.
5. "Look out"! Holly yelled "The UFO has landed! Run for your lives"!
6. Have you read Poe's story "The Pit and the Pendulum?"
7. Alberto told me that the song Blue Suede Shoes by Elvis Presley was "totally rad."
8. Marilyn said fiercely to the group, "Get out of our way;" I simply glared.
9. I told her, "If you'd stop calling that dog "Patsy's little puppsie-wuppsie", maybe people would stop laughing."

10. Did Dale really utter the words "What makes you think it's up to you?"?

11.10 ITALICS (UNDERLINING)

Italic type is a special slanted type that is used in printing. *(This sentence is printed in italics.)* Indicate italics on a typewriter or with handwriting by underlining. (<u>This sentence is underlined</u>.) When you are using a computer, learn the special keystrokes for italics by referring to your software manual.

ITALICS WITH TITLES

Italicize (underline) the following: titles of books, long poems, plays, films, television series, paintings, sculptures, and long musical compositions. Also italicize (underline) the names of newspapers, magazines, ships, airplanes, and spacecraft.

A "long poem" or a "long musical composition" is any poem or musical composition published under its own title as a separate work.

EXAMPLES

Great Expectations [book]

Snow-Bound [long poem]

Romeo and Juliet [play]

Gone with the Wind [film]

Nova [television series]

Starry Night [painting]

The Thinker [sculpture]

Grand Canyon Suite [musical work]

the *Oakland Tribune* [newspaper]

Sports Illustrated [magazine]

USS *Enterprise** [ship]

Spirit of St. Louis [airplane]

Columbia [spacecraft]

*Don't italicize abbreviations such as USS in the name of a ship.

Italicize (underline) and capitalize articles (*a, an, the*) written at the beginning of a title only when they are a part of the title itself. It is common practice not to italicize (underline) the article preceding the title of a newspaper or a magazine. Do not italicize the word *magazine* unless it is a part of the title of a periodical.

EXAMPLES   *The Red Badge of Courage*
             A Light in the Attic

                        but

             a *National Geographic* magazine
             the *Chicago Tribune*

ITALICS WITH FOREIGN WORDS

Italicize (underline) foreign words and expressions that are not used frequently in English.

EXAMPLE   The motto of the U.S. Marine Corps is ***semper fidelis*** ("always faithful").

Don't italicize (underline) a foreign word or expression that is commonly used in English. Consult a dictionary; if a foreign word or expression is a dictionary entry word, don't italicize (underline) it.

EXAMPLE   I had **croissants** for breakfast.

ITALICS WITH WORDS AND OTHER ITEMS USED TO REPRESENT THEMSELVES

Italicize (underline) words, letters, and numerals used to represent themselves—that is, words used as words, letters used as letters, and numerals used as numerals.

For instance, if you were to say, "Don't start a sentence with *and*," you would pronounce the *and* in that sentence much differently than the *and* in the phrase "oranges and lemons." Your voice would make it clear that *and* was being used to represent itself. When you are writing, you don't have your voice to help, so you can use italic type to indicate a word that is being used as a word.

EXAMPLE Do not start a sentence with ***and*** or ***but.***

EXAMPLE Replace all the number signs (#s) with the word ***number.***

EXAMPLE In your report about Robert Finnegan, you have spelled his last name with an extra ***n.***

PRACTICE Italics (Underlining)

Rewrite each item, correcting errors in the use of italics (underlining) and other punctuation.

1. He pointed to the *hors d'oeuvres* and told me the *fromage* was good; I didn't realize he meant the cheese.
2. Jan subscribes to the magazine "Discover."
3. Rebecca read the first ten pages of the poem "Beowulf."
4. If you start a sentence with "however," the word should be followed by a comma.
5. The hyacinth's scientific name, "Hyacinthus orientalis," comes from Latin, as do other flowers' scientific names.

"Why is it that every time I say something in quotation marks you respond in italics?"

11.11 THE APOSTROPHE

APOSTROPHES TO SHOW POSSESSION

Use an apostrophe and –s for the possessive form of a singular indefinite pronoun.

Do not use an apostrophe with other possessive pronouns.

EXAMPLES

everybody's problem	*but*	**its** owner
each other's parents		**whose** talents
one's record		The bikes are **theirs.**
		The prize is **yours.**
		The plan is **ours.**

Use an apostrophe and –s to form the possessive of a singular noun, even one that ends in s.

EXAMPLES

the woman's briefcase   San Francisco's earthquake
the class's election   Robert Burns's poetry

There are some exceptions to this rule, however. To form the possessive of ancient proper nouns that end in *es* or *is*, the name *Jesus*, and expressions with words that end in an "*s*" sound, such as *conscience* and *appearance*, just add an apostrophe.

EXAMPLES

Isis' temple   Jesus' teachings
Moses' brother   for appearance' sake
Euripides' plays   his conscience' prodding

Use an apostrophe alone to form the possessive of a plural noun that ends in s.

EXAMPLES

the two countries' treaty   the Joneses' picnic
the trees' leaves   the Greens' barbecue

Use an apostrophe and –s to form the possessive of a plural noun that does not end in s.

EXAMPLES

women's clubs   children's videos
Women's Bar Association   oxen's harness
men's course   mice's tunnels

Put only the last word of a compound noun in the possessive form.

EXAMPLES

my sister-in-law's office   an attorney general's job
the court-martial's officers   the chief of staff's order

If two or more persons (or partners in a company) possess something jointly, use the possessive form for the last person named.

EXAMPLES

Barbara and Andy's children
Johnson and Johnson's baby-care products
Abbott and Costello's routines

If two or more persons (or companies) possess an item (or items) individually, put each one's name in the possessive form.

EXAMPLES

Tina Turner's and the Rolling Stones' songs
Chrysler's and the American Motor Company's cars

Use a possessive form to express amounts of money or time that modify a noun.

The modifier can also be expressed as a hyphenated adjective. In that case, no possessive form is used.

EXAMPLES one dollar's increase   *but*   a one-dollar increase

five minutes' drive   a five-minute drive

ten days' wait   a ten-day wait

APOSTROPHES IN CONTRACTIONS

Use an apostrophe in place of letters that are omitted in contractions.

A **contraction** is a single word made up of two words that have been combined by omitting letters. Common contractions combine a subject and a verb or a verb and the word *not*.

EXAMPLES you'd   *is formed from*   you had, you would

you're   you are

who's   who is, who has

it's   it is, it has

won't   will not

I'm   I am

doesn't   does not

Use an apostrophe in place of the omitted numerals of a year.

EXAMPLES the class of '99   the '96 presidential campaign

Rewrite each item, correcting errors in the use of the apostrophe and other punctuation.

1. Isnt it sad that the rain ruined the tulips in Jeffs' garden?
2. I visited both of Massachusetts' senator's offices.
3. Alexis' birthday is in late October, which means my birthday comes before her's.
4. The childrens' choir performed at the womens' request.
5. Gilbert's and Sullivan's operettas are performed by school's drama clubs and by professional companies.
6. Gabriels' computer game's were harder than Franks'.
7. If Id known that everyones friends were welcome, youd have been invited.
8. William Shakespeare and Eugene O'Neill's plays are widely performed.
9. My only nieces cousin's are twins who were born in 98.
10. After two hour's delay, my brother's-in-law's car was finally repaired.

11.12 THE HYPHEN

HYPHENS WITH PREFIXES

A hyphen is not ordinarily used to join a prefix to a word. There are a few exceptions, however. If you are in doubt about using a hyphen, consult a dictionary. Also keep in mind the following guidelines:

Use a hyphen after any prefix joined to a proper noun or a proper adjective. Use a hyphen after the prefixes *all-, ex-* (meaning "former"), and *self-* joined to any noun or adjective.

EXAMPLES

mid-Atlantic	post-Elizabethan
pre-Renaissance	all-city
trans-Pacific	ex-coach
all-American	self-confidence

Use a hyphen after the prefix *anti-* when it joins a word beginning with *i*. Also use a hyphen after the prefix *vice-*, except in *vice president*.

EXAMPLES

anti-icing
vice-mayor
but vice president

Use a hyphen to avoid confusion between words beginning with *re-* that look alike but are different in meaning and pronunciation.

EXAMPLES re-cover the couch
re-store the supplies
re-lease the apartment

but

recover the ball at the ten-yard line
restore one's confidence
release the brake

HYPHENS WITH COMPOUNDS AND NUMBERS

Use a hyphen in a compound adjective that precedes a noun.

In general, a compound adjective that follows a noun is not hyphenated.

EXAMPLES

dark-green eyes	*but*	Her eyes are dark green.
a fifteen-year-old aunt		Her aunt is fifteen years old.
a well-liked reporter		That reporter is well liked.

Don't hyphenate an expression made up of an adverb that ends in *–ly* and an adjective.

EXAMPLES   a nicely behaved dog   a fairly close race
a slightly rusted exterior   a hastily written report

Hyphenate any spelled-out cardinal number (such as *twenty-one*) or ordinal number (such as *twenty-first*) up to *ninety-nine* or *ninety-ninth*.

EXAMPLES   sixty-four   **Sixty-four** tickets were sold.

sixty-fourth   I was the **sixty-fourth** person to buy a ticket.

eighty-two   There were **eighty-two** in the marching band.

eighty-second   This is the **eighty-second** year of the annual parade.

Hyphenate a fraction that is expressed in words.

EXAMPLE   one-eighth teaspoon

EXAMPLE   one-quarter cup

EXAMPLE   one-half of a pound

Hyphenate two numerals to indicate a span.

EXAMPLE   pages 30–56

EXAMPLE   1986–1996

When you use the word *from* before a span, use *to* rather than a hyphen. When you use *between* before a span, use *and* rather than a hyphen.

EXAMPLE   **from** 1986 **to** 1996

EXAMPLE   **between** 2:00 **and** 3:30 P.M.

HYPHENS TO DIVIDE WORDS AT THE END OF A LINE

Words are generally divided between syllables or pronounceable parts. Because it is often difficult to decide where a word should be divided, consult a dictionary.

In general, if a word contains two consonants occurring between two vowels or if it contains double consonants, divide the word between the two consonants.

EXAMPLES	mar-gin	sup-per
	lin-ger	tomor-row
	profes-sor	

If a suffix has been added to a complete word that ends in two consonants, divide the word after the two consonants. Remember, the object is to make the hyphenated word easy to read and understand.

EXAMPLES	pull-ing	spelunk-er
	harsh-ness	strong-est

PRACTICE Hyphens

Rewrite each item, correcting errors in the use of hyphens and other punctuation. Then make a list of all the italicized words, showing where each would be divided if it had to be broken at the end of a line.

1. The recipe on page eighty four of my *cookbook* calls for one half of a teaspoon of salt and one quarter of a teaspoon of nutmeg.

2. Do you see the *handsome* man with the light brown hair over there? He is a selfemployed artist who paints in a flashy lively postmodern style.

3. I want to research the basement because my exfriend *distracted* me, when I searched the first time.

4. Tomorrow's test on the history of the TransSiberian Railroad will cover pages 67 110 in the text.

5. Ida B. Wells was a wellrespected activist and *journalist,* who was active in the antilynching *movement.*

11.13 ABBREVIATIONS

Abbreviations are shortened forms of words.

Abbreviations save space and time and prevent unnecessary wordiness. For instance, *M.D.* is more concise and easier to write than *Medical Doctor.* Most abbreviations have periods. If you are unsure of how to write an abbreviation, consult a dictionary.

Use only one period, not two, if an abbreviation that has a period occurs at the end of a sentence that would ordinarily take a period of its own.

If an abbreviation that has a period occurs at the end of a sentence that ends with a question mark or an exclamation point, use the abbreviation's period *and* the question mark or the exclamation point.

EXAMPLE   Gerry left at 8:00 A.M.

EXAMPLE   Did she really leave at 8:00 A.M.?

CAPITALIZING ABBREVIATIONS

Capitalize abbreviations of proper nouns.

EXAMPLES   37688 Lancaster **Blvd.**   **Rev.** Oral Roberts
            N. Michigan **Ave.**   **U.S.** Congress

Abbreviations of organizations and government agencies are often formed from the initial letters of the complete name. Such abbreviations, whether pronounced letter by letter or as words, don't have periods and are written with capital letters. Exceptions are *U.S.*, *U.S.A.*, and *Washington, D.C.*, which do have periods.

EXAMPLES　**YWCA**　**NAACP**　**IRS**　**CBS**　**NASA**　**UNICEF**

When abbreviating a person's first and middle names, leave a space after each initial.

EXAMPLES　**E. B.** White　　**A. E.** Housman　　**J.** Alfred Prufrock

Capitalize the following abbreviations related to dates and times.

A.D. (*anno Domini*, "in the year of the Lord" [since the birth of Christ]); place before the date: A.D. 5

B.C. (before Christ); place after the date: 1000 B.C.

B.C.E. (before the common era, equivalent to *B.C.*); place after the date: 164 B.C.E.

C.E. (common era; equivalent to *A.D.*); place after the date: 66 C.E.

A.M. (*ante meridiem*, "before noon"); place after exact times: 7:45 A.M.

P.M. (*post meridiem*, "after noon"); place after exact times: 2:30 P.M.

POSTAL ABBREVIATIONS

In ordinary prose, spell out state names. On envelopes, however, abbreviate state names using the two-letter abbreviations approved by the U.S. Postal Service.

A complete list of these abbreviations can be found in the Ready Reference section on pages 86–87.

EXAMPLES　Alaska　　**AK**
　　　　　　Hawaii　　**HI**
　　　　　　Maine　　　**ME**
　　　　　　Texas　　　**TX**

The postal abbreviation for the District of Columbia, for use on envelopes only, is **DC**. In ordinary prose, however, use periods to write **Washington, D.C.**

EXAMPLE We moved from **Washington, D.C.,** to Baltimore.

ABBREVIATIONS OF TITLES AND UNITS OF MEASURE

Use abbreviations for some personal titles.

Titles such as *Mrs., Mr., Ms., Sr.,* and *Jr.* and those indicating professions and academic degrees *(Dr., Ph.D., M.A., B.S.)* are almost always abbreviated. Titles of government and military officials and members of the clergy are frequently abbreviated when used before a full name.

EXAMPLES **Mrs.** Roosevelt   **Sen.** Jesse Helms
           Harry Connick **Jr.**   **Gen.** Robert E. Lee
           Rosalyn Ying, **Ph.D.**   Myron Greene, **D.D.S.**

Abbreviate units of measure used with numerals in technical or scientific writing. Don't abbreviate them in ordinary prose.

The abbreviations that follow stand for both singular and plural units. Notice that the first list of abbreviations uses periods but the second does not.

EXAMPLES

U.S. SYSTEM		METRIC SYSTEM	
ft.	foot	cg	centigram
gal.	gallon	cl	centiliter
in.	inch	cm	centimeter
lb.	pound	g	gram
mi.	mile	kg	kilogram
oz.	ounce	km	kilometer
pt.	pint	l	liter
qt.	quart	m	meter
tbsp.	tablespoon	mg	milligram
tsp.	teaspoon	ml	milliliter
yd.	yard	mm	millimeter

Rewrite each item, correcting errors in the use of abbreviations and punctuation.

1. I just sent a letter to my dentist, addressed as follows:
   GB Shaw DDS
   45 Englewood Rd
   Brewer, Va 22140
2. Ancient Egypt's decline began around 1070 bc; it was later conquered by Alexander the Great, then Rome; in 642 ad, it was conquered by Muslims from Arabia.
3. I live in Washington DC, but I was born in Juneau, AK.
4. The Norman Conquest occurred in 1066 A.D.
5. My aunt got a PhD, so now we call her Dr Omachi.
6. The label on the box reads as follows:
   Octoglomerate Airlines
   800 Richmond Ave
   Houston, Tx 77042
7. After her operation, Marissa was given 40 mg of morphine to help ease the pain.
8. When I doubled the recipe, I ended up needing three tsp of vanilla, so I just measured out one tbsp instead.
9. Every day, my friend goes to the gym at 320 n. Oak at 5:15 a.m..
10. Ivy takes swimming classes at the Y.M.C.A.

For more information on abbreviations, see pages 82–89 in the Ready Reference.

11.14 NUMBERS AND NUMERALS

In nontechnical writing, some numbers are spelled out, and some are expressed in figures. Numbers expressed in figures are called *numerals*.

NUMBERS SPELLED OUT

In general, spell out cardinal numbers (such as *twenty*) and ordinal numbers (such as *twentieth*) that can be written in one or two words.

EXAMPLE New Hampshire is one of the original **thirteen** colonies.

EXAMPLE There are **fifteen hundred** students in the school.

EXAMPLE Alaska was the **forty-ninth** state to join the Union.

Spell out any number that occurs at the beginning of a sentence. (Sometimes, it is better to revise the sentence to move the spelled-out number.)

EXAMPLE **Sixteen hundred seventy** delegates attended the conference.

BETTER The conference was attended by 1,670 delegates.

NUMERALS

In general, use numerals to express numbers that would be written in more than two words.

EXAMPLE Mount Mitchell, the highest mountain in the eastern United States, is **6,684** feet high.

EXAMPLE In 1790 the total population of the United States (according to the first census) was **3,929,214.**

EXAMPLE In 1984 Joe W. Kittinger covered **3,535** miles in eighty-three hours and fifty-three minutes, setting a new record for balloon flight.

Very large numbers are often written as a numeral followed by the word *million* or *billion*.

EXAMPLE The surface area of the earth is close to **197 million** square miles.

If related numbers appear in the same sentence and some can be written out while others should appear as numerals, use all numerals.

EXAMPLE Edgar ranked **5th** in the class; his brother ranked **119th.**

EXAMPLE They ordered **38** dollhouses and **112** toy robots.

Use numerals to express amounts of money, decimals, and percentages. Spell out the word *percent*, however.

EXAMPLES **$897** million   **1.2** kilograms   **5** percent

Amounts of money that can be expressed in one or two words, however, should be spelled out.

EXAMPLE **forty-five** cents   a **thousand** dollars

Use numerals to express the year and day in a date and to express the precise time with the abbreviations A.M. and P.M.

EXAMPLE The USSR launched *Sputnik I* on October **4, 1957.**

EXAMPLE She reached the doctor's office at **4:15 P.M.**

Spell out expressions of time that do not use A.M. or P.M.

EXAMPLE She set her alarm clock for **five** o'clock.

To express a century when the word *century* is used, spell out the number. Likewise, to express a decade when the century is clear from the context, spell out the number.

EXAMPLE The **twentieth** century saw great technological advances.

EXAMPLE The Great Depression of the **thirties** was an economic crisis.

When a decade is identified by its century, use numerals followed by an –s.

EXAMPLES   **1980s**   the **1940s** and **1950s**

Use numerals for numbered streets and avenues above ninety-nine and for all house, apartment, and room numbers. Spell out numbered streets and avenues of ninety-nine and below.

EXAMPLE   **1654** West **347th** Street

EXAMPLE   **4** North **Ninety-ninth** Street

EXAMPLE   Apartment **8C**

EXAMPLE   **20 Second** Avenue

PRACTICE   Numbers and Numerals

Rewrite each item, correcting errors in the use of numbers, numerals, and punctuation.

1. Marian Anderson sang at the Lincoln Memorial for seventy-five thousand people in nineteen thirty-nine.
2. Singer Etta James was in her church choir at the age of 5, and only nine years later she was a member of a rhythm and blues band.
3. There is a well-known publishing company at 175 5th Avenue in New York City.
4. The Great Wall stretches nearly 4000 miles across northern China.
5. Information about the French Riviera can be found on pages eight and 135 in the travel book on the shelf.
6. 10,000 people attended the concert.
7. The Queen of Sheba was the ruler of Yemen during the 10th century B.C.
8. The sun contains 99.8 % of the mass in the solar system.

Chapter 11 Punctuation, Abbreviations, and Numbers **359**

9. I was ranked fourth among the tournament's debaters while Andrea was 3rd.

10. The American Civil War ended in eighteen sixty-five.

PRACTICE   **Proofreading**

Rewrite the following passage, correcting errors in spelling, capitalization, grammar, and usage. Add any missing punctuation. Write legibly to be sure one letter is not mistaken for another. There are ten mistakes.

Before Jackie Robinson

[1]The history of african Americans and the game of baseball is a fascinating one. [2]In baseballs early years, some teams were integrated. [3]Even while the Civil War was raging Union army soldiers organized games of baseball. [4]At the time, a newspaper reported that "black players were much sought after as teammates because of their skills as ball handlers."

[5]Regrettably, by the late eighteen sixties, American baseball leagues began banning black teams and players. [6]In 1896 the last African American a man named Bert Jones was forced off of an integrated baseball team. [7]This did not mean however that African Americans stopped playing baseball. [8]Black Americans "formed barnstorming" teams, which traveled all over the country playing each other. [9]Finally, in 1920, the Negro Leagues were formed. [10]The year 1945 marked the end of an era; Jackie Robinson was signed to play with the previously allwhite Brooklyn Dodgers. [11]For more information about the Negro Leagues, read the book "The Story of the Negro Baseball Leagues," by Patricia and Frederick McKissack.

POSTTEST   **Punctuation**

Rewrite each sentence, correcting any errors in punctuation.

1. Tom run and get the doctor quickly

2. He may actually be in his nineties on the other hand he may just look old.

3. Hurry Renaldo is having a heart attack

4. My grandmother, who thinks that opera is the bee's knees said "How can you not respond to the beauty of such operas as Figaro or Aida"?

5. In his book of sayings, the Analects, Chinese philosopher Confucius wrote these words, "Have no friends not equal to yourself".

6. Beware: toxic chemicals may be present.

7. Heather went to Scotland, she wanted to visit relatives.

8. Joshua Johnston who was the first artist of African descent to gain fame as a portrait painter painted in the early 1800s.

9. I have lived in: Atlanta, which is in the South, Washington D.C., which is on the East Coast, and Santa Cruz, which is in California.

10. Watermelons; oranges; lemons; and spinach are all high in vitamin C.

11. An eager intelligent student makes a motivated teachers job easier.

12. Mikayla likes eggs not pancakes for breakfast, and insists on eating before seven o'clock.

13. Snoring loudly he slept like a log but I was up late watching Lerner's and Loewe's musical "My Fair Lady."

14. The adult lion—muscles rippling under her tawny hide approached the jeep—her eager hungry cubs waited impatiently in the distance watching carefully.

15. The orchid one of (the world's most beautiful flowers), is not often found in the wild these days unfortunately.

16. Whenever my father walked to the store hed ask my little sister and me to go with him.

17. "Run as fast as you can, he would say to my four year old sister and me, and I will time you to the end of the block".

18. My mother who is Lebanese, frequently uses the word "yulla," which means hurry.

19. I need to write an essay, that compares preRevolutionary and postRevolutionary economic conditions.

20. Tanya a film student loved the documentary *"The Civil War"* but she was disappointed that the show did'nt give more time to womens' work during the war.

POSTTEST **Abbreviations and Numbers**

Rewrite each item, correcting any errors in the use of abbreviations and numbers.

21. Are there 10 cm. in an in., or am I mixed up?

22. The Zhou Dynasty ruled China from around bc 1122 to bc 221, a period of more than 800 years.

23. The Industrial Revolution began in the 19th century.

24. A tithe is a donation of ten % of one's income.

25. I went to the D.M.V. to get my license, but the office closed at 500 p.m. on the dot.

26. The Neuman's used to live on One hundred and twenty-third street in Chicago, IL.

27. Did an ice cream cone ever cost only 5 cents?

28. A very good dentist in our neighborhood is Yuang Chow DDS.

29. Gen Ulysses S Grant served in the Civil War and then became a US president.

30. I feel warm only when it's seventy degrees or more outside.

Chapter 12

Sentence Combining

● ● ● ● ● ● ● ● ● ● ● ● ● ● ●

PRETEST   **Sentence Combining**

Read each group of sentences below. Combine the sentences in the way that seems best to you.

1. The sun set early in the evening. It was orange. It was glowing.
2. The swimmer jumped into the lake. It was cold. The swimmer jumped in quickly.
3. The asteroid fell toward Earth. It was a rock. It was fiery.
4. The lake shimmered in the distance. It reflected the sun.
5. I have no lunch. I do have a good snack.
6. Porpoises live underwater. They come to the surface to breathe.
7. Don and Terry Carter wanted to honor their favorite baseball player. They named their son Willie Mays Carter.

8. The actor learned his lines. They were Shakespearean.

9. The sun shone through the curtains. They were lace.

10. Eloise is a ballroom dancer. She dances the tango with grace. She dances it with drama.

11. George Custer received the temporary rank of general in his twenties. He graduated last in his class at West Point.

12. I will paint the walls pink. I will paint the ceiling white.

13. The large book fell with a loud thud. It was a world atlas.

14. Where is my hat? I wear it in the rain.

15. Edmund Gwenn played Santa Claus in *Miracle on 34th Street*. He won an Oscar for best supporting actor.

16. The runner slipped on the path. Wet leaves covered the path. The runner sprained his ankle.

17. My friend paints murals. She paints them for stores and schools. The murals are full of bright colors.

18. Many consider *Citizen Kane* the greatest movie of all time. It did not win the Oscar for best picture.

19. Jill read a short story. She completed a math assignment. She then went to bed.

20. The bird called a swift can fly at speeds of one hundred miles per hour. Therefore, it has the perfect name.

12.1 TIPS FOR SENTENCE COMBINING

A distinctive writing style is one way of communicating your personality. Developing a clear, expressive writing style requires practice, of course. By writing regularly in your journal and by trying out different kinds of writing—poems, essays, stories, letters to the editor—you practice a range of skills. Another excellent approach for developing style is sentence combining.

The process of combining short sentences into more complex ones is the focus of this chapter. Your goal, though, is not to make long sentences, but to make good ones. Sometimes you'll find that longer, complex sentences let you express your ideas clearly and precisely. At other times, shorter is better.

Sentence combining is easy and fun. Here are some suggestions that have worked for other high school students—suggestions you might try as you explore your style.

1. **Whisper sentences to yourself.** This is faster than writing, and it helps you decide on the best sentence to write down.

2. **Work with a partner.** By trying out sentences on a partner and hearing your partner's ideas, you often discover new, interesting ways to solve specific challenges. Feel free to borrow ideas.

3. **Use context when choosing sentences for a paragraph.** Each paragraph has an emerging context: the sentences you have already combined. Reading this context aloud helps you decide on the best next sentence.

4. **Compare your sentences with those of other students.** Seeing how others have solved combining tasks broadens your awareness of sentence options. Keep asking yourself, "Which do I prefer?"

5. **Look for stylistic patterns in your writing.** Calculate the average number of words per sentence; study your sentence openers; listen to rhythms in your style. Try new patterns to stretch yourself.

6. **Take risks.** It makes good sense to take risks and make mistakes as you combine sentences. Mistakes provide feedback. As you learn from them, you develop a personal style, a voice. You come to know yourself as a writer.

The point of sentence combining is to improve your revising and editing skills. Practice in combining sentences helps you see that sentences are flexible tools for thought, not rigid structures cast in concrete. The simple fact that you feel confident in moving sentence parts around increases your control of revising and editing. To acquire this sense of self-confidence—based on your real competence in combining and revising sentences—try strategies like these:

1. **Vary the length of your sentences.** Work for a rhythmic, interesting balance of long and short sentences, remembering that short sentences can be dramatic.

2. **Vary the structure of your sentences.** By using sentence openers occasionally and by sometimes tucking information into the middle of a sentence, you can create stylistic interest.

3. **Use parallelism for emphasis.** Experiment with repeated items in a series—words, phrases, clauses.

4. **Use interruption for emphasis.** Commas, colons, semicolons, dashes, parentheses—all of these are useful in your stylistic toolkit.

5. **Use unusual patterns for emphasis.** That you might sometimes reverse normal sentence patterns may never have occurred to you, but it can strengthen your writing.

You'll use these four main strategies when you combine sentences:

- deleting repeated words
- adding connecting words
- rearranging words
- changing the form of words

12.2 COMBINING SENTENCES BY INSERTING WORDS

When two sentences talk about the same idea, sometimes you can effectively combine them simply by taking a word from one sentence and inserting it into the other sentence. Occasionally the word or words you are inserting must change form.

ORIGINAL VERSION	COMBINED VERSION
The breeze brought the fragrance of spring flowers. The breeze was light. The fragrance was welcome.	The **light** breeze brought the **welcome** fragrance of spring flowers. [no change in form]
A gas log burned in the fireplace. Its burning was cheerful.	A gas log burned **cheerfully** in the fireplace. [The adjective *cheerful* changes to the adverb *cheerfully*.]

PRACTICE Combining Sentences by Inserting Words

Read each group of sentences below. Combine the sentences by inserting a word or words from the later sentences into the first sentence in each group.

1. Throw away the crackers. The crackers are stale.
2. The music played. The music played loudly. It was discordant music.
3. I'm going to the mall. I'm going tonight. The mall is new.
4. The boys walked through the park. The boys were happy. The park was sunny.
5. The dog lay at my feet. The dog was tired. My feet were sore.
6. The mountains sat in the distance. The mountains were snow-capped.
7. The cherry tree was blooming. It was tall.
8. The young athlete stopped trying to win the race. He was defeated
9. The horse was running. It ran fast. It was gray.
10. Ben Franklin was a skillful diplomat. He was a skillful inventor.

12.3 COMBINING SENTENCES BY INSERTING PHRASES

Another way to combine sentences is to insert a phrase from one sentence into another sentence. Sometimes you can use the phrase unchanged; at other times, you must turn the words into a phrase. The most useful phrases for this purpose are prepositional phrases, appositive phrases, and participial phrases.

PREPOSITIONAL PHRASES

ORIGINAL VERSION	COMBINED VERSION
Left behind was a single shoe. It was under the bed.	Left behind **under the bed** was a single shoe. [no change]
The job applicant answered the interviewer's questions. Her smile was nervous.	**With a nervous smile,** the job applicant answered the interviewer's questions. [The second sentence is changed into a prepositional phrase.]

NOTE: For more information on prepositional phrases, see pages 147–148.

PRACTICE Combining Sentences by Inserting Prepositional Phrases

Read each group of sentences below. Combine the sentences by inserting phrases.

1. I would like some Parmesan cheese. I would like it on my spaghetti.
2. I read the novel *The Color Purple*. I read it during my junior year.

3. The building was shaken. The shaking was caused by an earthquake.

4. The zebra is a fairly unintelligent, though interesting, animal. It is in the horse family.

5. An apple fell and hit Isaac. It came from a tree. It hit him on the head.

6. The school band played a lively song. They did it with spirited energy.

7. The painting was hanging. It was on the wall. The wall was in the dining room.

8. Marita enjoyed doing crossword puzzles. They were in the *Chicago Sun-Times*.

9. The old, battered ship was slowly sinking. It was going under the waves.

10. Charlie ate cereal. He ate it out of the box. He ate it in the morning.

APPOSITIVE PHRASES

ORIGINAL VERSION	COMBINED VERSION
Zora Neale Hurston's best-known novel is about an independent African American woman. It is called *Their Eyes Were Watching God.*	Zora Neale Hurston's best-known novel, ***Their Eyes Were Watching God,*** is about an independent African American woman.
	or
	Their Eyes Were Watching God, **Zora Neale Hurston's best-known novel,** is about an independent African American woman.

NOTE: For more information on appositive phrases, see pages 149–150.

Read each group of sentences below. Combine the sentences by inserting appositive phrases.

1. We watched *The Princess Bride*. It is a movie directed by Rob Reiner.
2. Vivian plays the cello well enough to be in an orchestra. She is my oldest cousin.
3. Wolves have a special habitat at the zoo. Wolves are my favorite animals.
4. I packed the suitcase carefully. It was my only piece of luggage.
5. Ulysses S. Grant was born in Ohio. He was a Civil War general.
6. I loved to watch Walter Payton play football. He was a great running back.
7. Millard Fillmore took office when President Zachary Taylor died. Fillmore was the thirteenth president.
8. President James Buchanan had his niece serve as White House hostess. He was a bachelor.
9. Four of the first five presidents were from one state. That state was Virginia.
10. The tree in the backyard was shedding its leaves. It was a maple.

PARTICIPIAL PHRASES

ORIGINAL VERSION	COMBINED VERSION
Moriah was doing a lazy side-stroke toward the raft. She felt her worries slip away.	**Doing a lazy sidestroke toward the raft,** Moriah felt her worries slip away.
	or

	Moriah, **doing a lazy side-stroke toward the raft,** felt her worries slip away.
Small whitecaps were formed by the rising wind. The whitecaps glinted in the sun.	**Formed by the rising wind,** small whitecaps glinted in the sun.
	or
	Small whitecaps **formed by the rising wind** glinted in the sun.

NOTE: For more information on participial phrases, see pages 151–152.

PRACTICE Combining Sentences by Inserting Participial Phrases

Read each group of sentences below. Using participial phrases, combine the sentences.

1. Patrick jogged eagerly along the path. He hoped to meet Cheri.
2. South Dakota is located north of Nebraska. It is hot in the summer and cold in the winter.
3. The vase fell off the table. It broke.
4. The police officer quizzed Laura. He was talking politely.
5. Lynn rehearsed her speech. She practiced in front of the mirror.
6. Mary Cassatt made a reputation as an Impressionist painter. She used women and children as subjects.
7. Harry sat on a rock to rest. He was tired of walking.
8. The fence stood out from the others on the block. It was painted red.
9. The house rocked with laughter. It came alive for the first time.
10. Clouds drifted across the sky. They looked like cotton.

12.4 COMBINING SENTENCES USING COORDINATION

To combine sentences that have equally important ideas, you can use a coordinating conjunction *(and, but, or, so, nor, for, yet)* to form a compound sentence part, such as a compound subject, predicate, or object. Or, you can use one of those conjunctions or a pair of correlative conjunctions *(both . . . and, just as . . . so, not only . . . but (also), either . . . or, neither . . . nor, whether . . . or)* to form a compound sentence. Alternatively, you can use a semicolon with or without a conjunctive adverb, such as *however, consequently,* and *furthermore.*

ORIGINAL VERSION	COMBINED VERSION
I need shoes. I also need socks.	I need shoes **and** socks.
He wants to study art. If not art, he wants to study music.	He wants to study art **or** music.
Pulling weeds is not all we will do. We will also plant flowers.	We will not only pull weeds **but also** plant flowers.
I need a week to read the book. As a result, I must start today.	I need a week to read the book; therefore, I must start today.

PARALLELISM

Parallelism consists of using the same grammatical constructions to express related ideas. Within a sentence, the words, phrases, or clauses joined by a conjunction must be parallel. A conjunction should not be used to link an adjective with a noun, a noun with a verb, or a phrase with a clause.

EXAMPLE   **INCORRECT**   People look for loyalty and the trait of being honest in their friends.

   CORRECT   People look for loyalty and honesty in their friends.

PRACTICE **Combining Sentences Using Coordination**

Read each group of sentences below. Combine the sentences, using conjunctions or conjunctive adverbs. Be sure your constructions are parallel.

1. Corn prices went down. Many farmers lost money.
2. Playing varsity basketball is something I want to do. To join the National Honor Society is also a goal of mine.
3. Mauricio didn't make the debate team. His best friend, Sanford, didn't either.
4. Sasha wore her heavy coat. She left her boots at home.
5. I need to eat a healthy diet. Getting enough exercise is something else I need.
6. Ducks like water. However, they do not like rain.
7. Constant loud noise can be irritating to the nerves. It can do damage to the eardrums, too.
8. Setting goals is good. Meeting goals is better.
9. A strong wind blew over the sea. The crew raised the sails.
10. Ostriches are bigger than other birds. They live longer.

12.5 COMBINING SENTENCES USING SUBORDINATION

Sometimes the ideas in two sentences are not equally important. Instead, one idea is more important than the other. You can combine these kinds of sentences by making the less important idea into a subordinate clause.

ADVERB CLAUSES

One kind of subordinate clause is an adverb clause, a clause that is introduced by a subordinating conjunction. An adverb clause modifies a verb, an adjective, or another adverb in the main clause. Following are some subordinating conjunctions you might use to show the relationship between the two clauses.

SUBORDINATING CONJUNCTIONS	
FOR EXPRESSING TIME RELATIONSHIPS	after, as, as soon as, before, since, so long as, until, when, whenever, while
FOR EXPRESSING PLACE RELATIONSHIPS	as far as, where, wherever
FOR EXPRESSING CAUSE-AND-EFFECT RELATIONSHIPS	as, because, since, so (that)
FOR EXPRESSING CONDITIONAL RELATIONSHIPS	although, as if, as long as, as though, considering (that), if, inasmuch as, in order that, provided (that), since, so (that), than, though, unless, whereas

In the following examples, some of the techniques you have already seen are used along with subordinating conjunctions to combine several sentences into one. Study the examples to see how the techniques can be used together.

ORIGINAL VERSION	COMBINED VERSION
Rain began to fall in drops. The drops were fat. Trees swayed like dancers. Trees jerked like dancers. The dancers were frantic.	**As** rain began to fall in fat drops, trees swayed and jerked like frantic dancers.
She had made her decision. Her decision was not to see him again. His apologies had been weak. His apologies had been pathetic.	She had made her decision not to see him again **because** his apologies had been weak and pathetic.

Suntans may suggest good health. They seriously damage your skin. They destroy its elastic fibers.	**Although** suntans may suggest good health, they seriously damage your skin by destroying its elastic fibers.

NOTE: For more information on using subordinating conjunctions in adverb clauses, see pages 168–169.

see pages 168–169.

PRACTICE Combining Sentences Using Subordination: Adverb Clauses

Read each group of sentences below. Using adverb clauses, combine the sentences.

1. The sculptor of the Statue of Liberty used his mother's face as his model. She looked strong and honest.
2. My family went to the Grand Canyon last summer. Lucy fed our cat.
3. I wanted to see Ben. I did my homework quickly.
4. I went to the movies. First I completed my chores.
5. Kent walked to town. He had to ask directions.
6. Lynn will like the movie. She won't like it if it's science fiction.
7. I had no fruit. I had crackers and cheese.
8. Jeri took a picture. I was not looking at the time she did.
9. My parents go to the movies. I baby-sit my brother.
10. Joseph helped Charles with math. At the same time, Theo helped Mark with spelling.

ADJECTIVE CLAUSES

An adjective clause is a subordinate clause that modifies a noun or a pronoun in the main clause. To combine ideas using an adjective clause, replace the subject of one sentence with the word *who, whose, which,* or *that.*

ORIGINAL VERSION	COMBINED VERSION
Octavio Paz was a diplomat, a teacher, an author, and a poet. He stood at the top of Mexican literature throughout the twentieth century.	Octavio Paz, **who stood at the top of Mexican literature throughout the twentieth century,** was a diplomat, a teacher, an author, and a poet.
	or
	Octavio Paz, **who was a diplomat, a teacher, an author, and a poet,** stood at the top of Mexican literature throughout the twentieth century.
Paz taught at Texas, Harvard, and Cambridge universities. His *Collected Poems* was published in 1987.	Paz, **whose *Collected Poems* was published in 1987,** taught at Texas, Harvard, and Cambridge universities.
Paz's *Collected Poems* offers a unique view of a poet's mind. I read the book of poems last summer.	Paz's *Collected Poems*, **which I read last summer,** offers a unique view of a poet's mind.
	or
	Last summer I read Paz's *Collected Poems*, **which offers a unique view of a poet's mind.**

NOTE: For more information on adjective clauses, see pages 167–168.

PRACTICE Combining Sentences Using Subordination: Adjective Clauses

Read each group of sentences below. Using adjective clauses, combine the sentences.

1. Andorra was once ruled by both the president of France and a bishop of Spain. It lies between France and Spain.
2. Harvard College was named after John Harvard. He gave the school his books and about two thousand dollars.

3. My hat is on the coat rack in the hall. I bought the hat in Russia.

4. Ants are not found in Antarctica. They are found on every other continent in the world.

5. That bird is a condor. It has the longest wingspan of any land bird.

6. Salukis are extremely fast dogs. They are not commonly used in dog racing.

7. Ruby and Wayne did not eat any of the pizza. They do not like anchovies.

8. Greta found the science book. Howie was looking for the book.

9. Eugene V. Debs received almost one million votes as a presidential candidate. He was in jail throughout the election.

10. The oldest presidents in United States history were Ronald Reagan and Dwight Eisenhower. They both served into their seventies.

NOUN CLAUSES

A noun clause is a subordinate clause used as a noun. To combine ideas using a noun clause, begin one sentence with one of the words in the following chart. (It will probably be necessary to change some other words in the sentence.) Then put the noun clause you have made into another sentence.

WORDS THAT CAN INTRODUCE NOUN CLAUSES			
how	whatever	which	whoever
that	when	whichever	whose
what	where	who, whom	why

ORIGINAL VERSION	COMBINED VERSION
He never learned something. The problem could be solved some way.	He never learned **how the problem could be solved.** [noun clause acting as direct object]
They want to hang rings from their noses. The reason for this is a mystery to their elders.	**Why they want to hang rings from their noses** is a mystery to their elders. [noun clause acting as subject]
Someone hires lifeguards. Send your application to him or her.	Send your application to **whoever hires lifeguards.** [noun clause acting as object of the preposition *to*]

NOTE: For more information on noun clauses, see pages 169–170.

PRACTICE Combining Sentences Using Subordination: Noun Clauses

Read each group of sentences below. Using noun clauses, combine the sentences.

1. Beavers never eat fish? Are you sure?
2. Who will the class president be? It's usually the person with the most friends.
3. Mom heard something about our new car. It should be shared with Dad.
4. Jonas Salk discovered the vaccine for polio. The vaccine is named for him.
5. Ria left the party before I arrived. I didn't understand why.
6. Chester would like to discover something. He wants to find the location of his dad's old swimming hole.

7. When will Mel begin her campaign? No one knows.

8. Does anyone know this? Where are my books for class?

9. Greg baked a pumpkin pie. It was a treat for us.

10. Someone will win the race. Give the blue ribbon to him or her.

Read each group of sentences below. Combine the sentences using adverb clauses, adjective clauses, or noun clauses.

1. Michael finished the landscaping. Then we had a garden party.

2. I didn't like reading that book. However, I learned a lot from it.

3. Kevin cares about children. He does volunteer work in the childcare center. He tutors twice a week at the branch library.

4. What is the oldest mountain range on the North American continent? Do you know?

5. I promised to lend you this volume of the encyclopedia. Here it is.

6. His friend moved away. It made Mark sad.

7. Thomas Edison was a productive inventor. He created the first practical incandescent lamp.

8. My teddy bear is getting ragged. I'm putting it on the shelf for safekeeping.

9. Did you like that book? I lent it to you last week.

10. My friends decided to take a trip to Wrigley Field. They can see the Cubs there. They can also get great Chicago-style hot dogs.

GRAMMAR/USAGE/MECHANICS

The following is a passage about the writer Edward Harrigan. Rewrite the passage, combining sentences that are closely related in meaning. Not all sentences have to be combined.

Edward Harrigan

Edward Harrigan was born in New York. He was born in 1845. His parents were Irish American. He was apprenticed to work in construction as a teenager. He ran away. He went to San Francisco. He began working in one of the variety theaters. These theaters came before vaudeville.

Harrigan had three partners in his act. The last one was Tony Hart. They worked very well together. Harrigan wrote their sketches. They were immensely popular. Then Harrigan started writing short plays. Finally he wrote full-length musical shows. Harrigan and Hart started producing their own shows. They produced them at the Theatre Comique on Broadway.

Harrigan and Hart presented *The Mulligan Guards' Ball*. They presented it in about 1879. It was a huge success. It was a spoof of paramilitary groups. These groups were popular at the time. Audiences demanded more plays about the Mulligan Guards.

Edward Harrigan also wrote about ethnic, working-class people. He wrote with sympathy. He wrote with some degree of realism. That had not been done before in American theater very often. Some of the songs Harrigan wrote were quite popular. They are now thought of as American folk music. Some critics compare Harrigan to England's Charles Dickens. Dickens wrote about the lives of poor people. So did Harrigan. Dickens recognized social injustice. So did Harrigan. Dickens was also a humorous writer. So was Edward Harrigan. Dickens was a greater writer. Even so, Harrigan made his mark on American culture.

Read each group of sentences. Combine the sentences in the way that seems best to you.

1. I made four cakes for the bake sale. They are chocolate.
2. The cat sits regally. She sits on the windowsill.
3. Tia was interested in the book. Her eyes were glued to the page.
4. Carmen seems very nice. She came to my house. She welcomed me to the neighborhood.
5. Two hatboxes sit on the shelf. They are old. They are black.
6. The captain of the debate team is a terrific speaker. He is my brother.
7. My neighbor pruned the hedge. He made an effort to improve his yard.
8. Mud slid down the mountain. The train was held up.
9. Roger whittled wooden deer for the bazaar. He whittled cats, too.
10. Felicia used velvet for the king's costume. It was purple.
11. A girl fell into the well. The firefighters saved that girl.
12. Our school cafeteria closes at 2:00 P.M. The chef gave me a cookie after school.
13. Only one state was named after a United States president. It is Washington.
14. How many states were named after rulers of England? Do you know?
15. We have long been free of England. However, six states are still named for English monarchs.
16. Mac is persistent. She shows this quality in her work.
17. Lola has long looked like her mother. She was a baby when the resemblance first appeared.
18. During part of the year, it is summer in the Northern Hemisphere. At this time, the northern half of Earth is tilted toward the Sun.
19. Someone has my English book. It is the person who sits in the seat behind me.
20. I have every intention of helping you. I will finish this chapter first.

Chapter 13

Spelling and Vocabulary

● ● ● ● ● ● ● ● ● ● ● ● ● ● ● ●

13.1 SPELLING RULES

The following rules, examples, and exceptions will help you master the spelling of many words. However, not all words follow the rules. When you're not sure how to spell a word, the best thing to do is check a dictionary.

Spelling *ie* and *ei*

An easy way to learn when to use *ie* and when to use *ei* is to memorize a simple rhyming rule. Then learn the common exceptions to the rule.

RULE	EXAMPLES
"WRITE *I* BEFORE *E*	achieve, believe, brief, chief, die, field, friend, grief, lie, niece, piece, pier, quiet, retrieve, sieve, tie, tier, yield
EXCEPT AFTER *C*	ceiling, conceit, conceive, deceit, deceive, receipt, receive
OR WHEN SOUNDED LIKE *A*, AS IN *NEIGHBOR* AND *WEIGH*."	eight, eighth, eighty, freight, neigh, reign, sleigh, veil, vein, weigh, weight

Some exceptions: *either, caffeine, foreign, forfeit, height, heir, leisure, neither, protein, seize, species, their, weird;* words ending in *cient (ancient)* and *cience (conscience);* plurals of nouns ending in *cy (democracies);* the third-person singular form of verbs ending in *cy (fancies);* words in which *i* and *e* follow *c* but represent separate sounds *(science, society)*

Words Ending in *cede*, *ceed*, and *sede*

The only English word ending in *sede* is *supersede.* Three words end in *ceed: proceed, exceed,* and *succeed.* You can remember these three words by thinking of the following sentence:

If you **proceed** to **exceed** the speed limit, you will **succeed** in getting a ticket.

All other words ending with the "seed" sound are spelled with *cede: concede, intercede, precede, recede, secede.*

Spelling Unstressed Vowels

Listen to the vowel sound in the second syllable of the word *or-i-gin.* This is an unstressed vowel sound. Unstressed vowel sounds can be spelled in many ways. Dictionary respellings use the schwa (ə) to indicate an unstressed vowel sound.

To spell a word that has an unstressed vowel sound, think of a related word in which the syllable containing the vowel sound is stressed.

The word *original*, for example, should help you spell the word *origin*. The chart shows some other examples.

SPELLING UNSTRESSED VOWELS

UNKNOWN SPELLING	RELATED WORD	WORD SPELLED CORRECTLY
leg_l	le**gal**ity	legal
fant_sy	fan**tas**tic	fantasy
host_le	hos**til**ity	hostile
opp_site	op**pose**	opposite
def_nite	de**fine**	definite

Adding Prefixes

To add prefixes, keep the spelling of the root word and add the prefix. If the last letter of the prefix is the same as the first letter of the word, keep both letters.

un- + happy = unhappy   co- + operate = cooperate

dis- + appear = disappear   il- + legal = illegal

re- + enlist = reenlist   un- + natural = unnatural

mis- + spell = misspell   im- + migrate = immigrate

Adding Suffixes

When you add a suffix beginning with a vowel, double the final consonant if the word ends in a **single consonant preceded by a single vowel** *and*

- the word has one syllable

mud + -y = muddy   sad + -er = sadder

put + -ing = putting   stop + -ed = stopped

- the word is stressed on the last syllable and the stress remains on the same syllable after the suffix is added

occur + -ence = occurrence

regret + -able = regrettable

begin + -ing = beginning

repel + -ent = repellent

commit + -ed = committed

refer + -al = referral

Don't double the final consonant if the word is not stressed on the last syllable or if the stress shifts when the suffix is added.

murmur + -ed = murmured

refer + -ence = reference

Don't double the final letter if the word ends in *s, w, x,* or *y: gases, rowing, waxy, employer.*

Don't double the final consonant before the suffix *-ist* if the word has more than one syllable: *druggist* but *violinist, guitarist.*

Adding suffixes to words that end in *y* can cause spelling problems. Study the following rules and note the exceptions.

When a word ends in **a vowel and y,** keep the *y.*

---

play + -s = plays   joy + -ous = joyous

obey + -ed = obeyed   annoy + -ance = annoyance

buy + -ing = buying   enjoy + -ment = enjoyment

employ + -er = employer

enjoy + -able = enjoyable

joy + -ful = joyful

boy + -ish = boyish

joy + -less = joyless

coy + -ly = coyly

SOME EXCEPTIONS: gay + -ly = gaily, day + -ly = daily,
pay + -d = paid, lay + -d = laid, say + -d = said

When a word ends in **a consonant and y,** change the y
to i before any suffix that doesn't begin with i. Keep
the y before suffixes that begin with i.

carry + -es = carries

deny + -al = denial

dry + -ed = dried

rely + -able = reliable

easy + -er = easier

mercy + -less = merciless

merry + -ly = merrily

likely + -hood = likelihood

happy + -ness = happiness

accompany + -ment =

beauty + -ful = beautiful

   accompaniment

fury + -ous = furious

carry + -ing = carrying

defy + -ant = defiant

baby + -ish = babyish

vary + -ation = variation

lobby + -ist = lobbyist

SOME EXCEPTIONS: shy + -ly = shyly, dry + -ly = dryly,
shy + -ness = shyness, dry + -ness = dryness,
biology + -ist = biologist, economy + -ist = economist,
baby + -hood = babyhood

Usually a **final silent e** is dropped before a suffix, but
sometimes it's kept. The following chart shows the
basic rules for adding suffixes to words that end in
silent e.

RULE	EXAMPLES
Drop the *e* before suffixes that begin with a vowel.	care + -ed = cared dine + -ing = dining move + -er = mover type + -ist = typist blue + -ish = bluish arrive + -al = arrival desire + -able = desirable accuse + -ation = accusation noise + -y = noisy
Some exceptions	mile + -age = mileage dye + -ing = dyeing
Drop the *e* and change *i* to *y* before the suffix *–ing* if the word ends in *ie*.	die + -ing = dying lie + -ing = lying tie + -ing = tying
Keep the *e* before suffixes that begin with *a* and *o* if the word ends in *ce* or *ge*.	dance + -able = danceable change + -able = changeable courage + -ous = courageous
Keep the *e* before suffixes that begin with a vowel if the word ends in *ee* or *oe*.	see + -ing = seeing agree + -able = agreeable canoe + -ing = canoeing hoe + -ing = hoeing
Some exceptions (There can never be three of the same letter in a row.)	free + -er = freer free + -est = freest
Keep the *e* before suffixes that begin with a consonant.	grace + -ful = graceful state + -hood = statehood like + -ness = likeness encourage + -ment = encouragement care + -less = careless sincere + -ly = sincerely

See next page for some exceptions

RULE	EXAMPLES
Some exceptions	awe + -ful = awful
	argue + -ment = argument
	true + -ly = truly
	due + -ly = duly
	whole + -ly = wholly
Drop *le* before the suffix *–ly* when the word ends with a consonant and *le*.	possible + -ly = possibly
	sniffle + -ly = sniffly
	sparkle + -ly = sparkly
	gentle + -ly = gently

Don't drop any letters when you add *–ly* to a word that ends in a single *l*. When a word ends in *ll,* drop one *l* when you add the suffix *–ly.*

real + -ly = really

cool + -ly = coolly

chill + -ly = chilly

full + -ly = fully

Don't drop any letters when you add the suffix -*ness* to a word that ends in *n.*

stubborn + -ness = stubbornness

mean + -ness = meanness

Compound Words

Keep the original spelling of both parts of a compound word.

Remember that some compounds are one word, some are two words, and some are hyphenated. Check a dictionary when in doubt.

foot + lights = footlights

busy + body = busybody

book + case = bookcase

light + house = lighthouse

fish + hook = fishhook

with + hold = withhold

book + keeper = bookkeeper

heart + throb = heartthrob

Spelling Plurals

A singular noun names one person, place, thing, or idea. A plural noun names more than one. To form the plural of most nouns, you simply add –s. Remember, however, that simple plural nouns never use apostrophes.

The following chart shows other basic rules.

GENERAL RULES FOR PLURALS		
NOUNS ENDING IN	**TO FORM PLURAL**	**EXAMPLES**
ch, s, sh, x, z	Add –es.	lunch → lunches bus → buses dish → dishes box → boxes buzz → buzzes
a vowel and *y*	Add –s.	boy → boys turkey → turkeys
a consonant and *y*	Change *y* to *i* and add –es.	baby → babies penny → pennies
a vowel and *o*	Add –s.	radio → radios rodeo → rodeos
a consonant and *o*	Usually add –es.	potato → potatoes tomato → tomatoes hero → heroes echo → echoes
	Sometimes add –s.	zero → zeros photo → photos piano → pianos

NOUNS ENDING IN	TO FORM PLURAL	EXAMPLES
f or *fe*	Usually change *f* to *v* and add *–s* or *–es.*	wife → wives knife → knives life → lives leaf → leaves half → halves shelf → shelves wolf → wolves thief → thieves
	Sometimes add *–s.*	roof → roofs chief → chiefs cliff → cliffs giraffe → giraffes

The plurals of **proper names** are formed by adding *–es* to names that end in *ch, s, sh, x,* or *z.*

EXAMPLE   The **Woodriches** live on Elm Street.

EXAMPLE   There are two **Jonases** in our class.

Just add *–s* to form the plural of all other proper names, including those that end in *y.* Remember that the rule of changing *y* to *i* and adding *–es* doesn't apply to proper names.

EXAMPLE   The **Kennedys** are a famous American family.

EXAMPLE   I know three **Marys.**

EXAMPLE   The last two **Januarys** have been especially cold.

To form the plural of a **compound noun written as one word,** follow the general rules for plurals. To form the plural of **hyphenated compound nouns** or **compound nouns of more than one word,** usually make the most important word plural.

EXAMPLE The two women's **fathers-in-law** have never met.

EXAMPLE The three **post offices** are made of brick.

EXAMPLE There have been three **surgeons general** in this decade.

EXAMPLE The list of **poets laureate** in Great Britain is short.

EXAMPLE The general presided over two **courts martial** today.

Some nouns have **irregular plural forms** that don't follow any rules.

---

man → men

woman → women

child → children

foot → feet

tooth → teeth

mouse → mice

goose → geese

ox → oxen

Some nouns have the same singular and plural forms. Most of these are the names of animals, and some of the plural forms may be spelled in more than one way.

---

deer → deer

sheep → sheep

head (of cattle) → head

Sioux → Sioux

series → series

species → species

fish → fish *or* fishes

antelope → antelope *or* antelopes

buffalo → buffalo *or* buffaloes *or* buffalos

Learning to Spell New Words

You can improve your spelling by improving your study method. Try the following method to learn to spell new words. You can also improve your spelling by thoroughly learning certain common but frequently misspelled words.

1. Say It
Look at the printed word and say it aloud. Then say it again, pronouncing each syllable correctly.

2. Visualize It
Picture the word in your mind. Avoid looking at the printed word on the page. Try to visualize the word letter by letter.

3. Write It
Look at the printed word again, and write it two or three times. Then write the word without looking at the printed spelling.

4. Check It
Check your spelling. Did you spell the word correctly? If not, repeat each step until you can spell the word easily.

How Do You Find a Word in the Dictionary If You Can't Spell It?

Write down letters and letter combinations that could stand for the sound you hear at the beginning of the word. Try these possible spellings as you look for the word in a dictionary.

Using a Computer to Check Spelling

A spelling checker is a useful computer tool. If you have misspelled any words, a spelling checker can find them for you. Not only will it save you time, but it will also show you words you need to learn to spell.

Although spelling checkers are handy, they can't do the whole job. When a spelling checker finds a misspelled word, it searches the computer's dictionary for words spelled in a similar way. *You* must choose the correct word from the options the computer gives you.

Furthermore, a spelling checker can't check for sense. If you type *right* instead of *write*, the spelling checker won't highlight the error because both *right* and *write* are correctly spelled words. You still need to know correct spellings.

PRACTICE **Spelling Rules**

Find the misspelled word in each group and write it correctly.

1. weight, shield, releive
2. succeed, precede, conceed
3. comparable, riducule, imaginative
4. ilegible, immovable, unnoticed
5. occurrence, committed, prefference
6. fateful, wasteful, achievment
7. bunchs, ponies, potatoes
8. truely, originally, cruelly
9. marries, hurrys, buries
10. pranceing, changeable, hateful

13.2 SPELLING DIFFICULT WORDS

Some words are more difficult to spell than others, and not all words follow basic spelling rules. Each person has an individual list of "problem" words. One useful strategy for learning difficult words is to develop a list of words that you frequently misspell and study them often.

A list of frequently misspelled words follows. Use it for quick reference.

FREQUENTLY MISSPELLED WORDS

abdomen
absence
abundant
academically
accelerator
accept
accessible
accidentally
acclimated
accommodate
accompaniment
accomplishment
acknowledge
acknowledgment
acquaintance
adequately
admission
admittance
adolescent
advantageous
advertisement
adviser
aerate
aerial
against
alcohol
allegiance
alliance
allot
allotting
all right
anonymous
answer
apologetically

apparatus
apparent
arctic
arousing
arrangement
atheistic
attendant
ballet
bankruptcy
beautiful
beginning
behavior
bibliography
biscuit
blasphemy
boulevard
buffet
bureau
bureaucrat
burial
business
cafeteria
calendar
camouflage
canceled
canoe
capitalism
carburetor
caricature
cataclysm
catastrophe
cemetery
changeable
chassis

choir
circumstantial
coliseum
colleague
colonel
coming
commercial
competition
complexion
concede
conceivable
connoisseur
conscience
conscientious
conscious
consciousness
consistency
controlling
controversy
convenient
cruelty
curriculum
decadent
decathlon
deceitful
deference
definite
deodorant
descend
descendant
descent
desirable
detrimental
devastation

develop
devise
dilemma
diligence
diphtheria
disastrous
disciple
discipline
discrimination
disease
diseased
dissatisfied
division
efficiency
eighth
elementary
eligible
embarrass
embarrassed
emperor
emphasize
endeavor
enormous
entertainment
entrance
environment
espionage
essential
exceed
except
exhibition
exhilaration
expensive
exuberant

familiarize
fascinating
fascism
February
feminine
financier
fission
foreign
forfeit
forty
fulfill
fundamentally
funeral
gaiety
galaxy
gauge
genius
government
grammatically
guarantee
guidance
harassment
height
hereditary
hindrance
hippopotamus
horizontal
hospital
humorous
hygiene
hypocrisy
hypocrite
ideally
idiomatic

immediate
incidentally
independent
inevitable
influential
ingenious
innocent
inoculate
institution
intellectual
interference
irresistible
jewelry
judgment
knowledge
knowledgeable
laboratory
larynx
legitimate
leisure
leisurely
library
license
livelihood
luxurious
magistrate
magnificence
maintenance
malicious
manageable
maneuver
marital
marriageable
martyrdom

GRAMMAR/USAGE/MECHANICS

mathematics
mediocre
melancholy
melodious
metaphor
miniature
mischievous
misspell
molasses
mortgage
mosquito
municipal
muscle
naive
necessary
necessity
negligence
negotiable
neighborhood
neurotic
newsstand
niece
nucleus
nuisance
nutritious
occasion
occasionally
occur
occurrence
occurring
omission
omitting
opportunity
orchestra

original
outrageous
pageant
pamphlet
parallel
paralysis
parliament
pastime
peasant
pedestal
perceive
permanent
permissible
personnel
perspiration
persuade
pharmacy
physical
physician
picnic
picnicking
pilot
playwright
pneumonia
politician
possessed
precede
preferable
presence
prestige
presumption
prevalent
privilege
procedure

proceed
propaganda
propagate
prophecy
prophesy
psychoanalysis
questionnaire
realtor
rebellion
receipt
receive
recognize
recommend
recommendation
reference
referred
rehearsal
reminiscent
remittance
repetitive
representative
responsibility
restaurant
reveal
rhythm
rhythmical
ridiculous
salable
schedule
seize
separate
separation
sergeant
significance

sincerely	symmetrical	undoubtedly
souvenir	synonymous	unmistakable
specimen	technique	unnecessary
sponsor	technology	unscrupulous
statistics	temperament	usually
strategic	tendency	vaccine
stubbornness	theory	vacuum
succeed	tolerance	valedictory
succession	tortoise	variety
sufficient	traffic	vaudeville
superintendent	tragedy	vehicle
supersede	transparent	vengeance
suppress	truly	versatile
surprise	twelfth	villain
susceptible	unanimous	Wednesday

GRAMMAR/USAGE/MECHANICS

PRACTICE Spelling Difficult Words

Find each misspelled word and write it correctly.

1. This isn't our permunent address; we're in temporary accommodations until the house is ready in Febuary.
2. Helen felt so giddy that she was barely concsious of her imediate dilema.
3. The building's magnificense was more appropriate for a king than for a bureuacrat.
4. The company's methods were fundamentaly sound, but they resulted in bankruptsy nonetheless.
5. An endevor to talk politics almost garantees controversy.
6. Kyle is knowledgable about both politics and goverment.
7. Intelectual activities are undoubtably their favorite kind of enertainment.

8. Dressing my cat in a camuflage suit made him look like part of the couch, and he didn't find that humorus.

9. Jane found it covenient and desireable to run her business from her residence.

10. Faced with a taxpayers' rebelion, the legislators gave unanamous support to the governor's recomendations on tax cuts.

13.3 EXPANDING YOUR VOCABULARY

Increasing your vocabulary improves your reading and writing skills and your chances of scoring well on standardized tests. The following tips suggest ways to expand your vocabulary and remember new words you encounter.

1. **Notice** new words when you're reading or listening. Write the words and their meanings in a notebook.

2. **Check** the meaning and pronunciation of a new word in a dictionary. Use the original context—surrounding words that are familiar—to understand the word's meaning and use.

3. **Relate** the new word to words you already know. Associate its spelling or meaning with a familiar word that will make the new word easier to remember.

4. **Verify** your understanding of the new word with someone else. A teacher, a parent, or a friend may be able to tell you if you correctly understand the meaning of the word.

5. **Practice** using the new word in your writing and conversation. Try to use the new word at least once a day for a week. Using a word repeatedly is the best way to remember it.

LEARNING FROM CONTEXT

You can often figure out the meaning of an unfamiliar word by looking for clues in the surrounding words and sentences, called the context.

"Your vocabulary is enlarged."

USING SPECIFIC CONTEXT CLUES

The following chart shows five types of specific context clues. It also lists clue words to look for. Finally, the chart gives examples of sentences with unfamiliar words whose meanings you should be able to figure out from the context. In the examples, the clue words are in bold type. The unfamiliar words and the helpful context are in italic type.

INTERPRETING CLUE WORDS IN CONTEXT

TYPE OF CONTEXT CLUE	CLUE WORDS	EXAMPLES
Definition The meaning of the unfamiliar word is stated in the sentence.	also known as in other words or that is which is which means	The course emphasized *demography,* **which is** *the study of human populations.* The lecturer was *verbose;* **that is,** he was *wordy.*

Example The meaning of the unfamiliar word is explained through familiar examples.	for example for instance including like such as	Osbert served as the old duke's *amanuensis;* **for example,** *he took dictation and copied manuscripts.* *Miscreants* of all kinds, **including** *pickpockets, thieves, and vandals,* roamed the streets of Victorian England.
Comparison The unfamiliar word is similar to a familiar word or phrase.	also identical like likewise resembling same similarly too	Joan's friend testified to her *veracity.* Her teacher, **too,** said Joan's *truthfulness* was evident to all who knew her. Consuela suffered from *acrophobia;* her father **also** had a *fear of heights.*
Contrast The unfamiliar word is the opposite of a familiar word or phrase.	although but however on the contrary on the other hand though unlike	**Unlike** his *despondent* opponent, Kwami appeared *hopeful, happy,* and *sure* he would win. Martin always *grouses* about doing his chores, **but** his sister does her work *without complaining.*
Cause and Effect The unfamiliar word is explained as part of a cause-and-effect relationship.	as a result because consequently therefore thus	Maria felt the stranger was being *intrusive* **because** he *asked too many personal questions.* Otis has a *loquacious* nature; **consequently,** the teacher is constantly telling him to stop talking.

USING GENERAL CONTEXT

Sometimes there are no special clue words to help you understand an unfamiliar word. However, you can still use the general context. That is, you can use the details in the words or sentences around the unfamiliar word. Read the following sentence:

EXAMPLE Ramon was in a *jocund* mood, laughing and joking with his friends.

Even if you don't know the meaning of *jocund,* you do know that it must be an adjective describing *mood.* From other details in the sentence (*laughing and joking*), you may guess correctly that *jocund* means "merry, cheerful, carefree."

PEANUTS reprinted by permission of United
Feature Syndicate, Inc.

PRACTICE Using Context Clues

Use context clues to figure out the meaning of the italicized word. Write the meaning. Then write definition, example, comparison, contrast, cause and effect, *or* general *to tell what type of context clue you used to define the word.*

1. As the dark sky and black clouds looked *ominous,* we all began to fear what would happen next.
2. We depended on Josie to recommend the best dishes on the menu; she's a true *epicure.*
3. Everyone makes mistakes; no one is *infallible.*
4. The girl's ability to sing on key seemed *innate,* something she was born with.

5. Jerry's self-conscious and unworldly manner is the opposite of Stanley's *debonair* style.
6. The referee's questionable call caused angry grumbling on the sidelines and then a noisy *altercation* on the field involving players and coaches from both teams.
7. "Written in stone" is simply a more colorful way of saying that a decision is *irrevocable*.
8. While Bette is outgoing and doesn't think about her feelings or motivations, her sister Bea is clearly a more *introspective* person.
9. John's apology, though sincere, did little to *mitigate* the unhappiness his careless words caused Ted.
10. The major *ideologies* of the twentieth century included communism, capitalism, and socialism.

13.4 ROOTS, PREFIXES, AND SUFFIXES

You can often figure out the meaning of an unfamiliar word by analyzing its parts. The main part of a word is its root. When the root is a complete word, it's sometimes called a base word. A root or base word can be thought of as the "spine" of a word. It gives the word its backbone of meaning.

A root is often combined with a prefix (a word part added to the beginning of a word), a suffix (a word part added to the end of a word), or another root. Prefixes and suffixes change a word's meaning or its part of speech.

Although the English language borrows words from many other languages, a large number of words we use have their origins in Latin and Greek roots. Knowing some of these Latin and Greek roots will help you analyze many unfamiliar words and determine their meanings.

encryption

Prefix	The prefix *en-* means "to put into."

Root	The root *crypt* means "hidden" or "secret." The word *encrypt,* therefore, means "to put into a hidden or secret form."

Suffix	The suffix *–ion* changes *encrypt* from a verb to a noun meaning "the state of being encrypted."

The word *encryption,* then, means "something that has been put into a secret code," in other words, "a coded message." Although this word's parts add up to its meaning in a fairly clear way, sometimes an analysis of a word's parts doesn't yield the word's meaning so readily. Use a dictionary to check your analysis.

ROOTS

When you're trying to determine the meaning of an unfamiliar word, think of words that might share a root with it. The meanings of these other words might give you clues to the meaning of the unfamiliar word. The following chart lists some common roots and some words that share them. Keep in mind that one or more letters in a root may change when the root is combined with other word parts.

ROOTS	WORDS	MEANINGS
ac or *ag* means "do"	action	act or process of doing
	agenda	list of things to do
agri or *agro* means "field"	agriculture	science of cultivating the soil
	agronomy	study of crop production and soil management
am means "love" or "friend"	amicable	friendly
	amorous	relating to love
anima means "life" or "mind"	animate	having life
	unanimous	being of one mind
anthrop means "human beings"	anthropology	study of human beings
	misanthrope	one who hates or distrusts human beings
aqua means "water"	aquarium	tank of water in which living animals are kept
	aqueduct	structure for moving water
arch means "rule" or "government"	anarchy	absence of government
	archives	government records
astr or *astro* means "star"	astronaut	traveler among the stars
	astronomy	study of stars
audio means "hear"	audience	group that hears a performance
	audiometer	device for measuring hearing
aut or *auto* means "self"	autistic	absorbed in the self
	autobiography	story of a person's life written by that person

ROOTS	WORDS	MEANINGS
bene means "good"	beneficial	good, helpful
	benevolent	inclined to do good
bibli or *biblio* means "book"	bibliography	list of books related to a particular subject
	bibliophile	lover of books
bio means "life"	autobiography	story of a person's life written by that person
	biology	study of living things
brev means "short" or "brief"	abbreviate	shorten a word or phrase
	brevity	shortness of expression
cand means "shine" or "glow"	candle	molded mass of wax that may be burned to give light
	incandescent	bright, glowing
capit means "head"	capital	place where the head of government sits
	decapitate	remove the head
ced means "go"	proceed	go forward
	recede	go back
cent means "hundred"	centimeter	one hundredth of a meter
	century	one hundred years
chron or *chrono* means "time"	chronological	arranged in time order
	synchronize	cause to happen at the same time
cid or *cide* means "kill"	germicide	agent that destroys germs
	homicide	killing of one human being by another

GRAMMAR/USAGE/MECHANICS

ROOTS	WORDS	MEANINGS
circ means "circle"	circumference	distance around a circle
	circus	entertainment usually held in a circular area
cis means "cut"	incision	surgical cut
	incisor	tooth adapted for cutting
cline means "bend," "lean," or "slope"	decline	slope downward
	incline	lean forward
cogn means "know"	cognition	knowledge; awareness
	recognize	know someone or something
corp means "body"	corps	body of military troops
	corpse	dead body
cracy means "government"	democracy	government by the people
	technocracy	government by technical experts
cred means "believe" or "trust"	credible	believable
	incredible	unbelievable
crypt or *crypto* means "hidden" or "secret"	cryptic	having a hidden meaning
	cryptogram	communication in secret code
culp means "blame" or "guilt"	culpable	guilty
	culprit	one who is guilty
cur or *curs* means "run"	current	water running in a stream or electricity running through a wire
	cursory	rapidly performed or produced

ROOTS	WORDS	MEANINGS
cycl means "circle" or "wheel"	bicycle cyclone	two-wheeled vehicle storm that rotates in a circle
dec or *deca* means "ten"	decade decathlon	ten years athletic contest consisting of ten events
dem or *demo* means "people"	democracy epidemic	rule by the people affecting many people
di means "two"	dichotomy dichromatic	division into two groups having two colors
dict means "say"	contradict dictate	say the opposite of speak for another to record
duc or *duct* means "lead" or "draw"	conductor deduct	one who leads take away from a total
ectomy means "surgical removal"	appendectomy mastoidectomy	surgical removal of the appendix surgical removal of part of the mastoid bone or process
equi means "equal"	equilateral equitable	having sides of equal length dealing equally with all
err means "wander" or "err"	aberration erratic	result of straying from the normal way inconsistent, irregular
eu means "good" or "well"	eulogize euphoria	praise feeling of well-being
exo means "outside" or "outer"	exoskeleton exotic	outer supportive covering of an animal, as an insect or mollusk outside the ordinary

GRAMMAR/USAGE/MECHANICS

ROOTS	WORDS	MEANINGS
fac or *fec* means "make" or "do"	effective factory	done well place where things are made
ferous means "bearing" or "producing"	coniferous somniferous	bearing cones, as a pine tree producing sleep
fid means "faith" or "trust"	confidant fidelity	person one trusts faithfulness
fin means "end" or "limit"	define infinite	limit the meaning of having no end
fix means "fasten"	fixate fixative	fasten one's attention intently substance that fastens or sets
frac or *frag* means "break"	fracture fragile	break easily broken
fus means "pour" or "melt"	effusive fusion	demonstrating an excessive pouring out of talk or affection joining by melting
gen means "class," "kind," "descent," or "birth"	general generate	affecting a whole class start or originate
geo means "earth," "ground," or "soil"	geocentric geology	measured from the center of the earth study of the earth
grad or *gress* means "step" or "go"	egress gradual	way to go out proceeding by steps or degrees
gram or *graph* means "writing"	autograph telegram	written signature written message sent over a distance

ROOTS	WORDS	MEANINGS
grat means "pleasing" or "thanks"	congratulate	express sympathetic pleasure
	gratuity	something given voluntarily to show thanks for service
hetero means "different"	heterogeneous	made up of different kinds of things
	heteronym	word spelled like another word but different in meaning and pronunciation, for example, *bow*
homo means "same"	homogeneous	made up of the same kinds of things
	homophone	word pronounced like another word but different in meaning and spelling, for example, *to, too,* or *two*
hydr or *hydro* means "water"	dehydrate	remove water
	hydrant	large pipe used to draw water
ject means "throw"	eject	throw out
	trajectory	path of something thrown
jud means "judge"	judicious	using good judgment
	prejudice	judgment formed without sufficient knowledge
junct means "join"	conjunction	word that joins other words
	junction	place where two things join

GRAMMAR/USAGE/MECHANICS

ROOTS	WORDS	MEANINGS
jur or *jus* means "law"	jurisprudence	system of law
	justice	determination of rights according to the law
lect or *leg* means "read"	lectern	stand used to support a book or paper for reading
	legible	capable of being read
like means "resembling"	businesslike	resembling the conduct of a business
	childlike	resembling the behavior of a child
loc means "place"	local	relating to a place
	location	position, site, or place
locut or *loqu* means "speak" or "speech"	locution	style of speaking
	loquacious	talkative
log or *logo* means "word," "thought," or "speech"	dialogue	speech between two people
	monologue	speech by a single person
logy means "science" or "study"	biology	science of living things
	genealogy	study of ancestors
	mineralogy	study of minerals
	pathology	study of disease
luc means "light"	lucid	suffused with light; clear
	translucent	permitting the passage of light
macro means "large"	macrocosm	world; universe
	macroscopic	large enough to be observed with the naked eye

ROOTS	WORDS	MEANINGS
magn means "large" or "great"	magnificent magnify	large and grand make larger
mal means "bad" or "badly"	maladjusted malice	badly adjusted desire to see another suffer
man means "hand"	manual manuscript	done by hand document written by hand or typed
meter or *metr* means "measure"	metric thermometer	relating to meter instrument for measuring heat
micr or *micro* means "small"	micrometer microwave	device for measuring very small distances a short electromagnetic wave
milli means "thousand"	millimeter million	one thousandth of a meter one thousand times one thousand
mis or *mit* means "send"	remiss transmit	failing to respond send across a distance
mon means "warn"	admonish premonition	express warning or disapproval in a gentle way forewarning
mon or *mono* means "one"	monarchy monochromatic	rule by one person having one color
morph or *morpho* means "form"	metamorphosis morphology	change in physical form study of the form and structure of animals and plants

GRAMMAR/USAGE/MECHANICS

ROOTS	WORDS	MEANINGS
mort means "death"	mortal	subject to death
	mortician	one who prepares the dead for burial
neo means "new"	neologism	new word, usage, or expression
	neonatal	affecting the newborn
nym means "name"	anonymous	not named or identified
	pseudonym	fictitious or pen name
octa or *octo* means "eight"	octagon	figure with eight sides
	octopus	creature with eight limbs
omni means "all"	omniscient	knowing all
	omnivorous	eating both animal and vegetable matter
oper means "work"	opera	musical and dramatic work
	operative	working
pan means "all" or "whole"	panacea	remedy for all problems
	Pan-American	relating to the whole of North and South America
path or *pathy* means "feeling" or "suffering"	pathology	study of disease
	sympathy	inclination to feel like another
ped means "child" or "foot"	pediatrician	physician who cares for children
	quadruped	animal having four feet
pend or *pens* means "hang" or "weigh"	pendant	something hanging or suspended
	suspense	feeling that leaves one hanging or unsure of an outcome

ROOTS	WORDS	MEANINGS
phil or *phile* means "loving" or "fondness"	bibliophile philanthropist	lover of books one who loves human beings
phobia means "fear"	acrophobia hydrophobia	fear of heights fear of water
phon or *phono* means "sound," "voice," or "speech"	phonics phonograph	method of teaching relationships between sounds and letters instrument for playing recorded sound
physi or *physio* means "nature" or "physical"	physiognomy physiotherapy	natural features of the face believed to show temperament and character physical therapy
poly means "many"	polyglot polygon	composed of numerous language groups a many-sided figure
pon or *pos* means "place" or "put"	exponent position	symbol placed above and to the right of a mathematical expression place where something is situated
port means "carry"	portable porter	capable of being carried one who carries
prehend means "seize" or "grasp"	apprehend comprehend	arrest by seizing grasp the meaning of
prim means "first"	primary	first in order of time or development

GRAMMAR/USAGE/MECHANICS

ROOTS	WORDS	MEANINGS
prim, continued	primitive	characteristic of an early stage of development
prot or *proto* means "first" or "beginning"	proton prototype	elementary particle original model
pseudo means "false"	pseudoclassic pseudonym	pretending to be classic fictitious or pen name
psych or *psycho* means "mind"	psychology psychotherapy	study of the mind therapy for the mind
punctus means "point"	punctual puncture	on time hole or wound made by a pointed instrument
quadr or *quadri* means "four"	quadrangle quadrilateral	four-sided enclosure having four sides
rect means "right" or "straight"	rectangle rectitude	figure with four right angles quality of being correct in judgment or procedure
reg means "rule" or "direct"	regular regulate	according to rule direct according to rule
rupt means "break"	interrupt rupture	stop or hinder by breaking in break
sang means "blood"	consanguinity sanguine	blood relationship marked by high color and cheerfulness; confident; optimistic
sci means "know"	omniscient science	knowing all things knowledge about the natural world

ROOTS	WORDS	MEANINGS
scope means "a means for viewing"	microscope	a means for viewing small things
	telescope	a means for viewing things at a distance
scrib or *script* means "write"	prescribe	write an order for medicine
	prescription	written order for medicine
secu or *sequ* means "follow"	sequel	installment that follows a previous one
	sequence	series in which one item follows another
sens or *sent* means "feel" or "sense"	sensation	feeling
	sentence	group of words that makes sense
sol or *solv* means "dissolve" or "solve"	solution	that which solves a problem
	solvent	that which dissolves
son means "sound"	resonant	continuing to sound
	sonorous	full of sound
soph means "wise" or "clever"	sophisticated	having wise and clever knowledge of the ways of the world
	sophomore	student in the second year of high school or college (a combination of wise and foolish)
spec or *spect* means "look" or "watch"	perspective	way of looking at something
	spectator	one who watches an event

GRAMMAR/USAGE/MECHANICS

ROOTS	WORDS	MEANINGS
spir means "breath" or "breathe"	inspire respiration	exert an influence on breathing
strict or *string* means "bind"	constrict stringent	draw together strict; severe
tact or *tang* means "touch"	contact tangible	touching of two things or people capable of being touched
tele means "far off" or "distant"	telephone television	instrument for hearing sound at a distance instrument for viewing pictures at a distance
terr means "earth"	extraterrestrial terrain	being from beyond earth physical features of a tract of land
therm or *thermo* means "heat"	thermal thermometer	relating to heat instrument for measuring heat
trac means "draw" or "pull"	extract traction	pull out friction caused by pulling across a surface; pulling force
tri means "three"	triangle triathlon	figure with three angles athletic contest consisting of three events
vac means "empty"	evacuation vacant	process of emptying out empty

GRAMMAR/USAGE/MECHANICS

ROOTS	WORDS	MEANINGS
ven or *vent* means "come"	intervene venue	come between place related to a particular event
verb means "word"	verbal verbose	having to do with words wordy
vers or *vert* means "turn"	avert reverse	turn away turn back
vid or *vis* means "see"	evident visible	plain to see capable of being seen
viv means "live" or "alive"	revive vivacious	bring back to life full of life; lively
vit means "life"	vital vitamin	necessary to the maintenance of life substance necessary for the regulation of life processes
voc or *vok* means "call" or "call forth"	evoke vocation	call forth job a person feels called to do
vol or *volv* means "roll"	evolve revolution	develop rotation

GRAMMAR/USAGE/MECHANICS

PREFIXES

Prefixes are word parts added to the beginning of a root or a base word to change its meaning. They are important tools for understanding and learning new words. The following chart shows common prefixes and their meanings. Notice that some prefixes have more than one meaning and that some prefixes convey the same meaning as others.

PREFIXES	WORDS	MEANINGS
a- means "without" or "not"; it can also mean "on," "in," or "at"	amoral	without morals
	atypical	not typical
	aboard	on board
	abloom	in bloom
ant- or *anti-* means "against" or "opposing"	antacid	agent that works against acidity
	antiwar	opposing war
ante- means "before"	antecedent	going before
	antediluvian	before the biblical flood
be- means "cause to be"	befriend	act as a friend to
	belittle	cause to seem little or less
bi- means "two"	bimonthly	once every two months *or* twice a month
	bisect	divide into two equal parts
cat- or *cata-* means "down"	catacomb	subterranean cemetery
	catastrophe	final stage of a tragedy
circum- means "around" or "about"	circumference	distance around a circle
	circumstance	surrounding condition
	circumvent	avoid by going around
co- means "with" or "together"	coworker	person one works with
	cowrite	write together
col-, com-, con-, or *cor-* means "together" or "with"	collaborate	work with others
	companion	one who accompanies another
	confer	consult with others

PREFIXES	WORDS	MEANINGS
col-, com-, con-, or *cor-,* continued	correspond	exchange letters with another
contra- means "against"	contradict contrary	speak against opposite
counter- means "opposite" or "opposing"	counterbalance counterclockwise	oppose with an equal weight or force opposite of clockwise
de- means "do the opposite of," "remove," or "reduce"	de-emphasize defrost devalue	do the opposite of emphasize remove frost reduce the value of
dia- means "through" or "across"	diameter diaphragm	length through the center of a circle a membrane stretching across an area
dis- means "not" or "absence of"	dishonest distrust	not honest absence of trust
e- or *ex-* means "out"; *ex-* also means "former"	eject exceed ex-president	throw out go beyond former president
en- means "cause to be" or "put into"	enlarge enthrall	cause to be made large put into thrall
extra- means "outside" or "beyond"	extralegal extraordinary	outside of legal means beyond the ordinary
for- means "so as to involve prohibition or exclusion"	forgive forgo	give up feelings of resentment give up pleasure or advantage
hemi- means "half"	hemicycle hemisphere	structure consisting of half a circle half a sphere

GRAMMAR/USAGE/MECHANICS

PREFIXES	WORDS	MEANINGS
hyper- means "excessive" or "excessively"	hyperbole hypersensitive	excessive exaggeration excessively sensitive
il-, im-, in-, or *ir-* means "not" or "into"	illegal illuminate immature immigrant inconvenient insight irregular irrigate	not legal bring light into not mature one who comes into a country not convenient power of seeing into a situation not regular bring water into
inter- means "among" or "between"	international interscholastic	among nations between schools
intra- means "within"	intramural intrastate	within the walls (of a school) within a state
intro- means "in" or "into"	introspection introvert	looking within oneself one who is turned inward
mis- means "bad," "badly," "wrong," or "wrongly"	misspell mistreat	spell wrong treat badly
non- means "not"	nonallergenic nonconformist	not causing allergies one who does not conform
over- means "exceed," "surpass," or "excessive"	overeat overqualified	eat to excess qualified beyond the normal requirements

GRAMMAR/USAGE/MECHANICS

PREFIXES	WORDS	MEANINGS
para- means "beside" or "beyond"	paramedic	one who works beside a physician
	paranormal	beyond the normal
peri- means "around"	perimeter	distance around a plane figure
	periscope	instrument for looking around
post- means "after"	postgame	after the game
	postwar	after the war
pre- means "before"	precede	go before
	premonition	advance warning
pro- means "in favor of," "forward," "before," or "in place of"	pro-American	in favor of America
	proceed	go forward
	prologue	introduction before the main text
	pronoun	word that takes the place of a noun
re- means "again" or "back"	recall	call back
	replay	play again
retro- means "back," "backward," or "behind"	retroactive	effective as of a prior date
	retrogress	move backward
semi- means "half" or "partly"	semicircle	half a circle
	semisweet	partly sweet
sub- means "under" or "less than"	subhuman	less than human
	submarine	underwater
super- means "over and above"	superabundant	having more than an abundance
	superhuman	over and above what is normal for a human being

GRAMMAR/USAGE/MECHANICS

PREFIXES	WORDS	MEANINGS
sym- or *syn-* means "with" or "together"	symbiosis	living together of two dissimilar organisms
	synchronize	make happen at the same time
trans- means "across"	transmit	send across
	transport	carry across
un- means "not" or "do the opposite of"	unhappy	not happy
	untie	do the opposite of tie
uni- means "one"	unicycle	one-wheeled vehicle
	unified	joined into one

PEANUTS reprinted by permission of United
Feature Syndicate, Inc.

SUFFIXES

Suffixes are word parts added to the end of a root or a base word to change its meaning and sometimes its part of speech. The following chart shows common suffixes and their meanings. Notice that some suffixes have more than one meaning and that some suffixes convey the same meaning as others. Notice also that the spelling of a root often changes when a suffix is added. Furthermore, more than one suffix may be added to many words.

SUFFIXES	WORDS	MEANINGS
-able or *-ible* means "capable of," "fit for," or "tending to"	agreeable	tending to agree *or* able to be agreed with
	breakable	capable of being broken
	collectible	fit for collecting
-age means "action," "process," or "result"	breakage	action or process of breaking
	marriage	action, process, or result of marrying
	wreckage	result of wrecking
-al means "relating to" or "characterized by"; it can also mean "action," "process," or "result"	fictional	relating to fiction
	rehearsal	action or process of rehearsing
-an or *-ian* means "one who is of or from"; it can also mean "relating to"	Bostonian	one who lives in Boston
	Elizabethan	relating to the reign of Queen Elizabeth I
-ance, -ancy, -ence, or *-ency* means "action," "process," "quality," or "state"	dependency	state of being dependent
	performance	action or process of performing
	persistence	quality of persisting
	vacancy	state of being vacant
-ant means "one who or that which"; it can also mean "being"	contestant	one who participates in a contest
	observant	being observing
-ar means "relating to" or "resembling"; it can also mean "one who"	liar	one who lies
	molecular	relating to molecules
	spectacular	resembling a spectacle

Chapter 13 Spelling and Vocabulary **423**

SUFFIXES	WORDS	MEANINGS
-ard or *-art* means "one who"	braggart dullard	one who brags one who is dull
-ary means "person or thing belonging to or connected with"; it can also mean "relating to or connected with"	complimentary functionary	relating to a compliment person who serves a particular function
-ate means "of," "relating to," or "having"; it can also mean "cause to be"	activate collegiate	cause to be active relating to college
-cy means "state," "quality," "condition," or "fact of being"	accuracy bankruptcy infancy	quality of being accurate condition of being bankrupt state of being an infant
-dom means "state of being"	boredom freedom	state of being bored state of being free
-ee means "receiver of action" or "one who"	escapee trainee	one who escapes receiver of training
-eer means "one who"	auctioneer engineer	one who runs an auction one who is concerned with engines
-en means "made of or resembling"; it can also mean "cause to be or become"	golden strengthen	made of or resembling gold cause to be strong
-ent means "one who"	resident superintendent	one who resides in a place one who superintends

SUFFIXES	WORDS	MEANINGS
-er means "one who" or "native or resident of"; it can also mean "more"	New Yorker reporter sooner stronger	resident of New York one who reports more soon more strong
-ery or *-ry* means "character," "art or practice," "place," or "collection"	bakery cookery jewelry snobbery	place for baking art of cooking collection of jewels character of being a snob
-ese means "originating in a certain place," "resident of," or "language of"	Japanese	originating in Japan; resident of Japan; language of Japan
-esque means "in the manner or style of" or "like"	picturesque statuesque	in the manner or style of a picture like a statue
-et or *-ette* means "small" or "group"	islet kitchenette quartet	small island small kitchen group of four
-fold means "multiplied by"	fourfold	multiplied by four
-ful means "full of" or "tending to"; it can also mean "amount that fills"	fearful forgetful spoonful	full of fear tending to forget amount that fills a spoon
-fy or *-ify* means "make or form into," "make similar to," or "become"	fortify glorify solidify	make similar to a fort make glorious become solid
-hood means "state," "condition," "quality," or "character"	childhood likelihood statehood	state of being a child quality of being likely condition of being a state

GRAMMAR/USAGE/MECHANICS

Chapter 13 Spelling and Vocabulary **425**

GRAMMAR/USAGE/MECHANICS

SUFFIXES	WORDS	MEANINGS
-ic or *-ical* means "having the qualities of," "being," "like," "consisting of," or "relating to"	angelic athletic atomic historical	like an angel having the qualities of an athlete consisting of atoms relating to history
-ile means "tending to" or "capable of"	contractile infantile	capable of contracting tending to be like an infant
-ine means "of," "like," or "relating to"	Alpine crystalline marine	relating to the Alps like crystal of the sea
-ion or *-ation* means "act or process," "result," or "state or condition"	pollution selection sensation	result of polluting process of selecting state or condition of feeling something
-ish means "like," "inclined to," "somewhat," or "having the approximate age of"	bookish foolish reddish thirtyish	inclined to be interested in books like a fool somewhat red about thirty
-ism means "act, practice, or process," "prejudice," "state or condition," "doctrine or belief," or "conduct or behavior"	criticism heroism Mormonism parallelism racism	act of criticizing conduct or behavior of a hero belief in the doctrines of the Mormon faith state of being parallel prejudice against a race of people
-ist means "one who"	violinist finalist	one who plays a violin one who takes part in the final playoff
-ite means "native or resident of"	Brooklynite	native or resident of Brooklyn

SUFFIXES	WORDS	MEANINGS
-ity means "quality," "state," or "condition"	humanity	condition of being human
	purity	quality of being pure
	sanity	state of being sane
-ive means "performing or tending toward"	active	tending toward action
	excessive	tending toward excess
-ize means "cause to be," "become," or "make"	Americanize	become American
	modernize	make modern
	sterilize	cause to be sterile
-less means "without"	hopeless	without hope
-ly means "like"; it can also mean "in a manner" or "to a degree"	easily	in an easy manner
	friendly	like a friend
	partly	to a partial degree
-ment means "result," "action," or "condition"	amazement	condition of being amazed
	astonishment	result of being astonished
	development	act of developing
-ness means "state," "condition," or "quality"	darkness	condition of being dark
	goodness	state of being good
	heaviness	quality of being heavy
-or means "one who or that which"	elevator	that which raises people or goods to a higher level
	inventor	one who invents
-ory means "place of or for"; it can also mean "relating to" or "characterized by"	contradictory	characterized by contradiction
	observatory	place for observing
	sensory	relating to the senses
-ose means "full of" or "having"	grandiose	having grand ideas
	verbose	full of words; wordy

GRAMMAR/USAGE/MECHANICS

SUFFIXES	WORDS	MEANINGS
-ous means "full of," "having," or "characterized by"	courageous	characterized by courage
	gracious	having grace
	joyous	full of joy
-ship means "state, condition, or quality," "office, dignity, or profession," or "art or skill"	ambassadorship	office of an ambassador
	friendship	state of being a friend
	horsemanship	art or skill of horseback riding
-some means "characterized by"; it can also mean "group of"	foursome	group of four
	troublesome	characterized by trouble
-th or *-eth* is used to form ordinal numbers	seventh	ordinal for *seven*
	twentieth	ordinal for *twenty*
-ty means "quality," "condition," or "state"	novelty	quality or condition of being novel
	safety	state of being safe
-ure means "act," "process," "state," or "result"	composure	state of being composed
	erasure	result of erasing
	exposure	act of exposing
-ward means "toward" or "in a certain direction"	afterward	at a later time
	homeward	toward home
-y means "characterized by or full of," "like," or "tending or inclined to"; it can also mean "state, condition, or quality" or "instance of an action"	chatty	tending or inclined to chat
	homey	like home
	inquiry	instance of inquiring
	jealousy	state, condition, or quality of being jealous
	juicy	full of juice
	waxy	characterized by wax

GRAMMAR/USAGE/MECHANICS

Use the following roots, prefixes, and suffixes to make a list of ten words you know or combinations you think might be words. Use at least one root, prefix, or suffix from the chart in each word you write. Check your words in a dictionary.

PREFIXES	ROOTS	SUFFIXES
anti-	am	-able, -ible
de-	audio	-ance, -ancy, -ence
dis-	ced	-ate
e-, ex-	cred	-dom
contra-	dict	-en
for-	equi	-ic, -ical
il-, im-, in-, ir-	lect, leg	-ion, -ation
pre-	loc	-ive
re-	ject	-ory
trans-	scrib, script	-ous

GRAMMAR/USAGE/MECHANICS

Part Three

● ● ● ● ● ● ● ● ● ● ●

Composition

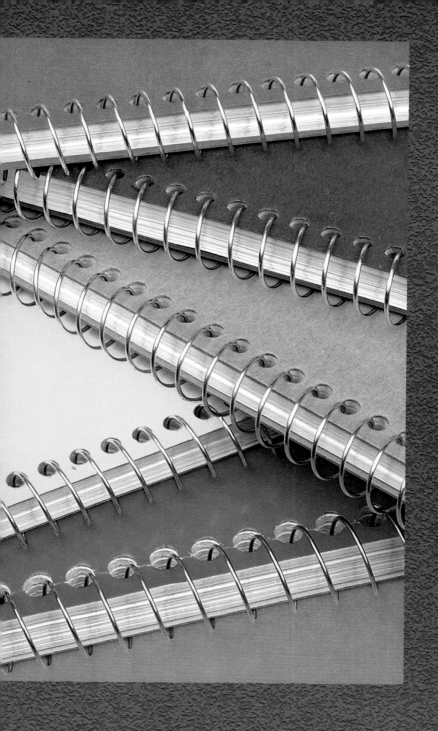

Chapter 14

The Writing Process

● ● ● ● ● ● ● ● ● ● ● ● ● ● ●

Writing is a process done in different stages: prewriting, drafting, revising/editing, proofreading, and publishing/presenting. These stages are recursive, that is, they do not necessarily follow one another in order; you can go back and forth among steps, repeating those that you need to until you end up with the result you want.

THE FAR SIDE By GARY LARSON

© 1982 FarWorks, Inc. All Rights Reserved/Dist. by Creators Syndicate

The Far Side by Gary Larson © 1982 FarWorks, Inc. Used with permission. All Rights Reserved.

The Writing Process

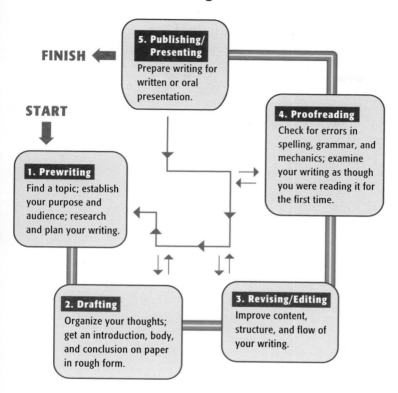

FINISH ←

5. Publishing/ Presenting
Prepare writing for written or oral presentation.

START

1. Prewriting
Find a topic; establish your purpose and audience; research and plan your writing.

4. Proofreading
Check for errors in spelling, grammar, and mechanics; examine your writing as though you were reading it for the first time.

2. Drafting
Organize your thoughts; get an introduction, body, and conclusion on paper in rough form.

3. Revising/Editing
Improve content, structure, and flow of your writing.

STAGE 1: PREWRITING

During Prewriting, you decide what you want to write about by exploring ideas, feelings, and memories. Prewriting is the stage in which you not only decide what your topic is, but

- you refine, focus, and explore your topic
- you gather information about your topic
- you make notes about what you want to say about it
- you also think about your audience and your purpose

Your audience is whoever will read your work. Your purpose is what you hope to accomplish through your writing.

After you've decided on a topic and explored it, making notes about what you will include, you will need to arrange and organize your ideas. This is also done during the Prewriting stage, before you actually draft your paper.

There are many techniques you can use to generate ideas and define and explore your topic.

CHOOSING AND EXPLORING YOUR TOPIC

Keeping a Journal

Many writing ideas come to us as we go about our daily lives. A journal, or log, can help you record your thoughts from day to day. You can then refer to this record when you're searching for a writing topic. Every day you can write in your journal your experiences, observations, thoughts, feelings, and opinions. Keep newspaper and magazine clippings, photos, songs, poems, and anything else that catches your interest. They might later suggest questions that lead to writing topics. Try to add to your journal every day. Use your imagination. Be creative and don't worry about grammar, spelling, or punctuation. This is your own personal record. It is for your benefit only, and no one else will read it.

Freewriting

Freewriting means just what it says: writing freely without worrying about grammar, punctuation, spelling, logic, or anything. You just write what comes to your mind. Choose a topic and a time limit and then just start writing ideas as they come to you. If you run out of ideas, repeat the same word over and over until a new idea occurs to you. When the time is up, review what you've written. The ideas that most interest you are likely to be the ones that will be most worth writing about. You can use your journal as a place for freewriting, or you can just take a piece of paper and start the process. The important thing is to allow your mind to follow its own path as you explore a topic. You'll be surprised where it might lead you.

1. Let your thoughts flow. Write ideas, memories, anything that comes to mind.
2. Don't edit or judge your thoughts; just write them down. You can evaluate them later. In fact, evaluating your ideas at this point would probably dry up the flow. Accepting any idea that comes is the way to encourage more ideas.
3. Don't worry about spelling, punctuation, grammar, or even sense; just keep writing.

Brainstorming

Brainstorming is another free-association technique that you can use to generate ideas. It is often most effective to brainstorm with others because ideas can spark new ideas. Start with a key word or idea and list other ideas as they occur to you. Don't worry about the order; just let your ideas flow freely from one to the next.

Brainstorming TIP

1. Choose someone to list ideas as they are called out.
2. Start with a topic or a question.
3. Encourage everyone to join in freely.
4. Accept all ideas; do not evaluate them now.
5. Follow each idea as far as it goes.

Clustering

Write your topic in the middle of a piece of paper. As you think about the topic, briefly write down everything that comes to mind. Each time you write something, draw a circle around it and draw lines to connect those circles to the main idea in the center. Continue to think about the secondary ideas and add offshoots to them. Draw circles around those related ideas and connect them to the secondary ideas.

Clustering TIP

1. Start with a key word or phrase circled in the center of your paper.
2. Brainstorm to discover related ideas; circle each one and connect it to the central idea.
3. Branch out with new ideas that add details to existing ideas.
4. Review your chart, looking for ideas that interest you.

COMPOSITION

Clustering

Collecting Information

Whether you're deciding on your topic or exploring a topic you've already chosen, you need to discover as many facts as possible about your topic or possible topic.

Asking Questions To discover the facts you need, begin by writing a list of questions about your topic. Different questions serve different purposes, and knowing what kind of question to ask can be as important as knowing how to ask it clearly. The chart that follows will help you categorize your list of questions.

KINDS OF QUESTIONS	
PERSONAL QUESTIONS	ask about your responses to a topic. They help you explore your experiences and tastes.
CREATIVE QUESTIONS	ask you to compare your subject to something else or to imagine observing your subject as someone else might. Such questions can expand your perspective on a subject.
ANALYTICAL QUESTIONS	ask about structure and function: How is this topic constructed? What is its purpose? Analytical questions help you evaluate and draw conclusions.
INFORMATIONAL QUESTIONS	ask for facts, statistics, or details.

Library Research If your topic requires information you do not already have, your school or public library is the best place to find it.

Library Research TIP

1. Search for books by title, author, and subject, using either the card catalog or the online computer system.
2. Use the subject heading for each listing as a cross-reference to related material.
3. Browse among other books in the section where you locate a useful book.
4. Jot down the author, title, and call number of each book you think you will use.
5. Record the titles of books that don't provide help (so you won't search for them again).
6. Examine each book's bibliography for related titles.
7. Try to be an independent researcher but ask a librarian for help if you cannot locate much information on your topic.

If you do your research on the Internet, evaluate your sources carefully and always find at least one more source to verify each point. The reliability of Internet information varies a great deal. Use print sources to verify information you find on the Internet, if that is possible.

Observing One good starting point for exploring a topic is simply to observe closely and list the details you see. After you've listed the details, arrange them into categories. The categories you choose depend on the details you observe and your writing goal. For example, you might want to organize your details using spatial order, chronological order, or order of importance.

Interviewing Get your information directly from the source; interview someone. You may choose someone whom you can interview in person, or you might investigate the possibility of an interview conducted over the telephone, through e-mail, or online. Follow these steps:

BEFORE THE INTERVIEW	Make the appointment.
	Research your topic and find out about your source.
	Prepare four or five basic questions.
DURING THE INTERVIEW	Ask informational questions (who, what, where, when, why, and how).
	Listen carefully.
	Ask follow-up questions.
	Take accurate notes (or tape-record with permission).
AFTER THE INTERVIEW	Write a more detailed account of the interview.
	Contact your source to clarify points or to double-check facts.

IDENTIFYING PURPOSE AND AUDIENCE

Purpose

Before you start to write, you must determine the primary purpose for your writing: to inform or explain, to explore or analyze, to persuade, to amuse or entertain, to narrate, or to describe. Sometimes you might want to accomplish more than one purpose, so you will have a primary purpose and a secondary purpose. To determine the primary purpose, answer these questions:

1. Do I want to tell a story?
2. Do I want to describe someone or something—a place, a person, a process, a relationship, an event, an impression?
3. Do I want to inform my readers about the topic or to explain something about it?
4. Do I want to persuade my readers to change their minds about something or take some action?
5. Do I want to amuse or entertain?
6. Do I want to explore or analyze a topic someone else has written about and perhaps argue with the conclusions he or she has drawn?

Audience

Your audience is anyone who will be reading your writing. Sometimes you write just for yourself. Most often, however, you write to share information with others. Your audience might include a few friends or family members, your classmates, the population at large, or just your teacher. As you write, consider these questions:

1. Who will my audience be? What do I want to say to them?
2. What do my readers already know about my topic?
3. What types of information will interest my audience?

ARRANGING AND ORGANIZING IDEAS

Once you have gathered your information and ideas, you can choose from many kinds of details—examples, facts, statistics, reasons, and concrete and sensory details—to support your main idea. As a writer, you need to put these details in order. Patterns of organization include

- chronological order (by time)
- spatial order (based on space, place, or setting)
- order of importance
- cause and effect (events described as reason and result, motive and reaction, stimulus and response)
- comparison and contrast (measuring items against one another to show similarities and differences)

Your organization might be as simple as making a list or an outline that groups details under larger subtopics or headings. You can also organize details visually by making a chart or a diagram similar to the clustering diagram on page 437. You might better be able to see a plan for organizing your paper when you see the relationships among the parts of your topic.

"It's our new assembly line. When the person at the end of the line has an idea, he puts it on the conveyor belt, and it passes each of us, we mull it over and try to add to it."

Sidney Harris

STAGE 2: DRAFTING

When you write your draft, your goal is to organize the facts and details you have accumulated into unified paragraphs. Make sure each paragraph has a main idea and does not bring in unrelated information. The main idea must be stated in a topic sentence, and it must be supported by details that explain and clarify it. Details can be facts and statistics, examples or incidents, or sensory details.

Writing a draft, or turning your ideas into paragraphs, is a stage in the Writing Process and a tool in itself. During Prewriting, you started to organize your details. You will continue to do this as you write your draft because you might find links between ideas that give new meanings to your words and phrases. Continue to organize your details using one of the methods discussed in Prewriting.

To make your sentences interesting, be sure to vary the length of sentences. Don't use too many short, choppy sentences when you can incorporate some of your ideas in subordinate clauses or compound or complex sentences.

Writing Tip

Your composition should consist of three parts: the introduction, the body, and the conclusion (see the Outlining Tip on page 476). Begin your paper with an **introduction** that grabs the reader's interest and sets the tone. The introduction usually gives the reader a brief explanation of what your paper is about and often includes the **thesis.** The thesis states your paper's main idea or what you're trying to prove or support.

Each paragraph in the **body,** or main part, of your paper should have a topic sentence that states what the paragraph is about. The rest of the paragraph should include details that support the topic sentence. Similarly, each topic sentence should support the thesis, or main idea of the paper.

Writing Tip (continued)

End your paper with a good **conclusion** that gives a feeling of "completeness." You might conclude your paper in any of the following ways:

- Summarize what you've said in the body of your paper.
- Restate the main idea (using different words).
- Give a final example or idea.
- Make a comment on or give a personal reaction to the topic.
- End with a quotation that sums up or comments on the topic.
- Call for some action (especially in persuasive papers).

STAGE 3: REVISING/EDITING

The purposes of Revising are to make sure that your writing is clear and well organized, that it accomplishes your goals, and that it reaches your audience. The word *revision* means "seeing again." You need to look at your writing again, seeing it as another person might. You might read your paper very carefully, you might tape-record yourself reading your paper aloud, or you might share your writing with another student, a small group of students, or your teacher. After evaluating your work, you might want to move things around or change them completely. You might want to add or cut information. Mark these changes right on your draft and then incorporate them.

The revision stage is the point at which you can

- improve paragraphs
- implement self-evaluation and peer evaluation
- check content and structure
- make sure the language is specific, descriptive, and nonsexist
- check unity and coherence
- check style and tone

Writing Tip

When you are writing about people in general, people who may be either male or female, use nonsexist language. That is, use words that apply to all people, not specifically to males or females. For example, instead of *mailman*, which is gender-specific, you could use the term *mail carrier*.

Traditional nouns for males and females in the same occupation (for instance, *poet* and *poetess*) are no longer encouraged. The noun *poet* now refers to both males and females. Refer to the following list for other gender-neutral terms to use in your writing.

Use	Instead of
actor	actress
Briton	Englishman
businesspeople	businessman/woman
chairperson, chair, moderator	chairman/woman
a member of the clergy	clergyman
craftspeople	craftsmen
crewed space flight	manned space flight
fisher	fisherman
flight attendant	stewardess
Framers, Founders	Founding Fathers
handmade, synthetic, manufactured	manmade
homemaker	housewife
humanity, human beings, people	mankind
it/its (in reference to ships, countries)	she/her/hers, he/his
land of origin, homeland	mother country
letter carrier/mail carrier	mailman
police officer	policeman
representative	congressman/woman
server	waiter or waitress
supervisor	foreman
watch, guard	watchman
worker	workman
workforce	manpower

Writing Tip (continued)

Masculine pronouns (such as *he, him, his*) were once used to refer to mixed groups of people. Females were understood to be included. That is, a sentence like *A reporter must check his facts* was understood to apply to both male and female reporters. Now everyone is encouraged to use gender-neutral wording. Some gender-neutral possibilities for that sentence are *Reporters must check their facts, A reporter must check the facts*, and *A reporter must check his or her facts*. (See page 243.)

STAGE 4: PROOFREADING

The purposes of Proofreading are to make sure that you've spelled all words correctly and that your sentences are grammatically correct. Proofread your writing and correct mistakes in capitalization, punctuation, and spelling. Refer to the chart on the next page for Proofreading symbols to help you during this stage of the Writing Process.

COMPOSITION

Proofreading Marks		
Marks	**Meaning**	**Example**
∧	Insert	My gran∧mother is eighty-six years old.
℘	Delete	She grew up on a dairᴇ̷y farm.
# ∧	Insert space	She milked#cows every morning.
◠	Close up space	She fed the chickens in the barn‿yard.
≡	Capitalize	t̲i̲m̲e̲s have changed.
/	Make lowercase	Machines now do the /Milking.
◯ Sp	Check spelling	Chickens are fed ⟨autommatically.⟩ Sp∧
◡	Switch order	Modern farms are ⟨like⟩ more ⟨factories.⟩
⁋	New paragraph	⁋Last year I returned to the farm.

STAGE 5: PUBLISHING/PRESENTING

This is the stage at which you share your work with others. You might read your work aloud in class, submit it to the school newspaper, or give it to a friend to read. You could illustrate a copy to send to a favorite relative or to hang on a school corkboard. You might find a web page on which to print it, or you might find an online chat room or bulletin board where its posting could spark comments. There are many avenues for Presenting your work.

Chapter 15

Modes of
Writing

• • • • • • • • • • • • • • •

15.1 DESCRIPTIVE WRITING

In descriptive writing, your goal is to help your reader experience the subject described. You will find descriptive writing in advertisements, stories, newspapers, travel guides, scientific journals, and many other places. It is important to appeal to as many senses as possible, allowing your audience to appreciate the subject fully.

BEFORE YOU WRITE

Before you begin to write a description, you must choose a topic, such as an object, a person, a place, or an event.

Observe and Take Notes If possible, spend some time directly observing your topic. As you observe, ask yourself

- What is the most striking thing about this subject?
- What colors do I see? What sounds do I hear? What do I smell? Taste? Feel?

447

- What should I include in the description so that my audience will see what I am seeing, feel as I am feeling?

As you observe, take detailed notes about the subject, recording your impressions.

Establish Your Vantage Point From your notes and observations, you will be able to establish your vantage point, or point from which you view the subject. You may choose a stationary vantage point, a fixed position from which you view your subject; or you may select a moving vantage point, which allows you to view your subject from different angles.

Whichever vantage point you choose, remember that it limits the available details.

Establish Order Once you have chosen your vantage point, it will be easy to decide how to order your description. The following chart contains a few possibilities.

ORGANIZING DETAILS	
SPATIAL ORDER	Spatial order is often used when observing from a stationary vantage point. You can organize details from top to bottom, left to right, front to back, east to west, clockwise, or counterclockwise.
ORDER OF IMPORTANCE	When you organize details according to their importance, you may want to begin with the least important detail and build to the most important. This builds the description to a climax.
ORDER OF IMPRESSION	Using order of impression, you give the reader the feeling of being there. Relay the details of the things that you noticed first. Keep in mind that the first impression is not always right—you can build on this and construct a suspenseful mood.

Writing Tip

Use transitions to make your writing read smoothly and to make your description coherent. Some common transitional words include *next to, across from, behind, after, above all,* and *finally.*

WRITE A DESCRIPTIVE ESSAY

Now that you have observed your topic, taken detailed notes, and established your organization, you are ready to write your description.

Topic Sentence The first step to forming a coherent paragraph is to write a topic sentence to give each paragraph unity and to help your readers identify your purpose. You can place a topic sentence at the beginning, in the middle, or at the end of a paragraph.

Use Descriptive Language Support each topic sentence with vivid, precise details.

- Try to stay away from overused modifiers, such as *good*, *bad*, *really*, *so*, and *very*. Consider these modifiers instead: *completely, definitely, especially, exceptionally, largely, mostly, notably, oddly, particularly, strikingly, surprisingly, terribly, thoroughly, unusually*.
- Use precise verbs to capture the essence of actions.
- Think of words that appeal to sight, sound, taste, smell, and touch. For your reader to experience your topic in the same way you did, you must appeal to the senses.

Writing Tip

Descriptive language brings writing alive. When you revise your work, use a thesaurus to find varied words that appeal to the senses and replace repetitive language. Keep in mind, though, that synonyms are very seldom interchangeable. When you have selected a synonym, look in a dictionary for its meaning. For instance, *eager* and *anxious* aren't exact synonyms, although both mean "looking forward to a future event." *Eager* means "anticipating with pleasure," but *anxious* means "anticipating with dread."

Use Analogies An analogy is an extended comparison between two things that are usually considered unlike but that do share some common features. An analogy makes an extended comparison, supported point by point with examples and details. It can last through several paragraphs or an entire essay.

CREATING SUCCESSFUL ANALOGIES

1. Find at least three similarities between the ideas you are comparing.

2. Use specific details and examples to support your comparisons.

3. Write a topic sentence that establishes the basis of the comparison.

4. Decide on a logical order for the points of the analogy and use transitions such as *similarly* and *also* to link them clearly.

Possible analogies:

- Going on a school field trip is a lot like going on a family vacation.
- The new baby at our house reminds me of a very young puppy.
- Being in a group science-fair project is like running in a relay race.

Create a Mood With the descriptive language and the organization you choose, you will produce a certain mood, or overall feeling, for your descriptive writing. To achieve a suspenseful mood, you could organize your description by order of importance, leaving the surprise for the end. To express excitement, you may choose the same order but change the descriptive language you use.

GUIDELINES FOR DESCRIPTIVE WRITING

- Gather vivid details that will help you describe a person or re-create a scene or an experience for your readers.

- Decide which kind of organization will be more appropriate for your subject—spatial order, order of importance, or order of impression.

- Write a thesis sentence that presents your central idea.

- Use transitions to clarify the organization and relationships among ideas.

- Use descriptive language and analogies to make your writing vivid.

COMPOSITION

15.2 NARRATIVE WRITING

A narrative is a story of an event. Narrative writing can be **personal,** allowing the author to focus on important events in his or her life; **historical,** capturing a moment from the past and presenting it in a story format; or **fictional,** using imagination to produce a short story. Here are the basic elements of a narrative:

- **Plot** is the story's action and events. When you tell what happened, you are relating plot. Plots have a **conflict,** a problem basic to human experience, and a **resolution,** the outcome of the conflict.
- **Characters** are the people, animals, or main actors in the plot. Their actions and thoughts enable you to express the **theme,** or overall idea, of the narrative.
- **Setting** is the time and place in which the events of a narrative occur. The setting helps create the **mood,** or general feeling, of a narrative.

DEVELOP YOUR NARRATIVE

Most authors do not just sit down and write. Usually they follow several steps before getting the first draft onto paper. These steps allow for planning and organization, as well as character and plot development.

Frank and Ernest

THE BROADWAY STAGE DELI

I'LL HAVE A THICK, JUICY PLOT WITH EXTRA THEME, HOLD THE NUANCE BUT HEAVY ON THE IRONY!

THAVES

© 1993 Thaves / Reprinted with permission. Newspaper dist. by NEA, Inc.

Find a Story Idea Your story should have a conflict, which can be external—a person struggling against another person, for example, or internal—such as a person torn between two ideals. You can search your everyday life for story ideas for a personal narrative, or you might try looking through newspapers and magazines for ideas. Talk about story ideas with friends.

After you have an idea for your narrative, evaluate it:

- Does the conflict concern a basic human experience, such as love, hate, loyalty, pain, survival, or death?
- Does the conflict matter deeply to the characters?
- Does the resolution grow directly out of the conflict?
- Is the resolution a result of the characters' efforts?
- Does the resolution provide a theme for the narrative?
- Do the characters grow or change by resolving the conflict?

Develop Character Your characters should be as lifelike as possible. Relate the characters' physical descriptions, thoughts, personality traits, actions, and reactions to one another. Include dialogue to let the reader witness the characters' conversations. Dialogue not only gives readers important information about the characters, but it also moves the plot along, foreshadows possible trouble, and produces a sense of time and place.

DIALOGUE GUIDELINES
• Use language that reflects the age, background, and personality of each character.
• Give your dialogue a purpose—to advance the action, to reveal a character's personality, to show relationships between characters, or to build the conflict.
• Enclose a quotation in quotation marks and begin it with a capital letter.
• Begin a new paragraph each time the speaker changes.

COMPOSITION

Set the Scene A setting includes information about time, place, weather, and historical period. Often the setting will affect the way your characters act. Setting also contributes heavily to mood. For instance, if the action of the narrative takes place in an old, abandoned house, the mood will most likely be suspenseful or scary. As you write, consider how each element of the setting can help advance your narrative.

Communicate a Theme The theme of a story is the insight into human life that the writer conveys through the narrative. One way to express the theme of your narrative is through your description of the setting. Ask yourself how you can create a mood and hint at the theme through scenery, props, color, and sound. Then use concrete words to describe these details.

PEANUTS reprinted by permission of United
Feature Syndicate, Inc.

Choose a Point of View Once you have decided on the characters, plot, and setting, you must choose the point of view from which you will tell the story.

- **First-person point of view:** The narrator is a character in the story; he or she uses the pronoun *I*.

- **Third-person point of view:** The narrator is not a character in the story but an observer of it. Using this point of view, you may choose a **third-person limited narrator,** who sees the world through the eyes of one character and knows and relays the thoughts and actions of only this character. Alternatively, you may choose a **third-person omniscient narrator,** who knows and relays the thoughts and actions of all of the characters.

Remember that the point of view you choose significantly affects the story. It can give the story a bias, or it can limit what the audience knows until the very end. Think carefully about the point of view and how it will affect the development of the plot.

ORGANIZE YOUR NARRATIVE

When you begin to organize the information you have decided to include in your story, review the basic plot structure diagram that follows.

You don't have to follow this curve precisely in your narrative, but it gives you a basis to follow. You might want to use **flashbacks** in the rising action that take you back to a time before the story began. You might also consider opening with the climax and then giving the background that led up to it. As you are writing, try several ways of organization, then evaluate the flow of the narrative to see which organization is most successful.

Most Plots Develop in Five Stages.

- **Exposition** is background information about the characters and setting. This sets the scene for the conflict that follows.
- **Rising action** develops the conflict.
- **Climax** is the point of highest interest, conflict, or suspense in the story.
- **Falling action** shows what happens to the characters after the climax.
- **Resolution** shows how the conflict is resolved or the problem solved.

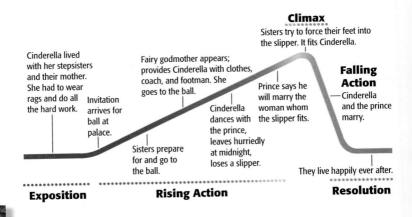

Climax
Sisters try to force their feet into the slipper. It fits Cinderella.

Cinderella lived with her stepsisters and their mother. She had to wear rags and do all the hard work. Invitation arrives for ball at palace.

Fairy godmother appears; provides Cinderella with clothes, coach, and footman. She goes to the ball.

Prince says he will marry the woman whom the slipper fits.

Falling Action
—Cinderella and the prince marry.

Cinderella dances with the prince, leaves hurriedly at midnight, loses a slipper.

Sisters prepare for and go to the ball.

They live happily ever after.

Exposition   **Rising Action**   **Resolution**

15.3 EXPOSITORY WRITING

Giving directions, explaining an idea or term, comparing one thing to another, and explaining how to do something are all forms of expository writing. The purpose of expository writing is to inform your audience or explain something to them. The chart on the next page describes several types of expository writing.

TYPES OF EXPOSITORY WRITING	
TYPE	EXPLANATION
EXPLAIN A PROCESS	Uses step-by-step organization to explain how something happens, works, or is done
CAUSE AND EFFECT	Finds the causes or effects or both of a system; examines the relationship between causes and effects
COMPARE AND CONTRAST	Examines similarities and differences to find relationships and draw conclusions
DEFINITION	Explains a term or concept by listing and examining its qualities and characteristics
PROBLEM AND SOLUTION	Examines aspects of a complex problem and explores or proposes possible solutions

Writing Tip

In expository writing, consider using graphs. Often expository writing includes so many statistics that it is hard to read. A visual element, such as a bar graph, a line graph, or a circle graph, will help your readers grasp your topic.

EXPLAIN A PROCESS

Before you begin to explain a process, you should do at least one of the following: go through the process yourself, watch someone go through the process, or research the process. Take detailed notes as you go.

Organization In most process explanations, you will use chronological order, or the order in which steps will occur. After you have placed the basic steps in order, elaborate on them, supplying necessary details to clarify your explanation.

Writing Tip

Consider your audience's knowledge of the process and the terminology used to describe it. If you explain a process in technical terms with which your audience is unfamiliar, your audience will not understand your explanation.

EXPLAIN A CAUSE-AND-EFFECT RELATIONSHIP

Cause-and-effect relationships occur when one event produces another event, or outcome. Cause-and-effect writing gives explanations for events, conditions, and behavior. For this kind of expository writing, you can

- start with one cause and lead to one effect
- start with one cause and lead to several effects
- start with several causes and lead to one effect
- start with several causes and lead to several effects
- start with one cause that leads to an effect, which in turn becomes a cause that leads to another effect, and so on. The result is a chain of events.

Organization When you describe a cause-and-effect relationship, you can

- describe the effect first and then explain its cause, or you can
- describe the cause first and then explain how it leads to the effect.

Whichever organizational method you choose, make sure that your cause-and-effect relationship is valid—that is, be sure you have not assigned an effect to the wrong cause or causes.

COMPARE AND CONTRAST

When you compare two topics, you're discussing their similarities. When you contrast two topics, you're addressing ways in which they are different. In a compare-and-contrast essay, you must choose two topics that share both similarities and differences, and you must explain these.

Organization As you organize your two topics, you might consider using a Venn diagram such as the one that follows.

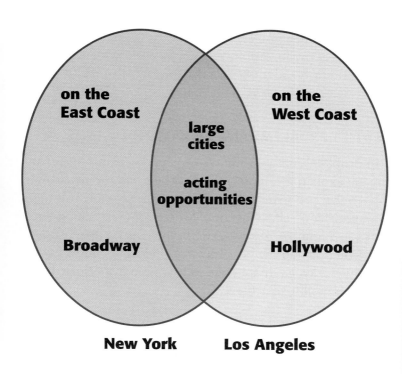

on the
East Coast

large
cities

on the
West Coast

acting
opportunities

Broadway

Hollywood

New York   **Los Angeles**

Once you have identified the similarities and differences of your topics, you can choose the most effective way to present the information—by subject or by similarities and differences.

EXPLAIN A DEFINITION

When you write to define a term or an idea, you can give a formal definition or a personal definition. If you are presenting a formal definition, you should provide specific qualities of the term you are explaining to help your audience understand. If you are presenting a personal definition, you might instead use real-life examples and vivid details to convey your personal feelings about the idea or term.

Organization Begin your research with a dictionary or other source. Once you have the basic definition or idea, you can add details. When you actually write your draft, try different orders of organization; you might want to start with the basic definition and move to a broader sense of the term or vice versa.

IDENTIFY PROBLEMS AND PROPOSE SOLUTIONS

In problem-and-solution writing, you investigate a problem and explain it to your readers. Then you propose solutions to that problem. As you think of the possible solutions, don't limit yourself to just one. Most problems can be solved in a number of ways, and by proposing many solutions you open up the possibility of finding a solution that actually works. Evaluate your solutions to make sure they aren't impossible to achieve.

Organization As you begin your research, consider the causes of the problem. You might want to include these in your writing to help your audience better understand the extent of the problem. You might also include different examples, such as personal anecdotes and statistics.

After you have thoroughly covered the problem, propose solutions. In your writing, you should address both the pros and the cons of the solutions you propose. Keep in mind that there is often no one solution that will fix the entire problem.

15.4 PERSUASIVE WRITING

Persuasive writing surrounds you in everyday life. You encounter persuasive writing in advertisements on television, radio, and billboards. Politicians give persuasive speeches during campaigns. Organizations persuade you to adopt their causes, encouraging you to donate time or money to them.

Persuasive writing is used to motivate readers—to change their minds about a topic, to convince them to buy a product, or to get them to vote for a certain candidate or issue. The main reason behind persuasive writing is to convince readers to take action, in whatever form that might be.

CHOOSE A TOPIC

When you write persuasively, make sure you choose a topic worth addressing. Consider the following when choosing a topic.

- **Are opinions concerning this topic varied?** In persuasive writing, you must argue a point and try to convince readers to support your opinion or somehow to take action. If your opinion is not disputed, it probably is not worth arguing. For example, it would be pointless to argue that pollution is bad because almost everyone would agree with you. However, you might argue for a certain antipollution law, such as mandatory carpooling, and try to convince your audience that such a law is necessary to battle pollution.

- **Will your audience be receptive to your argument?**
Take into consideration your audience and their
opinions and situations when you choose a topic. For
instance, it would be pointless to argue for mandatory
carpooling if your audience was too young to drive.
- **Does enough evidence exist to support your argument?** Briefly investigate the amount of supporting evidence for your argument. If little support for your
opinion exists, you will be fighting a losing battle.

Writing Tip

Before you begin writing, you must also identify your purpose. Do you
want to change the opinions of your audience? To motivate them to
take action? Or simply to encourage them to recognize the validity
of your opinion?

KNOW YOUR AUDIENCE

When you choose a topic, it is important to evaluate your
audience—to know their concerns, their general opinions
and beliefs, and their prior knowledge of or biases toward
the subject. After all, your purpose is to influence their
opinions and perhaps change their actions.

As you evaluate your audience, answer the following
questions:

- Does the issue apply to my audience's lives? Will their
action bring about positive change for them?
- What is the current attitude of my audience? Are they
likely to agree or disagree?
- What do they already know about the issue? Do I need
to provide background or clear up misconceptions?

- What types of evidence will have the strongest impact on my audience? Will facts and statistics alone be effective? Should I include emotional language to convey my point?

From your answers to these questions, you can evaluate the topic you have chosen. If the audience seems appropriate, your next step is to gather evidence to support your topic.

SUPPORT YOUR ARGUMENT

When you present an argument, you can appeal to emotion or to reason. To appeal to emotion, use words that elicit strong positive or negative reactions. Also, you might use real-life examples. For instance, if you were addressing the issue of homelessness, you might consider interviewing a homeless person to give your argument not only factual support but also emotional appeal. To appeal to reason, include facts, statistics, and expert opinions.

Use Evidence to Support Your Viewpoint Persuasive writing is more than just a statement of your opinion. You need to back up your opinion with evidence—facts and expert opinions that support your viewpoint.

Evaluate Your Evidence When gathering evidence, be careful to evaluate the type of support you include. Often opinions are presented as facts. Consider the following chart as you decide which information you will include in your persuasive writing.

RECOGNIZING FACTS AND OPINIONS	
FACTS	• are statements, statistics, observations, examples that can be verified, or experiments that can be repeated
OPINIONS	• are personal judgments • can be supported but not proven by facts • are often biased

Even though opinions are usually personal viewpoints, often they are influenced by supporting facts and statistics. When you evaluate opinions, including your own, make sure that enough supporting evidence exists. Expert opinions can be valuable in supporting your argument because an expert is likely to give an informed, reasoned opinion.

Use Inductive and Deductive Reasoning Either of two kinds of reasoning can support strong arguments. Both kinds of reasoning involve using facts to arrive at conclusions, but they work in opposite ways.

First, let's look at inductive reasoning. We rely on this kind of reasoning for much of our knowledge. When you use *inductive reasoning,* you follow these steps:

1. You begin with a series of facts you've observed.
2. You study the facts, looking for connections or patterns among them.
3. You draw a conclusion or a generalization.

Inductive reasoning proceeds logically from limited facts or observations to a general conclusion. An inductive argument will hold up only if the evidence is accurate and the conclusion follows reasonably from the evidence. Check your reasoning by asking whether any other conclusions can be drawn from the evidence.

EVALUATE INDUCTIVE REASONING

1. What are the specific facts or evidence from which the conclusion is drawn?
2. Is each fact or piece of evidence accurate?
3. Do the facts form a sufficiently large and representative sample?
4. Do all of the facts or the evidence lead to the conclusion?
5. Does the argument contain any logical fallacies?

The other kind of reasoning is called deductive. When you use *deductive reasoning,* you follow these steps:

1. You begin with a generalization.
2. You apply that generalization to a specific example.
3. You arrive at a conclusion.

Deductive reasoning may involve a **syllogism,** which consists of a *major premise,* which is a general statement; a *minor premise,* which is a related fact; and a *conclusion* based on the two.

SYLLOGISM

STRUCTURE	EXAMPLE
Start with a generalization, a MAJOR PREMISE.	Multimedia computers require fast modems.
State a related fact, a MINOR PREMISE.	Lou is getting a multimedia computer.
Draw a CONCLUSION based on the two.	Therefore, Lou needs a fast modem.

NOTE: A syllogism is *valid* if it follows the rules of deductive reasoning. A syllogism is *true* if the statements are factually accurate. A perfectly valid syllogism, then, can be untrue. Here is an example:

Major premise: All voters are good citizens. [There is more to good citizenship than just voting.]

Minor premise: My parents are voters.

Conclusion: Therefore, my parents are good citizens. [This conclusion is valid according to the premises; however, it isn't necessarily true, because the major premise is flawed.]

1. What are the major premise, the minor premise, and the conclusion?

2. Is the major premise a universal statement?

3. Are both premises true?

4. Does the conclusion follow logically from the major and the minor premises?

5. Does the argument contain any logical fallacies?

Recognize Logical Fallacies Faulty reasoning involves errors called logical fallacies. Learning to recognize your own and others' logical fallacies will strengthen your skills in persuasive writing. Here are three of the most common types of flaws.

- A **red herring** statement diverts attention from the issue at hand. A senator who is attacked for irregular attendance might describe her charitable work to prove she is productive. However, she has not addressed the criticism about the missed meetings.

- **Circular reasoning** is an argument that apparently leads to a logical conclusion but actually takes you back to where you started. The statement "Frank Sinatra was a great singer because he had such a wonderful voice" sounds true, but the statement doesn't prove anything; it merely repeats the point in different words. There is nothing to prove or disprove.

- **Bandwagon reasoning** The term "jumping on the bandwagon" means doing or thinking something because everyone else is doing or thinking it. This type of reasoning provides no evidence to support a decision or a viewpoint.

Address the Opposition As you research supporting evidence, take time to address opposing evidence and opinions. If you do not argue against opposing viewpoints, your argument may seem weak.

ORGANIZE YOUR ARGUMENT

To be a successful persuasive writer, you must state your case well. As you organize your argument, take the following steps.

GUIDELINES FOR ORGANIZATION			
INTRODUCE THE ISSUE.	**STATE YOUR OPINION.**	**SUPPORT YOUR POSITION.**	**DRAW YOUR CONCLUSION.**
Describe the issue, supplying any background information needed.	Take your stand in a clear, direct thesis statement.	Present your evidence and show the flaws in opposing viewpoints.	Summarize your ideas and state your purpose.

Chapter 16

Research Paper Writing

• • • • • • • • • • • • • •

"GRANTED, WE HAVE TO DO THE RESEARCH. AND WE
CAN DO SOME RESEARCH ON THE RESEARCH. BUT I
DON'T THINK WE SHOULD GET INVOLVED IN RESEARCH
ON RESEARCH ON RESEARCH."

Sidney Harris

When you write a research paper, you collect information from several sources, analyze and organize this information, and present it to your readers in a clear and interesting way.

To write a research paper, you need to

- choose a topic that interests you
- narrow the topic to fit your paper's length
- perform extensive research to gather information
- organize your research and write an outline
- form a thesis statement and support the thesis with the information you gathered in your research
- compile a list of your sources

16.1 PREWRITING

CHOOSE A TOPIC

One of your first decisions is what to write about. Try to find a topic that interests you. Researching and writing will be easier if you are curious about the topic you choose. Also consider how much information will be manageable given the length of your research paper. If the topic is very broad, you'll have too much information. If the topic is too narrow, you won't be able to uncover enough material. If you choose a topic either too broad or too narrow, your paper will probably lack substance.

TOO BROAD	NARROW	TOO NARROW
Art	Pablo Picasso	Picasso's painting *Les Demoiselles d'Avignon*
Tennis	The History of Wimbledon	2001 Wimbledon

Decide on a Central Idea

Once you have a topic, you need to decide on your paper's central idea. This idea will guide your thinking and your selection of research questions. Try to identify three to seven research questions, each question focusing on one aspect of the topic. Ask the *what*s, *why*s, and *how*s about your topic. As you begin to find answers, you'll come up with more sharply focused questions. Feel free to modify your central idea as you learn more about the topic.

Sample Questions for a Paper about Pablo Picasso

- How did Picasso learn to paint?
- What other art works, besides paintings, did he produce?
- Why is Picasso so famous?
- What inspired Picasso's art works?
- What is Cubism?

FIND INFORMATION ON YOUR TOPIC

Use two types of sources when you do your research—primary and secondary.

- A **primary source** is firsthand information that has not been evaluated or analyzed by someone else. If you are studying the painter Pablo Picasso, for example, a letter he wrote or a painting he created would be considered a primary source. Historical documents from the era you are researching and statistics are considered primary sources.
- A **secondary source** is information that has been organized and analyzed by someone else. An article analyzing

Picasso's paintings would be a secondary source. Most books and magazines are considered secondary sources.

Technology Tip

The Internet can be a valuable tool for finding both primary and secondary sources. Evaluate Internet sources carefully. Not all Internet sites contain accurate information. To make sure you are obtaining accurate data, find another source that contains the same information.

Take Notes

Once you have found some sources, you can begin taking notes and collecting information. Taking notes efficiently and accurately is one of the most important steps in writing a good research paper. You'll probably take many more notes than you'll use. It's better to have too much information than too little.

Prepare Note Cards Read your sources thoroughly for information, ideas, statements, and statistics that relate to your research topic and your main idea. When you find something you can use, write it on a three-by-five note card, with one piece of information per card, and record the number of that source's bibliography card (see Develop a Working Bibliography on p. 474). You can take notes in one of three ways:

- by quoting the sources directly. Use quotation marks to indicate direct quotations.
- by paraphrasing (writing the information in your own words)
- by summarizing (writing a brief summary of the information, highlighting the most important parts)

Types of Note Cards

EXAMPLE Direct Quotation Note Card

> Record **direct quotations** exactly as they appear, including punctuation. Put quotation marks around all quoted material.

An Introduction to Music and   Bib 8
Art in the Western World.

"Cubism was a style of twentieth-century
art that reduced nature to basic
geometric patterns.... Again, the artists
painted what they knew, not what they
saw. In pursuing this style, they
were concerned more with <u>how</u> a work
was painted and less with <u>what</u>
was painted."
            (quotation)   page 307

EXAMPLE Paraphrase Note Card

> A **paraphrase** is a restatement of someone else's original idea. In what other ways could you restate this information?

An Introduction to Music and   Bib 8
Art in the Western World

Cubists painted geometric patterns to
represent how they thought of a
subject, not what it looked like to
other people.

            (paraphrase)   page 307

EXAMPLE Summary Note Card

> When you **summarize,** you put together key points and important details.

An Introduction to Music and Bib- 8
Art in the Western World

Cubists focused on the method of painting, not on the painting's subject.

(summary) page 307

> The page number of the source is 307. Complete information about the source is on bibliography card #8.

Read Sources Critically As you read and research, evaluate your sources. A source may be biased; that is, the writer may be prejudiced toward one particular viewpoint. Using a biased source without recognizing it as such can hurt your argument. To detect bias, ask yourself, "Does this writer have a hidden purpose? Is she [*or* he] taking sides?"

When you take specific notes, pay attention to each idea's context, its relation to the ideas presented before and after it. Information out of its context may be misleading.

Avoid Plagiarism Presenting someone else's ideas or statements as your own is plagiarism. You must avoid even accidental plagiarism. Writers sometimes begin to paraphrase but instead present an idea almost as it was originally written and then take credit for it. Read your sources critically, keep complete and well-documented notes, and credit other writers when you should. If you have doubts about whether you may be plagiarizing, try rewriting the passage again in your own words, and then compare your new version with the source.

COMPOSITION

Develop a Working Bibliography

As you begin your research, assemble a record of the books, articles, Internet sites, and other sources you consult. This record is your working bibliography. When you find a useful source, record the publishing data on a three-by-five index card. This way you can easily find and use the information later. Complete bibliography cards will also help you write your list of works cited.

Different kinds of sources need different data on their bibliography cards. See the examples under A List of Works Cited on page 485 for more information about what you need to record on these cards.

Types of Bibliography Cards

EXAMPLE   Book

> 1
>
> Penrose, Roland. *Picasso.* London: Phaidon Press Ltd., 1991.

> 2
>
> "*Picasso and Cubism.*" Designer: Denise Hall. 7 Nov. 1996. University of Texas. 15 July 1998
>
> < http://ccwf.cc.utexas.edu~/ifeh 750/index.html >.

CHOOSE A METHOD OF ORGANIZATION

How can you decide on the best way to arrange the ideas
in your notes? You have a number of options, depending on
the nature of your information.

- **Chronological:** arrange the information according to
  when it happened. This organization is often used in
  papers describing historical changes. The outline about
  Picasso's life and work is organized chronologically.
- **Cause and Effect:** arrange items in causal order to
  show how one idea or event directly determines
  another. This organization is often used in papers
  exploring why something happened.
- **Cumulative:** arrange items according to how important or how familiar to the reader each one is. This
  organization is often used in papers evaluating results.

Develop an Outline

An outline is a summary of the main points and the ideas
that support them. As you take notes, look for ways to classify the facts and ideas you find and begin to group the note
cards accordingly. As you make decisions about how to
organize your cards, you are developing the information
you need to write a working outline. You'll continue to
write and revise this outline as you conduct your research.
The following tips will help you write a working outline,
which will eventually become the formal outline you will
use when you write your first draft.

COMPOSITION

Outlining TIP

1. Look for similarities among notes; group note cards on similar topics together. Use each group as a main topic in your outline.
2. Within groups, cluster similar note cards into subgroups that elaborate on the larger and more general topic. Use these subgroups as the subheadings in your outline.
3. Arrange main topics to build on your central idea. Under each topic, arrange subheadings so they elaborate on the heading, or main topic, in a logical way.
4. As you continue your research and learn more, revise and elaborate on your outline. Subdivide information in subheadings into outline entries if necessary.
5. Set aside note cards that don't fit under any heading. Don't discard them.
6. Before you begin your first draft, prepare a formal outline.

Title of Paper

I. Introduction
   Central idea (thesis statement)

II. Heading (main topic)
   A. Subheading (supporting detail)
      1. sub/subheading
      2.
   B. Subheading (supporting detail)
      1.
      2.

III. Heading (main topic)

IV. Heading (main topic)

V. Conclusion

Body — { II, III, IV

The Life and Work of Pablo Picasso

I. Introduction
Picasso was not content to paint in one style;
instead he experimented with different styles
and media, and he changed the style of his
art frequently over the course of his life.

II. Early life
   A. Talented by age 10
   B. Art school in Madrid
   C. Trip to Paris
      1. Influenced by other artists
      2. Use of color

III. Blue period
   A. Depression caused by friend's death
   B. Subjects of blue period

IV. Rose period
   A. Settles in Monmartre
      1. Meets artists
      2. Lighter mood
   B. Inspirations and influences

V. Les Demoiselles d'Avignon
   A. First work of Cubism
      1. Reaction of contemporaries
      2. Put away for twenty years
   B. Description of painting
      1. Motivation
      2. Philosophy

VI. Cubism
   A. Development
      1. Georges Braque
      2. Dates of Cubism
   B. Definition
      1. "Paint objects as I think them..."
      2. Goals of Cubists
      3. Influences

VII. Post-Cubist painting
   A. Realistic style portraits
   B. Political art
      1. Guernica
      2. History of Guernica
      3. Description of painting
      4. "Painting... instrument of war"

VIII. Other media
   A. Scene and set design
   B. Poetry and plays
   C. Sculpture
   D. Ceramics

IX. Conclusion

16.2 DRAFTING

DEVELOP A THESIS STATEMENT

So far, you have guided your research and your outline according to your central idea, or the basic question you've been exploring. You've probably rethought this idea as you have learned about the topic. Now it's time to turn that central idea into a **thesis statement**—that is, a concise idea that you try to prove, expand on, or illustrate in your writing. Your thesis statement will focus your writing from start to finish.

FOUR TYPES OF THESIS STATEMENTS

TYPE	DESCRIPTION	EXAMPLE
Original	Used to demonstrate new information you have developed	My survey of students and teachers at Lincoln High School has uncovered a desire for more and better computers.
Evaluative	Used when stating your opinion on a topic	Solar power provides our best option for future energy needs, taking into account both economic and environmental concerns.
Summary	Used when your paper primarily reports the ideas of others	High-speed trains have revolutionized long-distance travel in both France and Japan.
Combination	Combines any two or all three of the above approaches	Interviews with music store salespeople and CD owners lead me to believe that the CD has replaced the record once and for all.

USE YOUR OUTLINE AND NOTES

Using the structure you have given your formal outline, you will be able to transform your piles of note cards into a first draft. Look at your outline again to be sure you're satisfied with the way each idea leads to the next. Then begin drafting.

1. Try to draft as smoothly and logically as possible without getting stalled on details. Don't worry about finding the "perfect" word or phrase; you can revise later.
2. Write at least one paragraph for each heading in your outline. Each paragraph should have a topic sentence and supporting details.
3. When you use data from a note card, write the number of that card near the data in the text to help you document the idea later.
4. Use your outline as a "map" to guide you in your writing. The outline should remind you of what comes before or after a particular idea.

Write the Introduction and Conclusion

A good introduction should grab your reader's attention and make him or her want to read on. Consider the following techniques for capturing your reader's attention:

1. Summarize by providing an overview of the main headings in your paper to make your reader comfortable with the topic.

2. Include an unusual anecdote or fact about your topic.

3. Pose a question that you plan to answer or explore in your paper.

4. Use a quotation.

Your conclusion should alert the reader that you are wrapping up. You might summarize your main points or mention any new questions your paper raises.

RESEARCH PAPER FORMAT

Use the following format for your research paper:

- At the top, bottom, and both sides of each page, leave margins of one inch.
- Double-space every line, including the title if it is more than one line long.

- Unless you are told to include a cover page, write your name, your teacher's name, the name of the course, and the date on four lines along the left margin at the start of page one.
- Center the title on the next line.
- Except for the first page, put the first line of type one inch from the top edge of the paper.
- For all pages except the cover page: Put your last name and the page number in the upper right corner of each page, one-half inch from the top and even with the right margin. Number all pages consecutively.
- Indent each paragraph's first line one-half inch from the left margin.
- If you use a set-off quotation, indent each line of it one inch from the left margin.
- At the end of your research paper, on a new page, begin your list of works cited. Center the title, *Works Cited*, an inch from the top of the page. Begin each entry even with the left margin. If an entry is more than one line long, indent the next line or lines one-half inch from the left margin.

16.3 CITING SOURCES

Document Information In a research paper, you need to be careful to indicate the sources of the information you present—including all ideas, statements, quotes, and statistics you have taken from your sources and that are not common knowledge. One reason for documenting your sources is to enable your reader to check the source personally and to judge how believable or important a piece of information is. Another reason is to avoid plagiarism.

COMPOSITION

What to Document What kinds of information need documentation? You should document your information

- whenever you use someone's exact words
- whenever you paraphrase a particular idea or series of ideas
- whenever you use information that is not generally known or found in most books on the subject

You do not need to document widely known proverbs, famous quotations, and simple definitions.

Parenthetical Documentation One way to cite sources is to insert the author's name and a page reference in parentheses after the information that requires citation. Place this documentation at the end of the sentence containing the information. The following chart explains how to document different sources in the body of your paper.

DOCUMENTING SOURCES WITHIN THE RESEARCH PAPER	
Kind of Source	**Example**
Author named in text Insert the page number in parentheses.	As Hughes points out, by the time of Picasso's death, millions of people around the world could recognize his work (72).
Work with two authors Insert both authors' last names in parentheses before the page number.	In 1937 Picasso's work changed dramatically, becoming for the first time political (Smith and Jones 15).
Work with three or more authors Give the last name of the first author listed, followed by *et al.* ("and others") and the page number.	In 1907 Picasso painted *Les Demoiselles d'Avignon*, "an early experiment" in the Cubist style (Wold et al. 307–308).

Kind of Source	Example
Work with no author or editor Use the title or a shortened version of the title, and give the page number.	The distortion, especially the "presentation of multiple perspectives," shows early signs of Cubism ("Picasso and Cubism" 1).
Source on a page with no page number Use *n. pag.* ("no pagination") in place of the page numbers.	"When I was a child, my mother said to me, 'If you become a soldier you'll be a general. If you become a monk you'll end up as the Pope.' Instead, I became a painter and wound up as Picasso" (Clark n. pag.).
More than one work by the same author Use the author's name, the title or a shortened version of the title, and the page number.	As long as he lived, Picasso regarded Spain as his homeland and the source of his creativity (Jaffé <u>Picasso</u> 14).
More than one source at a time Include both sources and their page numbers, separated by a semicolon.	Picasso rolled up the just-finished *Les Demoiselles d'Avignon* and stored it for over twenty years (Penrose 12; McCully 861).

Use Quotations

You may quote from a source in the following ways:

1. You may quote one word or part of a sentence, including it in a sentence of your own.

In 1907 Picasso painted *Les Demoiselles d'Avignon*, which was "an early experiment" with the Cubist style (Wold et al. 308).

COMPOSITION

2. You may quote one or more complete sentences, which you should introduce in your own words.

   As Picasso once said about his work, "If you know exactly what you are going to do, what's the good of doing it? There's no interest in something you know already. It's much better to do something else" (Clark 24).

3. You may omit words or sentences from a quotation by using ellipses in place of the omitted words or sentences. Place brackets around words you have inserted in place of the omitted words or sentences. Be careful not to change the meaning of the original sentences.

   Picasso's interest in the Iberian figures and other primitive sculpture "urged along . . . [his] tendency to simplification and greater objectivity of form, to suppression of detail" (Jaffé 22).

4. You may use a quotation of more than four lines by starting a new line and indenting the quote. In this case, do not use quotation marks.

Compile a List of Works Cited

From your bibliography cards, record the publishing information about the sources in the form of a Works Cited list. The list should be alphabetized by the authors' last names. If a work has no author, alphabetize it by the title. Include this list on a new page at the end of your report.

The following chart shows the proper bibliographic style for various sources, as recommended by the Modern Language Association of America (MLA). If your teacher asks you to use a different style to document your sources, you can still refer to this chart to be sure you have included everything necessary.

A LIST OF WORKS CITED	
TYPE OF CITATION	EXAMPLE
Book with Single Author	Penrose, Roland. <u>Picasso</u>. London: Phaidon Press Ltd., 1991.
Book with Two Authors	Robb, David M., and J. J. Garrison. <u>Art in the Western World</u>. New York: Harper & Row, 1963.
Book with Three or More Authors	Wold, Milo, et al. <u>An Introduction to Music and Art in the Western World</u>. Dubuque: Brown and Benchmark, 1996.
Magazine Article	Hughes, Robert. "The Artist: Pablo Picasso." <u>Time</u> 8 Jun. 1998: 72-77.
Newspaper Article	Bradley, Jeff. "Picasso's Genius as a Graphic Artist on Display at New Metro State Center." <u>Denver Post</u> 10 Jun. 1998: F1.
Encyclopedia Article	McCully, Marilyn. "Picasso." <u>The New Encyclopaedia Britannica: Macropaedia</u>. 15th ed. 1998.
Internet Article	"Picasso and Cubism." Des. Denise Hall. 7 Nov. 1996. University of Texas. 15 July 1998 <http://ccwf.cc.utexas.edu/~ifeh750/ index.html>.

Not all sources fit the categories listed above. To cite such sources, check the *MLA Handbook for Writers of Research Papers*, and adapt one of the above entries, arranging the information in the following order:

Author information should appear at the beginning of the entry, with the author's last name first.

- If the source has two or more authors, reverse only the first author's name.

- If no author is listed, list the editor. If no editor is listed, begin with the title.
- If you use more than one work by the same author, you do not need to repeat the author's name for each entry; use a dash instead.

Title information follows any author information and lists the title of the article, essay, or other part of the book first if needed, then the title of the book.

Publication information follows the author and title, and as needed, lists the editor's name, edition number, volume number, and series name. Always list the city of publication, publisher's name, and the publication date.

Citing Online Sources

You won't need to include everything from the following list in a single citation; most sources don't require all the information in this list. If you cannot find all the information needed for a particular source, provide as much information as is available.

1. Author, editor, or compiler of the source
2. Title of the article, poem, or short work (in quotation marks); or title of a posting to a discussion line or forum followed by the phrase *Online posting.*
3. Title of the book (underlined)
4. Editor, compiler, or translator of the text (if not mentioned earlier)
5. Publication information for any print version of the text

6. Title of the scholarly project, database, periodical, or professional or personal site (underlined). If the professional or personal site has no title, add a description such as *Home page.*

7. Editor or director of the scholarly project or database

8. Version number of the source, or for a journal, the volume number, issue number, or other identifying number

9. Date of electronic publication, of the last update, or of the posting

10. Total number of pages (if they are numbered)

11. Name of the institution or organization sponsoring or associated with the Internet site

12. Date when you accessed the source

13. Electronic address of the source (in angle brackets)

Writing Tip

Page numbers in parenthetical documentation indicate the pages from which the information is taken. Page numbers in Works Cited entries are for the page span of the entire periodical or anthologized work.

16.4 REVISING/EDITING

When you revise your first draft, you can improve your choice of words, your transitions, and—most important—the way you present your ideas. Use the chart on the next page to help you revise your draft.

COMPOSITION

SOLVING REVISION PROBLEMS	
PROBLEM	SOLUTION
My first draft needs a clearer focus.	Review your thesis statement. Delete or rewrite anything in the paper that doesn't support it.
My argument should be easier to follow.	Add transitions. Rearrange and add ideas to make the paper more coherent. Delete irrelevant information.
My paragraphs don't flow smoothly from one to another.	Add or change transitions between paragraphs. Rearrange paragraphs to achieve a more logical order.
My introduction doesn't connect well with the rest of my paper.	Add transitions or rewrite the introduction to conform with the purpose and main idea.
My sentences sound repetitive.	Vary the sentence structure. Use precise, lively language. Find synonyms for repeated words.

16.5 PROOFREADING

After revising your draft, type or print a new copy of it with your corrections included. Then you can proofread your paper one final time, checking citations, grammar, spelling, punctuation, and word use. The following checklist can help you catch any remaining problems or errors.

Proofreading Checklist

1. Have I organized my ideas clearly?
2. Have I explained or defined any words that may be unfamiliar to the reader?
3. Have I discussed my topic completely?
4. Have I corrected all grammar and spelling errors?

5. Have I documented my sources properly?
6. Have I considered the meanings of the words I've used?
7. Have I capitalized everything correctly?
8. Is my final copy neat and easy to read?

16.6 PUBLISHING/PRESENTING YOUR RESEARCH PAPER

If your teacher requests it, include a cover sheet containing the title of the paper as well as your name and other identifying information. Your teacher may also ask you for other materials to check the extent of your research and the construction of your paper. For example, you may be asked to include a clean copy of your formal outline.

Your teacher may also ask you to include a summary statement. This is a brief restatement of your thesis statement, no more than two sentences long and inserted before your report.

SAMPLE RESEARCH PAPER

Lionel Washington

Ms. Kim

4th period English 10

May 7, 2001

The Life and Work of Pablo Picasso

In 1998 *Time* magazine confirmed what many already knew when it named Pablo Picasso the most influential artist of the twentieth century. Picasso, who lived from 1881 to 1973, was one of the first visual artists in history to achieve a mass audience in his own lifetime. By the time of his death at age ninety-one, millions of people around the world knew his name and had seen reproductions of his work (Hughes 72). What was it about Picasso that made him so famous? There were certainly many other talented and innovative artists in the twentieth century. One reason for Picasso's fame may be the fact that throughout his

> The thesis statement clearly states the main idea of the paper.

COMPOSITION

lifetime he constantly reinvented himself and his work. He distinguished himself as an adept painter from the time he was a child; his early paintings show his skill at what some would call the "traditional" art of copying objects and people exactly as they are. But Picasso was not content to simply continue painting in this style. As he once said about his work, "If you know exactly what you are going to do, what's the good of doing it? There's no interest in something you know already. It's much better to do something else" (Clark 24).

The son of a professor of art, Picasso was born in Spain. By the time he was ten, Picasso's talent as an artist was evident, and he soon surpassed his father in skill and technique. His family recognized his rare talents and promising future.

> When I was a child, my mother said to me, "If you become a soldier you'll be a general. If you become a monk you'll end up as the Pope." Instead, I became a

COMPOSITION

painter and wound up as Picasso (Clark

n. pag.).

Picasso's family hoped that he would become a

government-supported painter, so they sent Picasso

to art school when he was fourteen and to another

school in Madrid when he was sixteen. Unimpressed

with the teaching at the school in Madrid, Picasso

left to wander the streets and visit art galleries.

When he was eighteen, he returned to his family in

Barcelona and met a fellow artist named Carles

Casagemas. After one of his paintings was accepted

for an exhibit in Paris, Picasso, who was eager to

see the city of artists, left for Paris with Casagemas.

In Paris, Picasso discovered the bright colors used

by such artists as Vincent Van Gogh and Paul Gaugin.

He began to use these brilliant colors in his own

paintings.

Picasso returned to Spain after two months in

Paris. He became depressed after the death of his

friend Casagemas in 1901, and he expressed this

depression during his Blue Period, which lasted from 1901 until 1904. He abandoned the bright colors he'd begun using in France and instead painted works mostly in cold blue tones. During this time, Picasso moved back and forth between Barcelona and Paris and used street beggars and poor people in each city as his subjects. During the Blue Period, "allegories concerning poverty, blindness, love, death, and maternity were often in his thoughts" (Penrose 9).

In 1904 Picasso decided to settle permanently in Montmartre, Paris, where he met and befriended many artists and poets. His mood became lighter, and he replaced the cold blue tones of the Blue Period with the pinks and grays of his Rose Period (1904–1906). Picasso often took inspiration from the circus performers he saw around Paris. During this period, Picasso became interested in the Iberian sculptures he saw in the Louvre Museum in Paris (Penrose 10). These sculptures, dating from

COMPOSITION

before the Roman Empire, were simple depictions of people whose figures were out of proportion. Some of Picasso's portraits from this era depict women with similarly distorted figures. According to Hans L. C. Jaffé, Picasso's interest in the Iberian figures and other primitive sculpture "urged along . . . [his] tendency to simplification and greater objectivity of form, to suppression of detail." These tendencies would later lead Picasso to develop the style of art for which he is most famous, Cubism (22).

In 1907 Picasso painted *Les Demoiselles d'Avignon,* which was "an early experiment" with the Cubist style (Wold et al. 308). Instead of depicting beautiful women, Picasso painted what was considered to be a violent depiction of women— prostitutes with distorted figures and mask-like faces. Picasso once again found inspiration for these figures from sculpture, this time from African art (McCully 861), and the distortion in this painting,

especially the "presentation of multiple perspectives," shows the early signs of Cubism ("Picasso
and Cubism"). Picasso's contemporaries were outraged by this "violent" depiction of women, so he
rolled up the painting and put it away for more than
twenty years.

In 1909, for the only time in his life, Picasso
began working closely with another painter,
Georges Braque. Together, Picasso and Braque
developed the style of painting that became known
as Cubism. As a Cubist, Picasso said he began to
"paint objects as I think them, not as I see them"
(<u>Oxford</u> 514). His goal was no longer to copy what
he saw; instead he and Braque abandoned what
was known about perception and presented a new
kind of reality, in which objects were often depicted
from several different perspectives at the same time.
When one is looking at some Cubist paintings, one
seems to be looking at the same object from many
different angles. Cubists "were more concerned

COMPOSITION

with *how* a work was painted and less with *what* was painted" (Wold et al. 307).

Those who knew Picasso as a Cubist were surprised when he began once again to draw portraits in a realistic style in the late 1910s (Jaffé 31). Picasso, though, was never again to remain faithful to one style during his long life; he combined and developed different styles to create works that suited his purpose. During World War II, when he lived in German-occupied France, he painted one of the most famous political paintings of the twentieth century, *Guernica*. The Nazis bombed the Spanish city of Guernica in 1937, and in his painting, Picasso relates the violence and mutilation of the bombing, and of war in general, by depicting dismembered body parts and ferocious monsters. He added a new purpose to his art when he declared, "No, painting is not interior decoration. It is an instrument of war, for attack and for defense against the enemy" (Jaffé 12).

> The topic sentence of each paragraph supports or explains the thesis statement; the rest of the paragraph supports or explains the topic sentence.

COMPOSITION

Picasso's contribution to art was not limited to his work as a painter. In 1917 he created the costumes and sets for the Russian Ballet's performance of *Parade.* In the 1930s, he published two works of poetry, and he wrote a play in 1941.

He was also an innovative sculptor who was among the first to use found objects in his sculptures, such as the bicycle saddle and handlebar he made into *Head of a Bull, Metamorphosis* (Bradley F1). He also made ceramics, coloring and deforming plates and bowls until they could no longer be used as containers.

He created more than fifty thousand works of art in his lifetime (McCully 863) and did not slow down his creative output even during his last years. By then, Picasso's reputation had risen to almost mythological status.

Picasso himself put into words the theme of his whole career when he angrily said to a publisher who had criticized his work, "What is sculpture?

COMPOSITION

What is painting? Everyone clings to old-fashioned ideas and outworn definitions, as if it were not precisely the role of the artist to provide new ones" (Clark 29).

Picasso gained and kept the admiration of people worldwide throughout his life and even afterward. As stated in the introduction, twenty-five years after his death *Time* magazine declared him the most influential artist of the twentieth century. Why? His innovative approach to art and his constantly changing definition of what art should be kept his appeal fresh.

The conclus[ion] might restat[e] thesis stater[ment] summarize main points mention ne[w] questions th[e] paper raises

COMPOSITION

Works Cited

Bradley, Jeff. "Picasso's Genius as a Graphic Artist on
Display at New Metro State Center." <u>Denver Post</u>
10 Jun. 1998: F1.

Clark, Hiro ed. <u>Picasso: In His Words</u>. San Francisco:
Collins Publishers, 1993.

Hughes, Robert. "The Artist: Pablo Picasso." <u>Time</u>
8 Jun. 1998: 72-77.

Jaffé, Hans L. C. <u>Pablo Picasso</u>. New York: Harry N.
Abrams, Inc., Publishers, 1983.

McCully, Marilyn. "Picasso." <u>The New Encyclopaedia
Britannica: Macropaedia</u>. 15th ed. 1998.

"Pablo Picasso." <u>The Oxford Dictionary of
Quotations</u>. 4th ed. 1996.

Penrose, Roland. <u>Picasso</u>. London: Phaidon Press
Ltd., 1991.

"Picasso and Cubism." Des. Denise Hall. 7 Nov.
1996. University of Texas. 15 July 1998
<http://ccwf.cc.utexas.edu/~ifeh750/index.html>.

Wold, Milo, et al. <u>An Introduction to Music and Art in the Western World</u>. Dubuque: Brown and Benchmark, 1996.

Chapter 17

Business Writing

● ● ● ● ● ● ● ● ● ● ● ● ● ● ● ● ●

17.1 WRITING A LETTER OF COMPLAINT

Maybe your new sweatshirt shrank two sizes the first time you washed it, and now you can't even pull it over your head. Perhaps you ordered your favorite group's newest CD—but the company sent you a CD by a group you never heard before and don't care about. Maybe a waiter acted as if you and your friends didn't deserve good service. You might decide to write a letter of complaint to let your feelings be known.

TIPS ON WRITING A LETTER OF COMPLAINT

Here are some tips that will help you write an effective letter of complaint.

- Provide all the necessary information. Include the time and place the event occurred and the names and titles of the people involved. If you're complaining about a purchase, describe the exact item you bought or ordered, its stock number and price, and the date you bought or ordered it. If you called in your order and remember the clerk's name, include that, too.

- Objectively describe the problem. Vague, emotional words such as *awful* and *disgusting* won't help. Instead, calmly and clearly explain what happened, as a reporter would do. Remember that the person reading your letter needs clear information in order to help you.

- Request a specific, reasonable solution. Demanding that the recipient just "do something" about a problem isn't helpful. Instead, say what you would like to happen, such as having an item replaced or receiving a refund. Most companies will go out of their way to keep customers happy and will be glad to fulfill a reasonable request—if they just know what the customer wants.

- Be polite. Calling people names, insulting their intelligence, or making threats won't help the situation. Remember that everyone makes mistakes, and misunderstandings do happen. Even more to the point, in most cases the person who will read your letter is not the person who made the mistake. Don't make an enemy of the person who opens your letter.

- Keep a copy of your letter until your complaint has been resolved in some way. If you need to write a follow-up letter, attach copies of any previous correspondence.

159 West Street
Bethel, ID 89753
June 20, 2001

Add a heading with your own address and the date.

Karla Lessing
Manager, The Place
429 Carriage Drive
Bethel, ID 89753

Include an inside address: the recipient's name and title if available, the name of the business, and its address.

Dear Ms. Lessing:

If possible, address the reader by name. (Mel called the restaurant to learn the manager's name.) Otherwise, use a general salutation such as *Dear Manager* or *Dear The Place*.

Today, June 20, two of my friends and I ate dinner at The Place. We arrived about 6:20 pm, and our waiter's name was Lee. Provide the background information.

After we were seated, we had to wait fifteen minutes for Lee to bring us menus. Then we waited another twenty minutes before Lee took our order. After ordering, we had to wait forty-five minutes for our food.

We saw Lee a lot during this time, but he was always helping someone else. He seemed to be ignoring us. When our food finally arrived, it was not what we had ordered. Lee brought my friend Tony chicken even though Tony had asked for chili. My friend Erin never did get her French fries, but Lee still put them on our bill. Objectively describe the problem.

All in all, we were very dissatisfied with the service we received. We know the restaurant just opened and Lee is new at his job, so we would like to try again. Please send us a coupon or some kind of credit for the cost of our meal, so we can give your restaurant another chance. I am enclosing a copy of the receipt for our meals, which totalled $22.50 for the three of us. Request a reasonable solution.

Sincerely, Include the closing, followed by a comma.

Mel Adams

Mel Adams Sign your name above your typed name.

BE POLITE

Avoid using the pronouns *you* and *your*. Using these two pronouns in negative situations can seem like a personal attack on the reader, blaming the reader personally for whatever went wrong. These examples show the difference.

ATTACKING THE READER	STATING THE FACTS
You sent me the wrong CD!	I did not receive the CD I had ordered.
Your waiters are incompetent!	Lee did not bring the food we had ordered.
I *know* you don't want me to tell all my family and friends how you treated us.	A new restaurant, trying to build good public relations, has to try to give each customer an enjoyable dining experience.

Readers who feel they are being attacked or blamed may stop reading. Yet if you simply state the facts, they probably will read your entire letter and try to solve your problem.

To avoid insulting someone, don't mail anything you wrote while you were angry or upset. Wait until you cool off to revise. Here are some words and phrases that indicate an angry—or perhaps a rude—writer:

WORDS AND PHRASES TO AVOID

I'm sure you don't realize	you must realize
irresponsible	you don't expect me to
mistaken	I expect you to
incompetent	you should know
failed	if you care
inexcusable	you forgot to
obnoxious	why do you people always
ignorant	you leave me no choice
insist	your complaint
refuse	you say

You have a right to make complaints, but you also have a responsibility to make them courteously, without trampling on the reader's right to be respected.

WILL YOUR LETTER BE DIRECT OR INDIRECT?

Letters can be **direct**, getting to the point right away, or **indirect**, explaining the situation before getting to the point. Letters that offer good news should be direct, stating the reason for writing in the first sentence or two. Getting to the point immediately gives a busy reader the information he or she needs right away.

If you write with a simple request, you are asking a reader to do something he or she won't mind doing, such as attending a meeting or filling an order. These letters should also be direct, making the request in the first or second sentence.

However, sometimes you write to ask readers to do something that they might not want to do. If you make your request in the first or second sentence, the reader will probably say no. In these situations, readers are more likely to say yes if you use the indirect approach, which is more persuasive. To do this, you explain the situation first and then make your request.

TWO APPROACHES TO BUSINESS LETTERS	
DIRECT	Give the main point first, then provide details.
INDIRECT	Explain the situation first, then make a request.

Reread Mel's letter of complaint. Do you see that he explained the situation before making his request? Think for a minute about how the restaurant manager might have responded if Mel had used a direct approach, starting right off by asking for a refund of $22.50. Without knowing the situation, the manager might think Mel is unreasonable, decide not to grant his request, and stop reading. Yet because Mel first explained the situation politely and objectively, the manager will probably keep reading and send him a coupon for three free meals.

BE BUSINESSLIKE

Being businesslike means avoiding slang. Words such as *awesome* and *diss* have no place in business writing. Save them for letters—or e-mail—to your friends. Fortunately, however, being businesslike does *not* mean using really long sentences and words. Neither does it mean using old-fashioned words and phrases, such as *herewith* and *the aforementioned*. Today's business writing uses simple, straightforward language and avoids the stilted words and phrases that make letters boring and difficult to understand. Your letters, including your letters of complaint, will be much improved if you make these kinds of substitutions:

Instead of	*Write*
herewith	with this letter
aforementioned	previously mentioned
As per your request,	As you asked,
Enclosed please find	I am enclosing
At this point in time,	Now *or* Today
is in possession of	has
forward it to the undersigned	send it to me

Writing Tip

Write letters of complaint when the situation requires it—but write ones that will get good results!

17.2 WRITING A MEMO

When you become a working adult, you'll probably need to know how to write a memo. People who work for the same company often communicate with one another using memos. Memos can be sent from a manager to an employee, from an employee to a manager, or from an employee to another employee. The word *memo* is short for *memorandum,* which means "a written reminder." Memos help employees coordinate projects or request others' help or opinions. They also are used to introduce new staff members, announce meetings, explain recent decisions, describe changes in procedures, and just to get things done.

Unclear, unorganized memos can force other employees to guess what the writer is trying to communicate. Guessing can result in wasted time, missed deadlines, poor decisions, and expensive mistakes. Managers and supervisors often consider an employee's ability to write a clear, well-organized memo when they are contemplating a raise or a promotion. In other words, your skill in writing memos will probably be used as a measure of your competence on the job.

UNDERSTANDING THE DIFFERENCE BETWEEN A LETTER AND A MEMO

While you'll use memos to communicate with people within your organization, you'll use letters when you write to people outside it. Letters and memos are similar in many ways. Both can be either long or short, depending on how much the writer has to say. Both can be informal when they are written to someone the writer knows well, or they can be formal when they are sent to a stranger, a superior, or a group of people. A writer might spend a few minutes jotting down a letter or memo—or hours on either one if the situation is sensitive or complex.

Although letters go to people outside the organization, they aren't necessarily more important than memos. A memo to another employee can be just as important as a letter to a customer.

FORMATTING A MEMO

Although letters and memos are similar, they have different formats. That is, they look different on the page. A letter begins with a heading (the writer's address and the date) followed by the inside address and the salutation. A memo begins with a different kind of heading, as shown here. Notice that the first letters of the date, names, and subject all line up vertically.

Date: March 13, 2001
To: Louis Morgan
From: Melloni Pollanski *mp*
Subject: Changes in ordering office supplies

The order of the information in memo headings can vary, with the date placed last instead of first, for example. Some memos also have a line labeled "CC:" that lists the people who receive carbon copies. (Today the copies are usually xerographic, but "C:" or "CC:" is still the label.) Some traditional writers use the label "Re:" instead of "Subject:" to indicate the topic of the memo. *Re* is Latin for "in regard to the thing."

Many businesses use a special letterhead for memos. No addresses are necessary in the heading of a memo, as it is going to someone within the company. Memos usually have no closing or signature. Instead, writers put their initials beside their names in the heading to show that they wrote the memo and are responsible for its contents.

Though the paragraphs in letters can be indented, the paragraphs in memos are usually written in full block form, without any indentation. Insert two or three extra lines between the heading and the memo, and put an extra line between the paragraphs.

Frank and Ernest

© 1979 Thaves / Reprinted with permission. Newspaper dist. by NEA, Inc.

ORGANIZING A MEMO

These steps will help you organize an effective memo:

1. Determine your purpose for writing Think about your reason to write. What do you need to communicate or request? If you tell yourself, "I need to write to Joan about the Simpson order," you haven't identified your purpose clearly enough. Here are more specific reasons to write to Joan:

- to inform her about a change in the shipping schedule
- to ask her to check on a price for an item in the order
- to tell her that Mr. Simpson has canceled his order

A memo should have one main point or two or three closely related points.

COMPOSITION

2. Choose a direct or an indirect approach In a **direct** approach, you get to the point in the first sentence or two of the memo. Use a direct approach if your purpose is

- to give the reader good news or information that is not controversial or potentially upsetting
- to make a request that the reader will probably be willing to grant

The following is part of a "good news" memo that uses the direct approach. Notice that the main point is stated immediately.

> The company is introducing a flextime working schedule. Starting November 1, employees will be able to choose their own working hours, with their supervisor's approval, as long as they work eight hours a day. Application forms for schedule changes will be available from the Human Resources Department as of October 15.

In an **indirect** approach, you explain the situation before getting to the point. Use an indirect approach if your purpose is

- to give bad news
- to persuade the reader to do something he or she might not want to do

On the next page is part of a "bad news" memo, organized using the indirect approach. Notice that the writer explains the situation before offering the bad news. This approach prepares readers for the bad news and helps them understand why a difficult decision was made. That way, they will

COMPOSITION

be more likely to accept the bad news without becoming angry or upset.

> For the past three months, the Human Resources Department has been studying the practicability of a flextime working schedule. Flextime would enable employees to customize their hours at work to accommodate changeable responsibilities such as sick children or elderly family members, school holidays, and even community volunteering projects. The company supports employee responsibility to family and community and hopes to be able to offer flextime in the near future. However, as you know, the Simpson project has required a great deal of overtime recently. Because of the tight deadlines, supervisors have not had time to give us their input on flexible scheduling. They have asked us to delay our decision until after the Simpson delivery date, which is six months away. For that reason, we will put flextime on the back burner until the third quarter. In the meantime, employees are invited to contact the Human Resources Department with comments and suggestions for the flextime policy that we will eventually adopt.

3. Decide what information to include in the memo Ask yourself these questions:

- What does the reader *already know* about this topic?
- What does he or she *need* to know?
- What does the reader *want* to know?

Don't bore readers by repeating what they already know, but do provide any background information or details that you think are necessary. Sometimes, however, readers need to be reminded about the facts of a situation even though they are familiar with it.

4. Write the memo Skip the subject line for now. Start by explaining your main point, if you chose a direct approach, or the situation, if you're using an indirect approach. If your memo is long, organize the information in a logical way. For example, you might explain a situation chronologically—that is, in the order in which it happened. Alternatively, you might put the information in order of importance.

5. Write an effective subject line If you have chosen the direct approach, the subject line in your heading should summarize the memo. It should be short and specific. If the memo is going to all employees or to several departments, the subject line should attract the attention of those employees most affected by the memo.

Here are some subject lines that are poor choices, followed by some that are better:

TOO WORDY	New cafeteria schedule for the month of May because of the kitchen remodeling
BETTER	New cafeteria hours for May
TOO VAGUE	Survey results
BETTER	Employees' cafeteria preferences

If you're using an indirect approach, don't put the bad news or the request in the subject line. Your reader may stop right there and become angry at the bad news or reject your request. Instead, just mention the topic in the subject line.

TOO DIRECT	Problems in meeting the deadline on the conversion project
BETTER	Conversion project status
TOO DIRECT	Mandatory overtime for June
BETTER	New June work schedule

MAKING MEMOS MORE READABLE

The way your memo looks on the page—its format—will help determine whether anyone reads it. Following these tips as you edit and revise will help you invite people to read your memos:

- Break your memo into paragraphs, with one main topic per paragraph. A solid page of words can discourage readers.

- Use lists and bullet points whenever appropriate to add interest to the page and further break it into smaller "chunks."

- Use words that your readers will understand. Unfamiliar terms and abbreviations will only frustrate readers. Remember, the purpose of a memo is to communicate, not to impress readers with your vocabulary or to teach them new words.

- When you're finished, proofread. If you're working on a computer, use your computer's spell-checker, if possible, but also read the memo yourself word for word. A spell-checker will catch spelling errors, but only your careful reading will catch missing words or the wrong forms of words, such as *here* for *hear* or *it's* for *its.* Reading the memo aloud may help you spot these mistakes. Putting it aside for several hours and then rereading it will also help you see exactly what's on the page, instead of what you intended to say.

Writing effective memos takes some practice, but if you can learn to write clear, well-organized memos, your co-workers—and your supervisors or managers—will be glad to see your initials on a memo from you, and your job will be easier, more pleasant, and more productive.

COMPOSITION

THIS IS MY REPORT ON SERFS..

SERFS HAD TO WORK VERY HARD..

EVERY MORNING THE MASTER WOULD YELL, "SERFS UP!"

WELL, I'LL BET THEY DID IN CALIFORNIA...

PEANUTS reprinted by permission of United Feature Syndicate, Inc.

17.3 MAKING A PRESENTATION

Oral presentations aren't just schoolwork. Any time you've planned what to say to a parent or guardian, any time you've thought out beforehand how a discussion with a friend might go, you've prepared for an oral presentation. When you begin working, you might have to explain a project to people in another department or ask other employees to contribute to a worthy cause. Maybe you'll be part of a team that is trying to get your department's proposal accepted by upper management. All these will be opportunities for you to use the oral presentation skills that you are practicing now in school.

Many people, even businesspeople, dread giving oral presentations. They worry about "doing something stupid" or looking foolish. They're afraid they'll forget what they planned to say—or remember it but "bore everyone to death." They don't want everyone to see how nervous they are. They don't want to be the focus of everyone's attention.

These panicked people probably don't know how to plan an effective oral presentation. If they did, they would feel more confident and comfortable about it. This lesson will help you look forward to your next presentation. Here are the steps you'll learn:

- Consider Your Topic and Your Purpose
- Analyze Your Audience
- Choose the Form of Your Presentation
- Decide What to Say
- Organize Your Presentation
- Create Visuals for a Multimedia Presentation
- Practice Giving Your Presentation
- Look Professional and Speak Effectively

CONSIDER YOUR TOPIC AND YOUR PURPOSE

In school or at work, you might choose a topic or one might be assigned to you. First, make sure you understand what is expected from your presentation. Are you simply informing the audience about a noncontroversial topic? If so, you might need to narrow a topic that is too broad. You might have to think of an approach that will interest your audience. You definitely must find out what the audience needs to know about the topic.

Maybe you're expected to persuade the audience to think differently about the topic. Perhaps you're supposed to convince them to do something they might not want to do. Then you will need to devote some time to analyzing the audience's different needs and viewpoints so you can determine what will best motivate them to act.

Often your next step will be learning more about the topic. This may require some time at the library, on the Internet, or both. You might also interview experts over the phone, in person, or via e-mail. The more you know about the topic, the better you can decide what to say to your audience. Feeling confident and knowledgeable about your topic is the foundation of giving an effective presentation.

COMPOSITION

ANALYZE YOUR AUDIENCE

Consider how your audience might respond to your topic. With interest? With indifference? Even with hostility? If the audience is familiar with the topic, some listeners might already have strong opinions about it. You will need to respect these opinions, even if you intend to persuade the listeners to change their minds. If the audience has heard about this topic many times before, you will have to think of an interesting new approach.

If the topic is relatively new to this audience, find out what, if anything, they already know about it. Can you use technical terms or will you have to define them—or avoid them? What is the audience's educational level? What interests or experiences do they have that will help them understand this unfamiliar topic? How can you show them that the topic is important in their everyday lives?

In a work setting, you will also need to know whether your audience will be mostly co-workers, mostly management, or a combination of the two. Are your listeners the decision makers or the ones who carry out decisions? Will they accept your recommendations at face value, or will you have to support your conclusions with statistics and experts' opinions?

The answers to these questions will help you decide what your presentation should include to meet the audience's needs and to accomplish your own goals.

CHOOSE THE FORM OF YOUR PRESENTATION

Decide how much your audience will participate. Here are two possibilities, but your presentation may fall somewhere in between:

A traditional speech or lecture In this approach, you provide information on a topic and answer questions from the audience afterward. This approach is often used because it is a direct way to share information. However, it can be boring for the audience, who must spend most of their time merely sitting and listening.

An interactive presentation This approach is more like a conversation and works best with a smaller audience. You provide basic information and then ask the audience questions. Here are some possible goals for this type of presentation:

- to get the audience's feedback on an issue
- to convince the audience to act on an issue
- to help a group work together to solve a problem
- to encourage the audience to ask questions that explore the topic
- to guide the audience to see how they can apply a certain concept or technique in specific situations

For example, if you were trying to get the audience to volunteer to be tutors in the community's Right to Read program, you might begin by explaining what the program does. You might also introduce some of the current tutors.

Next, you could involve the audience by asking for reasons why some people decide not to be tutors. Someone might point out, for example, that young people don't know how to be teachers. Then you can ask the audience if they've ever taught anyone to do something. What was it? (Be ready with examples of your own, such as shooting a basket, braiding hair, accessing the Internet, or programming a VCR. You are reminding the audience that they do, indeed, know how to be teachers.) After they've participated in the presentation, your audience is more likely to participate in the program.

Interactive presentations get the audience more involved than a traditional speech or lecture does, but the presenter must be able to keep discussions on track and quickly adjust the questions to meet the audience's needs and interests. You don't want the meeting to disintegrate into an argument.

DECIDE WHAT TO SAY

Learning more about your topic and analyzing your audience will help you decide what to include in your presentation. The amount of time allowed for your presentation will also help determine how much information you can include. Instead of saying a little about many aspects of the topic, focus on two or three main points that will be meaningful to your audience. They won't remember lots of facts and statistics, but they are likely to remember two or three points if you offer interesting examples and solid evidence to support them.

Writing Tip

While planning your presentation, ask yourself these questions:
· What do I want the audience to learn?
· What do I want the audience to do after my presentation?

ORGANIZE YOUR PRESENTATION

Plan an opening that will grab the audience's attention and introduce your topic. Here are some possibilities:

Tell a story It can be a true story about yourself or others, as long as it won't embarrass anyone else. (You can embarrass yourself if you want to.) Alternatively, it could be a story you've made up that helps you introduce the topic of your presentation. Here's one example: "I wanted to get a job this year, because. . . ."

Ask a question Get the audience thinking about the topic. For example, you might ask, "Where would you be today if you didn't know how to read?"

Offer a surprising fact Get the audience's attention with a fact that challenges their opinions. Here's an example: "Did you know that one in five adults in the United States cannot read as well as the average fourth grader?"

Tell a joke Do this only if you're good at it. Choose a joke that relates to your topic, and make sure it does not insult any person or group of people. Most libraries have books of jokes compiled especially for public speakers. Try the joke on friends first to see if they think it is funny, doesn't insult anyone, and isn't too silly.

" 'How I Spent My Summer Vacation,' by Lilia Anya, all rights reserved, which includes the right to reproduce this essay or portions thereof in any form whatsoever, including, but not limited to, novel, screenplay, musical, television miniseries, home video, and interactive CD-ROM."

After deciding how to begin your presentation, make an outline that organizes your main points into a logical order. Be sure to include examples, quotations, or statistics to back up each point. Following are some organizational patterns you might use:

CHRONOLOGICAL	Describe a series of events or steps in the order in which they occurred.
PRIORITY	Persuade your audience by arranging the reasons they should do something from least to most important.
PROBLEM/SOLUTION	Describe a problem, explain why it happened (or will happen), and offer a solution (which usually involves some action by the audience).
COMPARE AND CONTRAST	Show how two events, people, or objects are similar and different. This approach can help the audience understand an unfamiliar concept or convince them that one course of action is better than another. A variation is the pro/con pattern, in which you give both the advantages and the disadvantages of a course of action.
CATEGORIES	Divide the topic into categories and explain each one. You might use this approach to explain new services offered by your school or by a community agency.

The ending of your presentation is just as important as the beginning. Here are two effective endings:

- Summarize your main points and then go back to your opening statement. Finish your story, repeat your question, or refer to the fact or joke you used. Going back to the beginning gives the audience a sense of closure.
- Repeat your strongest point and then ask the audience to do something specific in response, such as filling out an application form or making a donation.

After you've outlined your presentation, write the main points on separate note cards. On each note card, include any important details you want to mention, along with any quotations or statistics you think will be effective. Use words and phrases, not complete sentences. You aren't going to read these cards aloud. You'll just use them during the presentation to remind yourself of what you planned to say. Number the cards so you can keep them in order during your presentation.

CREATE VISUALS FOR A MULTIMEDIA PRESENTATION

Multimedia simply means "involving several media or channels of communication." Speaking is one channel of communication, and visuals are another. Some people prefer the auditory channel and like to listen to new information, while others prefer the visual channel and would rather read or view new information. This second group will certainly appreciate your use of visuals.

CLOSE TO HOME JOHN McPHERSON

After the slide projector broke,
Dave's presentation to the board of directors
took a drastic turn for the worse.

COMPOSITION

Visuals help interest the audience and explain your points. A series of visuals can serve as an outline for your presentation and reduce the number of note cards you need. Visuals have other important benefits: they give the audience something to look at besides you, they provide something for you to do with your hands, and they make you look professional and well organized.

Visuals can be as simple as a list printed on poster board or as complex as animated computer graphics. Visuals can include charts, tables, graphs, maps, models, samples, videotapes, drawings, photographs, or diagrams. They can be created by hand or by computer and presented on handouts, poster board, or overhead slides or transparencies.

When designing visuals

- Explain only one point with each visual. Keep the visual simple so your audience can grasp your point right away. If necessary, explain a complicated point with a series of visuals or with several overlays on a basic transparency.
- Give every visual an informative title that stresses the point you want to make. For example, instead of "Food Preferences in the Cafeteria," you could use "Increasing Preferences for Low-Fat Food."
- Use large enough type to enable your audience to read labels and explanations easily. Do not use all upper case, or capital, letters. ALL CAPS ARE MUCH HARDER TO READ, AND THEY "SOUND" LIKE SHOUTING!
- Don't try to include every detail in the visuals, just the main points.
- Avoid clutter, such as too many typefaces, colors, clip art graphics, or borders. Two typefaces are enough, and three colors are plenty. Choose art that closely relates

to your topic. You might use the same border on all your visuals to tie them together.

- Don't forget to proofread. Otherwise, a transparency might display a misspelled word or other error in three-inch letters!

Keep it simple! Limit each visual to
- one idea
- no more than 5 to 7 lines of type
- no more than 6 to 8 words per line
- no more than 35 words in all

Using Computer Software

Many software packages are being developed to aid in school and business presentations. Several programs can create slides and transmit them directly from a computer to an overhead screen. This allows you to make words, paragraphs, or graphics appear and disappear from the slide. You can also add sound effects and fade the picture between slides. Using a chart or a graph, you can make lines or bars "grow," or you can separate one bar into several.

Most of these software programs can also create (with the help of a properly equipped film developer) 35-mm slides to use in a projector, make color or black-and-white overhead transparencies, and print handouts. In addition, you can write notes to use during your presentation, with the appropriate slide or overhead printed right on the page.

Using Visuals

Before using the visual aids you've prepared, check your equipment. Check it one more time just before the presentation to make sure it works. A program that worked fine at home may not work in another setting. A power surge may have damaged the computer. The bulb on the overhead projector may have burnt out. Be ready with another way to share the information in case of disaster.

When using your visuals, face your audience and stand to one side of the visual. Do explain your visuals, but don't read them to the audience. Don't show a visual until you're ready to talk about it. Then leave it displayed until you are ready for the next visual. Turning equipment on and off can annoy an audience. Glaring white screens can also be distracting.

PRACTICE GIVING YOUR PRESENTATION

Rehearse your speech, using your visuals so that you will feel comfortable with them. After your opening, tell the audience the points you will cover so they know what to

COMPOSITION

expect. Practice making smooth transitions between your points so your presentation will flow well.

Ask a few friends or family members to listen and give you feedback on both the content of your presentation and your delivery. Perhaps you can videotape yourself and do your own critique. Watch for times when your words were difficult to understand or you didn't clearly explain a point. Were any points or examples a little dry and boring? If so, find more interesting examples to liven them up.

Check your timing and make adjustments if your presentation is too long or too short. (You might also find that you speak more quickly than usual in front of a larger audience.) Be careful not to practice so many times that you memorize your presentation. You want it to be fresh and interesting for both yourself and the audience.

FoxTrot

Bill Amend

LOOK PROFESSIONAL AND SPEAK EFFECTIVELY

If you feel nervous before speaking to a group, you're just like most speakers. Still, that doesn't mean you won't do well. Admit to yourself that you're feeling a little jittery and use that energy to focus your attention and do your best.

Getting Ready

Get a good night's sleep and arrive at the location at least a half hour ahead of time so you don't have to rush. To prevent burping, avoid carbonated beverages for several hours before your presentation. Also, don't drink any more caffeine than you usually do.

To help yourself relax just before the presentation, take several slow, deep breaths. Next, tighten and relax your muscles, working from your toes to the top of your head. Then take a few more slow, deep breaths for good measure. Gather your note cards in your hand and take your place in front of the group where your visuals are waiting for you. Pause and smile at the audience. DON'T apologize for being nervous. Just greet your audience and begin.

Using Your Body Effectively

- Stand up straight, but in a relaxed way.
- Maintain eye contact with the audience. Pretend you are talking to just one person, but focus on a different person in a different area of the audience every minute or so. (According to several studies, audiences believe that speakers who make eye contact are better informed, more experienced, friendlier, and more sincere than speakers who don't.)
- Use gestures when they're appropriate. They help show your enthusiasm and interest in your topic.
- Move around. Unless you're standing on a stage or must stay close to a microphone, try walking among the audience members. It will bring you closer to them physically and emotionally.

Using Your Voice Effectively

- Speak clearly and slowly. Let your voice rise and fall naturally, as if you were having a conversation. Try not to rush.
- Speak loudly enough to reach people in the back of the room. However, if you're using a microphone, let it do the work. Don't shout.
- Show enthusiasm in your voice. Get excited about your topic. Your audience will catch your excitement. Enthusiasm is contagious.

PUTTING IT ALL TOGETHER

Now you know how to do well on your next presentation. If you still feel nervous about it, imagine the worst thing that could happen.

FEARS	REALITIES
You'll forget what you were going to say.	No, you won't. Your note cards and your visuals will keep you on track.
You'll mispronounce a word.	If a word is giving you problems while you rehearse, ask someone how to say it, or use another word.
Your presentation will be boring.	No, it won't, not after all the thought you've put into it. You know your audience and your topic well. You're going to start with an interesting story, and you've found good examples to support your main points. You've also created excellent visuals.

So when is your next presentation? It's not too early to start planning. You'll amaze everyone with your new skills.

COMPOSITION

Part Four

● ● ● ● ● ● ● ● ● ● ● ●

Resources

Knowledge is of two kinds: we know a subject ourselves, or we know where we can find information on it.

—Samuel Johnson

Chapter 18

The Library
or Media Center

● ● ● ● ● ● ● ● ● ● ● ● ● ● ●

Although you've probably been in a library, you might not realize all the resources the library has to offer or how to find them. This chapter will guide you through the library and help you understand how and where to find what you need.

CIRCULATION DESK

At the circulation desk, you'll find a librarian who can answer your questions and check out your books. In addition to a circulation desk, some libraries have computers you can use to check out your own books. Larger libraries might station additional librarians in other sections of the library.

CATALOG

A computer or card catalog will tell you which books are available in the library and where to find them. You'll learn more about using both kinds of catalogs on pages 533–539.

STACKS

The stacks, or rows of book shelves, are called the "adult section" in some libraries, but you don't have to be an adult to use these books. The stacks are usually divided into sections for fiction (novels and short stories that are works of the imagination) and nonfiction (books based on fact about subjects such as history and science).

YOUNG ADULT AND CHILDREN'S SECTION

Young readers, including high school students, can find excellent resources in the young adult and children's section. Fiction, nonfiction, and biographies are usually grouped separately, with picture books for very young readers in their own section. All of these books are listed in the library's computer or card catalog.

REFERENCE AREA

The reference area might include encyclopedias, dictionaries, almanacs, yearbooks, atlases, and other reference materials. Books in this area can be used only in the library. By not allowing people to check out these books, the library ensures that all reference materials will always be available for anyone who needs to consult them.

NEWSPAPERS AND PERIODICALS

In the newspaper and periodical section, you can read local newspapers as well as papers from major cities in the United States and perhaps from other countries. You can also browse through periodicals, which include magazines and journals. You probably cannot check out the currrent issues, but you can usually take older issues home to read. The young adult and children's section might have its own periodicals area. You'll learn more about finding specific articles in newspapers and periodicals on pages 545–547.

AUDIO-VISUAL MATERIALS

The audio-visual section of the library may stock software programs, audiocassettes and compact discs (CDs) of your favorite music, books on tape, videos, and slides for you to borrow and enjoy at home.

COMPUTER AREA

Many of today's libraries offer the use of personal computers for research on the Internet or for writing reports and papers. You may have to reserve a computer ahead of time, and the library might set a time limit, such as two hours, on your use of it. Many library computer areas also have software programs for you to use there, such as a résumé-writing program, an accounting program, or even a program to teach you how to type. For a small fee per page, you can usually print the articles you've located or the papers you've written.

STUDY AREAS

Many libraries now have desks or small rooms set aside for quiet study. You might need to reserve them ahead of time.

SPECIAL COLLECTIONS

Some libraries set aside a special room or section for collections of rare books, manuscripts, and items of local interest, including works by local students.

Bizarro. by Dan Piraro

I was surfing AMAZON.COM & a piranha bit me.

Chapter 19

Using Print Resources

• • • • • • • • • • • • • •

Imagine how frustrating it would be if you had to walk up and down the stacks in a library, looking for a book that might—or might not—be anywhere on the shelves! To make life easier, libraries use cataloging systems to keep track of what's available and arrange books on the shelves according to their content.

19.1 UNDERSTANDING CATALOGING SYSTEMS

Whether you want information on a particular subject, books by a certain author, or a specific book, the catalog will help you find whatever you're looking for. Many libraries now use computerized catalogs, but some still rely on paper card catalogs. You should be able to use both kinds of tools. Then no matter what library you enter, its catalog will be at your service.

COMPUTER CATALOGS

Computer systems vary, so before you use one for the first time, read the instructions posted beside the computer or printed on the screen. Most catalog programs begin by asking whether you want to search by author, title, or subject. If you use the author's name, type the last name first, followed by a comma and the first name, as in *Johnson, Samuel.* (Some systems will allow you to type *Samuel Johnson* or even just *Johnson,* although in the latter case you'll have to search through a list of all the authors named Johnson to find the one you want.) If you search by title, enter the title but start with the first important word, ignoring *A, An,* and *The.* For a subject search, you'll use a **keyword,** a word or phrase that describes your topic. Whenever you search a computer database, including the Internet, to find books, articles, or other media, the keyword you choose will greatly affect the results you get.

Search TIP

1. **Be specific.** A general keyword, such as *animal,* will get you a long list of sources, sometimes called **matches** or **hits.** However, few of them will be helpful to you. If you use a more specific keyword, such as *dachshund,* you won't have to read screen after screen of possible sources, trying to find a few that might be helpful.

2. **Use Boolean search techniques,** which offer different ways to combine words. You can use these techniques to look for books in a computer catalog, to find articles in magazine databases (described later), or to locate information on the Internet (also described later).

Named for George Boole, an English mathematician who lived during the nineteenth century, Boolean techniques use the words *and, or, not,* and sometimes *near* or *adj.*

and:
: If you combine two keywords with *and* (such as *wetlands and conservation*), the computer will list only sources that have both words. This kind of search results in far fewer hits, but many more of them will relate to your topic. (Some programs use + in place of *and: wetlands + conservation.*)

or:
: If you want information on either one of two related topics, link them with *or,* as in *alligators or crocodiles.* The computer will conduct two searches at once.

not:
: To eliminate a category of information from a search, use *not.* For example, if you want information about genetic disorders but not Down Syndrome, you can enter *genetic and disorders not Down.*

near *or* adj:
: Some computer programs allow you to use *near* or *adj* (adjacent) to locate sources, usually articles, that have two keywords used near each other. For example, you might use *wildlife near preservation* as your keywords. One program may list only those sources in which the keywords are within eight words of each other. Another program might allow the keywords to be fifteen words apart. This search technique has

an advantage over linking words with *and,* which can generate a long list of articles in which both words appear but never in connection with each other.

Not all computer programs recognize Boolean techniques; some will treat *and, or, not, near*, or *adj* as part of your keyword/phrase. For some other computer programs, you must begin a Boolean search with *b/,* as in *b/wildlife and preservation.*

3. **Use quotation marks.** Enclosing a phrase in quotation marks (for instance, *"preserving natural resources"*) tells the computer to find every book or article with exactly those words.

4. **Try truncating.** If you **truncate,** or shorten, your keyword by using an asterisk (*), the computer will search for all words that begin with the letters before the asterisk. For example, using *experiment** as a keyword will tell the computer to list books or articles containing such words as *experiment, experimental, experimented, experimenting,* and *experiments.* By truncating your keyword, you make sure the computer doesn't overlook various forms of the word.

   You can also truncate when you aren't sure how to spell a word. For example, you could use *Azer** as a keyword if you couldn't remember how to spell Azerbaijan, a country in southeastern Europe.

5. **Use a "wildcard"** by inserting a question mark *(?)* into certain words. For example, if you aren't sure whether to use *woman* or *women,* enter *wom?n.*

Now that you know how to choose keywords, here is an example of their use. To use a computer catalog, you type in the author's name, the book title, or a keyword or phrase, and the screen will list any related sources available at that library. Let's say you type the keywords *credit card safety*. The screen will then show you a list similar to the one below. If the catalog program is connected to a printer, you could print this list.

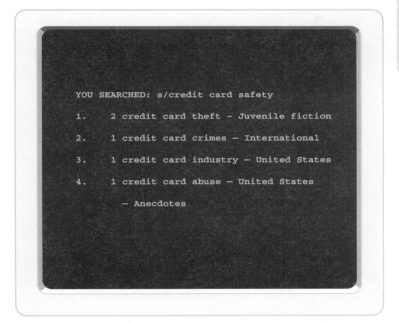

```
YOU SEARCHED: s/credit card safety

1.    2 credit card theft - Juvenile fiction

2.    1 credit card crimes — International

3.    1 credit card industry — United States

4.    1 credit card abuse — United States

      — Anecdotes
```

The first listing (1) tells you that the library has two books about credit card theft in the juvenile fiction category. Books listed in this category will be novels or collections of short stories that are appropriate for young readers. The second listing (2) tells you that the library has one book about international credit card crimes. This book isn't marked fiction, so it's nonfiction; it isn't marked juvenile, so it's for adults. To find out more about this book, enter the number of its listing, 2. The next screen might give you the following information.

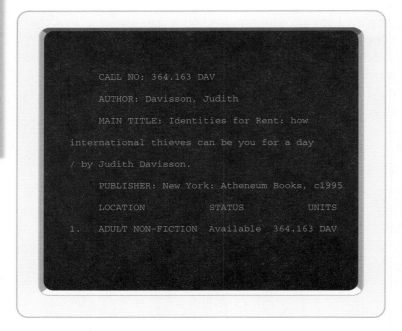

```
CALL NO: 364.163 DAV

AUTHOR: Davisson, Judith

MAIN TITLE: Identities for Rent: how
international thieves can be you for a day
/ by Judith Davisson.

PUBLISHER: New York: Atheneum Books, c1995

LOCATION          STATUS          UNITS

1.  ADULT NON-FICTION  Available  364.163 DAV
```

The status column indicates that no one has checked out this book, so it should be filed on a shelf. To find it, you would write down its call number, shown at the top of the listing. (**Call numbers** are numbers and letters used to classify books. They are explained on pages 539–544.) Then you would go to the location listed (the adult non-fiction stacks), find the shelf with call numbers between 360 and 370, and look down the rows for the book marked 364.163 DAV. The books are in numerical and alphabetical order.

If someone had checked out this book, the status column would state the date when it was due back at the library. If the library had several copies of the book, the status of each copy would be stated. Some catalog entries also include the number of pages in the book; whether it has illustrations, an index, a glossary, or a bibliography; and what kind of medium it is, such as a book or videotape. Many entries list additional headings you could enter into the catalog as keywords to find more information about the same topic.

The computer instructions will tell you how to move forward and backward as you search through the library's listings. For example, you might enter *ns* (next screen) or *f* (forward) to see more of a listing. To go backward, you might enter *ps* (previous screen) or *b* (backward).

CARD CATALOGS

Card catalogs are stored in long, narrow drawers. The drawers hold two or three small cards for every book in the library, arranged alphabetically. Fiction books have two cards each, one listing the book by its author and one listing it by its title. Nonfiction books have three cards each, listing the book by its author, title, and subject.

The cards list the same information as the computer catalog, although they don't, of course, tell you whether someone has checked out the book. A library may divide its card catalog into two categories: subject cards and author/title cards. Often cards are cross-referenced, listing other available books on the same subject or a related topic. A card catalog might also have separate cross-reference cards, filed alphabetically and listing related topics.

19.2 LOCATING BOOKS

The purpose of call numbers is to help you locate books. Most school and community libraries use call numbers based on the Dewey decimal system, while many college and university libraries use call numbers based on the Library of Congress system.

DEWEY DECIMAL SYSTEM

The Dewey decimal system, created in 1876 by a librarian named Melvil Dewey, divides nonfiction books into the ten categories listed below.

DEWEY DECIMAL CATEGORIES OF NONFICTION

NUMBERS	CATEGORY	EXAMPLES OF SUBCATEGORIES
000-099	General Works	encyclopedias, bibliographies, newspapers, periodicals
100-199	Philosophy	ethics, psychology, personality
200-299	Religion	theology, mythology, bibles
300-399	Social Sciences	sociology, education, government, law, economics
400-499	Language	dictionaries, foreign languages, grammar guides
500-599	Sciences	chemistry, astronomy, biology, mathematics
600-699	Technology	medicine, engineering, business
700-799	Arts	painting, music, theater, sports
800-899	Literature	poetry, plays, essays
900-999	History	ancient history, biography, geography, travel

Let's say you wanted to know more about Samuel Johnson, a seventeenth-century British author and dictionary writer. You would begin by entering his name as a keyword in a computer catalog or by looking under the *J*s in a card catalog.

The library might have many books about Johnson and his work, but the call numbers of these books could fall into different categories on the Dewey decimal chart, depending on their content. For example, one book listed by a computer catalog is *The Samuel Johnson Encyclopedia* by Pat Rogers. The 800 category, Literature, is broken down into subcategories; for example, 810 is American literature and 820 is English literature. Samuel Johnson was an English author, so this book has a call number of 820.

The more specific the topic, the more specific the call number. Some call numbers have decimals added to make them even more specific. We saw this earlier in *Identities for Rent*, which had a call number of 364.163 DAV.

Many libraries add the first three letters of the author's last name to the call number, in this case DAV for Davisson. Thus, in some libraries, the call number for *The Samuel Johnson Encyclopedia* would be 820 ROG (for Rogers).

Let's say our library also has a book titled *The Making of Johnson's Dictionary, 1746–1773* by Allen Reddick. Since this book is more about language than about Johnson, it's classified in the 400 category, Language, with a call number of 423. Another book is titled *Dr. Johnson's London*, by Dorothy Marshall. This historical account falls in the 900 category, History, so it has a call number of 942.1.

Research TIP

All libraries that use the Dewey decimal system use the same chart to assign call numbers to books. However, two librarians may put the same book into different categories. For this reason, the same book may have different call numbers in different libraries.

Biographies Our library has another book called *Everybody's Boswell: The Life of Samuel Johnson* by James Boswell. It has a call number of *B*, which stands for biography. Many libraries group their biographies together, with one biography section in the adult stacks and one in the young adult and children's department. Biographies are shelved alphabetically according to the last name of the subject of the book. *Everybody's Boswell: The Life of Samuel Johnson* will be in the *J* section of the biographies.

The library also has another biography of Johnson: *The Personal History of Samuel Johnson* by Christopher Hibbert. Two books about the same person will be shelved alphabetically by the author's last name. So Boswell's book will be before Hibbert's book in the *J* section of the biographies.

Fiction Most libraries that use the Dewey decimal system identify fiction with the call number *F* or *Fic*. The second line of the call number consists of the first three letters of the author's name or of the author's entire last name. Fiction is shelved alphabetically by the authors' last names. Books by the same author are shelved alphabetically by the first word in each title (not counting *A*, *An*, and *The*). Many public libraries have separate sections for some categories of fiction, such as mysteries or science fiction. In that case, usually a mark or label on the book's spine shows its inclusion on these special shelves. Within the mystery or science fiction section, books are shelved alphabetically by author's last name.

Reference Books Reference books, such as encyclopedias and current yearbooks, have an *R* or *Ref* preceding their call numbers. This will alert you that you cannot check out these sources and must use them in the library. An *OV* or another symbol added to a call number indicates that the book is oversized and kept in a section of the library with taller shelves. (Ask the librarian where this section is.)

LIBRARY OF CONGRESS SYSTEM

The Library of Congress system divides books into twenty-one categories, each represented by a letter as shown in the chart below. Like the Dewey decimal system, the Library of Congress system has subcategories identified by a second letter. For example, N is the category for fine arts. You would look under NA for books about architecture, NB for sculpture, ND for painting, and so on. Numbers added to the letter combinations identify more specific categories.

LIBRARY OF CONGRESS CATEGORIES

LETTER	CATEGORY	LETTER	CATEGORY
A	General Works	N	Fine Arts
B	Philosophy and Religion	P	Language and Literature
C–F	History	Q	Science
G	Geography and Anthropology	R	Medicine
H	Social Sciences	S	Agriculture
J	Political Science	T	Technology
K	Law	U	Military Science
L	Education	V	Naval Science
M	Music	Z	Bibliography and Library Science

In one library using the Library of Congress system, Pat Rogers' book, *The Samuel Johnson Encyclopedia,* has a call number of PR 3532.R64. *P* represents the general category of Literature, while *R* indicates a work by a British author.

The second *R* in the call number is from the author's name, Rogers.

Note that in the Library of Congress system, biographies are not filed separately but with the other books. Therefore, the call numbers of the biographies for Johnson begin with *PR*, indicating a British author.

FINDING INFORMATION IN NONFICTION BOOKS

Being familiar with the content and purpose of the parts of books will help you quickly determine whether a source will be useful to you. Not every book contains all the sections described below.

Information about a book

To find information about a book, check the following parts:

The **title page** contains the book title, the author's name, and usually the publisher.

The **copyright page**, which is usually printed on the back of the title page, gives the publication or copyright date. Check the copyright date to determine how current the information is.

The **table of contents** lists the main topics covered to help you decide whether the book has the information you're seeking.

The **foreword**, **introduction**, or **preface**, which is written by the author or an expert in the same field, may explain the purpose of the book or the author's outlook on the subject.

Information in a book

To find information in a book, check the sections below:

The **index** lists alphabetically the people, places, events, and other significant topics mentioned in the book and gives the pages where you can find references to them.

The **glossary** lists terms in the book alphabetically and defines them, taking into account the intended readers. (Books for young children define basic terms; those for adults define terms that would be unfamiliar to most adult readers.)

The **bibliography** suggests additional research sources that are appropriate for the intended readers of the book. It may also include the sources of the information in the book.

The **appendix** contains additional information related to the book, such as maps, charts, illustrations, or graphs.

The **afterword** or **epilogue** is used by some authors to make a final statement about the book, discuss implications, or offer additional findings.

19.3 LOCATING ARTICLES IN NEWSPAPERS AND OTHER PERIODICALS

If you need current information from newspapers, magazines, or journals, the two tools described below may make your search easier.

COMPUTER DATABASES

Many libraries subscribe to databases holding collections of magazine, journal, and newspaper articles that you can access using the library computers. Most of these databases allow you to search by topic, by type of publication, or by specific publication. Some programs also allow you to select the years you want to search. You might choose to browse through all the magazines or all the newspapers in the database that cover a certain period of time, or you could narrow your search to a specific magazine or newspaper, such as the *New York Times.* Some databases allow you to review the table of contents of one issue of a magazine and read any of the articles that interest you.

If you enter a keyword that describes your topic, the database will list the title of each article on that topic along with the author, the publication, the date, and a short description of the article. You can select any titles that seem especially relevant and read either a short summary or the whole article on the computer screen. For a small fee, you can print a copy of articles that you want to take home with you.

What kinds of articles you will find depends on the database you use. If you search using the keywords *natural remedies*, for example, one database might list articles on this subject from publications such as *Prevention, Newsday, Rocky Mountain Press,* and *USA Today.* If you enter the same keywords in a more academically oriented database, you might find articles from the *Journal of the National Cancer Institute, Annual Review of Psychology,* and *Biological Bulletin.* Don't check just one database and assume you've seen all the articles that are available.

READERS' GUIDE TO PERIODICAL LITERATURE

Not every library can afford to subscribe to computer databases, but nearly every library stocks the paper edition of *Readers' Guide to Periodical Literature.* This guide includes the titles of articles from nearly two hundred magazines and journals, with both subjects and authors listed alphabetically and cross-referenced. It's also available on a compact disc that you can search using a computer.

An update of the paper index is published every two weeks, and information about all the articles for the year is reprinted in a hardbound book at the end of the year. One index provided the following listing under *credit card crimes.*

CREDIT CARD CRIMES
    See also
    Credit cards—Security measures
    Identity theft
Are your theft fears overblown? S. Medintz. il
    Money v27 no6 p137-9 Je '98

If the article "Are Your Theft Fears Overblown?" in
Money sounds interesting, you must locate the June 1998
issue of this magazine and turn to page 137. (The *il* indicates
that the article is illustrated.)

Libraries often keep issues for the current year in their
newspapers and periodicals section. Issues from the previous one to five years may be stored in a different area, and
older issues may be on **microfilm** (a roll or reel of film) or
microfiche (a sheet of film). Both types of film must be
inserted into special projectors that enlarge the images so
you can read them. You can usually make photocopies of
these articles to take home.

Not every book or article in the library or on its databases
offers unbiased, valuable, reliable information. The following
steps will help you avoid sources that offer irrelevant, out-
dated information or biased opinions.

1. **Evaluate the author of each source of information**
   and read any biographical information about him or her.
   Consider whether the author is an expert in a certain field
   or simply someone who has opinions about it.

2. **Evaluate the information itself,** starting with whether it is directly related to your topic. If it's only loosely related and you try to include it in your report, your work may seem unorganized and disjointed.

3. **Evaluate the author's reasoning.** Are the "facts" in a source actually unsupported opinions or exaggerations? Does the author seem to make too many assumptions? Does he or she overgeneralize from one situation to another?

4. **Check the publication date.** Are certain statistics now out of date? Is it likely that the findings have been contradicted by more recent research? Information on many topics, such as Mark Twain's childhood, may be the same whether it was published last week or twenty years ago. However, you must use up-to-date information when discussing topics that are still being researched or debated.

5. **Gather information** on the same topic from several sources. This way, you'll be more likely to become familiar with different opinions on the issue or topic. Then compare and contrast facts from each source. If three sources agree and one disagrees, the latter source may be mistaken—unless it's more current than the other sources.

19.4 USING OTHER REFERENCE SOURCES

GENERAL REFERENCE SOURCES

General reference sources are easy to locate and easy to use. They also provide detailed information on thousands of topics. Following are some excellent examples of these sources.

TYPE OF REFERENCE	EXAMPLES
General Encyclopedias These encyclopedias usually consist of many volumes. Subjects are arranged alphabetically, with an index and cross-referencing to help you find related topics. Many encyclopedia publishers offer yearly updates.	*World Book Encyclopedia* *Encyclopædia Britannica* *Collier's Encyclopedia* *Grolier Encyclopedia* *Encarta Encyclopedia* (Some encyclopedias are also available on compact discs; *Encarta Encyclopedia* is available only on a CD-ROM. CD-ROMs are described in Accessing Electronic Resources, page 567.)
Specialized Encyclopedias Each of these references focuses on a certain subject. Most provide specialized information, while some, such as *Books in Print,* tell you where to look for the information you seek. You might be surprised at the number of specialized encyclopedias that are available.	*Encyclopedia of World Art* *Van Nostrand's Scientific Encyclopedia* *Encyclopedia of World Crime* *Encyclopedia of the Opera* *Encyclopedia of the Third Reich* *Encyclopedia of Vitamins, Minerals, and Supplements* *Encyclopedia of Western Movies* *Encyclopedia of the Geological Sciences* *Books in Print*
Almanacs and Yearbooks These references are published frequently to provide up-to-date facts and statistics.	*Information Please Almanac* *World Almanac and Book of Facts* *Guinness Book of Records* *Statistical Abstract of the United States*
Atlases Atlases can be historical or current; they contain maps and statistics about countries and continents, climates, exports and imports, and the spread of world cultures, among other topics.	*Hammond World Atlas* *Cambridge Atlas of Astronomy* *Historical Atlas of the United States* *Goode's World Atlas* *National Geographic Atlas of the World* *Atlas of World Cultures*

RESOURCES

TYPE OF REFERENCE, *continued*	EXAMPLES
Literary and Other Biographical Works These references include brief histories of notable people, living or dead, and are usually organized by fields instead of by names.	*Contemporary Authors* *American Authors 1600–1900* *European Authors 1000–1900* *Cyclopedia of Literary Characters* *Webster's New Biographical Dictionary* *Dictionary of American Biography* *Current Biography* *Biographical Dictionary of World War I (and II)* *Biographical Dictionary of Scientists (by field)* *Biographical Dictionary of Artists*
Government Documents Some large libraries hold the federal government documents that are available to the public. These pamphlets, journals, and reports offer information on agriculture, population, economics, and other topics.	*Monthly Catalog of United States Government Publications* *United States Government Publications Catalog* (both also available on compact discs and online)
Books of Quotations The indexes of these references help you look up quotations by certain people and by subject. The quotation from Samuel Johnson at the beginning of Part Four was taken from *The Harper Book of Quotations*. It was included in the category titled "Knowledge."	Bartlett's *Familiar Quotations* *The Harper Book of Quotations* *The Oxford Dictionary of Quotations* *The International Thesaurus of Quotations*

PLANNING LIBRARY RESEARCH

1. Start early. If you wait, other students may have checked out the sources you want to use.
2. Begin with the general reference sources rather than those that deal with specific fields or topics. A general source will offer an overview of your topic. It may

provide all the information you need, or it may guide you to additional sources.

3. List the sources you want to check and mark each one off your list after you've examined it so you won't check the same source twice.

4. Take careful notes and include the title, author, publisher, publication date, and page number of each source. (See pages 471–473 for more information about compiling note cards.)

5. Talk with the librarian about your project, its purpose, its length, and the kinds of sources you have been asked to use. Describe what you've done so far and be ready with specific questions you'd like answered. Librarians can often suggest valuable references you haven't considered and perhaps help you locate them.

19.5 MAKING THE MOST OF WORD RESOURCES

When you're visiting a library's reference department, you want to be able to go right to the information you need. Hunting aimlessly through the shelves and finding only irrelevant information is a waste of your time, no matter how interesting the information might be. This section will show you the different reference books that are available and what they are good for.

KINDS OF DICTIONARIES

Maybe you never stopped to think about it, but there are many kinds of dictionaries. Most of the dictionaries you've seen at school and in public libraries are general dictionaries, each including words from general English for a general reader. Then there are specialized dictionaries that define only words used in a particular field or profession, art or craft.

General Dictionaries

General dictionaries fall into these three categories:

School dictionaries contain fewer than 90,000 entries. They focus on common words and offer easy-to-understand definitions.

College dictionaries have about 150,000 entries. These references are used in homes, schools, and businesses. They answer most questions about spelling and definitions.

Unabridged dictionaries contain more than 250,000 entries and often fill several volumes. They are generally located in libraries and include extensive definitions and word histories.

Specialized Dictionaries

Specialized dictionaries list words used in a particular field. Following are some examples of the many kinds of specialized dictionaries:

Dictionary of Sports Idioms
Dictionary of Inventions and Discoveries
Facts on File Dictionary of 20th-Century Allusions
Dictionary of Italian Literature
Dictionary of Occupational Titles
Dictionary of Medical Folklore
Dictionary of Historic Nicknames

WORD ENTRIES IN GENERAL DICTIONARIES

Any one page in a dictionary probably *contains* a few thousand words, but it probably *defines* only a few dozen. A word entry discusses the meanings and the various forms of the entry word or headword, which is the word in bold-faced type that begins the word entry. When you look up a word in a dictionary, you are looking for its word entry.

Finding Words

Words are listed alphabetically in dictionaries, usually with no regard to hyphenated words or open compounds, as in this example:

> soften
> soft-focus
> soft pedal
> softshell

Words beginning with the abbreviation *St.* are listed as if the abbreviation were spelled out. So *St. Louis encephalitis* comes before the word *saintly*.

As you search for a word, don't forget to use the guide words at the top of every page. Guide words are the first and last entry words on the page. If the word you seek doesn't fall between these words alphabetically, it won't be on that page.

Search TIP

When you can't find the word you're looking for, consider these possibilities:

1. The word might have silent consonants, such as the *k* in *knight,* the *b* in *doubt,* or the *gh* in *blight.*
2. A consonant in the word might have an unusual spelling. For example, the *k* sound can be spelled with a *k (kindness), c (contract, lecture), ck (mackerel),* or *ch (chrysanthemum, chrome).*
3. A vowel in the word might have an unusual spelling, such as the first vowel sound in *beautiful* and *eerie.*
4. Your dictionary might not be large enough. An unusual word might not be listed in a school dictionary, for example.

Understanding Word Entries

Let's analyze a sample word entry to see what kinds of information it offers.

A   B   C   D

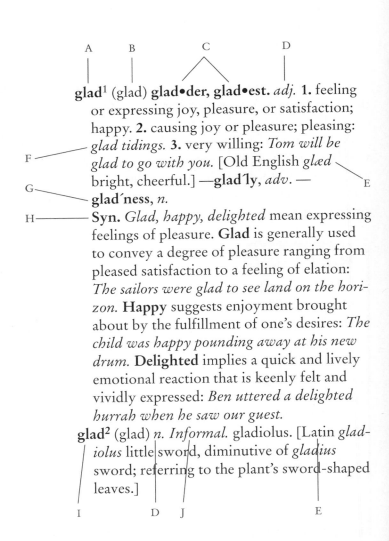

glad¹ (glad) **glad•der, glad•est.** *adj.* **1.** feeling or expressing joy, pleasure, or satisfaction; happy. **2.** causing joy or pleasure; pleasing: *glad tidings.* **3.** very willing: *Tom will be glad to go with you.* [Old English *glæd* bright, cheerful.] —**glad´ly**, *adv.* — **glad´ness**, *n.*

F

G

E

H——— **Syn.** *Glad, happy, delighted* mean expressing feelings of pleasure. **Glad** is generally used to convey a degree of pleasure ranging from pleased satisfaction to a feeling of elation: *The sailors were glad to see land on the horizon.* **Happy** suggests enjoyment brought about by the fulfillment of one's desires: *The child was happy pounding away at his new drum.* **Delighted** implies a quick and lively emotional reaction that is keenly felt and vividly expressed: *Ben uttered a delighted hurrah when he saw our guest.*

glad² (glad) *n. Informal.* gladiolus. [Latin *gladiolus* little sword, diminutive of *gladius* sword; referring to the plant's sword-shaped leaves.]

I   D   J   E

A. The Entry Word: The boldfaced word at the beginning of the entry is called the entry word. If this word can be divided at the end of a line, the divisions will be indicated by a raised dot. The word *explicate*, for example, is written ex•pli•cate. This means that you can divide the word after *ex* or after *expli.* In the sample word entry, *glad* cannot be divided; *gladder* and *gladdest,* however, can be divided. The entry word will also tell you when a compound word should be written as one word (as in *lighthouse*), when it should be hyphenated (as in *light-headed*), and when it should be written as two words (as in *light meter*).

B. Pronunciation: The correct way to say the word is shown immediately after the entry word and indicated in three ways: accent marks, phonetic symbols, and diacritical marks. In entry words with more than one syllable, accent marks indicate which syllable should be stressed. To check the meaning of the other marks and symbols, look at the pronunciation key that is usually located at the bottom of the page.

C. Inflected Forms: Plural forms of nouns, adjective forms, and forms of verbs in other tenses are included in an entry. In this case, we see that the comparative and superlative forms of *glad* are *gladder* and *gladdest.*

When two spellings are connected with *or,* they are equally acceptable. However, when they are joined with *also,* the first spelling is preferred. For example, the dictionary shows the plural of *alga* as "**algae** *also* **algas.**"

D. Parts of Speech: Abbreviations in italics indicate the part of speech of the entry word and other forms of the word. At the beginning of this entry, we see that *glad* is usually used as an adjective, but later we learn that the same spelling can be used as a noun.

E. Etymology: Many entries include the history of the word, or etymology. The entry for *glad¹* indicates that this word is based on an Old English word. The entry for *glad²* shows this word comes from Latin.

F. Definitions: If an entry has more than one meaning, each meaning is numbered. Example sentences using the entry word are often included in definitions to make meanings clearer.

G. Derived words: A definition may end with a variation of the entry word, preceded by a dash and followed by its part of speech. In the example, the derived words *gladly* and *gladness* are shown. When the meaning of the variation is taken from the entry word, the variation is not defined. If the pronunciation changes, it is given for each variation.

H. Synonyms: Many entries list words with similar meanings along with examples so you'll know when to use each word. Understanding small differences in meaning will keep you from using words incorrectly. Some dictionaries also include antonyms in entries.

I. Homographs: Homographs are words that are spelled the same but have different meanings and histories. Homograph entries are listed separately and are followed by small numbers. *Glad* has two homographs pronounced the same. (When homographs vary in pronunciation, their entries make that clear.) As you can see, the homographs of *glad* have quite different definitions and completely different etymologies.

J. Usage Information: Some entries also provide information on how words are used in different contexts. The entry *glad²* is labeled *Informal*. The following chart describes some usage guidelines you might encounter in a dictionary entry.

TYPE OF INFORMATION	DESCRIPTION	EXAMPLE FROM AN ENTRY
Capitalization	indicates that a word should be capitalized under certain conditions	**pilgrim** . . . *n* . . . **3.** *cap:* one of the English colonists settling at Plymouth in 1620
Out-of-Date Usage	identifies meanings that are obsolete (no longer used) or used only in special contexts	**play** . . . *n* . . . **1.b** *archaic:* GAME, SPORT
Special Field Usage	uses a phrase or label to indicate a definition used only in a particular field	**break** . . . *n* . . . **5.d** *mining:* FAULT, DISLOCATION
Informal	advises that the word be avoided when speaking and writing formally	**bloom•ing** . . . *adj* . . . **3.** *Informal.* complete, utter: *a blooming idiot.*
Regional Usage	explains how a word is used in a certain geographical area	**pet•rol** . . . *n.* *British:* gasoline
Usage Note	offers general guidelines for using— or not using—a word in a certain situation; often preceded by a dash and by the abbreviation *usu.* for *usually* or the words *called also.*	**fire away** *vi* . . . — usu. used as an imperative. **hun•dred•weight** *n* . . . —called also *long hundredweight.*

RESOURCES

OTHER KINDS OF INFORMATION IN GENERAL DICTIONARIES

When did Genghis Khan live? What does *omnia vincit amor* mean? You can find out by looking in the back of your dictionary.

Biographical Names

This section lists the spelling and pronunciation of the names of thousands of notable people. It also includes each person's birth and death dates, nationality, and field or title.

Geographical Names

In the geographical names section, you can find the correct spelling, pronunciation, and location of countries, regions, cities, mountains, rivers, and other geographical features.

Abbreviations and Symbols for Chemical Elements

Check this section if you can't remember the abbreviation for *kilometers per hour* (kmh or kmph), are confused by the abbreviation *PAT* (point after touchdown), or want to learn that *Fe* is the chemical symbol for iron.

Foreign Words and Phrases

The foreign words and phrases section defines unusual phrases, such as *Ars longa, vita brevis* (Art is long; life is short). Commonly used foreign phrases, such as *déjà vu,* are listed with the regular word entries.

Signs and Symbols

The signs and symbols section provides the symbols used in astronomy, business, math, medicine, weather forecasting, and other fields.

Style Handbook

Use the style section to check your punctuation or capitalization and for help with documentation of sources and ways to address people in certain positions, such as government officials.

THESAURUSES

A thesaurus, one kind of specialized dictionary, lists synonyms. The synonyms can be arranged categorically (traditional style) or alphabetically (dictionary style).

Traditional Style

To use a thesaurus arranged in the traditional style, begin by looking in the index for the word you want to change. For example, if you looked in the index under *require,* you might find these choices:

> **require** entail 76.4
> necessitate 637.9
> lack 660.6
> demand 751.4
> oblige 754.5
> charge 844.14
> obligate 960.11

If none of these words seems exactly right, you could look in the front of the book under 751.4 for more choices. On the page with the guide numbers 748.16–751.7, you find that word 751 is *demand.* Under this word are numbered paragraphs, each with possible synonyms for *demand.* The most commonly used words are printed in boldface type. Because *demand* can be a noun or a verb, the synonyms are separated into those two categories. You locate paragraph 751.4:

> VERBS **4. demand, ask,** make a demand; **call for,** call on *or* upon one for, come upon one for, appeal to for; cry for, clamor for; **require, exact,** require at the hands of; **requisition,** make *or* put in requisition, lay under contribution.

Some synonyms are marked *[coll.],* meaning "colloquial" or "informal." A page in the front or back of the thesaurus explains the other abbreviations that are used.

Dictionary Style

Looking up a word in a thesaurus organized alphabetically is just like looking up a word in a dictionary. Using the guide words at the top of the page, you locate the entry for the word *require:*

REQUIRE

Verb. **1.** [To need] want, feel the necessity for, have need for; see NEED. **2.** [To demand] exact, insist upon, expect; see ASK.

For more choices, you check *ask.*

ASK

Verb. request, query, question, interrogate, examine, cross-examine, demand, pose *or* raise *or* put a question, inquire, frame a question, order, command, challenge, pry into, scour, investigate, hunt for, quiz, grill, *needle, *sound out, *pump, *put through the third degree.

Antonym: see ANSWER, REFUTE, REJOIN.

Checking the front of the book, you learn that an asterisk (*) indicates that a term is colloquial or slang.

STYLE GUIDES

Should you capitalize a title when it follows a person's name? Should you write *87* or *eighty-seven?* You can find a number of style guides, such as *The Chicago Manual of Style*, that will answer these questions. Style guides are reference books with detailed indexes that allow you to look up specific questions. The index of one style guide, for example, devotes half a page to the uses of the comma. The answers in one style guide may contradict the answers in another guide, so everyone working on the same project should agree to use the same style guide. Perhaps some of your teachers have asked you to follow a certain style guide in your writing.

Chapter 20

Accessing Electronic Resources

● ● ● ● ● ● ● ● ● ● ● ● ● ●

The Internet is an increasingly important source of information for people of all ages worldwide, but CD-ROMs and other electronic resources not connected to the Internet also offer vast amounts of information.

20.1 USING THE INTERNET

The Internet is a computer-based, worldwide information network. The Internet uses telephone and cable lines and satellites to link personal computers worldwide. The World Wide Web, or WWW, is a set of programs and rules that determine how files are created and displayed on the Internet. To understand the difference, try this analogy: if the Internet were one computer, the WWW would be a program that runs on that computer. As you research a topic, the Internet and World Wide Web allow you to identify, retrieve, and study documents without leaving your home, school, or library. You can also use electronic mail, or e-mail, to communicate with others interested in a specific topic or with experts on that topic.

GAINING ACCESS

Your library computers can probably link you directly to the Internet at no cost to you. If you are using a computer at home, you'll need a **modem,** a device that connects your computer to a telephone or cable line. You must also subscribe to an **Internet service provider.** This service will connect you to the Internet for a fee.

UNDERSTANDING ADDRESSES

The information on the Internet is organized by locations, or sites, each with its own address. A Web address is also called a **Uniform Resource Locator,** or URL. Most addresses begin with *http://,* which stands for "hypertext transfer protocol" and identifies a way in which information is exchanged among computers connected by the Internet. The last part of an address, or its suffix, indicates the type of site it is. Here are some of the suffixes in use:

SUFFIX	TYPE OF SITE
.com	commercial
.edu	educational
.gov	government
.mil	military
.net	network organization or Internet service provider
.org	organization

USING BROWSERS

Each Internet service provider uses a specific **browser,** a program that locates and displays Web pages. Some browsers display only the text, or words, on a Web page;

most will display both text and **graphics** (pictures, photos, and diagrams). Browsers also allow you to print or download part or all of a Web site. (**Downloading** means copying information from Internet files onto a computer hard drive or a diskette.) Browsers permit you to move from page to page within a site or to jump from one site to a related site. Names of current browsers include Netscape Navigator and Internet Explorer.

ACCESSING WEB SITES

Let's say you are now connected to the Internet. If you want to see the information offered at a certain site, you can enter the site's address on the computer screen and be transferred there. You can also access specific reference sources this way, such as the *New York Times* or *Encyclopædia Britannica.* Some of these sources are free, but to gain access to others, you must subscribe and pay a fee in addition to the cost of the online service. A screen will explain any extra charges that are involved and let you choose whether to continue.

USING SEARCH ENGINES AND SUBJECT DIRECTORIES

If you don't have a specific address in mind, you can search by keyword with the help of a search engine or a subject directory.

Technology Tip

Be sure to read the Search Tip on pages 534–536, which provides information about using keywords. A keyword that is too general may generate hundreds of thousands of possible Web sites. It will take you a very long time to search them and find a few helpful sources.

Search Engines Search engines are a type of software that uses your keyword to compile lists of related Web sites. Internet service providers use certain search engines, but you can switch to a different one by entering its address. Many kinds of search engines are available, and they offer slightly different services. Some print the first sentence or two of the information offered at each Web site, while other search engines list only the site's title and address. Some search engines offer to list additional Web sites similar to those already on your screen.

Subject Directories Subject directories are a kind of software that provides an excellent place to start a search if you haven't selected a specific topic yet. A subject directory first lists general topics. After you choose one, the directory offers a list of possible subtopics from which to select. The directory then offers several more lists of subtopics for you to consider, allowing you to further narrow your topic. Finally, it provides a page of links to Web sites that are related to the specific topic you have now chosen.

For example, the search engine Yahoo! has a subject directory that offers fourteen general topics to choose from, such as Arts and Humanities. Then Yahoo! lists subtopics for you to choose from, helping you to narrow your search and define your topic until you reach a page of related Web sites.

MOVING AROUND WEB SITES

Often a word or phrase within the text of a Web page or at the end of the file will provide a link to a related Web site. These special words or phrases are called **hyperlinks.** They may be underlined or printed in a different color to make them easy to spot. When you click your mouse on a hyperlink, you'll immediately be transferred to another Web site. To get back, you can click on the back arrow or a similar symbol at the top of the computer screen.

EVALUATING TIP

Many Web sites are not checked for accuracy, so you must evaluate each site yourself. Begin by reviewing the Evaluating Tip on pages 547–548. This tip applies to Internet sources, too, especially the suggestions to use more than one source and to check for bias. Further suggestions follow.

1. Determine whether a Web site actually relates to your topic. A search engine will use every possible meaning of your keyword or phrase to compile a list of hundreds or thousands of sites. You may find that your keyword also happens to be the name of a computer game, a sports team, or even a cooking technique!

2. Pay particular attention to the source of the information in a Web site. (You may have to press the "move back" key several times to identify the organization sponsoring a site.) If a site is a personal Web page or if you cannot figure out its source or author, be sure to find another source to verify the information you find.

3. Evaluate the accuracy and fairness of the information. Is it based on more than one source? Are dissenting opinions included? After doing some of your own research elsewhere, are you aware of important information that was omitted from the site? Does the site include a bibliography and links to other sites? The answers to these questions can help you decide whether to use that source.

20.2 USING CD-ROMS AND DVDS

Technological advances create new research opportunities every day, so any discussion of the resources available quickly becomes out-of-date. Still, two resources are likely to be used for many years to come: CD-ROMs (Compact Disc-Read-Only Memory) and DVDs (Digital Video Discs). They can be used with a personal computer at home, at school, or at a library.

CD-ROM databases store both visual and audio information, such as photographs, maps, samples of different kinds of music, sound clips of famous speeches, and bird calls. Some CD-ROMs offer short videos of historical events and animated, narrated sequences that explain, for example, how acid rain forms or how airplanes fly.

One CD-ROM can store the same information as seven hundred diskettes; therefore, many dictionaries, encyclopedias, and other reference sources are now available as CD-ROMs. Many manufacturers offer yearly or monthly updates. To read a CD-ROM, your computer must have a CD-ROM drive. To broadcast sound effects, it must have speakers and a sound card.

Similar to a CD-ROM, a DVD has a larger storage capacity, enough space to store a full-length movie. DVDs require a DVD drive, which can also read CD-ROMs. (CD-ROM drives, however, cannot read DVDs.)

Library computer catalogs are another example of electronic resources that are not part of the Internet. Some of the databases available at the library are actually on CD-ROMs purchased by the library; other databases accessible from library computers are part of the Internet.

Knowledge often means knowing how to find information. Now you have knowledge. You can use it to find out more about the world and to take your place in it.

Index